METARACISM

METARACISM

Explaining the Persistence of Racial Inequality

Carter A. Wilson

LYNNE
RIENNER
PUBLISHERS

BOULDER
LONDON

Published in the United States of America in 2015 by
Lynne Rienner Publishers, Inc.
1800 30th Street, Boulder, Colorado 80301
www.rienner.com

and in the United Kingdom by
Lynne Rienner Publishers, Inc.
3 Henrietta Street, Covent Garden, London WC2E 8LU

Library of Congress Cataloging-in-Publication Data
Wilson, Carter A.
    Metaracism : explaining the persistence of racial inequality / Carter A. Wilson.
        p. cm.
    Includes bibliographical references and index.
    ISBN 978-1-62637-189-7 (hc : alk. paper)
    1. Race discrimination—United States—History—21st century.
2. Racism—United States—21st century. 3. Right and left (Political science)—
United States—21st century. I. Title.
    E185.615.W542 2015
    305.900973—dc23
                                                                2014028351

British Cataloguing in Publication Data
A Cataloguing in Publication record for this book
is available from the British Library.

Printed and bound in the United States of America

      The paper used in this publication meets the requirements
 ∞   of the American National Standard for Permanence of
      Paper for Printed Library Materials Z39.48-1992.

    5   4   3   2   1

Contents

Tables and Figures

Tables

Figures

1

What Is Metaracism?

The twenty-first century promises to be a paradoxical period in US race relations: an age of unparalleled progress, yet of unprecedented repression; an epoch of remarkable racial advancement, yet of persisting racial inequality; a season proclaimed to be one of postracial/post–civil rights politics, yet one of continuing racial strife. This paradox is not new. It has persisted throughout US history. It has just become more pronounced.

On the positive side of the ledger, African Americans serve in highly visible and prominent political positions. Barack Obama was elected the first black president in this nation's history and then reelected to a second term. Colin Powell became the first black man and Condoleezza Rice the first black woman to serve as secretary of state. Mo Cowan of Massachusetts and Tim Scott of South Carolina became the first two black men in history to serve simultaneously in the US Senate. Cory Booker was elected the first black senator from New Jersey. This is an age for the progress of black professionals, marked by a dramatic increase in the number of black physicians, black scientists, black university professors, black engineers, black attorneys, black chief executive officers (CEOs), and other black professionals. Indeed, between 1970 and 2008, the nationwide number of black physicians increased from 6,044 to 54,364, attorneys from 3,703 to 46,644, and college professors from 16,582 to 63,336.[1] This constitutes a period of visible and profound racial progress.

On the negative side, some consider this to be the new Gilded Age[2] and the new Jim Crow era.[3] This is a period in which the rich have grown richer; inequality has become more extreme; the black/white gap in income, wealth, and education has widened; equal opportunities have diminished; and upward mobility has declined. Incarceration rates among the poorer and darker citizens have soared, evoking complaints and condemnation

1

from international human rights organizations. Evidence of racial and class biases persists at every level of the criminal justice system. The minority voter suppression movement has intensified and the Supreme Court has struck down a part of the Voting Rights Act. Black poverty has increased and has become more concentrated and isolated in inner cities.

If African Americans have made tremendous progress, then why has the black/white gap in income, education, and wealth widened? If there is so much visible evidence of progress by black men, why are prisons massively overcrowded with them? What explains this regression in the face of what seems to be a period of progress?

In this book, I address these questions. I explain this paradoxical combination of progress and regression in terms of conflict between an egalitarian coalition and progressive political culture versus a conservative coalition and a reactionary political culture energized by a new form of racism—*metaracism*. The egalitarian coalition produced progress through the establishment of equal opportunity policies that emerged primarily during the 1960s and 1970s. The conservative coalition produced the regression not by reforming equal opportunity policies, but by assaulting, dismantling, dismembering, or shrinking them. The assault on equal opportunity policies contributed to the reversal of progress, an increase in racial repression, and the widening of the black/white gap in income, education, and wealth.

I examine the formation of metaracism, which arises out of concentrated urban poverty. Metaracism is associated with the development of a bifurcated black class structure, the rise of the black middle and professional class, and the growth of concentrated black poverty isolated in the inner city. Metaracism is a revised, refined, and subtle form of racism. As the originator of this concept, Joel Kovel, explains, "Metaracism is a distinct and very peculiar modern phenomenon. Racial degradation continues on a different plane, and through a different agency: those who participate in it are not racists—that is, they are not racially prejudiced—but metaracists, because they acquiesce in the larger cultural order which continues the work of racism."[4]

Metaracism is a form of racism without hateful bigots. It replaces biological determinism with cultural determinism. It no longer dehumanizes all blacks. It accepts the black middle class, but promotes dehumanizing images and stories of welfare queens, teenage girls having babies to get welfare, and black teenage thug culture. It involves the strategic use of race in the assault on progressive policies and the support of extreme inequality. It provides images and narratives that support and boost neoconservative and neoliberal ideologies and that energize reactionary political movements.

Metaracism can be seen in increasingly virulent antiblack rhetoric directed toward the president. Rather than signaling the end of racism and the emergence of a postracial/post–civil rights age, the election of President

Obama pushed to the surface a racism that had been lurking in the dark recesses of US culture. An article entitled "The Coon Caricature: Blacks as Monkeys" describes this resurgence of racism:

> Anti-black monkey imagery came back into the open during the 2008 campaign of Barack Obama. Several T-shirts and buttons were created and openly sold on the auction website eBay depicting Obama as a banana-eating monkey. . . . Though many Americans wanted to believe his election victory was a sign that the country had entered a "post-racial" era, the racist imagery associating the President with apes, and as a chicken and watermelon eating coon suggest otherwise. In fact, several public incidents have linked the proliferation of these images to elected officials in the Republican Party. . . . A Tea [Party] activist and Orange County Republican Party official Marilyn Davenport made headlines when it was revealed that she had sent out an email with the President depicted as the offspring of chimpanzees. The text of the email read, "Now you know why no birth certificate." She claimed to have not thought about the "historic implications" of the image, despite the fact that she had earlier defended a fellow Orange County Republican for having sent out an image of the White House lawn as a watermelon patch with the message, "No Easter egg hunt this year."[5]

Recounted in the same article is an incendiary political cartoon published in the *New York Post* in February 2009:

> Two officers, one with a smoking revolver in hand, stood over the corpse of an ape that [they] had just gunned down on the street. The ape, eyes open, tongue hanging out, several bullet holes in his torso, lay on his back in a large, splattered pool of his own blood. One cop is shown saying to the other, "They'll have to find someone else to write the next stimulus bill." While the cartoon was published in the wake of a high profile killing of a chimpanzee in Connecticut that had mauled its owner, the political nature of the caption, and common knowledge of the all-too-familiar incidents of police shootings of Black suspects, caused many to immediately recognize the old anti-Black monkey stereotype. And it seemed to be aimed squarely at President Obama.[6]

Just as sadly, other members of the first family have not been immune to discrimination and hate:

> In November 2009, a photoshopped, racist image of First Lady Michelle Obama made international news. . . . The image also reappeared on at least one blog, in which the author questioned why it was unacceptable to caricature the First Lady in this way, and yet it seemed to be acceptable that President George W. Bush was likewise caricatured. He re-presented numerous monkey comparisons of President Bush. . . . The blogger was attempting to justify racism using a variation on one of the common excuses, that it's okay to stereotype one group if others are likewise being stereotyped. . . . Ironically, this blog quickly drew in White Supremacists, who proceeded to completely undermine the blogger's original premise by unabashedly engaging in racist, hate-filled rants about the First Family in the comment section.[7]

The election of President Obama activated many racist images, epithets, and comments that percolated into the public space. Some people were unable to accept the president as a full-blooded American. It was evident in the birther and Tea Party movements, in the racially polarized elections, and in the racial polarization over the fatal shooting of Trayvon Martin by George Zimmerman and Zimmerman's subsequent acquittal. It was evident in the use of expressions like "shuck and jive" by Rush Limbaugh and John Sununu to describe the president's decisionmaking style. A major feature of metaracism includes a shift away from blatant hard-core racism to a more subtle and softer form of racism, one that uses coded language.

Metaracism also accommodates the reality of the rise of the black middle class. It focuses on the black poor and a so-called culture of poverty. At the same time, metaracism denies the existence of racism. Indeed, conservative commentators compete with each other over the extent to which they deny the existence of racism and rationalize the racist attacks on the president.

What is new about the current paradox is the tremendous progress made by African Americans that coincides with persisting racial inequality and severe racial repression. Scholars have attempted to explain this paradox, but with little success. They often provide analyses that overlook contradictory cultural trends, grossly underestimate the persistence of racism, misdiagnose the nature of prejudice, miss the adaptability and changing forms of racism, and ignore the extent to which racism has been deeply imbedded in US society. At its core, racism is tied into the US economy, integrated into its dominant culture, and exploited by reactionary political leaders.

In the 1940s, Swedish sociologist and economist Gunnar Myrdal attempted to explain this paradox in terms of what he called "the American dilemma." Myrdal saw a moral struggle within each individual, a struggle between individual prejudices and higher moral values and ideals emanating from the American creed and Christian values. Myrdal believed that the possession of these higher moral values tempered racial prejudices: "The moral struggle goes on within people and not only between them. As people's valuations are conflicting, behavior normally becomes a moral compromise."[8] Rather than seeing a conflict of cultures, Myrdal saw a unity of culture and a conflict within the individual:

> The unity of a culture consists in the fact that all valuations are mutually shared in some degree. We shall find that even a poor and uneducated white person in some isolated and backward rural region in the Deep South, who is violently prejudiced against the Negro and intent upon depriving him of civic rights and human independence, has also a whole compartment in his valuation sphere housing the entire American Creed of liberty, equality, justice and fair opportunity for everybody. He is actually also a good Christian and honestly devoted to the ideals of human brotherhood and the Golden Rule.[9]

Myrdal's optimism and faith was misplaced. There was no unity of US culture. Neither the American creed nor Christian values mediated or tempered the brutality of the institution of slavery. The Southern fundamentalist brand of Christianity and a reactionary political culture supported the institution of slavery and other forms of racial oppression.

Another attempt to explain the paradox of the great progress made by African Americans but persistent racial inequality and racial repression comes from William Julius Wilson who wrote in the late twentieth century. Wilson identifies a paradox of tremendous racial progress and increasing concentrations of black poverty in urban areas. He observes that black poverty had become more concentrated even after an aggressive affirmative action campaign. He concludes that economic changes related to class subordination rather than racism produced the black poverty—that the significance of race was in decline relative to the power of social class.[10]

In yet another view, Nancy DiTomaso insists that black unemployment and poverty rates are substantially higher than white rates, but not because of racism. In her book *The American Non-dilemma*, a reference to Myrdal, she demonstrates that these higher black unemployment and poverty rates were the result of a structure or network of advantages that privileged whites and disadvantaged blacks. This structure includes networks of whites helping other whites get jobs, the location of white communities in areas of job growth, and the greater social capital and community resources within white communities. These advantages contrast with multiple and cumulative disadvantages of poor black communities: isolation from areas of job growth and inadequate social capital and community resources. Like Wilson, she concludes that racial inequality was increasing in spite of the decline of racial prejudice and antiblack hostility. However, unlike Wilson, she draws from a wealth of survey data that indicate that although whites rhetorically abhor racism, many operate with a large amount of misinformation and stereotypes of inner-city blacks.[11]

Wilson and DiTomaso are correct in their observations that racism is no longer as brutal and overt as it was in the past. However, it has not disappeared. It has adapted to profound changes in the black class structure, to the growing concentration of poverty in urban areas in the midst of the rise of the black professional and middle class, and to the rise of extreme inequality.

George Fredrickson, renowned scholar on the history of racism, captures this changing nature of racism: "The term racism is often used in a loose and unreflective way to describe the hostile and negative feeling of one ethnic group or 'people' toward another and the actions resulting from said attitude. . . . The climax of the history of racism came in the twentieth century in the rise and fall of what I will call 'overtly racist regimes.'"[12] He insists that after World War II the old racist regimes based on blood and biological determinism declined because of their association with Hitler and Nazi Germany. He adds that newer racist regimes emerged based on cultural particularism. Nevertheless, he argues that cultural deterministic forms of racism were just as effective as the biologically deterministic forms, depending on how extreme and distorted its characterization of racial minorities. For example, he says, that "extreme racist propaganda, which represented black males as ravaging beasts lusting after white women, served to rationalize the practice of lynching."[13] He adds, "Deterministic cultural particularism can do the work of biological racism quite effectively as we shall see in more detail in later discussions of *volkisch* nationalism in Germany."[14] He demonstrates that current forms of racism tend to be grounded in cultural particularism and associated with various types of contemporary ideologies. Racism is therefore "a scavenger ideology, which gains its powers from the ability to pick out and utilize ideas and values from other sets of ideas and beliefs in specific historical contexts."[15] In other words, the old regimes of overt, brutal, and biologically based racism have ended, as newer culturally based and milder forms have emerged. The old racist frames have been replaced by a new, more subtle racist regime that has accommodated itself to contemporary social and economic realities. The new racism has adapted itself to the rise of the black middle class. It operates to legitimize the growth of concentrated black poverty and a repressive criminal justice system. The term *metaracism* best captures these features of the new racism.

Understanding the Dynamics and Forms of Racism

Like Myrdal, most people in the United States see the American creed and Christianity operating to extinguish racism. Most oppose blatant discrimination and hate speech. Most see racism as an individual phenomenon, involving the actions of a few uneducated, hateful, and prejudiced poor people; a few extremists in the Tea Party movement; or the rare and bizarre behavior of an eccentric basketball team owner. Most see racism as un-American, a marginal issue unrelated to mainstream US values and ideas. Racism is something they would like to forget and bury in the past. Most people are uncomfortable with discussing the subject of racism. Many are unfamiliar with the dynamics of racism because the study of racism has long remained outside the purview of traditional disciplines of literature, history, political science, and law. Even though it has been an integral part of US culture, the subject has only recently moved to center stage in many of these disciplines.[16]

Understanding the dynamics of past racism is critical to understanding contemporary metaracism. My review of the literature on racism underscores the following principles:

- Race and racism are historical and cultural constructs strongly associated with patterns of oppression and the drive to accumulate wealth.
- The constructions of race and racism typically present dominant and subordinate racial groups as binary opposites.
- These constructs function to legitimize patterns of oppression and to desensitize society to the suffering of the oppressed.
- The constructs of racism and race allow for the formation of white identity, which also functions to reduce class conflict and increase tolerance for extreme inequality.
- Racist perspectives have long been accepted as normal and valid precisely because these perspectives have been promoted, validated, and normalized by religious, intellectual, scientific, political, and media elites.
- While the dynamics of racism are similar, the forms of racism change as their structural, cultural, and political dimensions vary.
- "American exceptionalism" is a myth contradicted by a reactionary racist culture that has operated to sustain racial oppression and has periodically clashed with a progressive antiracist culture.

Racism as Historical and Cultural Constructs

Ancient Greek and Roman societies were devoid of the type of modern racism that is based on skin color and biology. In these ancient societies, differences in skin color meant nothing more than differences in variations in degrees of exposure to the sun.[17]

Race is a social construct and racism is a modern phenomenon that emerged out of the process of oppression. Oppression involves acts of violence, genocide, conquest, enslavement, exploitation, subjugation, or exclusion. Oppression also entails organized and systematic efforts that inhibit or obstruct the development of human potentials; arrangements that block access to food and nutrients necessary for adequate human growth; efforts that cut people off from educational and job opportunities; efforts that deny people living wages; and actions that dilute people's votes, silence their voices, and render them powerless in the political community.[18]

According to anthropologist Audrey Smedley, the word "race" entered the English language at the same time the English were conquering the Irish. The English conquest and treatment of the Irish was extremely violent. Men, women, and children were killed. Land was confiscated.[19]

This oppression of the Irish was associated with their racialization by the English. The English constructed negative images, stories, and ideas about the Irish that portrayed them as not just belonging to a different race but as being fundamentally different from and the binary opposite of the English. The English defined the Irish as savage, drunken, irrational, and immoral and themselves as civilized, sober, rational, and moral. A number of scholars insist that the English even characterized the Irish as apelike, much as they later characterized Africans and African Americans.[20] This portrayal of the Irish operated to legitimize the conquest. It desensitized the English to the suffering experienced by the Irish and made it easier for the English to live with themselves as good Christians while committing horrible atrocities on the Irish. This treatment and stereotyping of the Irish by the English set the stage for their violent treatment and stereotyping of Native Americans and African Americans.

As the English settlers conquered the Native Americans, they defined them in oppositional terms. The English considered themselves as civilized and the Indians as savages. The same dynamics arose with African slaves. Black slaves were said to be biologically inferior, savage, irrational, impulsive, ignorant, dangerous, immoral, and repulsive. White English settlers were biologically superior, tame, civilized, rational, calculating, safe, moral, and acceptable. This portrayal of oppressed African Americans evoked strong emotional responses toward them—contempt, repulsion, and hostility—so deep that it shaped decisions and drove behavior sometimes unconsciously and in ways that defied reason and ignored facts.

The Social Functions of Racism: Desensitize Society and Sustain Oppression

As a cultural construct, racism incorporated a complex array of categories, language, symbols, images, narratives, and ideas—all of which served a number of social functions. Racist culture operated to legitimize, normalize, enable, or enforce patterns of oppression and extreme inequality. This culture desensitized society to the suffering of the oppressed. This point is graphically illustrated by Mark Twain in a passage from his book, *The Adventures of Huckleberry Finn,* where Huck is explaining the delay of a steamboat to Tom Sawyer's Aunt Sally:

"It warn't the grounding—that didn't keep us back but a little. We blowed out a cylinder-head."
"Good gracious! Anybody hurt?"
"No'm. Killed a nigger."
"Well, it's lucky; because sometimes people do get hurt."[21]

Through this brief dialogue, Twain shows the extent to which Southern culture dehumanized blacks. In other words, Southern racist culture had so alienated the African American from the human species that the sudden, violent, and traumatic death of a black man from an explosion meant nothing. Indeed, whipping a slave was not like whipping a human being. It was considered a good thing, like whipping an animal to teach it discipline for its own good.

Racist culture also provoked oppression. During the era of slavery, the portrayal of Africans as dangerous savages when unrestrained by slavery encouraged the enslavement and the physical abuse of black slaves. During the era of Jim Crow segregation, the portrayal of blacks as foul-smelling, chicken-thieving, ignorant, and repulsive fools encouraged and provoked their exclusion from white society.

White Identity, Class Conflict, and Increased Tolerance for Extreme Inequality and Repression

The cultural construction of race and white identity operated within several different historical and social contexts to undermine the American creed, reduce class conflict, and increase tolerance for extreme inequality. First, white identity contributed to the formation of what Alexander Saxon refers to as the white republic.[22] From 1787 to 1865, the white United States was like an oppressive settler nation besieged by Native Americans and threatened by potential slave revolts. These potential threats intensified the bond and security created by white identity.[23] "White republicanism" was the idea of a white nation in which citizenship was reserved for whites only.[24] This notion of a white republic was built into the Naturalization Acts of 1790 and 1795, which restricted naturalization to immigrants who were "free white persons" of "good character."[25]

Race and white identity enabled the formation of a strand of political culture that promoted a racially exclusive notion of citizenship and a political community open to whites only. This strand of political culture redefined the American creed and constitutional protections as applying to whites only. Chief Justice Roger B. Taney provides the best illustration of this strand of political culture in the *Dred Scott* decision. In this decision, Taney argues that "it is too clear to dispute" that the Declaration of Independence, the Constitution, and citizenship applied to whites only.[26] In regards to the Declaration of Independence Taney said, "We hold these truths to be self-evident: that all men are created equal. . . . The general words above quoted seem to embrace the whole human family. . . . But it is too clear for dispute that the enslaved African race were not intended to be included and formed no part of the people who framed and adopted this declaration."[27]

Taney makes the same argument in reference to the preamble of the Constitution. He insists that the expression "We the people" refers to people who were members of the political community that produced the Constitution. He claims that this community excluded blacks. He argues further that representatives to the Constitutional Convention passed laws restricting citizenship to whites. Specifically, he adds, "the first of these acts is the naturalization law, which was passed at the second session of the first Congress, March 26, 1790, and confines the right of becoming citizens 'to aliens being free white persons.'"[28] Taney concluded that blacks were not only excluded from citizenship and the political community, they were considered members of an inferior race that could be rightly and justly enslaved and denied rights granted to whites. Taney stated:

> But there are two clauses in the Constitution which point directly and specifically to the negro race as a separate class of persons, and show clearly that they were not regarded as a portion of the people or citizens of the Government then formed. . . . They [blacks] had for more than a century before been regarded as beings of an inferior order; and altogether unfit to associate with the white race, either in social or political relations; and so far inferior that they had no rights which the white man was bound to respect and that the negro might justly and lawfully be reduced to slavery for his benefit.[29]

Second, white identity gave poor European ethnic groups immigrating to the United States, especially Irish, Italians, Germans, and Eastern Europeans, a level of acceptance and entitlement that they would not ordinarily have. These immigrants faced prejudice and hostility from native-born white Anglo-Saxon Protestant (WASP) Americans who saw these immigrants as threats to their jobs and status. For example, if Irish immigrants staked a claim on skilled jobs as Irish, they would face fierce opposition from native-born WASP craft workers. However, by acquiring a white identity and adopting antiblack prejudices, European ethnic immigrants were able to deflect the prejudice and hostility toward them and gain a sense of acceptance among the WASPs.[30]

A number of scholars make this point illustrating the transformation of European immigrants from ethnics who are victimized by prejudice to people who defined themselves as white and who directed their hostility and frustrations toward people of color. For example, B. J. Widick states, "Using the odious term 'niggers' gave the foreign-born worker (mainly Polish) a sense of identity with white society, and by throwing the spotlight of prejudice on the Negro, he turned it away from himself."[31] Other scholars describe how the Irish changed from a group that identified with African Americans as an oppressed group to a group that defined itself as white and that directed its prejudice toward African Americans. Theodore Allen provides a detailed analysis of this transformation in New York City. He focuses on the role of the Irish in the 1863 New York draft riot. During this riot, Irish participants targeted African Americans. Rejecting the idea that the Irish were provoked to riot by a fear that freed blacks would take their jobs, Allen says, "No European immigrants were lynched, no 'white' orphanages were burned, for fear of 'competition' in the labor market."[32]

Third, white identity created what W. E. B. DuBois refers to as a psychological wage that compensated for extremely low wages:

> It must be remembered that the white group of laborers, while they received a low wage, were compensated in part by a sort of public and psychological wage. They were given public deference and titles of courtesy because they were white. They were admitted freely with all classes of white people to public functions, public parks, and the best schools. The police were drawn from their ranks, and the courts, dependent upon their votes, treated them with such leniency as to encourage lawlessness.[33]

Whiteness explained tolerance of extreme poverty in the South. It gave Southern whites a sense of privilege and superiority over people of color. No matter how downtrodden or severely poor a white person was, he or she was always above people of color in intelligence, morality, status, and social acceptance. Because white identity allowed poor whites to identify more with rich whites than with poor blacks this identity suppressed class-consciousness and increased tolerance for the extreme inequality in the South.

According to historian Howard Zinn, rich Southern landowners deliberately pitted poor whites against poor blacks in order to superexploit both. Zinn cites Tom Watson, a white Populist Party leader, warning poor whites and poor blacks of this use of racial antagonism to exploit them both. Speaking in 1890 Watson said: "You are kept apart that you may be separately fleeced of your earnings. You are made to hate each other because upon that hatred is rested the keystone of the arch of financial despotism which enslaves you both. You are deceived and blinded that you may not see how this race antagonism perpetuates a monetary system which beggars both."[34]

White racial identity retarded class consciousness and allowed for a level of superexploitation, extreme inequality, and repression not tolerated in nonracist societies. White identity and racial tensions allowed members of the dominant class to pit white workers against workers of color. During the late nineteenth and early twentieth century, mine owners deliberately used blacks as scabs to break strikes organized by white workers. As long as black and white mine workers fought each other, mine owners could suppress the wages of both, thus increasing their own wealth.

In a hierarchical labor market, white skilled laborers enhanced their status, privileges, and wages by excluding blacks. Historically, up until the passage of the Civil Rights Act of 1964, most skilled trade unions had clauses in their constitutions or charters that explicitly excluded blacks.[35]

White skilled workers found more in common with the white manager or owner of a production facility than with lower-wage unskilled black workers. In this sense, racism prevented the formation of the Marxist notion of class consciousness among the proletariat—black and white.

Finally, white identity allowed for the construction of nonwhite scapegoats. During economic crises that caused whites to lose their land, jobs, and livelihood, racial divisions provided them with scapegoats, which allowed the most destitute among them to shift their attention away from the dominant class and direct their rage and frustration to people of color. The history of race relations in the United States is filled with periods of economic crisis precipitating episodes of white rage and extreme violence directed at people of color. The recession of 1882–1885 was associated with white mine workers and railroad workers violently targeting Chinese workers. Opposition to Chinese workers led to the passage of the Chinese Exclusion Act of 1882, which barred Chinese workers from entering the United States. The 1885 Rock Springs, Wyoming, massacre is but one of many examples of attacks on Chinese workers "where whites refused to work in the same mine with Chinese laborers; armed with rifles and revolvers, they invaded the Chinese section of town, shot Chinese workers as they fled, and burned the buildings."[36] The Panic of 1910–1911 and the depression of 1913–1914 were associated with the period of ethnic cleansing documented by Elliot Jaspin. Thousands of blacks were violently forced out of predominantly white counties throughout the Deep South and Midwest. The Great Depression of 1920–1923 was associated with several race riots in which white mobs destroyed entire black communities, most notably Rosewood, Florida, on which the movie *Rosewood* was based, and Tulsa, Oklahoma. In the Tulsa race riot, white mobs wiped out the "Black Wall Street," a strip in the downtown areas with a string of prosperous black retail businesses and black banks. The riot left over 10,000 African Americans homeless.[37]

White identity and racial tensions took a toll on society in other ways. As black laborers were pitted against white laborers, class solidarity collapsed and the wages and living standards of both blacks and whites declined. As white rage arising from economic crises was directed at people of color, attention was redirected away from the role of the dominant class in dismantling state programs designed to promote upward social mobility. Instead, programs were designed to enrich the wealthy. White identity accelerated the process of the rich becoming richer and poor whites becoming poorer.

The rise of race consciousness and the Redeemer period following the Reconstruction era illustrate this point. During the Reconstruction era, state governments had increased property taxes by as much as 400 percent. The additional resources were used to provide an adequate public education system, to build roads, and to assist the poor blacks and whites. The state government also operated to ensure fair payment to sharecroppers.

The Redeemer movement emerged as an all-out assault on the Reconstruction programs. This movement was led by the dominant class in the South, which consisted of the Southern land aristocracy, merchants, mine owners, and mill owners. This class had formed an alliance with Northern industry and finance.[38] This dominant class was hell-bent on dismantling Reconstruction programs and using the state government for the benefit of the dominant class. When this class captured the state government, it used it to enforce a crop lien system and to take away voting rights from almost all blacks and most poor whites. This class reduced taxes, violently suppressed labor unions, and reallocated public education funds to the benefit of the dominant class and to the detriment of both poor whites and poor blacks. Jack Bloom illustrates this well: "The inequalities produced by this system were immense. The extremes are illustrated by two counties in Mississippi in 1907, one majority black, one majority white. The white county, Itawamba, had a per capita expenditure of $5.65 for whites and $3.50 for blacks. Washington County, whose majority was black, spent $80.00 per capita on whites and $2.50 on blacks."[39] Most of these Washington County whites represented the dominant landowning class.

The Role of Elites in Promoting, Validating, and Normalizing Racist Perspectives

Racist stereotypes, narratives, and perspectives come to be accepted by the public as normal and factual because of the role of political, intellectual, religious, and media elites. These elites play a key part in promoting racism. Chief Justice Taney was noted above as promoting the idea of black inferiority. Southern religious leaders often used the story of Noah's curse of Ham to argue that black slavery was endorsed by the Bible and ordained by God. Southern political leaders spoke openly about how the lack of intelligence in blacks made them suitable for slave labor. Historians lectured and wrote about the absence of civilization in an Africa that was ravaged by cannibals and black savages. In the latter decades of the nineteenth century and the first half of the twentieth century, an entire industry of scientific racism emerged in which academia was inundated with scholarly works promoting racism. Racism was promoted in the specialized disciplines of craniology, heredity, and eugenics. It was well established in the disciplines of biology, psychology, criminology, and sociology. Social Darwinism embraced a racist ideology as it attacked social programs intended to help the poor. In their works, Stephen Jay Gould[40] and Thomas F. Gosset[41] provide extensive reviews of this promotion of racism by the scholarly community and intellectual elites.

The problem of scientific racism was somewhat like the paradigm problem in natural science popularized by the research of Thomas Kuhn.[42] The scientific paradigm was a worldview and set of assumptions that structured the thinking of scientists and shaped their research questions, hypotheses, and conclusions. Gould demonstrates that racist paradigms biased the most conservative and exacting scientists. By promoting the old paradigms of biological- and genetic-based racism, intellectual elites not only normalized and legitimized racism—they popularized and privileged it. They gave it a heightened sense of credibility and validity. To a large degree, the paradigms of biological determinism have now been replaced by the paradigms of cultural determinism found in the culture of poverty and urban underclass literature. For example, the old paradigms claimed that blacks were biologically and genetically predisposed to commit violent crimes. The new paradigms claim that black values, black underclass subculture, and young black male thug culture predisposes blacks to commit violent crimes.

Structural, Cultural, and Political Dimensions of Racism

Racism takes different forms, even though the dynamics within each form are similar. The forms of racism change as their structural, cultural, and political dimensions vary. Understanding the structural, cultural, and political dimensions of past forms of racism illuminates the dynamics of contemporary metaracism.

The structural dimension. Racism initially emerged out of the drive to accumulate wealth, which led to conquest and exploitation. The structural component arose as the dominant class established a system of accumulating wealth through the organized and systematic exploitation of the subordinate classes. The structure of racism is its economic base: the dominant mode of production, the organization of production, the manner in which labor is exploited, and the way wealth is accumulated. As the economic base of racism changes, so does the form of racism. At least four different forms of racism, each with a different economic base, can be identified: dominative racism, dominative/aversive racism, aversive racism, and metaracism.

The economic base of dominative racism was the institution of plantation slavery. Racial animus did not produce this institution. Greed did. The drive of plantation owners to make money and accumulate wealth led to the construction of the institution of slavery. The organization of the Southern plantation system formed the economic base of a brutal and sadistic form of racism. Once the institution of slavery was established, plantation owners defined African Americans as fundamentally different from other people, as biologically inferior and subhuman.

The term *dominative* is appropriate because this form of racism involved a system of intense, sadistic, and direct control to produce the maximum or superexploitation of the slave. Dominative racism ended with the destruction of the institution of slavery in 1865. The economic base of dominative/aversive racism that came next was the coexistence of the sharecropping system of plantation labor with an emerging system of mills and other production facilities. Dominative/aversive racism was the Jim Crow system of Southern segregation. The sharecropping system was dominative because it involved some elements of the old slave system. The former master maintained ownership and control over the land. The dominant class in the South—landowners, merchants, and mill owners—superexploited sharecroppers through the crop lien system. Although most sharecroppers were white, they were thought of as mostly black in the public mind. This racializing of sharecroppers enabled a more intense form of exploitation and repression. The dominant class pressured blacks to remain on the land, excluded blacks from the mills, and imposed a rigid system of racial segregation in public spaces. The combination of domination and segregation made the term *dominative/aversive racism* appropriate. This system lasted from 1865 to 1965.

Aversive racism emerged in the North around the same time period (1880–1970), as Northern industries and urban areas exploded in growth. Organizationally, this form of racism was associated with racially segregated cities, resulting in racially segmented and hierarchical labor markets ranging from professional, elite skilled labor, semiskilled labor, and unskilled labor. Aversive racism was marked by a hierarchy of labor that concentrated blacks in the lowest paying, least desirable unskilled industrial jobs and excluded them from higher paying skilled jobs. Aversive racism also involved segmented labor markets and racially segregated residential areas.

The cultural dimension. Culture is the learned and shared language, images, narratives, myths, ideologies, and ways of thinking that operate to shape perceptions and influence emotions. The cultural component of racism has involved the social construction of racial groups and the use of culture in ways that legitimize and normalize racial oppression. The cultural content of racism has changed as the economic base of racism has changed. The culture of dominative racism characterized blacks as animals, biologically and genetically predisposed to plantation labor, needing to be tamed and whipped into submission. As noted above, this culture normalized, legitimized, and promoted the institution of slavery. The culture of dominative/aversive racism characterized blacks as repulsive with an offensive odor, childlike and passive when employed in heavy farm labor, but a dangerous would-be chicken thief or rapist when not controlled. This culture normalized and encouraged racial segregation and an occasional lynching.

The culture of aversive racism depicted blacks as supermasculine menials, suitable for heavy physical labor and unsuitable for mental labor. In the first quarter of the twentieth century, racist cultural images and narrative overlapped with two opposing racist ideologies—eugenics and social Darwinism. Eugenics called for government intervention for the purpose of genetically breeding superior races and reducing the breeding of inferior races. Social Darwinism opposed government intervention in society, as it promoted laissez-faire capitalism and the notion of the survival of the fittest. Although the racist component is downplayed or denied by neo–social Darwinists today, social Darwinists envisioned rich white people as the superior species that would survive and become the dominant race while the inferior races, poor people of color, would eventually die out. The image of poor people as inferior people of color made it easier for social Darwinists to oppose public education, public assistance, and any other programs that would ease the suffering of the poor or assist in upward social mobility. Almost every aspect of the cultural component of racism functioned to legitimize oppression, exonerate society, and desensitize members of society to the difficulties and suffering of the oppressed.

The political dimension. The political component of racism has involved struggles over power and ideas; that is, conflicts between political interests opposed to racial oppression and those supportive of racial oppression. Because racial oppression has involved economic exploitation, supportive interests have generally included the dominant economic class.[43] This point is well illustrated by the extreme aggression in which Southern plantation owners defended the institution of slavery.

The struggles over ideas have involved conflicts between progressive and reactionary ideologies. Progressive ideology argues for using the powers of the state to ameliorate oppression, to protect the weak and vulnerable, to promote equal opportunities, and to improve the quality of the lives of all citizens. Reactionary ideology argues in support of economic and political arrangements that benefit the dominant economic classes, and against the use of state powers for the protection and benefit of subordinate classes or oppressed races.

These struggles over the power and ideas that shape US politics have been obscured by the myth of American exceptionalism, which denies both the existence of this struggle and racism. These struggles have also been obscured by compromises and alliances, and by the dominance of one political ideology over the other.

Nevertheless, these struggles explain the paradox of progress and regression. They explain episodes of political polarization, the most severe of which erupted into the Civil War. They explain major shifts in political regimes: the shifts from the slavery regime, to the Reconstruction regime, to the Redeemer regime, and to other regimes throughout history. Indeed, the outcome of these struggles have determined whether the state will operate to promote or ameliorate racial oppression.[44]

This perspective on US politics contradicts the notion of American exceptionalism. Exceptionalism insists that the United States is great and exceptional because of its revolution against a monarch, its rejection of centralized governmental powers, its lack of a feudal past with hereditary upper classes and titles of nobility, its possession of an open frontier, and its promotion of Christian values. These exceptional experiences allegedly explain the absence of class struggle and US commitment to equality, freedom, limited government, state's rights, individualism, and free and open markets. The myth of exceptionalism assumes that all of the founding fathers had the same values and vision, which produced a homogeneous and distinct political culture. Racial oppression and conflicting political cultures are excluded from this myth.

However, these conflicts and racism were an integral part of US history and politics. The struggle between progressive and reactionary political movements is a major feature of US history from the American Revolution to today. Understanding this struggle is critical to understanding the racial politics of the twenty-first century.

Thomas Paine and Progressive Ideology

Thomas Paine promoted progressive ideology. His ideas inspired the American Revolution, spawned the abolitionist movement, and gave full expression to a progressive political culture from the Revolution to today. For Paine, governments were established to protect the most vulnerable from the most powerful, to ameliorate oppression, to end poverty, to promote equal opportunity, and to improve the quality of the lives of all of its citizens beyond what it would be before the establishment of government.

Paine accepted natural inequality—that arising from differences in talents, skills, frugality, work effort, and luck. However, he was appalled by unnatural and extreme inequality. He argued that extreme and unnatural inequality arose from "landed monopoly" and was "the greatest evil." He added that "the contrast of affluence and wretchedness continually meeting and offending the eye, is like dead and living bodies chained together."[45] He insisted that, since the accumulation of wealth can occur only within society, the rich owed a debt to society. This debt was to be paid through taxes. He believed in taxing the rich to redistribute resources to the poor. Indeed, he believed that taxation was the price of civilization (a view often attributed to Supreme Court Justice Oliver Wendell Homes). According to Paine,

> To understand what the state of society ought to be, it is necessary to have some idea of the natural and primitive state of man. . . . There is not, in that state, any of those spectacles of human misery which poverty and want present to our eyes in all the towns and streets in Europe. Poverty, therefore, is a thing created by that which is called civilized life. It exists not in the natural state. . . .
>
> Taking then the matter upon this ground, the first principle of civilization ought to have been, and ought still to be, that the condition of every person born into the world, after a state of civilization commences, ought not to be worse than it if he had been born before that period.[46]

For Paine, freedom was not freedom from government or its powers. This concept of freedom was negative freedom, truncated freedom and reactionary freedom (as will be demonstrated later). For Paine, freedom required a positive role of the use of governmental resources and powers to improve the quality of the lives of its citizens beyond what it would be in the state of nature. Whereas many scholars attribute this positive concept of freedom to Franklin Roosevelt, it originated with Paine. It was part of a progressive, antiracist culture from the time of the Revolution to today. Paine's ideas not only inspired the Revolution, but they influenced other Revolutionary leaders, abolitionists, civil rights leaders, and progressive leaders throughout history and provided the foundations for modern liberalism.[47]

Paine's legacy was not without some controversy. Rogers Smith claims that he ascribed to male privilege and was biased in favor of Europeans.[48] However, Christopher Hitchens describes Paine's passionate defense of Native Americans against the theft of their land and the use of the Bible to justify conquest and slavery. Hitchens also notes Paine's opposition when Thomas Jefferson allowed slavery to expand into the Louisiana Territory. Paine had urged Jefferson to allow free African Americans to migrate into this territory. According to Hitchens,

> As the 19th century progressed, Paine's inspiration resurfaced, and his influence was felt . . . in the agitation against slavery in America. John Brown, ostensibly a Calvinist, had Paine's books in his camp. Abraham Lincoln was a close reader of his work, and used to deploy arguments from the Age of Reason in his disputes with religious sectarians. . . . The rise of the labour movement and the agitation for women's suffrage saw Paine's example being revived and quoted. When Franklin Roosevelt made his great speech to rally the American people against fascism after the attack on Pearl Harbor he quoted an entire paragraph from Paine's *The Crisis*.[49]

Reactionary Ideology

Paine may well have been the most exceptional intellectual leader of the American Revolution. Few of the other leaders of the Revolution or the new nation were as committed to the ideals of freedom and equality as Paine.[50] At the same time, none were reactionary—all were concerned with building a workable government. But they were divided on many issues, particularly the proper allocation of governmental powers between the states and the federal government. Jefferson initially opposed the US Constitution for shifting too much power to the federal government. He believed in states' rights and limited federal powers. In contrast, Alexander Hamilton had a vision of a strong federal government that maintained a central banking system and promoted the rise of a modern industrial state.[51]

All of the intellectual leaders of the Revolution opposed the institution of slavery. However, because the economy depended on this institution, these leaders were constrained to tolerate slavery. The constraints of this institution and the drive of the nation to accumulate wealth eventually pulled the entire nation down into the pit of reactionary politics. Later, support for slavery gave rise to reactionary ideology.

If Paine gave full expression to the American creed, Jefferson provided the Southern compromise that allowed for the formation of reactionary ideology. While in his early years as a revolutionary, Jefferson opposed slavery and promoted the ideas of equality. In his later years, he supported slavery and the notion of the racial inferiority of blacks.

Although he promoted these ideas in reaction to the excessive and abusive use of federal powers in enforcing the Alien and Sedition Acts of 1798, Jefferson promoted the notion of states' rights and (with James Madison) introduced the concepts of nullification, interposition, and secession. These same ideas were historically used by Southerners to defend slavery and Jim Crow segregation from federal restrictions and encroachments.

Reactionary and racist ideology emerged as political leaders defended slavery and conquest. For example, John Calhoun, Andrew Jackson's vice president, claimed that slavery was good for US society, good for whites, and good for blacks. He insisted that slavery was the basis of US wealth and civilization: "There never has yet existed a wealthy and civilized society in which one portion of the community did not, in point of fact, live on the labor of the other."[52]

Although he is portrayed in US history as a common self-made man of modest background and with a disdain for the air of superiority and exclusivity that had defined the Southern aristocracy, Jackson was also a slave owner. He started with a small cotton plantation with 9 slaves; at the height of his career, he owned over 1,000 acres of land and over 150 slaves. As president, he supported the institution of slavery and used the US Army to forcibly remove the Cherokee Indians from their homeland.[53]

Most antebellum presidents were slave owners who openly supported slavery. John Tyler believed that slavery brought Christianity and civilization to the slave. James Polk, the president who conquered half of Mexico and acquired land for the expansion of slavery, claimed that masters must discipline their slaves before showing them any regard or respect. Zachary Taylor, another slave owner, claimed that the South must defend slavery with the sword.[54] As political leaders became more comfortable in supporting slavery and conquest, they became more aggressive and uncompromising in promoting their right to accumulate wealth.

Whereas Paine and progressive ideology called for government to use its powers to ameliorate oppression, reactionaries defined "tyranny" as governmental powers interfering with the right to accumulate wealth through the oppression of others. This concept of tyranny became part of an aggressive, uncompromising, and sometimes violent reactionary ideology and movement.[55]

This reactionary concept of tyranny drove the Texas independence movement. Although most people romanticize this movement in the stories of Davy Crocket, Jim Bowie, and the Alamo, this independence movement was precipitated largely by a Mexican government that opposed slavery after winning independence from Spain. Richard Parker points out that the movement was initiated by slave plantation interests to separate Texas from Mexico in order to protect and expand the institution of slavery:

> However, Mexico's sudden independence from Spain in 1821 brought a new government both decidedly hostile to slavery and keen to control its most northern province which was filling up with Americans. Mexico restricted slavery and eventually abolished it, though at the pleading of Stephen F. Austin. . . . Texans gained narrow exceptions. Austin himself vacillated, alternately encouraging plantation owners to come, pleading with Mexico for leniency and questioning whether slavery was worth it, though he ultimately came down in favor of slavery, declaring, "Texas must be a slave country." Mexico in turn banned immigration from the United States. Texans retaliated by declaring independence. Slavery became legal and Austin himself purchased a male slave that year for $1,200, for no apparent purpose. By the end of the 1830s the Texan slave population had blossomed to 5,000.[56]

Thus, the state of Texas was born out of an independence movement provoked by slave owners who believed in their right and freedom to own slaves. For them, tyranny was the Mexican government interfering with their right to own and exploit slaves.

This reactionary concept of tyranny played a major role in the Southern secessionist movement and the Civil War. The Confederacy was not a rebel movement born out of the ideas of states' rights and individual freedom; it was an aggressive and uncompromising movement led by the dominant planter class that was determined to expand slavery. The political leaders of these states were driven by their uncompromising support for slavery, by their drive to expand into other territories, and by their unwavering belief that it was tyranny for any government to block this expansion or to regulate slavery. Despite President Abraham Lincoln's efforts to compromise, the Southern states seceded from the union.

The Constitution of the Confederate States of America reflected this obsession with the defense of slavery. It contained numerous provisions providing strong and clear support for the institution of slavery: provisions that prohibited the Confederate government from passing any "law denying or impairing the right of property in negro slaves," that guaranteed the rights of slave owners to travel throughout any state without interference from any state government, and that upheld the rights of slave owners in any federal territory.

This reactionary ideology, with its reactionary concept of tyranny is reemerging today. It is reflected in the Tea Party charges that President Obama is a tyrant for enacting the Affordable Care Act and the economic stimulus bill. It is evident in Southern political leaders calling for secession.

Struggle and Progress

Progressive and reactionary movements have clashed periodically throughout US history. As noted above, the most severe clash produced the Civil War. When the Southern reactionary forces were defeated, the Reconstruction regime emerged. This regime reflected the ideals of Paine: ameliorate oppression, protect the vulnerable from the powerful, alleviate the pain of poverty, and improve the quality of the lives of people beyond what it would have been in a state of nature.

The two movements clashed again in the period following Reconstruction. The Redeemer movement emerged to redeem the glory of the Old South. This aggressive and uncompromising movement was dedicated to overthrowing the Reconstruction regime. Once it succeeded, it established the racial caste system of the South that lasted until 1964.

Progressive and reactionary movements coexisted during the New Deal era. This coexistence produced progress and regression. Progress came through the New Deal programs and later through industrial production during World War II. Whereas blacks suffered severe repression in the South—extreme poverty, exclusion from job markets, and lynchings—they made gains from some of the New Deal programs, even though racial discrimination restricted their benefits. President Franklin Roosevelt took bolder stands against discrimination with the formation of the Fair Employment Practices Commission in 1941.

African Americans progressed with the collapse of the Southern sharecropping system, with the expansion of war production, and with their mass migration from rural to urban areas. This progress was accelerated by the emergence of the equal opportunity regime of the 1960s, which was created by several political movements and political coalitions: civil rights, civil liberties, and antipoverty. These coalitions joined the New Deal coalition and formed one of the most progressive and powerful coalitions in US history. The New Deal, civil rights, antipoverty, and civil liberties coalitions constituted an egalitarian coalition, which produced the equal opportunity regime. This regime produced a flood of progressive policies.

During the 1930s, the New Deal had established a plethora of programs in several areas: income transfer (social security benefits, unemployment benefits, Aid to Dependent Children, Aid to the Blind, and Aid to the Permanently and Totally Disabled), public service jobs (Civilian Conservation Corps, Public Works Administration, Works Progress Administration); improved working conditions (minimum wage, National Labor Relations Board); agriculture (Agricultural Adjustment Act); and financial regulations. These policies contributed to the improvement in the quality of the lives of most US citizens, black and white.

Progress continued during the 1960s with the civil rights, antipoverty, and civil liberty movements. The civil rights movement produced the Civil Rights Act of 1964, Voting Rights Act of 1965, Fair Housing Act of 1968, and many others. The antipoverty movement produced food stamps, Medicaid and Medicare, the National School Lunch Program, the Head Start Program, Upward Bound, the Elementary and Secondary Education Act of 1965 (now No Child Left Behind), and others. It also included the expansion of Aid to Dependent Children to Aid to Families with Dependent Children. The civil liberties movement brought about the liberalization of criminal justice policies.

Like a tsunami, this flood of progressive policies swept aside the old racist regime, ushered in a new progressive era, and produced the equal opportunity regime. This regime did much to ameliorate racial oppression in the United States. The egalitarian coalition and the progressive political culture suppressed racial prejudices. Racist culture was under siege. Blatant racial prejudices became unpopular, rejected, and despised within popular culture in the United States. Aggressive affirmative action programs emerged. African Americans experience remarkable progress. A strong and educated black middle class emerged. But the equal opportunity regime came under attack by the end of the 1970s.

The Emergence of Metaracism

Several factors contributed to the ascension of metaracism in the early 1980s. First, the structural situation of African Americans changed. In the

1950s, most black families lived below the poverty line. Blacks had experienced great progress during the 1960s and 1970s, so that black/white gaps in education, income, and wealth declined. By the end of the 1970s, most blacks had moved out of poverty and the black middle class had increased substantially due to black migration out of poor rural areas, to their movement out of sharecropping and into industrial and professional jobs in urban areas, to the success of the public programs of the 1960s, and to a dramatic increase in black education. With the rapid rise of the black middle class, a biologically based racism defied reality and made no sense. Old racism declined as it no longer fit contemporary reality. But this progress came to a halt in the 1980s. The manufacturing sector contracted. Manufacturing jobs declined. Unemployment and urban poverty increased. As the black middle class moved out of inner cities, urban poverty became more isolated and concentrated. This isolated and concentrated poverty emerged as the structural basis for metaracism.

A second factor that contributed to the rise of metaracism had to do with the decline of progressive ideology and interests and the emergence of reactionary ideology and interests. Reactionary interests attacked the equal opportunity regime. However, because this regime was well established and enjoyed strong public support, the attacks involved more subtle racist innuendos and code language. A new form of racial politics emerged involving racial euphemisms, innuendoes, and code words. As Stephen Steinberg suggests,

> What is all the more remarkable is that racial issues have dominated recent elections with scarcely any mention of race in general or of African Americans in particular. . . . If race were given explicit mention, this would invite charges of "racism" which not only arouses opposition among sympathetic whites, but runs the risk of antagonizing blacks and setting off a race war. Through these code words it is possible to play on racial stereotypes, appeal to racial fears, and heap blame on blacks without naming them. Thus, in this cryptic vernacular we have a new and insidious form of race-baiting that is so well camouflaged that it does not carry the political liabilities that were evident, for example, in David Duke's abortive campaign for the United States Senate in 1990.[57]

Political leaders began to exploit these subtle biases in politically expedient and strategic ways.

Ian Lopez traces this strategic use of racism back to George Wallace, Barry Goldwater, Richard Nixon, and others. He notes that, when George Wallace first ran for governor of Alabama, the National Association for the Advancement of Colored People (NAACP) endorsed him and the Ku Klux Klan (KKK) endorsed his opponent. Wallace had a reputation for treating all people fairly, regardless of race. He even campaigned among workers and spoke of the welfare of the poor. His opponent was a blatant racist.

Wallace lost the election, but he learned how to use racism strategically. He ran again four years later on a promise to maintain segregation. In 1963, he stood in front of the door of the main building at the University of Alabama to defy a court order to allow blacks to register for the university. Wallace avoided blatant racist statements; he couched his opposition in terms of the "illegal usurpation of the power by the Central Government."[58] Lopez notes that Wallace received over 100,000 telegrams and letters from all over the country in response to his opposition to desegregating Alabama public universities. Ninety-five percent of them praised him for his courage to standing up to the federal government. Lopez suggests that Wallace learned the lesson of using racism strategically without the use of racist language:

> At his inauguration, Wallace had defended segregation and extolled the proud Anglo-Saxon Southland, thereby earning national ridicule as an unrepentant redneck. Six months later, talking not about stopping integration but about states' rights and arrogant federal authority—and visually aided by footage showing him facing down a powerful Department of Justice official rather than vulnerable black students attired in their Sunday best—Wallace was a countrywide hero. "States' rights" was a paper-thin abstraction from the days before the Civil War when it had meant the right of Southern states to continue slavery.[59]

Lopez insists that Wallace had become a pioneer of a new soft form of racism in which he could exploit racial fears without mentioning race. Wallace focused on arrogant and excessive federal powers, states' rights, crime, and welfare.

However, this color-blind, dog whistle racism predates Wallace. It was quite evident in "The Southern Manifesto," a document written in 1956 and signed by nineteen US senators and eighty-two representatives in protest of the *Brown v. Board of Education* decision.[60] The document condemned the Brown decision as a form of tyranny, an excessive and unconstitutional exercise of federal judicial powers in violation of the reserved powers of the states. It said nothing about preserving racial segregation, nothing about white supremacy, and nothing demeaning about blacks. It mentioned race only in the context of explaining how this liberal decision disrupted the racial harmony of the South and precipitated racial conflict. Indeed, the whole idea that the use of federal powers to protect the rights of oppressed minorities constitutes a form of tyranny has long been a part of Southern reactionary and racist culture.

To some degree color-blind, dog whistle politics was evident in the Redeemer movement's assault on the Reconstruction regime. Leaders of this movement claimed that the Reconstruction regime overtaxed wealthy farmers, allowed illiterate and irresponsible voters of bad character to vote, and overextended state budgets, spending too much money on public programs and driving state governments to the brink of bankruptcy. These leaders insisted that the Reconstruction regime gave too much power to blacks at the expense of whites. They used seemingly innocuous language as they promoted laws to mandate racial segregation. They claimed that segregation was needed to maintain racial harmony and to secure public safety. See *Plessy v. Ferguson.*[61]

The Redeemer movement was a reactionary movement because it revolted against a progressive regime. Indeed, the entrenchment of the Radical Republicans (members of Congress who were most passionate in their promotion of social justice and their opposition to racism, racial segregation, and Ku Klux Klan violence)[62] may have constrained the racism of the Redeemers. It is quite feasible that the entrenchment of the equal opportunity regime and the egalitarian coalition may be constraining the blatant racism of the reactionary movement today.

Wallace, Nixon, and Ronald Reagan all used color-blind, dog whistle, racial politics, but they did so in different ways and for different reasons. Wallace and Nixon were both opportunists because they used dog whistle politics strategically. They both had populist sides: neither opposed the New Deal and both supported white labor. Wallace supported white labor unions and jobs programs but, at the same time, he opposed the entire civil rights agenda.

President Nixon used dog whistle politics in a more limited, opportunistic, and two-faced manner. That is, he used it primarily as his "Southern strategy" to expand his political base in the South and win over Southern voters. Nixon campaigned in the South on a promise to oppose court-mandated busing and to promote law and order. Overall, he was moderate by today's standards. He continued most of Lyndon Johnson's Great Society programs. He combined many of the War on Poverty and urban renewal programs into block grants, creating for example, the Comprehensive Employment Training Act, the Community Development Block Grant, and others. Block grants gave state and local governments more flexibility and discretion over federal programs. Nixon created the General Revenue program, which operated like President Obama's economic stimulus bill; it allocated federal money to state and local governments to assist them during downturns in the economy. Nixon also introduced the Philadelphia Plan, the first federal set-aside program for minority business enterprises.

President Reagan was different from Wallace and Nixon. He was more like the Redeemers in the sense that he supported the rich at the expense of the poor. He was decidedly pro-business, pro–upper class, and antiunion. He substantially cut taxes on major corporations, businesses, and the rich; pursued pro-business and anti-labor policies; and attempted to cut spending on programs for the poor. Like Wallace, Reagan used subtle racial signals strategically. He told stories that contrasted hardworking taxpaying whites with lazy welfare-cheating blacks. Lopez quoted Reagan as telling the story of the "Chicago welfare queen [with] eighty names, thirty addresses, [and] twelve Social Security cards [who] is collecting veteran's benefits on four non-existing deceased husbands. She's got Medicaid, getting food stamps, and she is collecting welfare under each of her names. Her tax-free cash income is over \$150,000." [63] Lopez added,

> More directly placing [the] white voter in the story, Reagan frequently elicited supportive outrage by criticizing the food stamp program as helping "some young fellow ahead of you to buy a T-bone steak" while "you were waiting in line to buy hamburger." This was the toned-down version. When he first field-tested the message in the South, that "young fellow" was more particularly described as a "strapping young buck." The epithet "buck" has long been used to conjure the threatening image of a physically powerful black man often one who defies white authority and who lusts for white women. When Reagan used the term "strapping young buck," his whistle shifted dangerously toward the full audible range. [64]

The strategic use of racial politics combined with the growth of con-centrated poverty contributed to the formation of metaracism. Metaracism was different from and similar to earlier forms of racism. It was different in the sense that it was not hard-core racism. It was not as blatant, egregious, or hateful as earlier forms. It rejected the biological and genetic determin-ism, the mythology of pure blood and pure races, the extreme hostility, and the revulsion characteristic of old style racism. Metaracism no longer toler-ated racial exclusion or racial prejudices; it was racism without visible racists.

Metaracism was similar to earlier forms of racism. It exhibited some of the same dynamics and functions of older forms of racism. Like them, metaracism has particular structural, cultural, and political components. Its structural component is associated with the growth of concentrated poverty and extreme inequality. It is related to the expansion of black poverty, the spatial concentration and isolation of the black poor, a split between the black poor and the black middle class, and the rise of mass incarceration, with more black men in jail and prison than ever before in US history.

Metaracism is compatible with the rise of the black middle class and black professionals. It depicts the black middle class favorably. It accepts and applauds people like Herman Cain (former presidential candidate and president of the National Federation of Restaurants), Condoleezza Rice (former secretary of state), Clarence Thomas (associate justice of the US Supreme Court), Benjamin Carson (brain surgeon and Fox News commen-tator), and other blacks who reinforce its view of exceptionalism and neoliberalism.

Metaracism is well integrated within an emerging reactionary political culture. This culture characterizes real US citizens as believing in small government, individualism, and self-reliance. It portrays blacks as being dependent on government, having a sense of entitlement, and feeling that government and society owe them something—jobs and acceptance into prestigious universities—not through hard work like everyone else, but through affirmative action.

The new metaracism is a hodgepodge of new and old stereotypes, images, narratives, and ideologies. It supports neoconservatives and neoliberalism and conflates race, ideology, and nationalism. Joel Kovel argues that "metaracism exists wherever the ends of the large-scale system of the modern Industrial State are considered more important than the human needs of men."[65]

The most malicious and oppressive aspect of metaracism arises in the space where race and class intersect. In this space, metaracism demonizes the black poor as being trapped in a culture of poverty and hostile to education and hard work. It portrays concentrated poverty areas as inhabited by a dangerous, predatory, and repulsive underclass and infested with hyperviolent, wild youth gangs that have no regard for human life.

Like older forms of racism, metaracism continues to be associated with patterns of oppression and the drive to accumulate wealth. It continues to desensitize society to the pain and suffering of the oppressed, to legitimize and enable oppression, and to present dominant and oppressed groups in binary oppositional terms. It portrays the black poor as the binary opposite of the white middle class. It rationalizes concentrated poverty and extreme inequality. It is promoted by the dominant economic class in order to divide lower-class whites and blacks to superexploit both. It enables and encourages an exceedingly repressive and racially biased criminal justice system. It has shifted the blame for concentrated poverty to the poor themselves and provided a strong ideological basis for shrinking or dismantling the equal opportunity state.

By the twenty-first century, metaracism had emerged with a corporate-centered coalition and a new reactionary ideology. This coalition, fueled by metaracism and neoliberal and neoconservative ideology, is leading a reactionary movement and an assault on the equal opportunity state. This assault has produced public policy changes that have contributed to a rise in racial inequality and racial oppression. In this book, I examine metaracism and this reactionary political movement.

The rest of the book is organized as follows. In Chapter 2, I focus more closely on the structural dimension of metaracism, the rise of concentrated urban poverty, and economic insecurity. In Chapter 3, I examine the culture of metaracism, the racialization of the poor, the social construction of the black underclass, and images and stories of young poor black men as dangerous street criminals. In Chapter 4, I analyze the rise of the corporate-centered conservative coalition: the alliance among corporate leaders, multibillionaires, conservative think tanks, the religious right, and the Tea Party movement. Then, I discuss the growth of inequality in Chapter 5. I cover the dismantling of the welfare state and the superexploitation of the working poor in Chapter 6. I look at race and the criminal justice system in Chapter 7. I describe the minority voter suppression movement in Chapter 8. Finally, in Chapter 9, I sum it all up and portray US politics at a crossroads.

Notes

1. Desmond S. King and Rogers M. Smith, *Still a House Divided: Race and Politics in Obama's American* (Princeton, NJ: Princeton University Press, 2011), p. 271.

2. Paul Krugman, "Why We're in a New Gilded Age," *New York Review of Books,* May 8, 2014; Thomas Piketty, *Capital in the Twenty-First Century* (Cambridge: Harvard University Press, 2014).

3. Michelle Alexander, *The New Jim Crow: Mass Incarceration in the Age of Colorblindness* (New York: New Press, 2010).

4. Joel Kovel, *White Racism: A Psychohistory* (New York: Columbia University Press, 1984), p. 211.

5. Authentic History Center, "The Coon Caricature: Blacks as Monkeys," July 20, 2012. authentichistory.com/diversity/African/3-coon/6-monkey/.

6. Ibid.

7. Ibid.

8. Gunnar Myrdal, *An American Dilemma* (New York: Harper, 1944), p. xlvii.

9. Ibid.

10. William J. Wilson, *The Declining Significance of Race: From Racial Oppression to Economic Class Subordination* (Lanham, MD: Rowman and Littlefield, 2006), p. 151; William J. Wilson, *The Truly Disadvantaged: The Inner City, the Underclass, and Public Policy* (Chicago: University of Chicago Press, 1987), pp. 1–10.

11. Nancy DiTomaso, *The American Non-Dilemma: Racial Inequality Without Racism* (New York: Russell Sage Foundation, 2013), pp. 241–255 and 304–308.

12. George Fredrickson, *Racism: A Short History* (Princeton: Princeton University Press, 2002), pp. 1–2.

13. Ibid., pp. 1–2.

14. Ibid., p. 8.

15. Ibid.

16. There is indeed a large body of literature on the study of race and racism going back to the time of W. E. B. DuBois, including a list of scholars too long to mention. However, only since 1984 has it been argued that it is impossible to understand US history, culture, literature, and politics without an understanding of the role of race. A few deserve mention such as Toni Morrison, *Playing in the Dark: Whiteness and the Literary Imagination* (Cambridge, MA: Harvard University Press, 1992). Some of the associations between race and the understanding of mainstream US literature are made in Kovel, *White Racism.* This connection of race and US politics and political culture is made by Rogers Smith, *Civic Ideas: Conflicting*

Visions of Citizenship in U.S. History (New Haven: Yale University Press, 1997); Aziz Rana, *The Two Faces of American Freedom* (Cambridge: Harvard University Press, 2010).

17. Frank Snowden, *Blacks in Antiquity* (Cambridge: Harvard University Press, 1970). See also Audrey Smedley, *Race in North America: Origin and Evolution of a Worldview* (Boulder, CO: Westview Press, 1993); W. E. B. DuBois, *The World and Africa* (Millwood, NY: Kraus-Thomson Organization, 1976). In Greek mythology, the god Helios (the Titan, rather than Apollo, the Olympian) let his son, Phaethon, drive the sun chariot. When he drove the chariot too close to the earth, people turned darker. They turned lighter when he drove too far away from the earth. See Thomas Gossett, *Race: The History of an Idea in America* (New York: Schocken, 1971), p. 6.

18. Paulo Freire, *Pedagogy of the Oppressed,* trans. Myra B. Ramos (New York: Continuum, 1993); Iris M. Young, *Justice and the Politics of Difference* (Princeton, NJ: Princeton University Press, 1990), pp. 39–63.

19. Smedley, *Race in North America.*

20. Louis Kushnick states, "In a development very similar to that adopted earlier vis-à-vis the Irish Catholics whose land and freedom had been stolen by England, all of the victims of these processes, whether they were Irish or Africans, were defined as apelike, less than human, savage." Quoted in Louis Kushnick, "The Political Economy of White Racism in the United States," in Benjamin Bowser and Raymond Hunt, eds., *Impacts of Racism on White Americans* (Thousand Oaks, CA: Sage, 1996), p. 51. See also Michael Hechter, *The Celtic Fringe in British National Development, 1536–1966* (Berkeley: University of California Press, 1975); Bill Rolston, "The Training Ground: Ireland, Conquest and Colonization," *Race and Class* 34, no. 4 (1993): 13–24.

21. Mark Twain, *Adventures of Huckleberry Finn* (New York: Random House, 1996/1885), p. 281.

22. Alexander Saxon, *The Rise and Fall of the White Republic: Class Politics and Mass Culture in Nineteenth-Century America* (New York: Verso, 1990).

23. Aziz Rana makes this argument. See Rana, *The Two Faces of American Freedom*, pp. 114–120. See also Woody Holton, *Forced Founders: Indians, Debts, Slaves, and the Making of the American Revolution in Virginia* (Chapel Hill: University of North Carolina Press, 1999); Simon Schama, *Rough Crossings: Britain, the Slaves and the American Revolution* (New York: HarperCollins, 2006); Judith N. Shklar, *American Citizenship: The Quest for Inclusion* (Cambridge: Harvard University Press, 1991).

24. See Saxton, *The Rise and Fall of the White Republic.*

25. Ian Lopez, *White by Law: The Legal Construction of Race* (Philadelphia: Temple University Press, 1995).

26. *Dred Scott v. Sanford,* 60 U.S. 393 (1857).

27. Ibid.

28. Ibid.

29. Ibid.

30. Theodore Allen, *The Invention of the White Race, Volume 1: Racial Oppression and Social Control* (New York: Verso, 1994); Noel Ignatiev, *How the Irish Became White* (New York: Routledge, 1995); David Roediger, *The Wages of Whiteness: Race and the Making of the American Working Class* (New York: Verso, 1991); Stephen Steinberg, *The Ethnic Myth: Race, Ethnicity, and Class in America* (Boston: Beacon Press, 1989); Branko J. Widick, *Detroit: City of Race and Class Violence* (Detroit: Wayne State University Press, 1989), p. 28.

31. Widick, *Detroit*, p. 28.

32. Allen, *The Invention of the White Race*, p. 197.

33. W. E. B. DuBois, *Black Reconstruction in America: An Essay Toward a History of the Part Which Black Folk Played in the Attempt to Reconstruct Democracy in America, 1860–1880* (New York: Atheneum, 1969/1935), pp. 700–701.

34. Howard Zinn, *A People's History of the United States* (New York: Harper Perennial, 2010), p. 291.

35. Philip Foner, *Organized Labor and the Black Worker, 1619–1981* (New York: International, 1982); Herbert Hill, *The AFL-CIO and the Black Worker: Twenty-Five Years After the Merger* (Louisville, KY: National Association of Human Rights Workers, 1982); Herbert Hill, *Black Labor and the American Legal System: Race, Work, and the Law* (Madison: University of Wisconsin Press, 1985).

36. Ronald Takaki, *Iron Cages: Race and Culture in Nineteenth-Century America* (New York: Oxford University Press, 1990), p. 248.

37. Elliot Jaspin, *Buried in the Bitter Waters: The Hidden History of Racial Cleansing in America* (New York: Basic Books, 2008).

38. Eric Foner, *Reconstruction: America's Unfinished Revolution, 1863–1877* (New York: Harper and Row, 1988); W. E. B. DuBois, *Black Reconstruction in America*.

39. Jack Bloom, *Class, Race, and the Civil Rights Movement* (Bloomington: Indiana University Press, 1987), pp. 55–56.

40. Stephen Jay Gould, *The Mismeasurement of Man* (New York: W. W. Norton, 1996).

41. Thomas F. Gosset, *Race: The History of an Idea in America* (New York: Schocken, 1971).

42. Thomas Kuhn, *The Structure of Scientific Revolutions* (Chicago: University of Chicago Press, 1970).

43. See Carter A. Wilson, *Racism from Slavery to Advanced Capitalism* (Thousand Oaks, CA: Sage, 1996).

44. See Noel Cazanave, *The Urban Racial State: Managing Race Relations in American Cities* (Lanham, MD: Rowman and Littlefield, 2011). Cazanave identifies different forms of the racial state, ranging from ameliorative to oppressive. See Antonio Gramsci, *Selections from the Prison Notebooks of Antonio Gramsci,* Quintin Hoare and Geoffrey N. Smith, ed. and trans. (New York: International, 1980).

45. Thomas Paine, "Agrarian Justice," in Philip S. Foner, ed., *The Complete Writings of Thomas Paine* (New York: Citadel Press, 1969), p. 617, quoted in Robert Lamb, "Liberty, Equality, and the Boundaries of Ownership: Thomas Paine's Theory of Property Rights," *Review of Politics* 72, no. 3 (Summer 2010): 483–511.

46. Thomas Paine, "Agrarian Justice," in Jessica Kimpell, ed., *Peter Linebaugh Presents Thomas Paine: Common Sense, Rights of Man and Agrarian Justice* (New York: Verso, 2009), pp. 299–300.

47. See Susan Jacoby, *Freethinkers: A History of American Secularism* (New York: Metropolitan Books, Henry Holt, 2004).

48. See, for example, Smith, *Civic Ideals*.

49. Christopher Hitchens, "Bones of Contention," *The Guardian,* July 15, 2006. Excerpt from Christopher Hitchens, *Thomas Paine's Rights of Man: A Biography* (New York: Grove Press, 2006).

50. Rana identifies William Manning as sharing Paine's views of freedom. Rana, *The Two Faces of American Freedom.*

51. See Alexander Hamilton, "Report on Manufacturers," December 5, 1791.

52. Richard Hofstadter, *The American Political Tradition* (New York: Vintage Books, 1948), p. 81.

53. Ibid.

54. Melvin Steinfield, *Our Racist Presidents: From Washington to Nixon* (San Ramon, CA: Consensus Press, 1972).

55. *Webster's Dictionary* defines a *tyrant* as an oppressive or cruel ruler. John Locke defined tyranny not as concentrated governmental powers, but as governmental powers used in the self-interest of the ruler and against the interest and to the detriment of the people. See John Locke, *Second Treatise on Government* (New York: New York University Press, 2002). Garry Wills in his introduction to *The Federalist Papers* claimed that James Madison saw tyranny arising when a faction or majority took over the government. See Alexander Hamilton, James Madison, and John Jay, *The Federalist Papers,* with an introduction and commentary by Garry Wills (New York: Bantam Classic, 2003 [1787–1788]), p. xxi. Of course, the implementation of the Alien and Sedition Acts of 1798 constituted a form of tyranny. However, this new concept of tyranny reflected the perspective of the slave-owning class of the South of which James Madison and Thomas Jefferson were members. In this new concept, tyranny became federal powers that interfered with their right to own slaves and to oppress and exploit subordinate groups.

56. Richard Parker, "Sam Houston, We Have a Problem," *New York Times,* January 31, 2011.

57. Stephen Steinburg, *Turning Back: The Retreat from Racial Justice in American Thought and Policy* (Boston: Beacon Press, 1995), pp. 213–214.

58. Ian Lopez, *Dog Whistle Politics: How Coded Racial Appeals Have Reinvented Racism and Wrecked the Middle Class* (Oxford: Oxford University Press, 2014), p. 15.

59. Ibid., p. 16.

60. Howard Smith of Virginia, chairman of the US House of Representatives Rules Committee introduced "The Southern Manifesto," US Congress, Congressional Record, 84th Cong., 2d Sess., 1956, 102, pt. 4: 4515–4516; Senator Strom Thurmond was the principal author. *Brown v Board of Education of Topeka, Kansas, et al.* 347 U.S. 483 (1954).

61. *Plessy v Ferguson* 163 U.S. 537 (1896).

62. Radical Republicans reflected the ideas of Thomas Paine. They were former abolitionists, passionate in the promotion of racial inequality and racial segregation. Examples of the Radical Republicans include James Ashley, a nemesis of Chief Justice Taney, who considered slavery a violation of the Constitution prior to the Civil War; Charles Sumner, who had campaigned to racially integrate Boston public schools before the Civil War; Thaddeus Stevens, who was so committed to racial integration that when he died he was buried in a predominantly black graveyard. See Rebecca Zielow, *The Forgotten Emancipator: James Mitchell Ashley and the Ideological Origins of Reconstruction* (Cambridge University Press, forthcoming); David Donald, *Charles Sumner and the Rights of Man* (New York: Da Capo Press, 1996); Hans Trefousse, *Thaddeus Stevens: Nineteenth-Century Egalitarian* (Chapel Hill: University of North Carolina Press, 1997).

63. Ronald Reagan, "'Welfare Queen' Becomes Issue in Reagan Campaign," *New York Times,* February 15, 1976, quoted in Ian Lopez, *Dog Whistle Politics: How Coded Racial Appeals Have Reinvented Racism and Wrecked the Middle Class* (Oxford: Oxford University Press), p. 58.

64. Lopez, *Dog Whistle Politics,* p. 59.

65. Kovel, *White Racism,* p. 218.

2

The Structure of Metaracism

Metaracism is associated with concentrated black poverty and economic insecurity. But metaracism did not produce concentrated black poverty; it emerged to legitimize that poverty. Just as racial animus was not the driving cause of the initial construction of the institution of slavery, it was not the primary cause of the growth of concentrated urban poverty. Just as greed and the drive to accumulate wealth contributed to the construction of the institution of slavery, the same greed and drive contributed greatly to the growth of concentrated urban poverty. Just as racism emerged to legitimize slavery, a new form of racism emerged to legitimize concentrated poverty.

After the period of stagflation (high inflation, high unemployment, low productivity, and low profits) of the late 1970s, US corporations engaged in an intensified campaign to increase profits and accumulate wealth. This campaign impacted different sectors of the economy and areas of the country in diverse ways and in varying degrees. Combined with public policy changes, the campaign contributed to the growth of concentrated urban poverty, the growth of inequality, and the growth of concentrated rural poverty. Those public policy changes and their impacts are the subject of Chapter 3. With regard to the emergence of metaracism, the impact of the campaign to increase profits and accumulate wealth was most significant on older industrial cities.

Industrial corporations increased profits through consolidation, downsizing, and reduced labor costs. They reduced labor costs through investment in new technology such as robotics; through the increased mobility of capital, moving production facilities to areas where wages were dirt cheap and unions nonexistent; and through outsourcing to nonunion, low-wage companies.

These changes resulted in the decline of US industrial production and industrial facilities. With African Americans concentrated in the manufacturing sector and the lower rung of the industrial working class, this campaign impacted them the most severely. These changes contributed to the rise of concentrated poverty. The combination of progressive civil rights laws and antipoverty programs and the decline of industrial production facilities produced this contradictory trend: the dramatic rise of the black middle class and the growth of concentrated urban poverty.

Growth of Concentrated Poverty

In the last half of the twentieth century, black poverty decreased dramatically nationwide, yet urban poverty became more concentrated. As Table 2.1 indicates, national poverty rates among blacks declined from 53.5 percent in 1960 to 33.5 percent in 1970. By 1975, these rates had declined to 31.3 percent. This national decline in black poverty was largely the result of the collapse of the sharecropping system, the rise of the industrial sector, and the mass movement of blacks from sharecropping in high-poverty rural areas to working on assembly lines in industrial jobs in urban areas. With the enactment of civil rights and antidiscrimination laws, public policy changes contributed to the decline of the black poor and the rise of the black middle and professional class.

The equal opportunity policy changes of the 1960s and 1970s improved the conditions of whites as well as blacks. White poverty rates declined along with black rates, although not quite as sharply. As Table 2.1 indicates, white poverty rates declined from 17.5 percent in 1960 to 13.4 percent in 1965. These rates declined further to 9.9 percent by 1970 and to 9.7 percent by 1975.

The 1980s was a period of economic stagnation. It was also a decade marked by increasing assaults on the social programs of the 1960s. Both black and white poverty rates increased marginally and stagnated. White poverty rates increased to 10.2 percent by 1980 and to 11.4 percent by 1985, but declined to 10.7 percent by 1990. The black poverty rate increased to 32.5 percent by 1980, declined to 31.3 percent by 1985, and then increased to 31.9 percent by 1990.

Poverty rates declined again during the 1990s, but increased during the first decade of the twenty-first century for both blacks and whites. Black poverty rates were at an all-time low of 22.5 percent by 2000 while white poverty rates were at an all-time low of 9.5 percent. Poverty rates for both blacks and whites increased from 2000 to 2010. By 2010, the black poverty rate had risen to 27.4 percent; the white rate had increased to 13.0 percent.

Table 2.1 Poverty Rates by Race, 1960–2011 (in percentage)

Year	All	White	Black	Hispanic
1960	22.2	17.5[a]	53.5[a]	n/a
1965	17.3	13.4[a]	43.0[a]	n/a
1970	12.6	9.9	33.5	n/a
1975	12.3	9.7	31.3	26.9
1980	13.0	10.2	32.5	25.7
1985	14.0	11.4	31.3	29.0
1990	13.5	10.7	31.9	28.1
1995	13.8	11.2	29.3	30.3
2000	11.3	9.5	22.5	21.5
2005	12.6	10.6	24.9	21.8
2010	15.1	13.0	27.4	26.5
2011	15.0	12.8	27.6	n/a

Source: US Bureau of Census, *Current Population Survey, Annual Social and Economic Supplement* (Washington, DC: Government Printing Office, 2012).
Note: a. Estimates.

The concentration of poverty increased during the 1970s and 1980s, declined in the 1990s, but increased again from 2000 to 2010. A 2011 Census Bureau report identified four categories of poverty tracts: Category I (less than 13.8 percent of the individuals in poverty); Category II (between 13.8 percent and 19.9 percent); Category III (between 20.0 percent and 39.9 percent); and Category IV (40.0 percent or more). (See Table 2.2.)

The Census Bureau defines "poverty areas" as "census tracts with poverty rates of 20 percent or more."[1] Category III and IV tracts constitute concentrated poverty tracts. With poverty rates at 40 percent and higher, Category IV tracts constitute severe concentrated poverty. According to the Census Bureau, about 66.9 million people reside in concentrated poverty tracts (Category III and IV combined). About 10.31 million people reside in severe concentrated poverty census tracts (Category IV alone), of which 43 percent are white alone; 26.3 percent are white, not Hispanic; 38.1 percent are black; 29.5 percent are Hispanic; 3.2 percent are Asian; and 2.1 percent are Native American and Alaska Native. Also, about 47.1 percent of the black population (17.1 million) reside in concentrated poverty areas (calculated from Table 2.2). About 10.8 percent of the black population (about 3.93 million people) reside in Category IV severe concentrated poverty areas (calculated from Table 2.2). The bureau concludes that "Whites and Asians were more likely to live in tracts with lower poverty rates than in tracts with higher poverty rates. In contrast, Blacks, American Indians and Alaska Natives, and those reporting 'Other Races' were over-represented in tracts with higher poverty rates and under-represented in tracts with lower poverty rates."[2]

Table 2.2 Distribution of People by Poverty Level of Census Tracts, 2006–2010

	Category I < 13.8%	Category II 13.8–19.9%	Category III 20.0–39.9%	Category IV 40.0% +
Total number of people	181,881,914	47,305,181	56,644,210	10,309,844
Percentage of total population	61.4	16.0	19.1	3.5
Percentage in each category				
White alone	81.0	73.2	58.8	43.0
White, not Hispanic	74.4	62.1	43.3	26.3
Black alone	7.2	13.0	23.3	38.1
Hispanic	10.7	18.7	27.2	29.5
Asian alone	5.5	3.6	3.4	3.2
Native Am./Alaska N.	0.5	0.9	1.5	2.1
In poverty	6.9	16.7	27.3	49.0
Estimated number of poor	12,549,852	7,899,965	15,463,869	5,051,824
Estimated number of blacks alone	13,095,498	6,149,674	13,198,101	3,928,051

Source: US Census Bureau, "Areas with Concentrated Poverty: 2006–2010," American Community Survey Briefs (Washington, DC: US Census Bureau, US Department of Commerce, Economic, and Statistics Administration, December 2011).

Note: Native Am. = Native American; Alaska N. = Alaska Native.

Between 2000 and 2010, poverty became more concentrated throughout the nation: among Native Americans on reservations, among whites in rural areas, among whites and blacks in the Deep South, and among blacks in older industrial cities.[3] Major economic and demographic changes contributed to this increase in concentrated poverty in both rural and urban areas. The rise of agribusiness and the mass foreclosures of family farms increased rural poverty. The restructuring and decline of the industrial sector combined with the exodus of the black middle class from older industrial cities increased the concentration of urban poverty, particularly among blacks.

Concentrated poverty increased among blacks, largely in older industrial cities between 1970 and 1990. This increase was largely the result of the economic and demographic changes in urban areas, the decline of the industrial sector, and the exodus of the black middle class from poverty areas. Poverty became more concentrated among blacks, even though national black poverty rates were stable between 1975 and 1990. (See Table 2.1.) The number of blacks living in Category IV census tracts increased sharply between 1970 and 1990. This number declined between 1990 and

2000: the economy had expanded, allowing inequality to lessen. (See Chapter 4 for details.) However, poverty and concentrated poverty increased again from 2000 to 2011: black poverty rates increased from 22.5 percent in 2000 to 24.9 percent in 2005 and to 27.6 percent by 2011 (see Table 2.1).

Poverty increased among blacks in older industrial cities, where there were huge losses of industrial jobs that had generally required less than a high school diploma but paid a middle-class wage. Many of these former industrial workers had to find jobs in the service and retail sectors, which paid considerably lower wages. The increase in these lower-paying jobs contributed to an increase in the number of working poor. The totality of these labor market changes contributed to the growth of concentrated poverty in central cities

The city of Detroit offers a prime example of these trends. Detroit's economy shifted during the 1970s and 1980s when the city suffered catastrophic losses of industrial jobs and substantial losses in the retail and wholesale sectors. Between 1972 and 1982, Detroit lost 69,300 industrial sector jobs, 24,900 jobs in retail, and 17,000 jobs in wholesale.[4] There was some job growth in the service sector. However, the new service sector jobs were largely in low-paying positions such as security guards, nurse's aides, home health aides, and janitors. Professional jobs in the service sector tended to be in social work, teaching, and related professional areas. The rise of poverty was most clearly associated with the city's loss of decent-paying industrial jobs in the automobile industry. Poverty in Detroit increased from 14.9 percent to 21.9 percent between 1970 and 1980.[5] In 2008, while the national poverty rate was 13.2 percent, the Detroit poverty rate was 33.1 percent. By 2010, the Detroit poverty rate had risen to 40.9 percent.[6]

Of course, Detroit was not alone in experiencing economic restructuring, massive job losses, and poverty increases. Most older industrial cities of the northeastern and Great Lakes regions experienced similar changes. The industrial decline in this region has continued in the twenty-first century. Between 2000 and 2005, seven states—Michigan, Ohio, Illinois, Pennsylvania, New York, Indiana, and Wisconsin—lost over 3 million manufacturing jobs. The older industrial central cities in the Great Lakes region were hit the hardest. According to Alec Friedhoff and Howard Wial,

> Of the 25 metropolitan areas examined in this report, only Peoria, IL, gained manufacturing jobs from 1995 to 2005, and even Peoria suffered manufacturing job losses after 2000. Eighteen of the metropolitan areas (Akron, OH; Allentown, PA; Ann Arbor, MI; Buffalo, NY; Canton, OH; Chicago, IL; Cleveland, OH; Dayton, OH; Detroit, MI; Flint, MI; Fort Wayne, IN; Lancaster, PA; Milwaukee, WI; Reading, PA; Rochester, NY; Scranton, PA; York, PA; and Youngstown, OH) lost a higher percentage of their manufacturing jobs from 1995 to 2005 than did the entire United States.

Five metropolitan areas (Ann Arbor, MI; Canton, OH; Flint, MI; Rochester, NY; and Youngstown, OH) had declines in manufacturing employment that exceeded 30 percent from 1995 and 2005. The Flint, MI region was the hardest hit, losing more than one-half (55 percent) of its manufacturing jobs over the course of the decade.[7]

Several factors have contributed to the decline in the industrial manufacturing sector: the development of new technology, the rise of global markets, and the corporate decisions driven by the need to retain competitive advantages and increase profits. With advances in air and trucking transportation and with developments in robotics, production facilities have become more mobile. Because these facilities are smaller, rely on fewer workers, and are no longer attached to railroads, they can be moved easily; that is, it is now easier to close down a production facility in Detroit and reopen it in Mexico or China. Other industries, like steel, have declined because of the developments in new technology and materials (e.g., advances in plastics and aluminum that have reduced the reliance on steel) and increased international competition.

In their drive to cut costs, industrial corporations broke the grand bargain with labor. This bargain is sometimes referred to as "Fordism" because it arose out of the realization by Henry Ford that automobile companies could sell more cars if their own workers were paid a decent wage. It is also referred to as the "Treaty of Detroit" because it arose out of labor negotiations initiated by President Harry Truman and held in Detroit.[8] This treaty meant that the automobile companies would provide generous wages and benefits in exchange for labor peace and labor's acceptance of management prerogatives. The collapse of this bargain meant that corporations no longer felt committed to paying high wages and accepting and working with labor unions.

Industrial corporations engaged in a range of practices designed to cut wages and weaken labor unions: downsizing (reducing the size of the labor force); outsourcing (closing down a division and contracting with a nonunion company to produce the parts once produced by the unionized division); using a two-tiered labor force (hiring new workers at lower wages and fewer benefits); and moving production facilities to regions or countries with lower wages and no unions.[9]

These corporate decisions contributed to the rise of poverty, unemployment, and labor force nonparticipation, that is, unemployed people dropping out of the labor force entirely. They had their most severe impact on declining industrial cities with large populations of African Americans.

The 1970s and 1980s witnessed a dramatic increase in blacks graduating from high school, going to college, and entering professional careers. Members of this black professional class began to move out of the inner cities, eventually following whites out of the cities into the suburbs. This exodus of blacks from central cities accelerated in the last decade of the twentieth century and the first decade of the twenty-first century. Some cities, like Detroit, lost more than half of their population. These economic and demographic changes contributed to the growth of concentrated poverty, which formed the structural basis of the new metaracism.

Just as the old racism legitimized slavery and the racial caste system, metaracism legitimizes the growth of concentrated and isolated black poverty. Metaracism involves the racialization of the poor and the construction of new racial stereotypes that desensitize society to the conditions of the urban poverty class and generate strong feelings of fear and disgust for this class. Stereotypes have emerged that characterize the so-called urban underclass as drug addicts, dangerous street predators, violent gang members, conniving welfare queens, and promiscuous teenage girls having babies to get welfare. These stereotypes have become major features of metaracism. They generate antipathy and disgust toward welfare recipients. They provoke fear of young black men and enable police repression. They contribute to labor market discrimination.

The combination of the separation of the urban poor from areas of job growth and the presence of labor market discrimination perpetuates urban poverty. This poverty reinforces racial stereotypes. As the black middle class moves out of the inner city and succeeds while the black poor languish in the inner city, this trend reinforces the paradox of simultaneous black progress and black poverty.

The Farm Crisis and the Rise of the Racist Right

Metaracism is grounded in concentrated black poverty produced by the drive for corporate profits and the exodus of the black middle class from inner-city areas. Stereotypes of poor blacks have emerged to legitimize this poverty. However, there is another economic dimension of metaracism— one that is grounded in economic insecurity and anxiety, the type of massive economic dislocation that has historically produced social movements and authoritarian politics, the type of politics based on in-group/out-group dynamics, and the use of scapegoats. This connection between economic insecurities and authoritarian extremist politics has been well documented, especially by Eric Hoffer, Erich Fromm, Theodor Adorno and colleagues, and Barrington Moore.[10]

Fromm argues that the economic dislocation associated with the worldwide depression of the 1930s generated unbearable insecurity and anxiety.[11] Individuals strove to allay this anxiety by retreating from the frightening world and anxiety-producing freedom into the security of large organizations that offered a strong sense of certainty and direction. By losing themselves in a large organization and submitting to the authority of the organization, these individuals became authoritarian. They engaged in what Gordon Allport referred to as in-group/out-group dynamics. That is, they found security and identity in their membership in their in-group.[12] They used outgroups (Jews, blacks, foreigners, immigrants, Muslims, gay men, lesbians, and others) as the targets of their anger and frustration.

Poverty itself does not produce the levels of insecurity, despair, and anger that spawn social movements. In Hoffer's view, the poor who struggle to survive, scrapping for food and shelter every day, live purposeful and meaningful lives. Stable poverty does not produce social movements. Rather, it is stability abruptly interrupted by earth-shaking economic dislocation that produces the level of insecurity and anxiety that spawns social movements, as if the ground that had been solid for a long period of time suddenly gives way and crumbles beneath the feet. Social movements are precipitated by the type of economic dislocation that shatters lives and destroys that which is most valuable and meaningful in life. Economic upheavals such as the loss of family farms or the collapse of an industry create conditions for mass movements. Hoffer explains,

> Not all who are poor are frustrated. Some of the poor stagnating in the slums of the cities are smug in their decay. They shudder at the thought of life outside their familiar cesspool. Even the respectable poor, when their poverty is of long standing, remain inert. They are awed by the immutability of the order of things. It takes a cataclysm—an invasion, a plague or some other communal disaster—to open their eyes to the transitoriness of the "eternal order."
>
> It is usually those whose poverty is relatively recent, the "new poor," who throb with the ferment of frustration. The memory of better things is as fire in their veins. They are the disinherited and dispossessed who respond to every rising mass movement.[13]

Thus, Hoffer insists that it is not the abject, hopeless poor that creates social movements but the mass of the dispossessed (farmers pushed off their farms and into cities), descending artisans or skilled craft workers who lost their vocation as a result of the Industrial Revolution, or as in the case of the civil rights movement, ascending middle classes and returning troops (returning from World War II and the Korea War) with something to lose or much to gain. Hoffer claimed that during the 1930s, "In Germany and Italy the new poor coming from a ruined middle class formed the chief support of the Nazi and Fascist revolutions."[14]

The farm crisis of the 1980s produced massive economic dislocation and contributed to the development of a racist right political movement. The farm crisis has deep roots in US history that are related to the rise of the use of motorized, high-tech farm equipment, chemical herbicides and pesticides, and agribusiness. US farm production had increased dramatically during the 1970s as a result of greater investments in farm machinery, chemical fertilizers, chemical pesticides, and the opening up of the grain market in the Soviet Union. Bank loans for farmers increased along with farm production. The crisis began when the Federal Reserve Board increased interest rates in order to reduce inflation. When interest rates increased, the loans dried up and farm values declined. Carolyn Gallaher describes the beginning of this crisis:

> The crisis began in 1979, when the chairman of the Federal Reserve Board Paul Volker, instituted the first of several sharp interest rate hikes to curb inflation. The effect on farms was doubly incapacitating. Because FmHA loans carried floating interest rates, farmers saw their monthly payments skyrocket. The intensity of the rate hikes was also devastating. . . . As rising interest rates led to deflating land values, farmers also saw their principal equity, farmland, dry up. The price "adjustments" were harsh. . . . In Iowa, the value of the state's farmland decreased by 63 percent in five years. From 1982 to 1985, U.S. farmland as a whole lost $146 billion in value.[15]

Gallaher argues that the restructuring of US farms was cataclysmic, contributing to massive foreclosures of family farms and the rise of a radical right-wing movement, the Patriot movement:

> By the end of the 1980s, approximately one million family farms had been lost to foreclosure. Many of the foreclosed farms were not however, purchased by other small and medium-size farmers. Rather, non-farmers purchased almost half the available land with two of the largest purchasers being insurance giants and farm-management companies. Indeed, while the personal crises associated with farming tended to make the news, the most significant result of the farm crisis was the underlying structural changes it enacted in U.S. agriculture. Today, approximately 75 percent of U.S. farmland is owned by the top 5 percent of landowners, while 78 percent of owners control, in total, only 3 percent of the available land.[16]

Millions of families lost their farms to foreclosure. The farm crisis was aggravated by the predatory expansion of a multinational farm industry as well as the federal government, which contributed to the worsening of the crisis through changes in the farm price stabilization programs that favored agribusiness over family farms, the deregulation of antitrust policy that allowed corporate farms to push family farms out of the market, and the construction of free-trade policy that favored agribusiness over family farms.[17] The federal government supported the large corporate farms and neglected family farms, which generated a great deal of antigovernment anger. Leaders of racist organizations exploited this anger by using it to build a racist right political movement.

Several scholars and human rights organizations have documented the rise of this racist right movement and its association with the farm crisis.

Sara Diamond argues, "The backdrop to the racist Right's 1980s resurgence was a crisis in the U.S. agricultural economy, more severe than any since the 1920s."[18] The Southern Poverty Law Center, the Center for Democratic Renewal, and Political Research Associates have documented the rise of the racist right.[19] Racist leaders moved from one organization to another, from the KKK to the neo-Nazis to the Christian Identity movement, and into new organizations such as the Posse Comitatus and the militia and Patriot movements.

The farm crisis did not automatically generate an upsurge in the racist right community; rather, white supremacists and anti-Semitic leaders effectively exploited the farm crisis to recruit more members. Two of their recruitment techniques stand out. First, recruiters were effective in responding to the psychological needs of the farmers who were losing their farms by giving them meaning, purpose, and grounding in their life. They made sense out of the inexplicable events occurring to them.

Joel Dyer provides a vivid description of the appeal of the Posse Comitatus to farmers who had lost their farms. This organization offered these farmers an invitation to live by bringing meaning and value to their lives when others had seemed to encourage them to die. Dyer explains:

> The invitation to die comes from others in our lives. A spouse strikes out because of heavy stress, the equipment dealer repossesses the equipment, and the land bank forecloses on the land. The lenders announce publicly in the newspapers that you have failed. Embarrassed and humiliated, you withdraw from all community activities and go into hiding. Where can you go and what can you do? There doesn't seem to be at this point but one thing to do. Suicide.[20]

Imagine a farmer who had worked hard all of his life for a farm that had been in his family for possibly six generations. He had borrowed money during the 1970s to buy heavy farm machinery and expand production. Now, he has to default on his farm equipment. He is publicly humiliated. His farm is foreclosed. His bank turns against him. His government abandons him. His wife leaves him. He has nothing else to live for. He followed the rules, made all the right decisions, and worked hard—only to lose everything. Why? The Posse Comitatus leaders empathize with him in ways that no other political leaders could and provide him with a clear and cogent answer: they say that it was not his fault. It was instead the fault of the Jewish bankers, the government, the blacks, and the immigrants. They also tell him that there are things he can do to fight back. According to Gallaher,

> To explain these apparent paradoxes, Posse leaders assured farmers that they had worked hard. Their efforts were fruitless, however, because there were

sinister forces at work against them. The government, they claimed, had been secretly hijacked by members of an internationally organized Jewish cabal, whose ultimate goal was to seize U.S. farmland, make slaves of its former occupants, and reap the benefits of free land and labor. . . . Posse leaders also took their message to the airwaves, spreading their conspiracy ideas on talk radio programs.

The Posse explanatory framework was further reinforced by concrete "solutions" farmers could take to save their farms and, while they were at it, erase the corrupting influence of the federal government from their lives. Arguing that the lending practices of "Jewish" banks were exploitative and unconstitutional, Posse leaders showed farmers how to file liens against the property of bankers, judges, and other officers of the state responsible for foreclosure proceeding.[21]

A second significant recruitment technique was that these racist right organizations were sufficiently sensitive to the feelings of nonracist farmers so that they never imposed their racist ideology on them. Instead, they provided a smorgasbord of issues designed to attract individual members and other organizations. Although antiabortion, prayer in schools, anti–same sex marriage, pro-gun rights, and other issues involved separate organizations disconnected from the racist right, according to Gallaher's rather extensive research, leaders of the racist right drew many of these single-issue groups into its movement. For example, the Patriot movement expanded to include these single-issue groups.

In addition to militias, the Patriot Movement would grow to include issue oriented groups, such as pro–Second Amendment organizations, the Fully Informed Jury Association, home-schooling coalitions, and pro-life alliances. Although these causes are advocated by groups on the mainstream right, patriots generally view them as "soft" on the issues or corrupted by their proximity to Washington. In general, patriot groups tend to support more radical measures than their "mainstream" counterparts. . . .

Holding these diverse groups together are usually larger umbrella groups. Umbrella groups tend to have innocuous sounding names, such as Nebraskans for Constitutional Government, or Citizens for a Constitutional Kentucky.[22]

Gallaher describes a recruitment process that operates like a funnel. It begins with discussions of wide appeal issues such as gun control, environmental restrictions, and other issues of concern to most residents of the Western states. The discussion funnel narrows to immigration issues. Gradually, the discussion funnels narrows to racist, anti-Semitic, homophobic, Islam-phobic issues interwoven with conspiracy theories.

These recruitment efforts were made possible by a political void left by the political parties. Neither Democrats nor Republicans responded adequately to the farm crisis, and both parties supported the North Atlantic Free Trade Agreement (NAFTA). But the leaders of the Aryan Nations,

National Alliance, Christian Identity movement, militia movement, Patriot movement, Posse Comitatus, white survivalists, and other racist organizations exploited the anger and frustration of white farmers over the loss of millions of family farms. These organizations offered a new community for these farmers to associate with. They gave them a strong and powerful identity group. The racist leaders of these organizations gave them scapegoats at whom to direct their anger: the government, blacks, Jews, Muslims, Latino immigrants, gays, and lesbians.

They exploited several incidents to build a racist right movement. They exploited the farm crisis to recruit farmers. They exploited the role of the Federal Bureau of Investigation (FBI) in the assault on the Branch Davidians in Waco, Texas, and the killing of Randy Weaver's wife and son at Ruby Ridge during the standoff while US Marshals were attempting to arrest Weaver on federal gun charges.[23] They used the FBI violence to promote the idea that the federal government was the enemy of the people.

Leaders of the Patriot, militia, and Posse Comitatus movements vehemently denied that these movements were racist or had anything to do with the bombing of the Murray Federal Building in Oklahoma City in 1995. Nevertheless, the person convicted of the bombing, Timothy McVeigh, was actively affiliated with these movements and also associated with the Christian Identity movement. He was influenced by the book *The Turner Diaries,* written by William Luther Pierce under the pseudonym of Andrew Macdonald.[24] The book imagined a violent overthrow of the US government by white supremacist organizations and the extermination of gays, lesbians, Jews, blacks, and other nonwhites. Pierce had founded the National Alliance, an extremist white supremacist organization that advocated the extermination of nonwhites; the organization fell apart shortly after he died in 2002, but reemerged under new leadership by the beginning of 2014. As I show in Chapter 3, some of the leaders of the Tea Party movement came from the Patriot and Posse Comitatus movements, as they imported their antigovernment and anti-immigrant messages into the new, broader and more mainstream movement.[25]

Urban Crisis and the Emergence of Metaracism

Economic crisis in the manufacturing sector and urban areas contributed to the emergence of metaracism in ways similar to the farm crisis. The restructuring of US industries, the closing of manufacturing facilities in Northeastern and Midwestern cities, and the decline of high-paying blue-collar jobs traditionally held by white workers generated insecurity in the urban United States. As the Democratic Party focused more on civil rights and antipoverty programs, white workers increasingly felt abandoned by this party. Working-class whites became increasingly angry toward the government because of their perception that the government was abandoning them, angry at immigrants because of their perception that immigrants were taking their jobs, and angry at blacks because of their perception that blacks were given jobs that whites deserved. They perceived the government as taxing them and helping poor blacks. They no longer saw equal opportunity programs as benefiting white workers, but assisting undeserving minorities. Although the War on Poverty programs of the 1960s helped more whites than blacks, they perceived these programs as essentially for blacks. Social programs such as the Supplementary Nutrition Assistant Program (SNAP, better known as food stamps), Temporary Assistance for Needy Families (TANF, formerly AFDC), and Unemployment Insurance are race neutral programs that benefit working-class whites as well as working-class blacks. However, these programs have increasingly been characterized as benefiting blacks rather than whites.

Nancy DiTomaso's surveys of white working-class men illustrate this point.[26] She surveyed white men who resided in industrial cities and were the most vulnerable to layoffs, plant closings, outsourcing, downsizing, reorganization, or technological changes. This cohort of white men would therefore seem to be the most in need of government assistance. However, DiTomaso found that this group tended to be the most hostile toward government programs, toward the federal government, and toward blacks. They saw the poor as largely being undeserving blacks. They saw government promoting affirmative action and welfare measures that gave jobs and assistance to unqualified and undeserving blacks at the expense of more qualified and deserving whites. DiTomaso explains how the language of the political parties cultivated these feelings in these white men:

> Democratic Party talk about fairness, inequality, and expansion of opportunity is interpreted by many white voters as support for policies that benefit blacks at whites' expense. Republican Party talk about responsibility, getting government out of our lives or off our backs, and reducing taxes so that people can keep their own money is translated by many white voters into opposition to policies that are thought to benefit blacks. Politicians do not have to mention race explicitly. They can frame their messages in terms of value differences or morality.
>
> One might think that such themes as fairness, inequality and expansion of opportunity are about class rather than race, but poverty has been racialized in the United States since the civil rights movement. The War on Poverty initially included whites in Appalachia and other rural areas, but it soon took on the image of blacks in the inner city because of the association with civil rights policies.[27]

Residual Racism and Southern Party Realignment

Economic trends in growth of concentrated poverty and rural economic dislocation certainly contributed to the emergence of metaracism. However, another part of this new racism came from residual racism, particularly in the South where it is evident in racial and class polarization in voting patterns.

This polarization was most clear in the 2012 presidential election. Contrary to the notion of a postracial society, the vote for Barack Obama exhibited this racial polarization. As Table 2.3 indicates, President Obama was elected with only 41 percent of the white vote. Most whites (59 percent) voted for Mitt Romney. People of color voted overwhelmingly for the president: blacks voted for Obama by 93 percent, and Asians and Hispanics by 73 percent and 71 percent, respectively.

Lower-income voters have been more likely to vote for the Democratic presidential candidate for over three decades, and the 2012 election was no exception. As Table 2.4 indicates, 60 percent of voters earning less than $50,000 a year voted for Obama. As income increased, the vote for Obama declined. Romney captured 54 percent of the vote of those earning $100,000 and over.

Residual racism is evident in the voting patterns of Southern whites in presidential elections. Figure 2.1 vividly illustrates this difference between

Table 2.3 Voters' Race and Ethnicity in the 2012 Presidential Election (in percentage)

	Barack Obama	Mitt Romney
White	41	59
Black	93	7
Hispanic	71	29
Asian	73	27

Source: New York Times Exit Polls, http://elections.nytimes.com/2012/results/president/exit polls.

Table 2.4 Voters' Income in the 2012 Presidential Election (in percentage)

	Barack Obama	Mitt Romney
> $50,000	60	38
$50,000–90,000	46	52
$100,000 +	44	54

Source: Roper Center Polls, http://www.ropercenter.uconn.edu/elections/how_groups_voted /voted_12html.

white voting patterns in the South and white voting patterns in the non-South in the 2012 election. Whereas the vote for Obama increased among lower-income voters nationwide, white Southern voters were substantially more likely to vote against Obama than white voters anywhere else in the nation. Moreover, low-income white voters in the South were substantially more likely to vote against Obama than low-income white voters anywhere else in the nation. Southern white voters seemed to be more sensitive to race than non-Southern white voters.

This sensitivity to race among white Southerners has not been limited to the election of President Obama. Southern white voters have shifted over en masse from the Democratic Party to the Republican Party. This shift, which constitutes a Southern party realignment, began after the passage of the Voting Rights Act of 1965. Prior to that time, less than 10 percent of Southern voters voted for Republican candidates. And before the passage of the Civil Rights Act of 1964, a large percentage of white Southern Democrats supported racial segregation and opposed civil rights. These Southern Democrats were called Dixiecrats. They were concentrated in the former Confederate states: Alabama, Georgia, Louisiana, Mississippi, and South Carolina of the Deep South; and Arkansas, Florida, North Carolina, Tennessee, Texas, and Virginia of the Outer South. After the passage of the Voting Rights Act, Dixiecrats began to shift over to the Republican Party.

Figure 2.1 Share of Vote for Barack Obama by Income, 2012 (whites only)

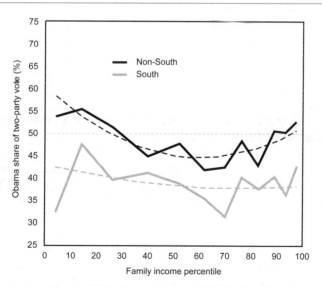

Source: Larry Bartels, "White Vote by Income, 2012," Monkey Cage, May 11, 2013, http://www.themonkeycage.org/2013/05-11/white-vote-by-income-2012/.

Although the conservative ideology and policy agenda of the Republican Party attracted Dixiecrats, race and racism played a much larger part of this shift that was already evident in the election of Richard Nixon whose opposition to school busing appealed to Southern voters. It became even more apparent in the election of Ronald Reagan. And it was complete in the 2000 presidential election when the Democratic candidate, Al Gore, lost every single Southern state, including his own (Tennessee). Today, the Republican Party is the majority party in the South.

Conventional wisdom tells us that the racial polarization in Southern voting patterns, the dramatic increase in white Southerners voting for Republican candidates, the astounding success of Republican presidential candidates in the South, and the anti-Obama vote even among low-income whites most likely had nothing to do with race and racism. They are more likely related to moral issues, conservative ideology, policy preferences, and perspectives on race issues. That is, white Southern Christian evangelicals are overwhelmingly supportive of the Republican Party, not because of race but because of moral issues such as abortion, same-sex marriage, and drugs. White Southerners are more likely to support Republican candidates because the party represents their views and offers a policy agenda more consistent with their own policy preferences. This wisdom insists that Southern whites are not opposed to blacks. Rather, they are opposed to racial preferences, racially targeted welfare programs, race-conscious drug rehabilitation, and prison reentry programs. They are opposed to big government, high taxes, gun regulations, and low defense spending. Conventional wisdom insists that researchers that see racism in racially polarized voting patterns and policy preferences confuse conservatism with racism. Indeed, the tendency of researchers to conflate conservatism and racism has long been a contentious issue among social scientists studying racism.[28] The debate over whether Southern voting patterns are driven by conservatism or racism can be resolved only with enough survey data to allow researchers to measure racial attitudes while controlling for ideology and policy preferences.

Research of this kind was conducted by Nicholas A. Valentino and David O. Sears and published in the *American Journal of Political Science* in 2005, three years before the election of President Obama.[29] Valentino and Sears used large multiple and cumulative survey data sets, General Social Surveys, and National Election Studies from the 1970s through 2000. Their survey data measured ideology (conservative vs. liberal), policy preferences (lower taxes, abortion, defense, spending), and racial attitudes. Racial attitudes were grouped in terms of Jim Crow racism, symbolic racism, negative black stereotyping, and white/black feeling thermometers (warm or cold). Two survey questions related to Jim Crow racism were asked from 1976 to 1996 regarding "white people's rights to keep blacks out of their neighborhoods . . . and laws against racial intermarriage." Survey questions measuring negative black stereotyping included three item-scaling questions pertaining to whether blacks were hardworking or lazy, intelligent or unintelligent, and peaceful or violent. Because of the controversy over whether symbolic racism was conflated with conservatism, Valentino and Sears were careful to use a widely accepted survey instrument with a high degree of validity and reliability. Symbolic racism was measured with responses to these statements: "Irish, Italians, Jewish, and many other minorities overcame prejudice and worked their way up. Blacks should do the same without any special favors. Over the past few years blacks have gotten less than they deserve. It's really a matter of some people not trying hard enough; if blacks would only try harder they could be just as well off as whites."[30]

The results of Valentino and Sears's study are astonishing. Their data demonstrate that Jim Crow racism had declined dramatically in the South and throughout the nation. However, a residue of Jim Crow racism remained. Moreover, there was evidence of increasing levels of symbolic racism in the South. More importantly (after controlling for conservative ideology and policy preferences), symbolic racism, negative racial stereotypes, and cold feelings toward blacks played a much stronger role in explaining racial polarization in voting preferences, the rise of the Republican Party, and the white vote for Republican candidates in the South than would be expected. Valentino and Sears argue that a new form of racism has arisen in that

> the Southern parties today are split quite decisively along racial lines. Republicans are almost all white, and blacks are the dominant core of the Southern Democratic Party. All this leads us to suspect that racial attitudes, in particular, might be found to structure partisan divisions today, particularly in the white South. Having said that, we see major changes in the role of race in the South along with such continuities. In the 1950s and 1960s, white Southerners strongly supported Jim Crow or "old-fashioned" racism, focused on rigid social distance between the races, legalized segregation, formal racial discrimination, and beliefs in the inherent inferiority of blacks. But much of that support for formal racial inequality has disappeared in the New South, and is now too skimpy to be the foundation of the party alignment. Instead we argue that its political influence has been replaced by that of a new form of racism, variously described as "symbolic racism," "modern racism, or "racial resentment," blending racial animus with perceptions that blacks violate traditional American values, such as individualism. It is reflected in beliefs that blacks continuing disadvantages reflect their own lack of work ethic rather than continuing racial discrimination and that blacks make excessive demands and get too many undeserved advantages.[31]

After controlling for ideology, policy preferences, and demographics (age and income), Valentino and Sears demonstrated that symbolic racism and racial stereotypes have a strong, independent influence on the Southern white voter. However, they also suggest, "Given the considerable evidence that racial attitudes have spilled over into some other domestic policy issues such as welfare, crime, and taxes and spending, seemingly race-neutral conservatism may itself have become partially racialized. If so, our tests may in fact 'over-control' for nonracial conservatism, and so underestimate the effects of racial conservatism."[32] Valentino and Sears demonstrate that contrary to conventional wisdom, racial polarization in Southern voting is a function of racism. Whereas Southerners are and have been more conservative than the rest of the nation and this conservatism influences their voting decisions, race, symbolic racism, and negative racial stereotypes have a much larger impact on their voting preferences than would be expected.

Thomas Edsall has long argued that racial attitudes were a major factor in explaining not only the shift of Dixiecrats, but also the shift of Northern white workers from the Democratic Party to the Republican Party (i.e., the Reagan Democrats). (See Chapter 3.) Edsall also notes in a *New York Times* article that the low white vote for Obama in the 2008 and 2012 presidential elections was not unusual.[33] With the exception of the election of Lyndon Johnson in 1964, Democrats have been unable to obtain a majority of white votes since the 1952 election of Dwight Eisenhower. What is different since the 2008 election of President Obama is that party attachments have become more polarized around racial issues and that racial resentments have increased. Edsall explains,

> Supporting the Tesler-Sears findings, Josh Pasek, a professor in the communication studies department at the University of Michigan, Jon A. Krosnick, a political scientist at Stanford and Trevor Tompson, the director of the Associated Press-National Opinion Research Center at the university of Chicago, use responses from three different surveys in their analysis of "The Impact of Anti-Black Racism on Approval of Barack Obama's Job Performance and on Voting in the 2012 Presidential Election." Pasek and his collaborators found a statistically significant increase from 2008 to 2012 in "explicit anti-black attitudes"—a measure based on questions very similar to those used by Tesler and Sears for their racial-resentment scale. The percentage of voters with explicit anti-black attitudes rose from 47.6 in 2008 and 47.3 in 2010 to 50.9 percent in 2012. Crucially, Pasek found that Republicans drove the change: "People who identified themselves as Republicans in 2012 expressed anti-Black attitudes more often than did Republican identifiers in 2008." In 2008, Pasek and his collaborators note, the proportion of people expressing anti-Black attitudes was 31 percent among Democrats, 49 percent among independents, and 71 percent among Republicans. By 2012, the numbers had gone up. "The proportion of people expressing anti-Black attitudes," they write, "was 32 percent among Democrats, 48 percent among independents, and 79 percent among Republicans."[34]

Edsall makes it clear that the major changes in attitudes are occurring within the Republican Party. He concludes, "In fact, the shifts described by Tesler and Pasek are an integral aspect of the intensifying conservatism within the right wing of the Republican Party. Many voters voicing stronger anti-black affect were already Republicans."[35]

The old Jim Crow racism has declined, but not disappeared. Symbolic racism has worsened. Undoubtedly, it has blended with negative racial stereotypes and other forms of racism that had emerged with the growth of concentrated poverty. These other forms of racism associated with poverty include images of lazy, irresponsible blacks who make unreasonable demands on others, have no sense of individual responsibility, and expect preferential treatment, and of poor blacks who use and sell drugs, prey on others, are prone to violence, and are long-term welfare recipients. This blending of the many different forms of racism with conservative ideology defines metaracism.

Poor White Support for the Republican Party

Southern racism and the lower-class white vote for Republican candidates beg further explanation. A number of scholars have attempted to explain why poor whites would support public policies that benefit the rich and hurt the poor. Four explanations stand out and tie together the literature on class and racism. First, white identity and black subordination gives whites a sense of status, prestige, and privilege that they would not ordinarily have. W. E. B. DuBois and David Roediger use the expression "the wages of whiteness."[36] By identifying themselves as white, poor whites acquired a level of social esteem, privilege, and worth above blacks that compensated for the loss of wages and the poverty they experienced by accepting programs that benefited the rich at the expense of the poor.

Second, Southern culture tends to be authoritarian. Authoritarianism explains the connection between racism and moral conservatism. Thomas Frank insists that the Republican Party appealed to poor white voters on the basis of a morality agenda: antiabortion, prayer in schools, pro-family, and anti-same-sex marriage. Frank argues that when Republicans were elected they delivered on the economic agenda that benefited the rich, but did little to deliver on the morality agenda.[37] However, the literature on authoritarianism ties the moral vote to the race vote.

George Lakoff distinguishes between strict parent morality and nurturing parent morality.[38] The "strict parent morality" is a variation of the concept of authoritarian morality or the authoritarian personality developed by the Frankfurt School of Social Science.[39] The strict parent or the authoritarian orientation views the world as a fearful place divided in absolute black and white terms, between the good and the evil. It promotes a strict or authoritarian morality that sees premarital sex as sin, abortion as murder, birth control as promoting promiscuity, same-sex marriage as a threat to traditional families, and gay men and lesbians as an abomination before God. At the same time, it sees immigrants and racial minorities as threatening to jobs, security, communities, and lifestyles.

Third, the pervasiveness of racist culture, particularly in the South, influences perceptions of blacks and public policies even among poor whites. This culture is filled with images of welfare queens, black teens having babies to get welfare money, undeserving blacks taking jobs from poor whites, and black youth gangs threatening working-class whites. As a result of decades of the mass media and political leaders portraying the poor as black and irresponsible, conceptualizing notions of fairness and equality in black and white terms, and claiming that white taxpayers pay for black programs, this racialized way of talking and conceptualizing social issues and public policies has become so deeply ingrained in US culture that this cultural context now operates like a racializing prism. Messages about justice pass through this prism and come out as messages about race. This prism effect of racist culture explains why, as DiTomaso so eloquently puts it, when Democrats talk about fairness, equality, and social justice white workers hear a message about welfare programs that take money from whites to finance programs that benefit blacks.[40] It explains why, when Republicans talk about promoting individual responsibility and reducing taxes, white workers hear that cutting black programs will reduce white taxes. In Chapter 5, I discuss more about the racializing of social programs and the use of racial stereotypes by the mass media and political leaders in ways that have generated hatred for welfare programs. The point here is that racist culture distorts the way people think about justice and fairness, and this distortion cuts across class lines to influence rich and poor alike.[41]

Fourth, the Democratic Party has not connected well with poor whites, particularly in rural areas. Liberal Democrats who believe that poor whites operate with a false consciousness when they vote Republican have forgotten that it was Democrats who promoted NAFTA, which many poor rural whites believe hurt them. Moreover, conservative Republicans have been effective in characterizing Democrats as liberal elites who are out of touch with poor whites.

Conclusion

In summary, several economic changes created the context out of which metaracism emerged. These economic changes included the drive of the corporate sector to increase profits and accumulate wealth. In pursuit of this drive, corporations consolidated, automated, and moved production facilities and manufacturing jobs out of high-wage, unionized, older industrial cities to low-wage, non-union areas, producing economic changes that contributed to economic insecurity and declining wages. These changes began to occur during the 1970s at the same time the black middle class was expanding and leaving inner cities. The exodus of the black middle class from inner cities occurred at the same time these cities were hemorrhaging high paying manufacturing jobs. The loss of both manufacturing jobs and the middle class contributed to the rise of concentrated urban poverty. The contraction of the manufacturing sector in urban areas and mass farm foreclosures in rural areas generated economic insecurity. These economic changes provided the context out of which metaracism emerged during the first two decades of the twenty-first century.

Metaracism involves both culture and politics. It is associated with a pervasive and racialized culture that operates to normalize the status quo, to legitimize concentrated poverty, and to account for the black middle class. The culture of metaracism functions to racialize and dehumanize the poor, to desensitize people to the suffering of the poor. It offers a world view that provided outlets for and makes sense of the economic insecurity and frustration. The politics of metaracism involves a marriage of the corporate sector with political organizations and leaders that exploit race in subtle ways to reinforce this racialized culture. Chapter 3 examines the cultural form of metaracism. Chapter 4 examines the politics of metaracism, the formation and operation of a reactionary political coalition.

Notes

1. Alemaye Bishaw, "Areas with Concentrated Poverty: 2006–2010," *American Community Survey Briefs* (Washington, DC: US Department of Commerce, Economics and Statistics Administration, US Census Bureau, 2011).

2. Ibid., p. 6.

3. Ibid., p. 1. See also David Erickson, Carolina Reid, Lisa Nelson, Anne O'Shaughnessy, Alan Berube, eds., A Joint Project of the Community Affairs Office of the Federal Reserve System and the Metropolitan Policy Program at the Brookings Institution, *The Enduring Challenge of Concentrated Poverty in America: Case Studies from Communities Across the U.S.* (Richmond, VA: Federal Reserve Bank of Richmond, 2008).

4. Carter Wilson, "Restructuring and the Growth of Concentrated Poverty," *Urban Affairs Quarterly* 28, no. 2 (1992): 198.

5. Ibid., p. 188.

6. US Department of Commerce, Census Bureau (2013).

7. Alec Friedhoff and Howard Wial, "Bearing the Brunt: Manufacturing Job Loss in the Great Lakes Region, 1995–2005" (Washington, DC: Urban Institute, 2006).

8. Timothy Noah, *The Great Divergence: America's Growing Inequality Crisis and What We Can Do About It* (New York: Bloomsbury Press, 2012), p. 134.

9. Bennett Harrison and Barry Bluestone, *The Great U-Turn: Corporate Restructuring and the Polarizing of America* (New York: Basic Book, 1990).

10. Eric Hoffer, *The True Believer: Thoughts on the Nature of Mass Movements* (New York: Harper and Row, 1966 [1951]); Eric Fromm, *Escape from Freedom* (New York: Holt, Rinehart and Winston 1964/1941); Theodor Adorno, Else Frenkel-Brunswik, Daniel Levinson, and R. Nevitt Sanford, *The Authoritarian Personality* (New York: Harper, 1950); Barrington Moore, *Social Origins of Dictators and Democracy: Lord and Peasant in the Making of the Modern World* (Boston: Beacon Press, 1967).

11. Fromm, *Escape from Freedom*.

12. Gordon Allport, *The Nature of Prejudice* (Garden City, NY: Doubleday, 1958).

13. Hoffer, *The True Believer*, p. 12.

14. Ibid.

15. Carolyn Gallaher, *On the Fault Line: Race, Class, and the American Patriot Movement* (Lanham, MD: Rowman and Littlefield, 2002), p. 77.

16. Ibid., p. 79.

17. Gallaher, *On the Fault Line*; Wenonah Hauter, *Foodopoly: The Battle over the Future of Food and Farming in America* (New York: New Press, 2012).

18. Sara Diamond, *Roads to Dominion: Right-Wing Movements and Political Power in the United States* (New York: Guilford Press, 1995), p. 259.

19. See Morris Dees with James Corcoran, *Gathering Storm: America's Militia Threat* (New York: Harper Collins Publishers, 1996). See also the Southern Poverty Law Center's journal, *Intelligence Report,* especially Mark Potok, "The Year of Hate and Extremism," no. 153 (2014).

20. Joel Dyer, *Harvest of Rage: Why Oklahoma City Is Only the Beginning* (Boulder, CO: Westview Press, 1998), p. 45.

21. Gallaher, *On the Fault Line*, p. 83.

22. Ibid.

23. Jess Walter, *Ruby Ridge: The Truth and Tragedy of the Randy Weaver Family,* US Department of Justice Report of the Ruby Ridge Task Force to the Office of Professional Responsibility of the Investigation of Allegations of Improper Governmental Conduct in the Investigation, Apprehension and Prosecution of Randall C. Weaver and Kevin Harris (Washington DC: United States Printing Office, June 10, 1994).

24. Andrew Macdonald, *The Turner Diaries: A Novel* (Hillsboro, WV: National Vanguard Books, 1995/1980). (Written by William Luther Pierce under the pseudonym Andrew Macdonald.)

25. For an excellent study of the transformation of racist, right-wing extremist organizations into mainstream white nationalist organizations, see Leonard Zeskind, *Blood and Politics: The History of the White Nationalist Movement from the Margins to the Mainstream* (New York: Farrar, Straus and Giroux, 2009).

26. Nancy DiTomaso, *The American Non-Dilemma: Racial Inequality Without Racism* (New York: Russell Sage Foundation, 2013).

27. Ibid., p. 188.

28. See Paul Sniderman and Edward Carmines, *Reaching Beyond Race* (Cambridge: Harvard University Press, 1997); Paul Sniderman and Thomas Piazza, *The Scar of Race* (Cambridge: Harvard University Press, 1993).

29. Nicholas A. Valentino and David O. Sears, "Old Times There Are Not Forgotten: Race and Partisan Realignment in the Contemporary South," *American Journal of Political Science* 49, no. 3 (2005): 672–688.

30. Ibid, p. 676.

31. Ibid., p. 674. (Some references in the original have been deleted.)

32. Ibid., p. 685.

33. Thomas Edsall, "The Persistence of Racial Resentment," *New York Times,* February 6, 2013. http://opinionator.blogs.nytimes.com/2013/02/06the-persistence -of-racial-resentment/?php=blogs&_r=0. See also Michael Tesler and David O. Sears, *Obama's Race: The 2008 Election and the Dream of a Post-racial America* (Chicago: University of Chicago Press, 2010); Michael Tesler and David O. Sears, "President Obama and the Growing Polarization of Partisan Attachments by Racial Attitudes and Race," paper presented at the annual conference of the Midwest Political Science Association, Chicago, April 2010.

34. Edsall, "The Persistence of Racial Resentment"; Josh Pasek, Jon Krosnick, and Trevor Tompson, "The Impact of Anti-Black Racism on Approval of Barack Obama's Job Performance and on Voting in the 2012 Presidential Election," National Opinion Research Center at the University of Chicago, unpublished paper, October 2012.

35. Edsall, "The Persistence of Racial Resentment."

36. David Roediger, *The Wages of Whiteness: Race and the Making of the American Working Class* (New York: Vergo, 1991).

37. Thomas Frank, *What's the Matter with Kansas: How Conservatives Won the Heart of America* (New York: Henry Holt, 2005). The entire book explains how Kansas transformed from a New Deal Democratic stronghold to a strong Republican state, see chapter 5.

38. George Lakoff, *Moral Politics: How Liberals and Conservatives Think* (Chicago: University of Chicago Press, 2002).

39. Theodor Adorno, Else Frenkel-Brunswik, Daniel Levison, and R. Nevitt Sanford, *The Authoritarian Personality* (New York: Harper, 1950); Robert Altemeyer, *The Authoritarian Specter* (Cambridge: Harvard University Press, 1996). There is a large volume of literature on the authoritarian personality. Theories of the authoritarian personality were popular in the 1960s and early 1970s. However, they were discredited by the psychometric discipline because the instrument that Adorno and colleagues used to measure this personality lacked sufficient validity and reliability. However, Altemeyer, a psychometrician, responded to the criticism by revising the instrument and resuscitating the authoritarian personality as a useful psychological construct. See Altemeyer, *The Authoritarian Specter,* chapter 1.

40. DiTomaso, *The American Non-Dilemma*, p. 307.

41. See Robert Bellah, Richard Madsen, William Sullivan, Ann Swidler, and Steven Tipton, *Habits of the Heart: Individualism and Commitment in American Life* (Berkeley: University of California Press, 2008), p. 26. The authors conducted a massive study of US culture and found that, compared to other cultures, US culture has an underdeveloped concept of justice. Whereas these authors attribute that inadequate concept of justice to the strong sense of individualism in the United States, an alternative explanation is that US culture is infected with a form of racism that inhibits citizens' understanding of justice. I develop this point further in Chapter 3.

3

The Culture of Metaracism

In Chapter 1, I introduced the structural and cultural dimensions of racism. In Chapter 2, I elaborated on the structural component of metaracism. In this chapter, I examine the cultural aspects of metaracism. As noted in Chapter 1, culture is learned and shared patterns of behavior. It includes learned and shared values, language, images, myths, stories, discourse, ideologies, and basic assumptions about the world. Culture shapes both perception and emotions.

I demonstrated that racism is associated with patterns of racial oppression in Chapter 1. Racist culture tends to emerge out of narcissistic assumptions about racially oppressive societies that they are just and morally good. For example, during the era of slavery, those who assumed that slavery was just and morally good were more likely to believe that slavery benefited both society and slaves by providing food, shelter, and the benefits of Christianity and civilization to the slaves. These assumptions and beliefs contributed to the cultural formation of dominative racism. In Chapter 1, I insisted that historically, racist culture operated to legitimize and normalize patterns of racial oppression. It defined the *oppressed* as fundamentally different from and the binary opposite of white people in the United States. That is, it described whites as moral, hardworking, rational, and normal, and blacks as immoral, lazy, irrational, and abnormal. It diminished the dignity and humanity of the oppressed. It desensitized society to their suffering, and exonerated society and the economy from any blame or responsibility. Racist culture was promoted by the academic literature and political elites.

In this chapter, I demonstrate that the culture of metaracism has characteristics and dynamics similar to earlier forms of racism. The chapter is divided into four parts. In the first section, I review the contributions of the academic literature to the formation of the culture of metaracism. I focus on the culture of poverty, neoconservatism, and urban underclass literature. Next, I examine the psychocultural aspects of metaracism. I draw from the disciplines of experimental psychology and neuroscience to analyze the phenomenon of black phobia and contemporary racial issues. I then consider other nuances of metaracism such as the notion of white nationalism. Finally, I look at the role of neoliberalism in the current assault on the equal opportunity regime.

The Academic Literature

Because metaracism is structurally related to the rise of concentrated black poverty, a large part of the culture of this form of racism emerged from the poverty literature. This literature is broad and complex. It involves several schools of thought explaining poverty from various perspectives. These schools can be classified in terms of the culture of poverty, the neoconservative, and the urban underclass perspectives. Because some neoconservatives focus on the lack of value for education as a major cause of poverty, a separate neoconservative/education perspective is examined.

This literature is not inherently racist. What makes this literature racist is not its unflattering portrayal of the poor, its focus on self-defeating values, or its identification of self-destructive behavior. Indeed, there are many particular values and forms of behavior that contribute to the formation of poverty. What makes the literature racist is the extent to which it mimics the social functions and dynamics of earlier forms of racism. It is racist to the extent to which it portrays the poor as the binary opposite of the white middle class and as essentially and fundamentally different, dark, unprincipled, immoral, promiscuous, irrational, dangerous, and predatory. These portrayals diminish the humanity of the poor and evoke fear, disgust, revulsion, and hostility.

The Culture of Poverty

The concept of the culture of poverty is thought to have originated with the anthropologist Oscar Lewis[1] and the antipoverty activist Michael Harrington.[2] There are many branches of the culture of poverty literature. Harrington saw poverty as resulting from market failure and institutional racism. He saw the culture of poverty emerging out of the situation and conditions of poverty. Elliot Liebow insisted that the culture of poverty arose out of the adaptation of traditional values to the situation of poverty.[3] A number of other scholars, such as Kenneth Clark and Lee Rainwater, saw the situation of poverty creating a culture of poverty that produced a "tangle of pathology" that in turn perpetuated poverty.[4]

While serving in the Johnson administration, Daniel Patrick Moynihan wrote a short but controversial report entitled *The Negro Family: The Case for National Action*, better known as "The Moynihan Report."[5] In this report, he claimed that the legacy of slavery, racism, and "incredible mistreatment" impacted the black family and precipitated an increase in the rates of female-headed households, which in turn created the "tangle of poverty" that not only sustained poverty but destroyed communities and created crime and social disorder.[6] He also claimed that because the rules of the welfare system only provided payments when the man had left the household, it contributed to the breakup of black families. Moynihan advocated replacing the welfare system with a more liberal system that guaranteed the annual incomes of poor families.[7]

In the 1970s, Edward Banfield added another perspective to the culture of poverty. He defined the middle class and the lower class, or poverty class, in terms of values and orientation. For Banfield, the middle class was future oriented and the lower class was present oriented. The orientation both defined and determined the class. In other words, people fell into the lower class because they were present oriented and committed to immediate gratification. People moved into the middle class because they were future oriented. They saved. They earned an education. They delayed gratification and sacrificed for the future.[8]

Today, the culture of poverty is part of the mainstream poverty literature. This perspective has been popularized by Ruby Payne's manuals for community agencies dealing with the poor. Payne reflects Banfield's perspective in her discussion of what she calls the "hidden rules among classes."[9] These rules allegedly demonstrate how the culture of the poverty class differs from the culture of the middle class. Payne suggests that members of the poverty class are impulsive in spending, present oriented, and unappreciative of the value of education in facilitating social mobility. In contrast, members of the middle class are good at saving and managing money, future oriented, and appreciative of the value of education.

According to Patricia Cohen, the culture of poverty has been a forbidden and controversial subject.[10] Reporting in the *New York Times* on a collection of essays on the decline of marriage released by Princeton University and the Brookings Institution and presented at the annual meeting of the American Sociological Association, Cohen claims that the general consensus was that for forty years social scientists investigating poverty avoided discussing the role of culture in producing poverty because of the intellectual assault on sociologist Daniel Patrick Moynihan after he published "The Moynihan Report." In her article Cohen states:

> For more than 40 years, social scientists investigating the causes of poverty have tended to treat cultural explanations like Lord Voldemort: That Which Must Not Be Named.

The reticence was a legacy of the ugly battles that erupted after Daniel
Patrick Moynihan, then an assistant labor secretary in the Johnson administration, introduced the idea of a "culture of poverty" to the public in a startling 1965 report.[11]

Cohen was not alone in her assessment. She reported on the consensus
expressed at the conference. Moreover, Bryce Christensen claims that
Moynihan was silenced and that the debate over the report and the culture
of poverty ended because social scientists feared being called racists or fascists by liberals.[12]

Contrary to this claim, Moynihan was never silenced and the debate
never ended. What followed the Moynihan Report was a rich, vibrant, and
healthy debate.[13] A few civil rights leaders criticized Moynihan for blaming the poor for poverty and trivializing the role of racism and racial discrimination in producing poverty.[14] Feminists criticized Moynihan for
characterizing male dominated families as healthy and female headed
households as the source of social pathology.[15] Kenneth Clark and other
black scholars such as William Julius Wilson came to Moynihan's
defense. Clark argued that the term, "tangle of pathology," which he had
originated, was a legitimate description of social problems in the ghetto.
Lee Rainwater and William Yancey edited a book, *The Moynihan Report
and the Politics of Controversy*, which featured pro and con articles on
this debate.[16]

The debate continued throughout the next forty years. Three branches
of the literature emerged—a liberal, a centrist, and a far right. The liberal
branch emphasized the strengths of black families and communities, despite
the devastation of poverty.[17] This branch cautioned against blaming the victims of poverty for poverty itself and emphasized the structural determinants of poverty and pathology: inequality, market failure, and the racial
and class segregation of the poor. The centrist branch continued in the
Moynihan tradition. Indeed, as noted above, William Julius Wilson revived
Moynihan's position. Moreover, in his book *The Audacity of Hope*, President Obama agreed with both Wilson and Moynihan and insisted that the
far right branch gained the upper hand in the debate because liberals
refused to acknowledge that the values and behavior of the poor were contributing to their poverty. Obama says:

> The response of liberal policy makers and civil rights leaders didn't help; in
> their urgency to avoid blaming the victims of historical racism, they tended
> to downplay or ignore evidence that entrenched behavioral patterns among
> the black poor really were contributing to intergenerational poverty. (Most
> famously, Daniel Patrick Moynihan was accused of racism in the early six-
> ties when he raised alarms about the rise of out-of-wedlock births among the
> black poor.) This willingness to dismiss the role that values played in shap-
> ing the economic success of a community strained credulity and alienated

working-class whites—particularly since some of the most liberal policy makers lived lives far removed from urban disorder.[18]

A third but problematic branch of this literature emerged—the far right or neoconservative literature. The problem with this literature is not that it explained poverty in terms of culture or recognized the role of values and behavior in contributing to poverty. "The question," as Stephen Steinberg puts it, "is not whether culture matters, but whether it is an independent and self-sustaining factor in the production and reproduction of poverty."[19] As I will demonstrate shortly, this neoconservative branch of the literature has focused almost exclusively on culture, bad behavior, bad values, and government as the causes of poverty. This literature has been excessive and extreme in its rejection of economic determinants of poverty. It has ignored structural changes in the economy and racial biases in the job market. It has been obsessive and single-minded about proving that bad values, bad behavior, and government programs are the exclusive determinants of poverty to the point of dehumanizing the poor and demonizing government.

Neoconservatism

Neoconservative ideology is not inherently racist. It openly opposes racism. It is based on a number of race-neutral assumptions about the government, the economy, and poor people. It assumes that markets are efficient, that governments provide perverse incentives, and that poor people are largely responsible for their own poverty. It calls for paternalistic approaches to poverty designed to change the values and behavior of poor people. (See Chapter 5.)

Neoconservative George Gilder argues that government welfare programs provided incentives for people not to work, for women to leave their husbands, and for teenaged girls to have babies. He maintains that these programs destroyed black families and contributed to the rise of black female-headed households and the growth of youth crime.[20]

Neoconservative Charles Murray claims that the liberal policies of the 1960s created a culture of dependency and poverty and that the expansion of welfare programs of the 1960s created the social ills of today. Like Gilder, he argues that these programs provided incentives for bad values and dysfunctional behavior, paid people not to work, gave teenaged girls money to have babies, and produced long-term, intergenerational, pathological dependency. He insists that, as social programs provide more generous benefits, they attract more people who do not need the benefits and pull them into this tangle of social pathology.[21]

In making his case, Murray presents data that demonstrate that poverty rates declined during the 1960s, but stagnated during the 1970s, precisely at the time when spending for cash transfer and in-kind programs were sky-rocketing. He concludes that increases in welfare spending produced the dramatic increase in black illegitimacy rates.[22]

These neoconservatives draw conclusions about values and behavior without examining values and behavior. This flaw becomes most evident in the face of alternative research that actually examines the values and behavior of the poor. For example, William Julius Wilson refutes the assertions that black teenaged girls were having more and more babies in order to get more welfare money. He provides data indicating that fertility rates among black teenagers declined sharply in the 1970s and early 1980s. The rise of the welfare rolls was associated with a decline in black fertility rates, contradicting the neoconservative assertions. Moreover, Wilson demonstrates that marriage rates among blacks declined at precisely the time that rates of joblessness and incarceration were increasing dramatically among black men. Wilson concluded that female-headed households increased because the pool of marriageable black men shrunk. When the sharp decline in the welfare rolls after the passage of the 1996 Personal Responsibility and Work Opportunity Act failed to produce any increase in the black marriage rate, the association between welfare spending and the rise of female-headed households lost credibility. This association was spurious during the 1970s and 1980s (produced by economic factors, not welfare) and nonexistent during the 1990s and the twenty-first century.[23]

Several other scholars have confirmed Wilson's conclusions. In a large study of the rise of female-headed households, Heather Ross and Isabel Sawhill found increases in these households among both blacks and whites, although the increase was more dramatic among blacks. They associated the increases in female-headed households with the rise of feminism and changes in the economy. They argue that women were no longer willing to stay in bad relationships and that marriage rates declined in times of economic recessions.[24]

In a short paper, Erol Rickets provides one of the most insightful and comprehensive discussions of the research on the rise of black female-headed households. After reviewing the literature, he concludes that lower marriage rates among blacks were more strongly related to higher levels of economic uncertainty.[25]

Education and Neoconservatism

Since most people in the United States see education as the path out of poverty, the view that black poverty is perpetuated by a low value for education among blacks has become a common belief among neoconservatives. John Ogbu's research provides academic support for this view. One of his major research projects targeted Shaker Heights, a suburb of Cleveland. He compared middle-class blacks with middle-class whites in this suburb, demonstrating that middle-class blacks had lower scores on standardized tests than middle-class whites. He claims that his data demonstrates that the lower educational performance among blacks was not a function of social class, but a function of a self-defeating cultural attitude that portrayed working hard and getting a good education as undesirable because it is "acting white."[26] His research suffered from two flaws. He conflated suburban residency with middle-class status and he based his conclusions about values and attitudes on anecdotal stories.

Ronald Ferguson surveyed over 40,000 middle school and high school students directly from fifteen different school districts, including Shaker Heights, the same district examined by Ogbu. Ferguson's study contradicted Ogbu's assertions. The study demonstrates that black students worked just as hard and valued education just as much as white students. He also found that teachers did not provide black students with as much encouragement as they provided white students.[27]

A growing body of empirical research contradicts Ogbu and supports Ferguson. David Bergin and Helen Cooks at the University of Toledo conducted extensive focus group interviews of black students to get a better understanding of the use of the term "acting white." What they discovered was that the expression "acting white" referred to people who had an arrogant and condescending disposition and lacked empathy, rhythm, and soul.[28] It was not an expression of hostility to education.

Karolyn Tyson, William Darity Jr., and Domini Castellino studied the attitudes of black and white high school students in eight North Carolina high schools. They found no difference in black and white high school students' attitudes toward education. Black and white students valued education equally high; however, there were some groups within each that stigmatized high achievers as "geeks" or "nerds." Moreover, these researchers discovered that high school students are generally sensitive to and critical of peers who are arrogant and condescending and who act like they are better or smarter than others. Although this behavior is typical among both black and white high school students, it is generally interpreted more negatively when seen among blacks.[29] A growing body of literature suggests that the idea that black students are hostile to education is contradicted by direct surveys.[30]

A 2012 survey of Houston, Texas, parents conducted by Rice University's Kinder Institute for Urban Research found that a higher percentage of the parents of black grade-school students (90 percent) believed that having a postsecondary education was essential for success than the parents of white grade-school students (64 percent).[31] The study concludes: "These universally high aspirations on the part of the parents with school-aged children who participated in the survey clearly contradicted a common explanation for ethnic differences in educational attainment—namely that blacks and Hispanics simply do not put as high a value on their children's education compared to Anglos and Asians."[32] Despite the higher aspirations, the achievement levels of African Americans and Hispanics in terms of test scores and college attendance were much lower than the achievement levels of whites. The report concluded that the lower achievement rates were more likely associated with the combined effects of the concentration and isolation of poor blacks and Hispanics in high poverty areas, with low quality schools. The Houston survey was corroborated by a national survey by the Pew Foundation, which also found a higher percentage of African American and Latino respondents compared to white respondents agreeing that higher education was important for success.[33] The cumulative evidence suggests that the view that African Americans are hostile to education is largely a myth. This myth is part of the culture of metaracism.

The Urban Underclass

Because metaracism is closely associated with concentrated urban poverty, a core feature of metaracism is the social construction of the underclass and the literature associated with it. The urban underclass literature practically defines the underclass as a criminal class. For example, Ken Auletta offers this definition:

> Although individuals often defy categories, in general members of the underclass seem to fall into four distinct groups. First are the hostile street and career criminals who openly reject society's dominant values, a surprisingly small number of whom are responsible for the majority of crimes in most cities. The second group consists of the hustlers, those who out of choice or necessity operate in the underground economy, peddling hot goods, reefers, or hard drugs, gambling, and pimping. . . . Third are the passive, those who have become dependent over the years on welfare and government support. The fourth group is made up of the traumatized—those whose minds have snapped and who have turned to drink and drugs or roam city streets as helpless shopping bag ladies, derelicts—or sadistic slashers.[34]

According to this construction, members of the underclass are not just considered to be poor people with less money and resources than everyone else. Even though they are not biologically different, they are thought of as fundamentally different from other people in the United States. They are the new version of the "undeserving poor."[35] They represent a repulsive class that poses a threat to the rest of society: the career street criminals, the pimps, the drug dealers, the welfare queens, the social parasites who live off the government, the alcoholics, the drug addicts, and the crackheads. This description of the underclass makes empathy almost impossible. It legitimizes targeted police enforcement in high-poverty areas.

This is not to say that there is no crime in high-poverty areas. On the contrary, there is indeed a disproportionately higher rate of crimes and violence in these areas. However, this fact alone does not mean that the majority of the people living in these areas are fundamentally different from people living in other areas of the country. These people are different only in the sense that they experience more hardships. They suffer more from the acts of desperation from others and, thus, are more likely to be exposed to violence.

Two well-publicized shootings that occurred on Chicago's South Side are illustrative of this point. The first shooting occurred in January 2013 just after the inauguration of President Barack Obama. Hadiya Pendleton—a fifteen-year-old honor student and majorette, with an insatiable appetite for reading books and with everything to live for—was shot and killed a few days after she had performed at the president's inauguration.[36] A month later Janay McFarlane, an 18-year-old young woman with a three-month-old baby, was shot and killed just after her younger sister had attended an address by President Obama on gun violence.[37] Both victims were innocent bystanders, and both shootings were gang related. These shootings dramatize the violence in black neighborhoods. But as horrible as these shootings are, people who live in inner-city areas are no different from people anywhere else. The parents of these children, like any other parents, work hard, love their children, and desire the best for them.

Charles Derber responds to the idea of violent inner-city youth gangs with this axiom: "a fish rots from the head first." He notes that these gangs are often characterized as engaging in "wildings," that is, having no regard for human life, taking pride in gang culture, and preying on the weak and helpless.[38] The concept of wildings came from the arrest of five black juveniles in the spring of 1989 for brutally assaulting and raping a twenty-eight-year-old jogger who was an investment broker. The jogger was so severely beaten that she was not expected to live. Her face was disfigured, her skull fractured, and her eye destroyed. For years the case was used to exemplify the pathology of the urban underclass and the need for police repression of inner-city black men.

Twelve years later, deoxyribonucleic acid (DNA) tests proved that the five black men were innocent. A serial rapist had beaten and raped the woman. Ken Burns has recently produced a documentary on this case that shows the rush to judgment was tainted by racial biases.[39]

Nevertheless, Derber's point is that bad values—the unrestrained drive to accumulate money and material things to the disregard of others—cut across class lines.[40] Where these values exist among a few members of the urban poor, they originate from the top. They are the same values found among members of the dominant class. They are just imitated by members of the lower class. These values have been exhibited by the large finance

companies that made fortunes from predatory lending and illegal foreclosures; by the tobacco manufacturers that increased the nicotine content in
cigarettes knowing that it was addictive and lethal; by the mining companies that used poisonous chemicals to extract precious metals, but saved
money by leaving the poison in the rivers; by the executives from the now
bankrupt Enron Corporation, who made fortunes by controlling the California electricity market and artificially raised electric bills (and even joked
openly about the shock the elderly would experience when their new electric bill was double the previous bill); and by the US companies that relo-
cated abroad to exploit child labor. These corporations made fortunes and
had little regard for human lives.[41] They engaged in wildings.

The problem is not the acknowledgment or lack of acknowledgment of
violence in high-poverty areas. There is no question that gangs and violent
crimes are a problem in high-poverty areas of large cities and that the government needs to do something to reduce the violence. The problem is the
characterization of young black men as being fundamentally different from
everyone else and in ways that diminish their humanity, provoke fear and
rage, and encourage a repressive government response.

Values and Poverty

Liberal scholars have long argued that inner-city residents have values that
are no different from the values of the white middle class or other people in
the United States. As noted earlier, Elliot Liebow came to this conclusion in
the 1960s. After extensive long-term and in-depth interviews with poor
people, he concludes that the values of poor people were not much different
from the values of people from any other social class. He saw the culture of
poverty arising out of the application of middle-class values to the social
context of inner-city poverty.[42]

More recently, Jennifer Hochschild made the case that the values and
worldview of inner-city drug dealers are indistinguishable from those of
CEOs of major corporations. Unlike the neoconservatives, she bases her
conclusions, not on conjectures but on direct evidence from interviews of
inner-city drug dealers. Hochschild argues,

> Finally, many drug sellers bear an uncanny resemblance to American cap-
> tains of industry. They work their way up the ladder: "I had to convince peo-
> ple I could do it. I didn't have my hand out for no charity. I worked hard to
> get established." They are self-disciplined and work-oriented: "Selling coke
> is just like any other business. You gotta work hard, stay on your toes, pro-
> tect what's yours." . . . They defer gratification: "I never use cocaine: it's not
> real when they say that a person that sells ends up using his drugs; that's not
> true." . . . They develop detailed job descriptions for subordinates, write man-
> uals to rationalize the flow of goods, learn salesmen's manners, use brand

names to distinguish their product from their competitors', and provide discount coupons, two-for-one sales, and contests for employees.

In the end, it is sellers' resemblance to junior members of the Chamber of Commerce that makes them and their trade so frightening to other Americans.[43]

Also, more recently, Barbara Ehrenreich engaged in extensive participatory research into the lives of the working poor. She too concludes that the problem with poor people is not that they have different values or different forms of behavior, but that they lack money. They did not save because they had no money to save. They manage extraordinarily well with the little money they have. If they seem to be present oriented, it is because their survival depends on it. They value education as much as anyone. They have been held back by real and pressing financial needs: the need to pay rent, utilities, and other bills.[44]

When the Academic Literature Contributes to Racism

The academic literature does not become racist when it portrays unflattering images of blacks or when it identifies self-destructive values or forms of behavior. This literature becomes racist when it racializes the poor; that is, when it talks about the poor and welfare recipients as if they are predominantly black, when it constructs poor people as if they are fundamentally different and the binary opposite of the white middle class, when it defines poor blacks and middle-class whites as having fundamentally different values and engaging in profoundly different forms of behavior, and when it characterizes the white middle class as moral, hardworking, independent, committed to education, law-abiding, sober, rational, decent, and normal and characterizes the black poor as immoral, lazy, welfare dependent, hostile to education, criminal prone, drug addicted, irrational, promiscuous, and abnormal.

In his large study, Theo David Goldberg included a section on the urban underclass literature. He suggests that this literature contributes to metaracism insofar as it racializes and dehumanizes the poor and, at the same time, denies the existence of racism. He observes, "So, in general, the notion of the underclass explicitly erases the exclusionary experiences of racism from social science analysis while silently enthroning the demeaning impact of race-based insinuations and considerations."[45] He even points to Wilson's moderate study that avoids dehumanizing stereotypes of the urban poor while recognizing the pathology of violence in concentrated poverty areas. He takes issue with Wilson's thesis of the declining significance of race.[46]

Wilson rejects the racist assumptions found in the neoconservative literature and explains the rise of poverty in structural economic terms. For

Wilson, urban poverty resulted from the economic restructuring of urban areas, the shift from an industrial-based economy to a knowledge-based economy associated with corporate headquarters, financial institutions, and information technology. Wilson concludes that urban poverty arose from the mismatch between the high level of education required for the knowledge-intensive economy and the low level of education attained by inner-city residents.[47] This mismatch thesis has been challenged by other scholars using direct empirical evidence of changes in urban labor markets that indicated a dramatic decline in industrial jobs, but a rise in service sector jobs requiring a range of education from low levels (for janitorial, security, and retail jobs) to high levels (for accounting, legal, medical, engineering, and high-tech jobs). A great deal of the increase in poverty has been explained by the rise of lower-paying service sector jobs. The literature also has demonstrated that institutional racism played a role in two ways: racial segregation isolated inner-city blacks from areas of job growth and labor market discrimination disadvantaged black workers.[48] I discuss this further in later chapters. Goldberg argues that

> Wilson's understating of the force of race and the effects of racism in the account of contemporary poverty in a deeply racialized social order like the United States rests upon his underestimating the perpetual disadvantages blacks continue to suffer, irrespective of their class position. Employment opportunities for whites are considerably greater than for blacks across the class spectrum. Geographically defined unemployment rates for blacks are often double that for whites. The rates of unemployment for both male and female blacks with one or more years of college are greater than those for whites who failed to complete high school.[49]

In other words, the mismatch thesis falls apart in the face of data indicating that blacks with higher levels of education have more difficulty in finding jobs than whites with lower levels of education.

A Bifurcated Class and Black Susceptibility to Metaracism

Whereas Wilson neglected the continuing influence of institutionalized racism, he correctly noted the growing class division among blacks—the increase in the black middle class offset by the growth of concentrated black poverty in inner-city areas. With this new class division and the rise of neoconservative/underclass literature, racism has changed in two important ways. The first and most obvious change is that metaracism is based on a split or dual image of blacks: a positive image of middle- and upper-class blacks and a negative image of low-income blacks. A good example of this split image in popular culture is found in the 1998 movie, *American History X*.[50] The movie is about race relations among black and white teenagers in an integrated working-class high school. The principal of the high school is an intelligent and compassionate black male character with a PhD. This positive black middle-class role contrasts sharply with the role of the lower-class black male students who are gang members. They indiscriminately harass, assault, and rob white students. The central character, a white student, has the courage to stand up to this black gang. At the same time, this student has been struggling against racism because his brother is part of a white supremacist group. At the end of the movie, without provocation, the black gang leader murders this innocent white teenager. In an effort to present the race problem in a balanced perspective, the movie depicts young black men as fundamentally different from normal middle-class and white working-class people; that is, as erratic, irrational, impulsive, violent, and extremely dangerous.

The second change that has occurred with the new metaracism is that dehumanizing images of the black poor are now pervasive, and these images affect the perspectives of middle-class blacks. That is, the black middle class is now susceptible to accepting stereotypes of the black poor. This change is the result of a paradox of civil rights. Prior to the civil rights movement, middle-class and poor blacks lived in the same neighborhoods. This class integration among blacks was the result of racial segregation and the small size of the black middle class. After the civil rights movement and especially during the 1970s, 1980, and 1990s, the black middle class grew and migrated out of inner-city areas. By the twenty-first century, the black middle class was much more disconnected from the black poor than ever before. Prior to the civil rights movement, when the black middle class lived in the same neighborhoods as the black poor and racism applied to all blacks, demeaning images of blacks in the larger culture had little impact on the black middle class. Today, with the black middle class disconnected from the black poor and with metaracism targeting the black poor and sparing the black middle class, racist images of the black poor have more impact on the black middle class.

Nevertheless, the literature on the susceptibility of blacks to antiblack stereotypes is mixed.[51] Robert Smith and Richard Seltzer suggest that historically the black middle class has been more conservative than the black lower class, and that the recent and dramatic expansion of the black middle class and the decline of the black poor has produced more of a convergence of ideological beliefs.[52] More research is needed on this subject. However, I demonstrate with the experimental research, black images prevalent in the media seem to impact both blacks and whites.

Several years ago, the *Washington Post,* Henry J. Kaiser Family Foundation, and Harvard University conducted a large survey to assess perceptions of black males. The study interviewed 2,864 people (blacks, whites, men, and women), which included 1,328 black males.[53] The survey asked participants what they valued and believed and what they believed black males valued and believed. The survey found that almost all of the black men surveyed valued marriage, education, and hard work. However, when asked about their perceptions of other black men, a majority of the black males surveyed saw themselves as the exceptions and other black men as not valuing marriage, education, and hard work as much as they did. In writing a *Washington Post* article on the results of the survey, Kevin Merida consulted with sociologists across the country to explain the results. Sociologists tentatively concluded that the media and academic literature may have produced biased perceptions of black men even among black men.[54]

One such example is the case of Bill Cosby. Aside from his personality, philanthropy, and the controversies surrounding him, including the accusations of sexual assaults, Cosby's comments at an NAACP dinner in May 2004 illustrates this point about dehumanizing racial stereotypes infecting middle-class blacks:

> Ladies and gentlemen, the lower economic people are not holding up their end in this deal. And these people are not parenting. They are buying things for kids—$500 sneakers, for what? . . .
> They're standing on the corner and they can't speak English. . . . There are people going around stealing Coca-Cola. People getting shot in the back of the head over a piece of pound cake! Then we all run out and are outraged, [saying] "The cops shouldn't have shot him." What the hell was he doing with the pound cake in his hand?[55]

Because he has toned down his harsh depiction of poor inner-city blacks and engaged in constructive community building in inner cities throughout the nation, these comments should be viewed apart from the person of Cosby and understood in the context of a society that has become increasingly hostile to poor blacks and increasingly tolerant of the repression of black men.

There are two problems with Cosby's image in his comments at the NAACP dinner. First, the image is false. Sociologist Eric Michael Dyson presents substantial data that contradict this image and demonstrate that an overwhelming majority of poor black children tend to be much more cost conscious and willing to settle for cheaper clothing products precisely because they are aware of limited family resources.[56]

Second, the image of poor black parents purchasing $500 sneakers for their children provokes disgust and contempt. It makes it almost impossible to sympathize with the struggles of poor blacks. Cosby's comment suggesting that the police are justified in shooting an unarmed juvenile because he stole a piece of cake is a profound expression of contempt for young poor black men. It denies their humanity and dignity.

The Emotional and Psychocultural Dimension of Metaracism

Fear has been a major component of the old racism: fear of the black African cannibals with bones in their noses; fear of the ape-looking black man lurking in the woods of the Deep South to rape a helpless white woman. Frantz Fanon refers to this fear as "Negrophobia."[57] Metaracism involves fear of black men. This fear comes from the undercurrent images of black men in contemporary US culture, images promoted by the urban underclass and neoconservative literature and popularized in the media; images of black street predators, violent black youth gangs, and crazed black crack addicts. However, given the intolerance for racism, most people deny black phobia.

This denial can generate controversy, which flares up periodically, particularly after police offers shoot and kill black male suspects. It did so in February 1999 after four New York City undercover police officers fired forty-one shots at unarmed Amadou Diallo as he stood outside of his apartment. The police were acquitted because they mistook Diallo reaching for his wallet as him reaching for a gun.[58] The controversy flared up again in the fall of 2013 when Charlotte, North Carolina, police officers shot and killed unarmed Jonathan Ferrell as he ran toward them seeking assistance after an automobile accident. The Charlotte police were responding to a 911 call from a woman who claimed that a stranger had knocked on her door.[59] It flared up again in the fall of 2014 when New York police choked Eric Garner to death when he was stopped for allegedly selling single cigarettes.[60]

The best example of this pattern of fear, denial, and hostility is the case of the February 6, 2012, shooting of Trayvon Martin. This incident attracted national attention when the police decided not to arrest George Zimmerman, the unofficial Neighborhood Watch leader who shot the unarmed seventeen-year-old high school student who wore a hoodie, possessed a bag of Skittles, and consumed an Arizona iced tea as he walked to his father's house while talking on his cell phone with a female friend. The NAACP called for a federal investigation and suggested that the shooting was racially motivated.[61]

Conservative news commentators engaged in extreme efforts to deny that the incident had anything to do with race. Geraldo Rivera commented on Fox News, "I'll bet you money, if he didn't have that hoodie on, that nutty neighborhood watch guy wouldn't have responded in that violent and aggressive way."[62] He claimed that the Unabomber wore a hoodie and that the hoodie made Martin look like a street criminal. Bill O'Reilly offered this explanation: "Trayvon Martin was killed because circumstances got out of control. He was scrutinized by a neighborhood watchman, George Zimmerman, because of the way he looked. Not necessarily his skin color, there is no evidence of that but because he was a stranger to Zimmerman and was dressed in clothing sometimes used by street criminals."[63]

On *The Last Word,* Lawrence O'Donnell challenged the O'Reilly's and Rivera's explanations. He showed videos featuring Harvard University students wearing Harvard hoodies and pictures of O'Reilly and Rivera wearing hoodies. He noted that O'Reilly even sold Fox News hoodies on his website. O'Donnell concluded that O'Reilly and Rivera were correct in noting that Zimmerman reacted to Martin because of the way Martin looked, but not because Martin was wearing a hoodie. Instead, race was a major factor explaining Zimmerman's actions and the public's reaction.[64]

Conservative commentators like Glenn Beck insisted that Martin was the aggressor and that anyone would have considered him dangerous. According to Alex Pareene,

> Glenn Beck's site, the Blaze, led the charge, suggesting without much in the way of evidence that Martin was "the aggressor," based on nothing other than the fact that he had been suspended from school. (The site also threw in some speculation that Martin may have been an arsonist.) The sole reason for this was a pathological need to deny the existence of any form of racism that doesn't take the form of liberals hating white people.[65]

When President Obama extended his sympathy to the Martin family and said that, if he had a son he would look like Trayvon, it ignited a firestorm of opposition. Journalist Adam Serwer reported Newt Gingrich saying that the president's comments were "disgraceful." Serwer adds that columnist Michelle Malkin accused Obama of "political opportunism" and "pouring gas on the fire" for empathizing with Martin's parents.[66]

This controversy has been complicated by the lack of understanding of the psychological dynamics of prejudice and the ugly image of the typical prejudiced individual in US culture. A prejudiced individual is usually portrayed as uneducated and hateful, much like Gunnar Myrdal's description of the uneducated, lower-class backwoods Mississippian that I featured in Chapter 1. Moreover, the act of prejudice is presumed to be deliberate, intentional, and hateful. The charge of prejudice conjures up images of KKK members, hateful people who act deliberately and with malice to target blacks.

For a long time, the idea that people reacted out of fear provoked by popular but frightening cultural images of young black men was largely speculation, a theory promoted by liberal intellectuals. However, recent developments in experimental psychology and neuroscience that offer a more accurate picture of prejudice have provided substantial support for the theory. Most of these discoveries have been made possible because of technological advances in brain research, especially with the construction of functional magnetic resonance imaging (fMRI) brain scanning. Researchers have been able to use fMRI to scan the regions of the brain that involve fear and reasoning. The fear region is the amygdala; the reasoning region involves the right ventrolateral prefrontal cortex (RVLPFC). First, neuroscience and experimental psychology research demonstrates that images of young black male faces indeed stimulate the amygdala. In other words, black phobia is real and confirmed by scientific research.[67]

Second, neuroscience and experimental psychology research shows that specific black characteristics are likely to stimulate stronger responses. These features include skin color, lip thickness, nose width, and hair texture, with dark skin provoking the strongest reaction. Moreover, dark skin stimulates the amygdala even in faces with distinctively white-looking noses, lips, and hair.[68]

Third, according to neuroscience and psychology research, this reaction is not limited to whites. These images also provoke fear in blacks. This finding confirms the hypothesis that the new racism is the product of a dominant culture filled with images and narratives that provoke fear in blacks as well as whites. It therefore also has implications for black-on-black violence.[69]

Fourth, neuroscience research shows that the responses are automatic and unconscious. In other words, Zimmerman may have been truthful when he said that he believed that he would have reacted no differently if Martin was white, even though in reality he indeed might have acted differently. Moreover, experimental research has demonstrated that subjects without any conscious awareness of prejudices are more likely to perceive harmless but ambiguous objects held by blacks as guns, and to perceive ambiguous behavior as aggressive when displayed by blacks, than subjects who are at least aware of the possibility of prejudice. Subjects in experimental situations in which they had to shoot when a picture of a man with a gun appeared before them were more likely to shoot at pictures of unarmed men when the men were black. Jennifer Eberhardt, Vallerie Purdie, and colleagues discuss some of these findings:

> The stereotype of Black Americans as violent and criminal has been documented by social psychologists for almost 60 years. Researchers have highlighted the robustness and frequency of this stereotypic association by demonstrating its effects on numerous outcome variables, including people's memory for who was holding a deadly razor in a subway scene, people's evaluation of ambiguously aggressive behavior, people's decision to categorize non-weapons as weapons, the speed at which people decide to shoot someone holding a weapon, and the probability that they will shoot at all. Not only is the association between Blacks and crime strong (i.e., consistent and frequent), it also appears to be automatic (i.e., not subject to intentional control).
>   The paradigmatic understanding of the automatic stereotyping process—indeed, the one pursued in all of the research highlighted above—is that the

mere presence of a person can lead one to think about the concepts with which that person's social group has become associated. The mere presence of a Black man, for instance, can trigger thoughts that he is violent and criminal. Simply thinking about a Black person renders these concepts more accessible and can lead people to misremember the Black person as the one holding the razor. Merely thinking about Blacks can lead people to evaluate ambiguous behavior as aggressive, to miscategorize harmless objects as weapons, or to shoot quickly, and at times, inappropriately.[70]

Prominent neuroscientist Joseph Le Duox has summarized brain research that shows the evolution of the brain and the distinction between the lower emotional brain controlled by the limbic system (consisting of the amygdala, hypothalamus, and hippocampus) and the upper brain (consisting of the cerebral cortex).[71] The lower brain controls emotions related to instinctual reactions like fear. Such reactions are considered instinctual because they are automatic and uncontrollable. Research into prejudice demonstrates that an individual may sincerely or intellectually believe in racial equality. This belief is deliberate and it takes place within the upper brain. But the same individual may react with fear to black faces, which takes place in the lower brain. Kerry Kawakami and colleagues explain this reaction: "According to aversive racism theory, even individuals who embrace egalitarian beliefs may continue to harbor nonconscious negative feelings toward blacks. Recent research demonstrates that, whereas egalitarian beliefs typically guide thoughtful, deliberative responses, lingering negative feelings toward blacks often emerge in the context of more spontaneous responses."[72]

Thus, prejudice has both an emotional side and an intellectual side. The emotional side is automatic and uncontrollable. The intellectual side has to do with the use or construction of stories and ideas that operate to explain or justify feelings of aversion or fear. These stories and ideas come from political and intellectual leaders, and from the literature that explains social arrangements and processes. They constitute intellectual biases that justify the behavior of Zimmerman and police shootings. Research suggests that those with intellectual biases are more likely to also have emotional biases, and are more likely to act on these biases. They are more resistant to the idea that they have biases, but are more likely to promote these biases.[73]

Fifth, neuroscience and psychology research shows that these emotional and intellectual biases have systematic and enduring consequences. For example, a large body of research demonstrates that these emotionally based racial biases and stereotypes explain more severe sentencing, including capital sentencing for people with more black physical characteristics. Jennifer Eberhardt, Paul Davis, and colleagues sum up this research:

Race matters in capital punishment. Even when statistically controlling for a wide variety of nonracial factors that may influence sentencing, numerous researchers have found that murderers of White victims are more likely than murderers of Black victims to be sentenced to death.

A growing body of research demonstrates that people more readily apply racial stereotypes to Blacks who are thought to look more stereotypically Black, compared with Blacks who are thought to look less stereotypically Black. People associate Black physical traits with criminality in particular. The more stereotypically Black a person's physical traits appear to be, the more criminal that person is perceived to be. A recent study found that perceived stereotypicality correlated with the actual sentencing decisions of judges. Even with differences in defendants' criminal histories statistically controlled, those defendants who possessed the most stereotypically Black facial features served up to 8 months longer in prison for felonies than defendants who possessed the least stereotypically Black features.[74]

Finally, neuroscience and psychology research applied to the legal field indicates that impartial and unbiased judgments do not come from the denial that racial prejudices exist, but from self-reflection and the acknowledgment of the possibility of stereotypes unconsciously influencing judgments. Linda G. Mills concludes, "Deliberate self-reflection becomes the only method by which to purge stereotypes entirely from experiences. Stereotypes were more likely to influence the decisions of judges who believed themselves to be unprejudiced."[75] The implication of these findings is that people who are the most adamant about being unprejudiced are the most likely to be the most prejudiced.

Nuances of Metaracist Culture

White Nationalism

Just as there is a progressive and reactionary political culture, there is a progressive and reactionary vision of nationalism. The progressive vision imagines the United States as a diverse, multicultural nation made up of a mix of people from all over the world; people of different colors, cultures, languages, and religions. This acceptance of others and tolerance of difference are very much a part of contemporary US culture. To some extent, it defines the people of this country. It is part of a sense of nationalism that unites everyone across class, ethnic, and racial boundaries with a common image, a common set of values, a common sense of identity, and a common definition of who we are as a nation. Progressive nationalism brings people together from all classes and walks of life. However, this notion of the United States as a tolerant and diverse country is not the only view of nationalism.

Conversely, the reactionary vision of nationalism sees the United States as a white nation. Indeed, in the past, political leaders worked to exclude people of color in order to maintain the nation as white. In the infamous Dred Scott decision, Chief Justice Roger B. Taney insisted that the United States was a white nation. He declared that the statement in the Preamble of the Constitution, "We the people of the United States," and the statement in the Declaration of Independence that "all men are created equal" referred only to white people, not people of color. In arguing his point, the chief justice cited immigration laws that allowed only white immigrants to become citizens as proof that political leaders intended for the United States to remain a white nation. He added that "the first of these acts is the naturalization law, which was passed at the second session of the first Congress, March 26, 1790, and confines the right of becoming citizens 'to aliens being free white persons . . .' but the language of the law above quoted shows that citizenship at that time was perfectly understood to be confined to the white race."[76]

Even Abraham Lincoln proposed sending blacks to Liberia after they were freed because he did not believe they could become part of white society in large numbers. Even after the Fourteenth Amendment granted citizenship to African Americans and anyone born in the United States, US immigration policy continued to favor whites. Congress passed the Chinese Exclusion Act of 1883 to maintain a white nation. In fact, US immigration policy favored northern European immigrants up until 1965.

In the late nineteenth and early twentieth century, white Anglo-Saxon Protestants (WASPs) were hostile toward Irish, Italian, Polish, and other Eastern European immigrants. Part of this hostility came from the WASPs who were xenophobic and defined the United States in their own white Protestant image. However, non-WASP European immigrants learned that they could assimilate and redefine themselves as white. "Whiteness" gave them an identity, status, and privilege that they did not have with their ethnic identity. Whereas they were once the victims of discrimination from US WASPs, many second-generation immigrants joined whites in a chorus of hostility toward nonwhites. Like WASPs, those of the second generation envisioned the United States as a white Christian nation with a special set of values that made the country exceptional: hard work, self-reliance, individualism, capitalism, entrepreneurship, and Christian ethics. Consistent with the dynamics of racism, these values were also seen as the binary opposite of nonwhite values (see Chapter 1).

This reactionary vision of nationalism has reemerged with the current reactionary movement. Igor Volsky argues this point with quotations from John Sununu, former governor of New Hampshire:

> The former New Hampshire governor has repeatedly suggested that Obama or his policies are "foreign," European, and something less than American.

Here are some of his greatest hits:

• Obama is foreign. Obama doesn't understand the "American system" because "he spent his early years in Hawaii smoking something, spent the next set of years in Indonesia . . . , and frankly, when he came to the U.S. he worked as a community organizer, which is a socialized structure."

• Obama doesn't know how to be an American. During a conference call, Sununu claimed, "The men and women all over America who have worked hard to build these businesses, their businesses, from the ground up is how our economy became the envy of the world. It is the American way. And, I wish this president would learn how to be an American."

• Obama is a lazy idiot. Sununu described Obama's debate performance as "babbling," "lazy," and "disengaged" and dismissed the possibility that he could do better in the future. "When you're not that bright, you can't get better prepared."[77]

In short, Sununu contends that the president does not fit the image of a traditional citizen; does not understand the values of hard work and business know-how that built this country; and is "lazy," "not that bright," and "can't get better prepared."

To a large degree, the birther movement is driven by people who do not believe President Obama fits the image of a US citizen. The strong association between racial stereotypes of the president and the birther movement is no coincidence. The belief in the United States as a white nation and the difficulty in accepting a black president are closely associated with each other.

Another example of this association between the image of the United States as a white nation and metaracism comes from O'Reilly in his analysis of the results of the 2012 election:

It is a changing country. The demographics in America is changing. It's not a traditional America anymore; and there are fifty percent of the voting public who want stuff. They want things. And who is going to give them things. President Obama. He knows it. He ran on it. . . . The white establishment is now the minority and the voters, many of them, feel the economic system is stacked against them and they want stuff. You are going to see a tremendous Hispanic vote for Obama; overwhelming black vote for Obama. Women would probably break Obama's way. People feel they are entitled to things and which candidate between the two is going to give them things. . . .[78]

If you look at the exit polling, you'll see that a coalition of voters put the president back into the oval office. That coalition was non-traditional, which means it veered away from things like traditional marriage, robust capitalism, and self-reliance. Instead each constituent that votes for the president—whether a single woman, Hispanic American, African American, whatever—had very specific reasons for doing so.[79]

O'Reilly makes a number of questionable and disturbing assertions. He asserts that Obama won the election because the United States is no longer a traditional white nation; that whites are now a minority; that blacks are dependent on government and have a sense of entitlement; that blacks reject US values such as traditional marriage, self-reliance, and robust capitalism; and that people of color voted for Obama because this president promises them public assistance.

Entitlements and Color-Blind Racism

Another feature of metaracism is the increasing tendency of political leaders to use the word "entitlement" as a weapon to attack both social welfare and civil rights policies. This code word has two connotations: undeserved welfare and undeserved rights. Rick Santorum's comment at the time of the 2012 Iowa caucuses illustrates the first use. He said, "I don't want to make black people's lives better by giving them someone else's money."[80] Another example comes from a Tea Party demonstration poster sign that reads: "You are not entitled to what I have earned."[81] In both uses, the term evoked racist images of blacks dependent on or feeling entitled to welfare paid for by white taxpayers. Thomas Edsall sums up the meaning of the code word *entitlement*: "The word entitlement has now taken its place in the pantheon of coded political rhetoric. The Republican coalition has proved over the past forty-five years that voters can be reached by code words or coded phrases that signal conservative values and interests and that, in target audiences, access or tap 'anger points.'" Edsall demonstrates that although the word *entitlement* denotes a value-neutral, nonracial right based in law, it has become a code word linked to every conservative talk show host and to every leading Republican politician—from Rush Limbaugh to Glenn Beck to Senator Rand Paul. Edsall maintains that the word has two political advantages: first, it softens what are in fact draconian cuts in federal benefits aimed at the poor and disabled, children, and the elderly; second, insofar as it refers to a government granted right, it appeals to a conservative hostility to the catalog, over the past fifty years, of government-sanctioned rights of all kinds, collectively known as the rights revolution—civil rights, gay rights, abortion rights, prisoners' rights, criminal defendant rights.[82]

Opponents have used the word *entitlement* to delegitimize civil rights laws. These opponents have redefined civil rights as undeserved entitlements promoted by powerful elitist minorities who believe they are entitled to special treatment denied to others. Thus, *entitlement* has emerged as an expression of contempt for civil rights policies and for the minorities these laws protect. It has been used as part of a larger assault on civil rights in general.

Supreme Court Justice Antonin Scalia provides a good example of the use of the term *entitlement* to attack civil rights policies. In his dissenting opinion in the *Romer v. Evans* decision, he supported a Colorado state constitutional amendment that nullified local laws that protected the civil rights of gay men and lesbians. Scalia argued that these local civil rights laws were entitlements because they granted special rights to gay men and lesbians.[83]

Scalia referred to the challenged provision of the Voting Rights Act as a "perpetual racial entitlement" and a violation of the Constitution. Linda Greenhouse offers this observation of Scalia's deliberations in this case:

> As I made clear in my most recent column, I wasn't expecting anything good to come out of this argument. But neither did I anticipate the ugliness that erupted from the bench. While Justice Antonin Scalia's depiction of the Voting rights Act as the "perpetuation of racial entitlement" quickly went viral . . . , that was not even the half of it. "Even the name of it is wonderful: the Voting Rights Act," Justice Scalia said, his voice dripping with sarcasm as he suggested that only political correctness, rather than a principled commitment to protect the right to vote, has kept the disputed Section 5 of the act alive through four successive Congressional re-enactments.[84]

Greenhouse's assessment of Scalia's dissent recognizes his contempt for civil rights. Like opponents of civil rights over 100 years ago, Scalia believes that civil rights protections are no longer necessary, that blacks have accumulated too much power, and that the Voting Rights Act constitutes a "perpetual racial entitlement."[85]

Carolyn Gallaher argues that white conservatives have used their advocacy of color-blind policies and opposition to bestowing "special rights" on select minorities to undermine civil rights and to reinforce white heterosexual male privileges. She explains,

> The right wing's largely successful campaign to depict affirmative action and hate crimes legislation as bestowing "special rights," for example, allows whites/heterosexuals to actively ignore targeted discrimination and violence through appeals to a "universality" disidentified from race or sexuality based privileges. Such invocations are especially insidious because they buttress class and racial privileges without referencing either.[86]

Denial of Racism

Another aspect of metaracism is its remarkable blindness to racism. One example of this blindness is Ann Coulter's defense of the White Citizen's Council (Citizens' Council of America), a pro-segregation organization that was active in opposing school desegregation during the civil rights era of the 1960s and today has been renamed the Council of Conservative Citizens (CCC):

There is no evidence on its Web page that the modern incarnation of CCC supports segregation, though its "Statement of Principles" offers that the organization opposes "forced integration" and "efforts to mix the races of mankind. . . ."

Apart from some aggressive reporting on black-on-white crimes—the very crimes that are aggressively hidden by the establishment media—there is little on the CCC website suggesting that the group is a "thinly veiled white supremacist" organization, as the New York Times calls it in one of its more charitable descriptions.[87]

Another example comes from a racist caricature of the president, which demonstrates both blatant racism and the denial of racism. In August 2013, a rodeo promoted by the Missouri Cowboy Rodeo Association featured a clown with a mask effigy of President Obama. Robin Abcarian describes the incident:

Perry Beam, a 48-year-old musician who describes himself as an "old country boy," was appalled by what he saw and blew the lid off this embarrassment by posting about it on Facebook. "One of the clowns ran up and started bobbling the lips on the mask and the crowd went crazy," Beam wrote, according to his friend, Bob Yates, who reposted the item on a politically liberal Missouri website called Show Me Progress. "Everybody screamed" and "just went wild" when the rodeo announcer talked about stomping the clown, Beam told the St. Louis Post-Dispatch.

"It was at that point I began to feel a sense of fear," Beam told the Dispatch. "It was that level of enthusiasm. . . . It was cruel. It was disturbing. I am still sick to my stomach over it. . . . I've never seen anything so blatantly racist in my life."

Later, in an interview with Missouri TV station KSDK, Beam said the scene was "like an effigy at a Klan rally."[88]

The Missouri Rodeo Cowboy Association publicly apologized for the incident, and Missouri's Democratic governor and Republican lieutenant governor both condemned it. Nevertheless, the next morning, Limbaugh was quoted as saying: "When the president of the United States more often than not connects with the American people on late-night comedy shows, what else can happen other than the diminishing of the office?"[89] He not only denied the racist implications of the incident, but practically blamed the incident on the president's appearance on a late night talk show—something other presidents had done in the past. Limbaugh demonstrates that racism may take the form of the inability to see racism.

The Foundations of Neoliberalism

Neoliberalism, like neoconservatism, is a major part of the contemporary conservative political culture. The hallmark of neoliberalism is its focus on economic principles of open markets, limited government, low taxes, deregulation, and privatization—all of which are calculated to expand production, grow the economy, and bring economic prosperity that benefits all classes in society, including the poor.

Some of the intellectual proponents of neoliberalism are Milton Friedman, Frederick Hayek, Robert Nozick, and Ayn Rand.[90] Rand has had a profound influence on contemporary political pundits and leaders. Her disciples include Ronald Reagan, Alan Greenspan (former chair of the Federal Reserve Board), Senator Rand Paul, Representative Ron Paul, and Representative Paul Ryan. Rand developed a broad political philosophy that combined theories of knowledge (epistemology), ethics, and politics. She advocated a scientific approach to knowledge and a form of ethics called rational self-interest that promoted individualism and selfishness as good and rejected altruism as bad, self-destructive, and irrational. Her politics was based on an opposition to all government programs except those that protected persons and property; an idolization of the rich, innovative, risk-taking elite; and a contempt for the poor masses. She viewed taxation as a form of coercion and theft. She campaigned against government programs of the Progressive, New Deal, and Great Society eras. She argued against antitrust, minimum wage, and child labor laws. She compared New Deal programs to Soviet totalitarianism. She opposed civil rights, public education, and all of the antipoverty programs of the 1960s, including food stamps, Medicaid, and Medicare.[91]

Rand idolized the special class of the wealthy elites—the innovators, risk takers, self-made men, and aggressive industrialists. She argued that business leaders were unfairly persecuted even though they made and sustained the modern world:

> While businessmen were rising to spectacular achievements of creative ability and self-confidently ambitious courage, challenging the primordial dogma of man's poverty and misery on earth, breaking open the trade routes of the world, releasing mankind's productive energy and placing in its service the liberating power of machines (against the scornful resistance of loafing, ex-feudal aristocrats and the destructive violence of those who were to profit most: the workers).[92]

In Rand's book *Atlas Shrugged* the protagonist, John Galt, symbolizes Atlas, the Greek mythological character that carried the world on his shoulders. As the modern Atlas, Galt epitomized the industrialist, the self-made man, the innovator, the risk taker, the intellectual, the John D. Rockefellers and the J. P. Morgans—the elites who made this world and carry it on their shoulders. For Rand, it was the business leader who unleashed productive and creative powers, created jobs, developed new technology, benefited humanity, and took the world to a higher level.[93]

Rand displayed contempt for workers. She saw them as loafers, resisters of progress, and irrational barbarians who engage in violence. Her contempt for the masses is displayed in the train crash in *Atlas Shrugged*. The scene ends with the narrator (Rand) noting the philosophical errors of the passengers (ordinary people) who died almost as if they deserved to die.[94]

Like Rand and other neoliberals, Milton Friedman saw capitalism as the economic system most suitable for attaining freedom. He defined "freedom" as capitalism, with the freedom to choose, to own property, to establish a business, to compete on the open market as a free individual directing his or her own destiny. He believed that open competitive markets were the most efficient way of allocating goods and services. He advocated limited government, opposed government regulations, called for tax cuts, and proposed privatization and market models as ways of stimulating economies and solving most public problems. He introduced the idea of vouchers and markets to improve education.[95]

Like Rand and other neoliberals, Friedman abhorred racism, but opposed civil rights laws. He believed that racial discrimination was wrong, irrational, and foolish. However, he believed that government interference in the market to prevent racial discrimination in employment was equally wrong. He argued that competitive markets would drive out racially discriminatory firms. He insisted that, when a nondiscriminatory firm hired hardworking, well-qualified blacks for a cheaper wage, the firm would be able to undersell and put out of business the racially discriminatory firms that had paid a higher labor costs for white employees. For Friedman, the market had almost magical powers that could counteract the most racially prejudiced of societies. The problem was that Friedman's idyllic view of market powers did not match the reality of a racially prejudiced society.[96]

The Ills of Neoliberalism

The problem with neoliberalism is not that it is racist. There is nothing racist about it. Neoliberal scholars are, in fact, antiracist. The problem with neoliberalism is that it reifies the free market in ways that favors the upper class at the expense of all other classes. It sanctifies private productive property, the source of the wealth of the upper class. It demands absolute unconditional protection for this property while insisting on the elimination of government regulations that protect the people. Though all markets operate under rules, neoliberalism calls for the elimination of rules that protect consumers, but disregard for rules that protect the dominant class. For example, recent changes in bankruptcy laws have allowed for the dissolution of workers' pensions while guaranteeing repayment to financial investors. Bankruptcy rule changes have already redistributed wealth and income upward. Neoliberalism insists on privatization because it assumes that markets are more efficient than government, but it ignores the manner in which privatization redistributes income and wealth upward and imposes higher costs on consumers: the costs of profits and monopolies. Greg Palast provides an example of the privatization of a city's water supply in Bolivia. The people were told that privatizing would reduce their water bills. But when the private company bought the public water utilities operation, it more than doubled people's water bills. This precipitated water riots because the price of the privatized water had become too expensive for the country's poor.[97]

As much as neoliberals insist that their policy principles of limited government, low taxes, privatization, and deregulation would fuel the economy and bring prosperity to all, in actual practice these policies have had disastrous impacts. They produce tremendous inequality. In practice, the policies of neoliberalism enrich the wealth and income of the upper class and diminish the income and wealth of all other classes. James Galbraith, Paul Krugman, Robert Reich, and Joseph Stiglitz discuss well the upward redistributive consequences of neoliberalism.[98]

In her book *The Shock Doctrine,* Naomi Klein provides examples of the consequences of implementing neoliberal economic policies in third world countries. She reported on the experiments of Friedman and his students from the Chicago School of Economics, who were invited as economic advisers to a number of countries such as Chile and Argentina. The results of the neoliberal experiment were mixed. Insofar as investors profited and the rich increased their wealth, Friedman's neoliberal approach was considered successful. But insofar as the inequality increased, the masses were further impoverished, the productivity declined, and the economy contracted, it was considered a disaster. Because the majority of the people of these countries opposed neoliberal programs, these programs were imposed on the people through force by brutal authoritarian regimes. These regimes reacted to opposition from the people with violence, death squads, and torture. Friedman loudly opposed government-run programs, but remained silent in the face of these authoritarian regimes and their violence against their own people.[99] Klein's book was an indictment of the uncompromising use of the neoliberal approach in attempting to improve economies.

Friedman and other neoliberals offered a false choice between a neoliberal free-market regime and a totalitarian regime such as that of Nazi Germany or the Communist Soviet Union. This false choice helps to explain why some neoliberal Tea Party extremists compare President Obama to Adolf Hitler and Joseph Stalin.

Whereas neoliberalism is not racist, whereas it does not contribute to the formation of metaracism, it is reactionary to the extent that it emerged in opposition to the New Deal and Great Society programs that have done much to reduce inequality. Neoliberalism rejects the social and educational programs that have done much to promote equal opportunities for both blacks and whites. Neoliberalism contributes to the reemergence of racial inequality by attacking the very programs that reduced this inequality.

As a disciple of Friedman, Thomas Sowell is an accomplished neoliberal scholar who has devoted much of his academic life to extolling the virtues of the free market and the evils of government. At the same time, he has done much to bridge the gap between neoliberals and neoconservatives. In his early years, he wrote extensively about the perceived connection between culture and the social mobility of ethnic groups.[100] He insisted that a number of minority groups came to the United States with nothing except the clothes on their backs and their determination to succeed. Sowell argued that these ethnic groups succeeded in the small business world in the face of racial discrimination and hostility and rose up high on the social ladder, without any government assistance. He used Asians as the model minority, attributing their success to their high value for education and their willingness to sacrifice, work hard, and save. The implications of his research goes beyond the importance of culture.[101] If Asian Americans can overcome racial discrimination and hostility to excel as entrepreneurs without the aid of government, then so can other minority groups, particularly African Americans. Within Sowell's framework, racism becomes irrelevant.[102]

The problem with Sowell's research is that it leaps over a great deal of disconfirming empirical data and jumps to broad conclusions. Steinberg argues that the success of Sowell's model minorities "is largely an artifact of selective migration—that is, the influx of large numbers of professionals and other educated and skilled workers."[103] These minorities never faced the same types of racist barriers that confronted African Americans.[104] Immigrants brought many advantages with them that help explain their success such as professional skills, education, experience, and financial capital. Many have had access to US and foreign banks that African Americans do not have.[105]

Sowell's focus on culture contains a number of innuendos about African American culture and poverty. However, there was never an expression of contempt until 2012 when he referred to government recipients as "losers" and "parasites":

> In politics few talents are as richly rewarded as the ability to convince parasites that they are victims. Welfare states on both sides of the Atlantic have discovered that largesse to losers does not reduce their hostility to society, but only increases it. Far from producing gratitude, generosity is seen as an admission of guilt and the reparations as inadequate compensation for injuries—leading to worsening behavior by the recipients.[106]

Even though the neoliberal literature's reification of the market and emphasis on privatization and limited government contribute to the formation of policies that advantage the wealthy and disadvantage everyone else, this literature does not directly contribute to metaracism. However, the characterization of welfare recipients as parasites does. This characterization does much to denigrate and dehumanize them. As will be demonstrated in later chapters, the combination of neoliberalism and metaracism accelerated opposition to equal opportunity programs and contributed to increases in racial inequality.

Notes

1. Oscar Lewis, "Culture of Poverty," in Daniel P. Moynihan, ed., *On Understanding Poverty: Perspectives from Social Sciences* (New York: Basic Books, 1969).

2. Michael Harrington, *The Other America: Poverty in the United States* (New York: Macmillan, 1964 [1962]).

3. Elliot Liebow, *Tally's Corner: A Study of Negro Street Corner Men* (Boston: Little, Brown, 1967).

4. Kenneth Clark, *Dark Ghetto: Dilemmas of Social Power* (New York: Harper and Row, 1965); Lee Rainwater, *Behind Ghetto Walls: Black Families in a Federal Slum* (Chicago: Aldine Publishing Co., 1970).

5. Daniel P. Moynihan, *The Negro Family: A Case for National Action* (Washington, DC: US Department of Labor, 1965).

6. Ibid.

7. Daniel P. Moynihan, *The Politics of Guaranteed Annual Income: The Nixon Administration and the Family Assistance Plan* (New York: Vintage Books, 1973). The Nixon administration proposed the Family Assistance Plan, but liberals opposed it because they thought it to be too stingy and conservatives opposed it because they thought it to be too generous.

8. Edward Banfield, *The Unheavenly City Revisited* (Boston: Little, Brown, 1974).

9. Ruby Payne, *A Framework for Understanding Poverty* (Highlands, TX: Aha! Process, 2005).

10. Patricia Cohen, "Culture of Poverty Makes a Comeback," *New York Times,* October 17, 2010. http://www.nytimes.com/2010/10/18/us/18poverty.html?pagewanted=all&_r=0

11. Ibid.

12. Bryce Christensen, "Time for a 'New Moynihan Report'? Confronting the National Family Crisis," *The Family in America* 18, no. 10 (October 2004). http://profam.org/pub/fia_1810.html.

13. Lee Rainwater and William Yancey, eds., *The Moynihan Report and the Politics of Controversy* (Cambridge: MIT Press, 1996 [1967]).

14. James Farmer, "The Controversial Moynihan Report," in Rainwater and Yancy, eds., *The Moynihan Report and the Politics of Controversy.* See also William Ryan, *Blaming the Victim* (New York: Random House, 1976 [1971]).

15. Laura Caper, "The Negro Family and the Moynihan Report," in Rainwater and Yancy, eds., *The Moynihan Report and the Politics of Controversy.*

16. Rainwater and Yancey, eds., *The Moynihan Report and the Politics of Controversy.*

17. Andrew Billingsley, *Climbing Jacob's Ladder: The Enduring Legacy of African-American Families* (New York: Simon & Schuster, 1993); Andrew Billingsley and Cleopatra H. Caldwell, "The Church, the Family, and the School in the African American Community," *Journal of Negro Education* 60, no. 3 (1991): 427–440.

18. Barack Obama, *The Audacity of Hope: Thoughts on Reclaiming the American Dream* (New York: Vintage Books, 2008), p. 301.

19. Stephen Steinberg, "Poor Reason: Culture Still Doesn't Explain Poverty," *Boston Review,* January 13, 2011.

20. George Gilder, *Wealth and Poverty* (New York: Basic Books, 1981).

21. Charles Murray, *Losing Ground: American Social Policy, 1950–1980* (New York: New York University Press, 2003 [1984]).

22. Ibid.

23. William J. Wilson, *The Truly Disadvantaged: The Inner City, the Underclass, and Public Policy* (Chicago: University of Chicago Press, 1987).

24. Heather Ross and Isabel Sawhill, *Time of Transition: Growth of Families Headed by Women* (Washington, DC: Urban Institute Press, 1975).

25. Erol Ricketts, "The Origin of Black Female-Headed Families." *Focus,* Institute for Research on Poverty, University of Wisconsin–Madison. www.irp.wisc.edu /publications/focus/pdfs/foc121e.pdf.

26. John Ogbu, *Black American Students in an Affluent Suburb: A Study of Academic Disengagement* (Mahwah, NJ: Lawrence Erlbaum, 2003).

27. Ronald Ferguson, "A Diagnostic Analysis of Black-White GPA Disparities in Shaker Heights, Ohio," in *Brookings Papers on Education Policy* (Washington, DC: Brookings Institution, 2001), pp. 347–414.

28. David Bergin and Helen Cooks, "High School Students of Color Talk About Accusations of 'Acting White,'" *Urban Review* 34, no. 2 (2002): 113–134.

29. Karolyn Tyson, William A. Darity Jr., Domini R. Castellino, "It's Not 'a Black Thing': Understanding the Burden of Acting White and Other Dilemmas of High Achievement," *American Sociological Review* 70, no. 4 (2005): 582–605.

30. See also Philip Cook and Jens Ludwig, "Weighing the Burden of Acting White: Are There Race Differences in Attitudes Toward Education?" *Journal of Policy Analysis and Management* 16, no. 2 (1997): 256–278.

31. Stephen Klineberg, Jie Wu, and Kiara Douds, "The 2012 Houston Education Survey: Public Perception in a Critical Time" (Houston: Rice University Kinder Institute for Urban Research, 2013), p. 15. http://kinder.rice.edu/uploadedfiles /kinder_institute_for_urban_research/SHEA%20education%20report.pdf.

32. Ibid.

33. Pew Hispanic Center and Kaiser Family Foundation, "National Survey of Latinos: Education," 2004. http:pewhispanic.org/files/reports/25.pdf.

34. Ken Auletta, *The Underclass* (New York: Random House, 1982), pp. 43–44.

35. See Michael Katz, *The Undeserving Poor: From the War on Poverty to the War on Welfare* (New York: Pantheon Books, 1989).

36. Don Babwin, "Hadiya Pendleton Dead: Chicago Teen Who Performed at Inaugural Event Fatally Shot," *Huffington Post*, January 30, 2013. http://www .huffingtonpost.com/2013/01/30/hadiya-pendleton-dead-chi_n_2581309.html.

37. "Janay Mcfarlane Dead: New Mom Shot Just Hours after Sister Attended Obama's Gun Speech," *Huffington Post*, February 17, 2013. http://www.huffington post.com/2013/02/17/janay-mcfarlane-dead_n_2707425.html.

38. Charles Derber, *The Wilding of America: How Greed and Violence Are Eroding Our Nation's Character* (New York: St. Martin's Press, 1996). This expression is taken from the title of chapter three, "A Fish Rots from the Head First: Washington and Wall Street Go Wild," pp. 37–59.

39. Ken Burns, David McMahon, and Sarah Burns, directors, *The Central Park Five* (Florentine Films and WETA, Washington, DC, 2013).

40. Derber, *The Wilding of America*, pp. 8–9.

41. Jeffrey Reiman and Paul Leighton, *The Rich Get Richer and the Poor Get Prison: Ideology, Class and Criminal Justice* (Boston: Pearson, 2013).

42. Liebow, *Tally's Corner: A Study of Negro Street Corner Men*.

43. Jennifer Hochschild, "The Politics of the Estranged Poor," *Ethics* 101, no. 3 (1991): 560–578. Quotes from Isabel Wilkerson, "Detroit Drug Empire Showed All the Traits of Big Business," *New York Times,* December 12, 1988, pp. 1, 42; Sari Horwitz, "A Drug-Selling Machine that Was All Business," *Washington Post,* April 24, 1988, pp. A1, A16.

44. Barbara Ehrenreich, *Nickel and Dimed: On (Not) Getting By in America* (New York: Metropolitan Books, Henry Holt, 2001).

45. Theo David Goldberg, *Racist Culture: Philosophy and the Politics of Meaning* (Cambridge, MA: Blackwell Press, 1994), pp. 170–173.

46. Ibid.

47. Wilson, *The Truly Disadvantaged*. The thesis used by Wilson originated with John Kasarda, "Urban Change and Minority Opportunities," in Paul Peterson, ed., *The New Urban Reality* (Washington, DC: Brookings Institution, 1985).

48. Norman Fainstein, "The Underclass/Mismatch Hypothesis as an Explanation for Black Economic Deprivation," *Politics and Society* 15, no. 4 (1986/1987): 403–451. Carter Wilson, "Restructuring and the Growth of Concentrated Poverty in Detroit," *Urban Affairs Quarterly* 28, no. 2 (1992): 187–205.

49. Goldberg, *Racist Culture,* p. 172.

50. Tony Kaye, director, *American History X* (New Line Cinema, 1998).

51. Ibid.

52. Robert Smith and Richard Seltzer, *Race, Class, and Culture: A Study in Afro-American Mass Opinion* (New York: State University of New York Press, 1992), p. 141.

53. *Washington Post,* Henry J. Kaiser Family Foundation, and Harvard University, "African American Men Survey" (Menlo, CA: Henry J. Kaiser Family Foundation, 2006), p. 1.

54. Ibid. See also, Kevin Merida, "Being a Black Man," *Washington Post,* June 2, 2006, which includes highlights of the study.

55. Bill Cosby, "Dr. Bill Cosby Speaks at the 50th Anniversary Commemoration of the *Brown v. Topeka Board of Education* Supreme Court Decision" (transcript provided by Bill Cosby's public relations representatives, www.eightcitiesmap.com ?transcript_bc.htm). The speech was delivered at the NAACP's 50th Anniversary of *Brown v. Board of Education,* May 17, 2004. The speech can also be found on YouTube, "Bill Cosby Famous Pound Cake Speech."

56. Eric Michael Dyson, *Is Bill Cosby Right or Has the Black Middle Class Lost Its Mind?* (New York: Basic Civitas Books, 2008), pp. 80–81. Dyson discusses not just the research that demonstrates the cost consciousness of poor children, but also the incredulity of whites who can't believe that these poor children and their parents do not fit the popular, racist stereotypes promoted in Bill Cosby's pound cake speech.

57. Frantz Fanon, *Black Skin/White Mask* (New York: Grove Press, 1967).

58. Michael Cooper, "Officers in Bronx Fire 41 Shots, and an Unarmed Man Is Killed," *New York Times,* February 5, 1999. http://www.nytimes.com/1999/02/05 /nyregion/officers-in-bronx-fire-41shots-and-an-unarmed-man-is-killed.html.

59. Mitch Weiss and Jeffrey Colins, "Jonathan Ferrell, Unarmed Man Killed in North Carolina Was Shot 10 Times by Officer; Police," *Huffington Post,* September 16, 2013. http://www.huffingtonpost.com/2013/09/16/jonathan-ferrell-shot_n _3937175.html.

60. Ray Sanchez, "Choke Hold by Cop Killed New York Man, Medical Examiner Says," CNN, August 2, 2014.

61. "Trayvon Martin Shooting Fast Facts," CNN Library, February 22, 2014. http://www.cnn.com/2013/06/05/us/trayvon-martin-shooting-fast-facts/index.html.

62. Geraldo Rivera, "Fox & Friends," Fox News, March 23, 2012.

63. Bill O'Reilly, "The O'Reilly Factor," Fox News, March 26, 2012.

64. Lawrence O'Donnell, *The Last Word,* MSNBC, July 24, 2013.

65. Alex Pareene, "Why Rush Limbaugh and the Right Turned on Trayvon Martin," *Salon,* April 2, 2012. www.salon.com/2012/04/02/why_rush_limbaugh_and _the_right_turned_on_trayvon_martin/.

66. Adam Serwer, "The Right Goes Nuts over Obama's Trayvon Comments," *Mother Jones,* March 23, 2012. www.motherjones.com/momo/2012/03/Obama -comments-trayvon-martin-case-and-right-goes-nuts.

67. Jennifer Eberhardt, Valerie Purdie, Phillip Goff, and Paul Davies "Seeing Black: Race, Crime, and Visual Processing," *Journal of Personality and Social Psychology* 87, no. 6 (2004): 876–893; Matthew Lieberman, Ahmad Hariri, Johanna Jarcho, Naomi Eisenberger, and Susan Bookheimer, "An fMRI Investigation of Race Related Amygdala Activity in African-Americans and Caucasian-American Individuals," *Nature Neuroscience* 8, no. 6 (2005): 720–722; Jaclyn Ronquillo, Thomas Denson, Brian Lickel, Zhong-Lin Lu, Anirvan Nandy, and Keith Maddox, "The Effects of Skin Tone on Race-Related Amygdala Activity: An fMRI Investigation," *Social Cognitive and Affective Neuroscience* 2, no. 1 (2007): 39–44; Eben Harrell, "Study: Racist Attitudes Are Still Ingrained," *Time,* January 8, 2009. http://content.time.com/time/health/article/0,8599,1870408.html.

68. Ronquillo et al., "The Effects of Skin Tone."

69. Lieberman et al., "An fMRI Investigation."

70. Eberhardt et al., "Seeing Black," p. 876.

71. Joseph Le Duox, *The Emotional Brain: The Mysterious Underpinnings of Emotional Life* (New York: Touchstone, 1996).

72. Kerry Kawakami, Elizabeth Dunn, Francine Karmali, and John Dovidio, "Mispredicting Affective and Behavioral Responses to Racism," *Science* 323, no. 5911 (2009): 276.

73. Linda G. Mills, *A Penchant for Prejudice: Unraveling Bias in Judicial Decision Making* (Ann Arbor: University of Michigan Press, 1999), p. 162.

74. Jennifer Eberhardt, Paul Davies, Valerie Purdie-Vaughns, and Sheri Johnson, "Looking Deathworthy: Perceived Stereotypicality of Black Defendants Predicts Capital-Sentencing Outcomes," *Psychological Science* 17, no. 5 (2006): 383.

75. Linda G. Mills, *A Penchant for Prejudice,* p. 162.

76. *Dred Scott v. Sanford,* 60 U.S. 393 (1857).

77. Igor Volsky, "John Sununu's History of Racial Remarks About Obama," *ThinkProgress,* October 26, 2012. http://thinkprogress.org/politics/2012/10/26 /1094491/john-sununus-history-of-racial-remarks-about-obama/.

78. Bill O'Reilly, Fox News, November 7, 2012.

79. Ibid.

80. Rick Santorum, "Iowa Caucus Victory Speech," *Washington Post,* January 3, 2012. www.washingonpost.com/blogs/post/-politics/post/santorums-iowa/text-and -video/2012/01/04/gIQA5Q!1naP_blog.html.

81. Ibid.

82. Thomas Edsall, *The Age of Austerity* (New York: Anchor Books, 2012), pp. 122–124.

83. *Romer v. Evans,* 517 U.S. 20 (1996).

84. Linda Greenhouse "A Big New Power," *New York Times,* March 6, 2013. http://opinionator.blogs.nytimes.com/2013/03/06/a-big-new-power/?_php =true&_type=blogs&module-Search&mabReward=relbias%3Aw&_r=0.

85. Ibid.

86. Carolyn Gallaher, *On the Fault Line: Race, Class and the America Patriot Movement* (Lanham, MD: Rowman and Littlefield, 2002), p. 62.

87. Ann Coulter, *Guilty: Liberal "Victims" and Their Assault on America* (New York: Crown Forum, 2008), p. 24.

88. Robin Abcarian, "Rodeo Clown with Obama Mask Has Big Defender: Rush Limbaugh," *LA Now,* August 12, 2013. http://articles.latimes.com/2013/aug/12 /local/la-me-ln-rodeo-clown-obama-mask-rush-limbaugh-20130812.

89. Ibid.

90. Milton Friedman, *Capitalism and Freedom* (Chicago: University of Chicago Press, 1962); Milton Friedman with Rose Friedman, *Free to Choose* (New York: Harcourt, 1980); Frederick Hayek, *The Road to Serfdom* (Chicago: University of Chicago Press, 1956 [1944]); Robert Nozick, *The State, Private Property, and Utopia* (New York: Basic Books, 1974); Ayn Rand, *Atlas Shrugged* (New York: New American Library, 1957); Ayn Rand with Nathaniel Branden, Alan Greenspan, and Robert Hessen, *Capitalism, the Unknown Ideal* (New York: Signet, 1985 [1967]).

91. Rand, *Capitalism, the Unknown Ideal.*

92. Ibid., p. 33.

93. Rand, *Atlas Shrugged.*

94. Ibid.

95. Friedman, *Capitalism and Freedom.*

96. Ibid.

97. Greg Palast, *The Best Democracy Money Can Buy: An Investigative Reporter Exposes the Truth About Globalization, Corporate Cons and High Finance Fraudsters* (London: Pluto Press, 2002).

98. James Galbraith, *The Predator State: How Conservatives Abandoned the Free Market and Why Liberals Should Too* (New York: Free Press, 2008); Paul Krugman, *The Conscience of A Liberal* (New York: W. W. Norton, 2007); Robert Reich, *Beyond Outrage: What Has Gone Wrong with Our Economy and Our Democracy and How to Fix It* (New York: Vintage Books, 2012); Joseph Stiglitz, *The Price of Inequality* (New York: W. W. Norton, 2012).

99. Naomi Klein, *The Shock Doctrine: The Rise of Disaster Capitalism* (New York: Metropolitan Books, Henry Holt, 2007).

100. See Thomas Sowell, *Migrations and Cultures: A World View* (New York: Basic Books, 1996).

101. Thomas Sowell, *Race and Economics* (New York: Longman, 1975).

102. This notion of the irrelevance of racial prejudice in market economies was promoted by Milton Friedman, *Capitalism and Freedoms.* As a student of Friedman, Sowell promoted this same notion.

103. Stephen Steinberg, *Turning Back: The Retreat from Racial Justice in American Thought and Policy* (Boston: Beacon Press, 1995), p. 140.

104. Ibid.

105. Tamara Nopper, "Beyond the Bootstrap: How Korean Banks and U.S. Government Institutions Contribute to Korean Immigrant Entrepreneurship in the United States," PhD diss., Temple University, 2008, p. 15.

106. Thomas Sowell, "Largesse for Losers," *National Review Online*, April 10, 2012, http://www.nationalreview.dom/articles/295600?largesse-for-losers-thomas-sowell.

4

Politics, the State, and the Maintenance of Racial Oppression

Chapters 2 and 3 covered the structural and cultural dimensions of metaracism. This chapter examines the political dimension. This dimension involves an epic conflict. On one side of the battle line is an egalitarian coalition and a progressive political culture supporting an equal opportunity regime. This regime produced a series of progressive public policies, including pro-labor, pro–civil rights, liberal criminal justice, and antipoverty programs. These policies have enabled upward mobility, ameliorated racial oppression, and created equal opportunities. On the other side of the battle line is a corporate-centered conservative coalition and a reactionary political culture. This coalition is engaged in an assault on the equal opportunity regime. As this conservative coalition increases in power, and as the egalitarian coalition weakens, public policies shift further to the right, equal opportunity programs erode, and racial inequality increases.

The Egalitarian Coalition

Several separate coalitions make up the egalitarian coalition, most notably the New Deal, civil rights, and antipoverty coalitions. The New Deal coalition was formed in the 1930s. It consisted of labor unions, progressive religious organizations, racial and ethnic minorities, liberal business leaders, large urban areas, and the South. This coalition started to break up during the 1960s with the rise of the civil rights movement and the defection of conservative Southerners and skilled labor. As noted earlier in the book, metaracism played a role in these defections. Remnants of the New Deal coalition make up part of the egalitarian coalition.

The civil rights coalition consists of older traditional civil rights organizations such as the NAACP and the National Council of Negro Women; post–World War II organizations such as the Congress on Racial Equality and the Southern Christian Leadership Conference (SCLC); 1960s organizations such as the Student Nonviolent Coordinating Committee; and post-1960s organizations such as the National Organization for Women (NOW), the American Indian Movement, the Mexican American Legal Defense and Educational Fund, the League of Latino Citizens, and lesbian, gay, bisexual, and transgender (LGBT) rights organizations. The antipoverty coalition consisted of some of the older and more aggressive but now defunct organizations such as the Physician Task Force on Hunger in America, the National Welfare Rights Organization (NWRO), and the Association of Community Organizations for Reform Now (ACORN). It also consists of a long list of other organizations that advocate for children, the homeless, and the hungry such as the Children's Defense Fund; the Association of Food Banks; the National WIC Association of the Supplemental Nutrition Program for Women, Infants and Children (WIC); and World Hunger Education, Advocacy & Training (WHEAT) as well as research organizations such as the Institute for Research on Poverty, the Center on Budget and Policy Priorities, and the Poverty and Race Research Action Council. Because of inadequate resources, these organizations have been politically weak.

The Corporate-Centered Conservative Coalition

Like the egalitarian coalition, the corporate-centered conservative coalition has several parts. (See Table 4.1.) It consists of thousands of business, corporate, and trade organizations such as the Business Roundtable, the US Chamber of Commerce, the National Association of Manufacturers, and the National Federation of Independent Business (NFIB). It has a large faith- or religious-based sector consisting of organizations such as the Christian Coalition, Focus on the Family, and the Traditional Values Coalition. It includes corporate-sponsored think tanks such as the American Enterprise Institute and the Heritage Foundation. Tea Party organizations and the National Rifle Association are also part of this conservative coalition.

Although business organizations have been around for a long time, the corporate-centered conservative coalition did not begin to emerge until the 1970s when the US political system began to change. For a variety of reasons, the business and corporate sector emerged in the political arena with a vengeance. Corporate and business leaders felt besieged by new special interest groups and by new aggressive government regulations. Older regulatory agencies such as the Federal Trade Commission, the Federal Com-

Table 4.1 Select Organizations of the Corporate-Centered Conservative Coalition

Corporate, Business, and Trade Associations	*Morality and Faith-Based Organizations*
Business Roundtable	Christian Coalition
US Chamber of Commerce	Focus on the Family
National Association of Manufacturers	Family Research Council
American Legislative Exchange Council	Operation Rescue
Alliance of Automobile Manufacturers	Traditional Values Coalition
American Bankers Association	
Americans for Prosperity	*Conservative Think Tanks*
Americans for Tax Reform	American Enterprise Institute
Americans for Tort Reform	Cato Institute
American Petroleum Institute	Heritage Foundation
Coalition for a Fair Judiciary	Hoover Institution
Freedom Works	Olin Foundation
National Federation of Independent Businesses	Pioneer Institute
National Restaurant Association	*Tea Party Organizations*
	Tea Party Patriots
Other	Tea Party Alliance
National Rifle Association	Tax Day Tea Party
	State and local Tea Parties

munications Commission, and the Food and Drug Administration had become more active, promoting new and more aggressive regulations. The older agencies were joined by the newer and zealous regulatory agencies: the Environmental Protection Agency, the Occupational Safety and Health Administration, and the Federal Highway Safety Administration. Environmental, consumer, and other public interests prevailed over corporate and business interests.[1] Also, with the stagflation of the late 1970s and early 1980s, corporate and business profits had declined. During that time, corporate and business leaders had become increasingly concerned about overly aggressive affirmative action programs and overly generous welfare programs.

Whereas the US political arena had been characterized as pluralistic, with many and different political interests competing in different issue areas,[2] the political system has generally favored the upper class and business interests.[3] Although politics involved bargaining, negotiations, and compromises among competing interests, there has always been a deference to business and corporate interests. What changed since the 1970s, and has continued to this day, is that business and corporate interests have become more visible, more organized, more coordinated, and more aggressive in the political arena.

A number of political scientists have documented the resurgence of a business and corporate–led conservative movement engaged in a revolt against the labor-management agreement that emerged from the New Deal era. This revolt was a reaction to a perceived assault on the business and corporate sector from hostile grassroots movements—including Ralph Nader's consumer movement, the environmental movement, and the labor occupational safety movement—and the business and corporate loss of political control in the face of wave after wave of rights movements such as civil rights, women's rights, and welfare rights. Some insist that this movement was well planned and well organized.[4]

Ian Lopez provides an excellent discussion of the role of Supreme Court Justice Lewis Powell's memo urging the US Chamber of Commerce and business interests to become more politically active. Lopez insists that the memo influenced the increase in the organization and political activism of the business sector as well as the role of corporate leaders and corporate-sponsored think tanks in setting the national policy agenda. He also notes the impact of the American Enterprise Institute's report *Mandate for Leadership* on the agenda of Ronald Reagan's administration.[5]

Thomas Edsall sums up the rise of business power in politics:

> During the 1970s, business refined its ability to act as a class, submerging competitive instincts in favor of joint, cooperative action in the legislative arena. Rather than individual companies seeking only special favors . . . the dominant theme in the political strategy of business became a shared interest in the defeat of bills such as consumer protection and labour law reform, and in the enactment of favorable tax, regulatory, and antitrust legislation.[6]

As with most major social movements the older business organizations grew and became more active while newer, even more aggressive, business organizations formed and grew rapidly. Older trade organizations such as the Tobacco Institute and the American Petroleum Institute have long been active in advancing their political agendas and putting resources into propaganda campaigns that promote their industries. Older organizations with business and corporate affiliations such as the National Association of Manufacturers (founded in 1895), the US Chamber of Commerce (founded in 1912), and the NFIB (founded in 1943) have long track records of political activism. In recent times, these organizations have become even more active and aggressive. The NFIB has been especially aggressive in pursuing tax cuts and opposing health care reform. It was the lead organization that took responsibility for defeating President Bill Clinton's health care reform. It also led the assault on the Affordable Care Act, challenging this act in the Supreme Court in *NFIB v. Sebelius* (2012).[7]

Among the new and more aggressive organizations was the American Legislative Exchange Council (ALEC) established by Charles and David Koch, the Koch brothers. Their father was Fred Koch, a founder and activists in the John Birch Society, a right wing, pro-capitalist, anticommunist, and anti–civil rights organizations that had little credibility in main street politics. Paul Weywich, a cofounder of ALEC, had been associated with the Koch brothers and affiliated with the creation of the Heritage Foundation and the Moral Majority.[8] ALEC has emerged as a major agenda-setting and policymaking organization for business and corporate interests. Today, it includes among its corporate contributors: BP, Coca-Cola, Dow, ExxonMobil, Pfizer, Shell, and Walmart.[9] ALEC sponsors and writes legislation for state legislators and for US congressmen and senators. It wrote and sponsored the Florida stand your ground law related to the shooting of Trayvon Martin.

The Citizens for a Sound Economy was formed in 1984, also by the Koch brothers. Its mission has been to "fight for less government, lower taxes and less regulations." It promotes neoliberal ideas and educational programs. In 2004, it split into two separate organizations: Americans for Prosperity and Freedom Works. Americans for Prosperity played a key role in mobilizing opposition to President Barack Obama's domestic policy programs, especially the American Recovery and Reinvestment Act (stimulus bill) and the Affordable Care Act.[10] Freedom Works was formed out of a merger of Citizens for a Sound Economy and Empower America. It has provided substantial financial support for the rise of the Tea Party movement. Another organization, Americans for Tax Reform, was established by Grover Norquist in 1984. It played a major role in extracting a pledge from Republicans not to raise taxes. Commitment to this pledge was largely responsible for temporarily shutting down the federal government in October 2013.

The number of political action committees and the amount of money spent on lobbying by business organizations has increased exponentially. The number of registered lobbyists increased from 5,500 in 1981 to 32,890 by 2005. The amount of money spent on lobbying increased from around $100 million in 1981 to over $2 billion by 2005.[11] Almost all of the increase was related to business organizations, Robert Reich explains:

> Almost all of this vast increase in lobbying has been financed by businesses. Lobbying by nonbusiness groups has been paltry in comparison. For example, in 2005, the AFL-CIO [American Federation of Labor–Congress of Industrial Organizations] had only six paid lobbyists on Capitol Hill. Of the one hundred organizations that spent the most on lobbying that year, the U.S. Chamber of Commerce headed the list, the AFL-CIO ranked seventy-fourth. Most public interest groups—advocating such causes as environmental protection, child welfare, or human rights—did not even make the list. . . .

Again, note that the escalation began in the 1970s. In 1950, fewer than one hundred companies maintained Washington offices. After the mid-1970s, the corporate lobbying business exploded. The National Association of Manufacturers moved its headquarters to the nation's capital in 1973, around the same time as the Business Roundtable—an association of chief executives who would travel to Washington to personally lobby—established itself there. By the 1990s, more than 500 American companies maintained permanent offices in Washington, and employed some 61,000 lobbyists, including lawyers who lobbied on their behalf. They were joined by corporate-sponsored foundations, centers, and institutes, staffed with their own policy experts and marketing personnel. To these were added companies specializing in advertising and marketing of public policies favored by one corporation or another.[12]

The political mobilization of business and corporate leaders has had three major impacts on the US political system: an increase in money-driven elections, a dramatic increase and presence of business and corporate lobbying, and an increase in the business sector seeking to influence public opinion.

First, this mobilization has contributed to an increase in the cost of elections. The cost of elections had been increasing over the past decades, but it has skyrocketed since the *Citizens United v. Federal Election Commission,* 558 U.S. 310 (2010) decision. The 2012 presidential election cost about $6 billion. Elected officials are now more dependent on donations than ever before; they spend more time raising money and are more careful not to offend major contributors. Andy Kroll summarizes the influence of wealthy donors:

Not since the years before the Watergate scandal has a small cadre of mega-donors influenced our elections as much as wealthy givers such as casino tycoon Sheldon Adelson, DreamWorks Animation CEO Jeffrey Katzenberg, Texas homebuilder Bob Perry, and Chicago media mogul Fred Eychaner did in 2012. These men and a few dozen others pumped hundreds of millions of dollars into Super-PACs and shadowy nonprofits and raised tens of millions more for presidential and Congressional campaigns.[13]

Adam Lioz and Blair Bowie documented the impact of the business and corporate political action committees (PACs) on the election. Their data indicates that less than 5 percent of PAC money comes from labor unions and that the top thirty-two super PAC donors "giving an average of $9.9 million each" matched the money raised by President Obama and Mitt Romney in the 2012 election.[14] Wealthy donors influence policy outcomes by contributing money to help elect officials who share their values and policy goals and by keeping issues off the policy agenda that are offensive to them.

This influence of money in elections has contributed to money-driven elections, which are by nature class-biased elections. More than ever before elected officials are predisposed to favor upper-class interests, the interests of their major contributors. Elected officials are less likely to consider lower-class interests because this class contributes little or nothing to their campaigns and is less likely to vote. This process perpetuates this electoral class bias.

Second, this mobilization signified the dominance of business and corporate interests to the detriment of other interests. William Hudson notes that with the rise in the lobbying activities of business, corporate, and trade industry PACs, the voices of workers, unions, community organizations, and antipoverty groups have been drowned out:

> These three kinds of business groups account for most of the interest-group activity in Washington, D.C. A recent study of the seven thousand or so groups active in the nation's capital found that corporations, trade associations, and general business organizations (including foreign business) accounted for 70 percent of all groups with Washington representation. By contrast, labor unions accounted for 1.7 percent of groups, social welfare groups and those representing the poor .6 percent, and citizens' groups 4.1 percent.[15]

The number and influence of corporate political action committees is even greater now than at the time of Hudson's study.

Third, the business and corporate sector has poured increasing resources into shaping public opinion in support of policies that favor it. One example is the role of the American Petroleum Institute and individual petroleum companies in funding public relations campaigns to promote neoliberal ideas and "undermine the scientific consensus on global clime change."[16] The business and corporate sector has also pumped large sums of money into think tanks, research organizations that have produced studies that promote corporate ideology. As I demonstrate in Chapters 5, 6, and 7, think tanks have produced a large amount of research to shape opinions on racial politics.

The Ascension of Corporate-Sponsored Think Tanks

Corporate-sponsored think tanks that emerged rapidly in the late 1970s and early 1980s, and have become part of the conservative coalition include: the American Enterprise Institute, the Hoover Institution, the Heritage Foundation, the Olin Foundation, the Pioneer Institute, and the Cato Institute.

The American Enterprise Institute's budget rose from $1 million in 1970 to over $10 million by the early 1980s.[17] Its sponsors include "the largest banks and corporations in America: AT&T contributed $125,000, Chase Manhattan Bank gave $171,000, Chevron donated $95,000, Citi-

Corp, $100,000, Exxon $130,000, General Electric, $65,000, General Motors $100,000, and Procter & Gamble, $165,000."[18]

The American Enterprise Institute played a major role in constructing and perpetuating contemporary racist culture and ideology. It provided substantial support for Charles Murray who is a senior fellow at the institute. Murray is the coauthor of the 1994 book, *The Bell Curve*[19] and the author of *Losing Ground*.[20] *The Bell Curve* exhumed the rotting corpse of old-style biological- and genetic-based racism, claiming that blacks were poor because of genetically predisposed low intelligence. *Losing Ground* argued that bad values, bad behavior, and government incentives produced poverty. As will be demonstrated in Chapter 5, Murray's book provided the ideological basis for dismantling the now defunct Aid to Families with Dependent Children (AFDC).

Like the American Enterprise Institute, the Hoover Institution has supported studies that promote police repression. For example, a study by Williamson Evers of the Hoover Institution insisted that rehabilitation programs do not work and that criminal justice policy should target career criminals and remove them from the streets permanently.[21]

A torrent of literature rushed out of these think tanks and flooded the academic world and the rest of society, contributing to the rise of metaracism. The literature deemphasized biology, with the exception of Murray's book *The Bell Curve*, but underscored the role of bad values and bad behavior in producing poverty, as discussed in Chapter 3. These books include the works of Gilder, Murray, and others to be discussed in Chapters 5 and 6.[22]

Many corporate-sponsored think tanks have a direct pipeline to the mass media. A good example of this pipeline is the case of Rupert Murdoch, who is the major shareholder and owner of News Corp. The subsidiaries of News Corp include 20th Century Fox, the *New York Post,* the London *Times, TV Guide,* HarperCollins, Fox News, Fox News Family Channel, National Geographic Channel, and several sports teams. David Brock describes Murdoch's connections:

> Beginning in the Reagan years, many of Murdoch's speeches were quietly written by his close adviser, Irwin Stelzer, an economist who linked Murdoch's media world to the world of the right-wing think tank network, which would come to supply a good deal of the content for his print and TV "news" divisions. Steltzer had been the "director of regulation" at AEI before joining the Hudson Institute. . . . Stelzer was published widely throughout the world in Murdoch publications, including in *The Weekly Standard,* William Kristol's neocon sinkhole. Stelzer arranged lucrative writing assignments for other think tank denizens, including Charles Murray, whose theories linking intelligence to genetics Stelzer supported. Murray called Stelzer "the Godfather."[23]

Not only is the material from conservative think tanks piped into Fox News, it is broadcast in an echo chamber. That is, the same information presented by Fox News is often echoed on other networks such as CNN, ABC, and MSNBC.[24]

These two major historical trends—the rise of money-driven elections and the emergence of corporate-sponsored think tanks—has affected the political arena and both political parties. Both political parties have come to depend more heavily on business and corporate contributions and support than ever before; both are impacted by studies flowing out of these corporate think tanks; both have become more favorable to business and corporate interests; and both have moved in a conservative direction.

The Rise of the Christian Right

The rise of the Christian right pushed the Republican Party even further to the right. The Christian right emerged in the late 1970s and became part of the conservative and Republican Party coalition. A popular story is that Christian right leaders met with President Jimmy Carter to persuade him to support the pro-life movement, but they left the meeting angry and frustrated when the president explained that *Roe v. Wade* was now the law of the land.[25] According to this story, that meeting prompted Reverend Jerry Falwell to organize the Moral Majority.[26]

Thomas and Mary Edsall offer a different interpretation. They claim that the aggressive enforcement of antidiscrimination policies provoked the rise of the Christian right:

> The seeds of the full-blown Christian right can be said to have been sown on May 21, 1969, when the Lawyer Committee for Civil Rights Under Law filed suit challenging the federal tax exemption granted to segregated private schools in Mississippi. The suit was the centerpiece of a civil rights drive to eliminate government subsidies to those private schools that had been created, in the era of "massive resistance," in order to evade integration orders. Many of these schools, known as "segregation academies," were set up across the south in cooperation with the White Citizens Council.[27]

Edsall and Edsall argue that many of these Christian schools were created in response to federal efforts to desegregate the public schools because of fear that black students would bring drugs, crime, violence, and sex with them to white schools. The director of the National Christian Action Coalition, Robert Billings Sr., led the battle against the Internal Revenue Service's decision to eliminate tax exempt status to schools established to maintain racially segregated schools. Billings had become the first executive director of the Moral Majority.[28]

Edsall and Edsall may be correct in citing opposition to school segregation as one factor contributing to the rise of the Christian right. However, this movement undoubtedly was spurred on by other issues such as women's rights, LGBT rights, reproductive rights (abortion and access to birth control), same-sex marriage, prayer in school, evolution, and secular humanism. Also, the emergence of televangelism—the Christian Broadcasting Network, now the Family Channel and the Trinity Broadcasting Network—provided the base for the emergence of this movement. In other words, these broadcasting networks provided leaders of the Christian right access to millions of viewers who would become millions of potential supporters and donors. Reverend Pat Roberson, who founded the Christian Broadcasting Network and still hosts the 700 Club, founded the Christian Coalition in 1989 after he lost the 1988 Republican primary election. He hired Ralph Reed as the CEO. The Christian Coalition emerged as one of the most powerful religious right political organizations in the nation. Today, Roberta Combs is its CEO.

A number of other Christian right organizations have emerged, including Focus on the Family, the Family Research Council, and the Traditional Values Coalition. They promote a range of moral issues such as opposing abortion, promoting traditional two-parent families, opposing same-sex marriage and LGBT rights, and supporting welfare reform. A number of single-issue organizations have emerged and joined the Christian right, such as Operation Rescue, the pro-life organization founded by Randall Terry.

The Christian right has had many connections with the corporate right. For example, Weyrich, who played a key role in the establishment of the Heritage Foundation and ALEC, takes credit for persuading Falwell to create the Moral Majority. David Harvey notes a new alliance between the religious and corporate right:

> But the moral values that have now become central to the neo-conservatives can best be understood as products of the particular coalition that was built in the 1970s, between elite class and business interests intent on restoring their class power, on the one hand, and an electoral base among the moral majority of the disaffected white working class on the other. The moral values centered on cultural nationalism, moral righteousness, Christianity (of a certain evangelical sort), family values, and right-to-life issues, and on antagonism to the new social movements such as feminism, gay rights, affirmative action, and environmentalism. While this alliance was mainly tactical under Reagan, the domestic disorder of the Clinton years forced the moral values argument to the top of the agenda in the Republicanism of Bush the younger. It now forms the core of the moral agenda of the neoconservative movement.[29]

Esther Kaplan describes this connection between Christian right organizations and the corporate right:

> Several Christian right groups joined forces with industry lobbies to form the Coalition for a Fair Judiciary. The Coalition, with its seventy-five member-

organizations, allows some of Washington's most influential mouthpieces for the Christian right, such as the Family Research Council, Concerned Women for America, the Free Congress Foundation, and the Christian Coalition, to work side-by-side with pro-business lobbies such as Grover Norquist's Americans for Tax Reform, which works to lower corporate taxes, the American Tort Reform Association, which seeks to limit corporate liability for wrongdoing, and the National Association of Manufacturers.[30]

Kaplan also describes the role of the Christian right in promoting the George W. Bush tax cuts:

For instance, as the president was building support for his first round of tax cuts in 2001, the *Wall Street Journal* reported, Tim Goeglein and Karl Rove enlisted help from the Christian right in promoting the proposal through a series of private meetings with social conservatives in Washington. When at one stage officials floated the idea of dropping the tax break for married couples, these religious leaders protested and the idea was dropped. Evangelicals returned the favor, as leaders such as Pat Robertson promoted the tax-cut package on popular programs such as his 700 Club. The day Bush was set to sign the bill, Christian radio stations across the country gave Goeglein access to their airwaves to praise it.[31]

Leonard Zeskind corroborates Kaplan's and the Edsalls' findings. Zeskind argues that this movement emerged as a reactionary movement to several political defeats: school desegregation, prayer in school, evolution, abortion, and traditional marriage. He demonstrates that the Christian Coalition consciously expanded its policy agenda. In the Heritage Foundation's monthly journal, *Policy Review*, Ralph Reed wrote:

The most urgent challenge for pro-family conservatives is to develop a broader issues agenda. The pro-family movement has limited its effectiveness by concentrating disproportionately on issues such as abortion and homosexuality. . . . To win at the ballot box and in the court of public opinion, however, the pro-family movement must speak to the concerns of average voters in the areas of taxes, crime, government waste, health care, and financial security.[32]

The Christian right has thus emerged as a powerful political movement and one that is allied with the corporate right. This alliance is part of the powerful conservative coalition, which not only supports the Republican Party but has been part of the transformation of this party.

The Transformation of the Republican Party

From 1970 to 2012, the Republican Party underwent a transformation. It moved from the center right to the far right. Several major changes spurred this process. The first change, which I discussed in earlier chapters, involved Southern Democrats switching to the Republican Party. Southern political leaders who had once supported racial segregation and opposed civil rights policies shifted to the Republican Party. Classic examples of this shift include Senators Jesse Helms of North Carolina, Strom Thurmond of South Carolina, and Phil Gramm of Texas.

As a Southern Democrat in the 1940s, 1950s, and early 1960s, Thurmond supported racial segregation and opposed federal civil rights policy. He switched to the Republican Party just after the passage of the Civil Rights Act of 1964. In the 1960s, Helms was a segregationist Democrat who opposed federal civil rights policy. He joined the Republican Party in the 1970s. Gramm switched from the Democratic Party to the Republican Party in the 1980s. Some of these shifts embarrassed the party such as that of David Duke, a former grand wizard of the Ku Klux Klan and Southern Democrat, who joined the Republican Party in the late 1980s. He was elected to the Louisiana State Legislature, and ran for governor of Louisiana but lost. Indeed, most Southern Democrats who supported segregation and opposed civil rights policies in the 1960s had switched to the Republican Party by the 1980s.[33]

This shift of Southern Democrats who opposed civil rights to the Republican Party was accompanied by an ideological shift to the right. While the Republican Party had initially opposed the New Deal programs, by the 1950s the party had come to accept these programs and Keynesian economic theory—the view that advocated the expansion of government spending during recessions. In the 1950s, government programs had expanded under the Dwight Eisenhower administration especially with the establishment of the federal interstate highway system and the Federal Housing Administration, which stimulated suburban housing expansion. But the Republican Party shifted to the right with the nomination of libertarian Barry Goldwater in 1964. However, after Goldwater's catastrophic defeat, the moderate Republicans reemerged and resumed control of the party. Examples of these moderate Republicans include Nelson Rockefeller, governor of New York from 1959 to 1973 and vice president of the United States from 1975 to 1976, and George Romney, governor of Michigan from 1963 to 1969, secretary of the housing and urban development under Richard Nixon, and a strong supporter of civil rights policy and opponent of Goldwater.

Nixon was elected president in 1968 and reelected in 1972. Although he campaigned using his Southern strategy to subtly exploit racial issues (see Chapter 1), Nixon was a moderate Republican. He promoted Keynesian economic policies. In terms of his economic and regulatory programs he was a liberal by today's standards, to the left of President Obama. He appeared conservative because of his Southern strategy.

When urban riots, busing, crime, and welfare expansion precipitated a white backlash, Nixon exploited the situation. He campaigned on a law-

and-order and antibusing platform to capture votes from the Solid South. He appealed to Northern white ethnics and white labor from the New Deal coalition as he promised to end busing, promote law and order, and reduce welfare rolls.

Although he catered to white conservative interests, Nixon continued to promote Keynesian economic policies. He gave local governments more discretion over the Great Society programs of the Johnson administration by creating block grants (Community Development Block Grants and the Comprehensive Employment Training Act). He established the General Revenue program for state and local governments, similar to President Obama's stimulus package.

The Nixon administration moved to the left in some ways. He promoted aggressive regulatory policy. He established the Environmental Protection Agency, the Occupational Safety and Health Administration, and the Consumer Product Safety Commission. He proposed a Family Assistance Plan to guarantee poor families a minimum income. He gained support from black businesses and civil rights groups by establishing the Philadelphia Plan, an aggressive affirmative action pilot program to increase the number of blacks employed by federal contractors. Nixon imposed administrative changes to end welfare fraud and reduce the welfare rolls.

The election of President Reagan in 1980 signaled the formation of a new Republican Party that combined anti-Keynesian neoliberalism with metaracism. Metaracism was the main factor explaining the shift of conservative Democrats to the new Republican Party. Noting the impact of race on Reagan Democrats, Edsall and Edsall cite the conclusion of a study of this shift written by Stanley Greenberg, president of the Analysis Group for the Michigan Democratic Party:

> These white Democratic defectors express a profound distaste for blacks, a sentiment that pervades almost everything they think about government and politics. Blacks constitute the explanation for their (white defectors') vulnerability and for almost everything that has gone wrong in their lives; not being black is what constitutes being middle class; not living with blacks is what makes a neighborhood a decent place to live. These sentiments have important implications for Democrats, as virtually all progressive symbols and themes have been redefined in racial and pejorative terms.[34]

The Edsalls discuss another study commissioned by the Democratic National Committee in 1985 based on surveys of 5,000 voters:

> The DNC study . . . found that race was a divisive issue among all of these groups, but it was most intense among the white ethnic voters (primarily Irish and Italian) and among southern Democratic moderates. . . . These white voters . . . believed "the Democratic Party has not stood with them as they moved from the working to the middle class. They have a whole set of mid-

dle class economic problems today, and their party is not helping them. Instead it is helping the blacks, Hispanics and the poor. They feel betrayed."[35]

Reagan promoted a distinctively conservative ideology, with racial and class undertones. He advocated smaller government, cuts in government spending, rollbacks in government regulations, and tax cuts for the rich as well as reductions in welfare, antipoverty, and unemployment programs. He popularized neoliberal and neoconservative ideas. He paraphrased Ayn Rand when he claimed that government was not the solution. Government was the problem, and "we need to get government off the backs of the American people."

The racial undertones of Reagan's conservative ideology were evident in a number of areas. As I noted in Chapter 1, Reagan quite frequently used racial images in his attacks on welfare and food stamps, expressions like "welfare queens," a term that conjured up images of an overweight black woman receiving multiple welfare checks and driving a Cadillac. He used the term "strapping young buck" in his image of a large, muscular young black man using food stamps to purchase T-bone steaks while middle-class whites struggled to buy hamburger meat. Reagan used these terms, stories, and images so frequently that it became obvious that, when he called for reducing dependency on welfare, he meant getting blacks off of welfare. Reagan's use of language combined with the role of the media helped racialize antipoverty programs. Programs to help the poor became programs to help blacks. The racializing of these programs desensitized the public and made it easier to eliminate them.

The use of race explains this contradiction. Reagan called for reducing the size of government while increasing the size of government. He targeted programs that had come to symbolize government assistance to blacks, such as the Comprehensive Employment Training Act and welfare, but expanded government police powers as he enlarged federal drug enforcement agencies and initiated a war on drugs. He also increased military spending.

Although Reagan was committed to a neoliberal policy agenda, he was constrained by the continued presence of the egalitarian coalition and by moderate Republicans. An alliance of Democrats and moderate Republicans constrained the Reagan administration and prevented Reagan from turning Medicaid into a block grant system and cutting social security, welfare, and other programs. Some of these moderate Republicans were John Chafee, Arlen Specter, Jim Jeffords, Nancy Kassebaum, and William Cohen. This alliance between Democrats and moderate Republicans continued into the George H. W. Bush and Clinton administrations. However, by the twenty-first century most of these moderate Republicans, if not all, were gone.

Some retired, some were defeated in general elections, and some were targeted by conservative Republicans and defeated in primary elections.

With the exodus of moderates, the mobilization of the business and corporate sector, the leadership of neoliberal corporate extremists, and the support of the Christian right, the Republican Party moved further to the right. It became more ideologically pure, more disciplined, and more uncompromising. With the emergence of the Tea Party movement, this party transformed completely into a reactionary party.

The Tea Party Movement

The Tea Party movement was a truly reactionary movement. Seeds of this movement were planted during the George W. Bush administration. Seething anxiety, frustration, anger, and fear provided the fuel for the movement. Conservatives were frustrated with the explosion of the budget deficit that occurred under that administration. This deficit was primarily attributable to major tax cuts and war spending on Iraq and Afghanistan. Spending for Medicare Part D, the pharmaceutical drug program, added marginally to the deficit. Frustrations grew as the budget deficit increased further with the bailouts of failing finance companies and the automobile industry and the near collapse of the financial sector.[36]

The ensuing recession became another factor. Frustration and anger intensified as the unemployment rate increased. As discussed in Chapter 1, massive foreclosures on homes of the middle class as well as the loss of family farms and displacement of farm families heightened this anger and frustration. Many of those affected were drawn to the militia and Patriot movements, both of which also had reputations as racist movements.

Anxieties turned to terror and anger among extreme conservatives with the election of a black president who was perceived to be a radical liberal. The election of President Obama, the passage of the stimulus bill, and the passage of the Affordable Care Act triggered panic and outrage.

The Tea Party became most active and visible just after the passage of the stimulus bill on February 17, 2009, and the bailout of the automobile companies. On January 19, 2009, a member of an Internet forum had posted a call to mail tea bags to members of Congress in protest of the bailout. On January 27, Rush Limbaugh called for a demonstration against the stimulus bill.[37]

The Tea Party movement gained momentum on February 19, 2009, when CNBC business newscaster, Rick Santelli, engaged in a loud rant against the Obama administration for passing the stimulus bill, rewarding bad behavior, bailing out companies, and subsidizing mortgages. He ended his rant with a call for a Chicago Tea Party demonstration. The next day, Fox News began promoting Tea Party demonstrations. The *Huffington Post* reported that on February 20 a Facebook page was created calling for Tea Party protests. Fox News played a crucial role in publicizing, sponsoring, and promoting Tea Party protest rallies.[38]

Theda Skocpol and Vanessa Williamson note the role of Glenn Beck and Fox News in promoting the April 15, 2009, and the July 4, 2009, protests:

> Aired on April 6, 2009, the Glenn Beck show included a clarion call for viewers to "celebrate" the upcoming Tax Day on Wednesday, April 15. Viewers were urged either to attend a Tea Party rally or watch Fox News Channel coverage of the protests. As Beck spoke, a map of the USA was displayed across the screen, highlighting the cities where Fox hosts would be present: Neil Cavuto in Sacramento, California; Greta Van Susteren in Washington DC; Sean Hannity in Atlanta, Georgia; and Beck himself in San Antonio, Texas.[39]

Fox News and key Fox officials such as Beck, Hannity, Van Susteren, and Cavuto did not simply cover Tea Party demonstrations; these news corporations and influential news personalities promoted the Tea Party demonstrations and helped organize the Tea Party movement. The overwhelming majority of people who identify with the Tea Party movement are regular Fox News viewers. Most are avid Beck fans.[40]

A number of scholars also have depicted this movement as emerging from the middle class. For example, in their study, Skocpol and Williamson provide both aggregate data and several case studies of local Tea Party organizations. They note that there are hundreds of local Tea Party organizations and organizers, that there is no central control over these local Tea Party organizations, that they are essentially autonomous, that they emerged spontaneously, and that they were formed by "ordinary people." Tea Party members tend to be older than the average citizen; most are of middle age and older. On average, they are more educated than the general public and have higher incomes. Many are retired professionals. Local organizers profiled by Skocpol and Williams include a stay-at-home mom, a retired contractor, a retired US Air Force pilot, real estate agents, insurance agents, a church organizer, and a number of Republican Party activists.[41]

Skocpol and Williamson suggest that the phenomenon of the movement is paradoxical. While one part of the movement consists of genuine grassroots organizations, formed spontaneously by ordinary middle-class people, the movement has also been well supported by corporate-sponsored organizations as described below. A number of conservative billionaires have played a major role in financing this movement and setting its agenda.[42]

For example, the Koch brothers played a major role. They have been obsessed with removing President Obama from office and remaking the Republican Party in their image:

> Even after President Obama ran the successful operation to kill Osama Bin Laden, David Koch was quoted belittling the president and renewing the out-landish claim that Obama is a "socialist." Blocking Obama's legislative agenda and setting up his defeat in 2012 has clearly been goal number one for the Koch coterie. . . . The Koch brothers are fighting not only against Democrats, but against other GOP powerbrokers like Karl Rove and Ed Gillespie, who have their own fundraising organizations to promote their preferred brand of Republicanism. . . . Charles and David Koch aim to "reorient the conservative political apparatus around free-market, small government principles and candidates," and away from the electability-over-principles approach they see Rove and Gillespie as embodying.
> The Tea Party eruption in early 2009 was just what the doctor ordered for far-right ideological billionaires like the Kochs, and others of their ideological ilk roving just beyond the edge of the GOP establishment. Suddenly, prospects were better for ultra-free-market funders and affiliated idea-pushers to try to link up with grassroots Tea Partiers.[43]

Koch-supported organizations moved immediately to assist in supporting and promoting the Tea Party movement. Freedom Works and Americans for Prosperity provided a great deal of initial support:

> Soon the organization's [Freedom Works] President Matt Kibbe and its Chairman Dick Armey teamed up to write a book they dubbed a "manifesto" for the Tea Party Movement. . . .
> With the opening provided by the Santelli rant, Freedom Works built activist connections. It helped to orchestrate the angry town hall protests against health reform in August 2009, co-sponsored Tea Party Rallies, and gained new leverage in 2010 with GOPers elected with its endorsement or the support of other Tea Party-identified groups. . . .
> Riding the Tea Party wave, the AFP [Americans for Prosperity] ballooned its contact lists from about 270,000 in 2008 to 1.5 million in 2011, while also expanding its network of coordinators to reach 32 states. AFP staffers and volunteer activists often appear at Tea Party rallies, and the organization regularly pays to transport protestors across the country and even to international events. AFP is also building extensive state networks.[44]

Other conservative organizations joined and helped set the policy agenda of the movement. The Cato Institute and the Heritage Foundation think tanks contributed studies and policy recommendations to Tea Party organizations.

ALEC holds annual "States and National Policy Summit" conferences. The purpose of the conference is not to discuss the development of a policy agenda, but to distribute model bills already developed by the ALEC. These bills fall into several policy areas: labor relations, voting rights, public education, business regulations, immigration reform, tax reform, tort reform, and criminal justice including mandatory sentencing and stand your ground laws.[45]

ALEC had been developing model bills for several years. However, the dramatic success of Tea Party candidates at the polls in the 2010 election provided ALEC with the opportunity to get these bills on the agendas of state legislators and Congress. ALEC aggressively pushed its policy agenda, which was similar to the Redeemer agenda in that it promoted laws designed to suppress voter rights, weaken labor unions, cut funding for public schools, and reduce taxes on the rich and on businesses.

Supporters insisted that this movement was not racist, but precipitated by the federal budget deficit, the bailout, and repressive federal laws, particularly President Obama's health care reform. Several analysts have argued that, although not overtly racist, the movement is tainted by racism.[46] There are three sources of support for this claim: public opinion polls, the nature of organizations supporting the movement, and the behavior of Tea Party enthusiasts at rallies.

Public opinion survey data presented by Skocpol and Williamson indicate some degree of racial bias among Tea Party members when compared to the general population. Tea Party supporters are more likely to view Obama as the Other, as foreign born, and as a non-Christian. He does not fit their image of a citizen. Whereas 42 percent of the general public doubt that Obama was born in the United States, 59 percent of Tea Party supporters doubt his US birth. While many people distinguish between hardworking, deserving, and taxpaying people and lazy, undeserving, and freeloading people, Tea Party supporters are more likely to divide these two groups along color lines. They are more likely to see blacks as lazy undeserving freeloaders living off of government programs financed by hardworking, taxpaying whites.[47] Support for the Tea Party movement is associated with racial resentment, even after accounting for ideology and partisanship. To some extent opposition to health care reform reflected fears that this program would provide health insurance primarily to poor people, particularly to lazy undeserving blacks. Tea Party supporters are also more likely than the general population to be angry about illegal immigrants crossing the border from Mexico into the United States.[48]

Another study led by Christopher Parker of the Washington Institute for the Study of Ethnicity, Race and Sexuality corroborates Skocpol and Williamson's research. Parker reported that 23 percent of whites surveyed strongly supported the Tea Party movement and 22 percent somewhat supported it.[49] In contrast, only 8 percent of blacks strongly supported the movement; 16 percent supported it somewhat. The survey labeled those who strongly supported the movement "true believers" and those who strongly opposed the movement "skeptics." It sorted out white true believers from white skeptics. The differences in select attitudes between these two groups were striking. See Table 4.2.

Parker's study revealed that compared to skeptics, true believer Tea Party supporters were substantially less likely to see blacks as hardworking (35 percent for true believers compared to 55 percent for skeptics), intelligent (45 percent for true believers compared to 59 percent for skeptics), and trustworthy (41 percent for true believers compared to 57 percent for skeptics). Similarly, most Tea Party supporters did not see Latinos as intelligent or trustworthy.[50]

Parker's study also suggests that the Tea Party movement is reactionary. An overwhelming majority of true believers (60 percent) agreed that "we have gone too far in pushing equal rights in this country," compared to only 23 percent of skeptics. Strong Tea Party supporters were more likely to support authoritarian government policies than skeptics. Few strong supporters (only 33 percent) disagreed with the statement that "government can tap people's phone," compared to 72 percent for skeptics.

Table 4.2 Racial, Ethnic, and Political Attitudes Among White Tea Party True Believers and Skeptics (in percentage)

	Responses	
Survey Question	True Believers	Skeptics
Blacks are hardworking	35	55
Blacks are intelligent	45	59
Blacks are trustworthy	41	57
Latinos are hardworking	54	58
Latinos are intelligent	44	56
Latinos are trustworthy	42	56
How likely is it that recent immigration levels will take jobs away from people already here? (Likely)	56	31
The number of immigrants from foreign countries should be (Decreased)	54	34
We have gone too far in pushing equal rights in this country (Agree)	60	23
We don't give everyone an equal chance in this country (Agree)	23	72
The government can tap people's telephone conversations (Disagree)	33	72
The government can detain people as long as they wish without trial (Disagree)	54	90

Source: University of Washington Institute for the Study of Ethnicity, Race, and Sexuality, *WISI Multi-State Survey of Race and Politics* (Seattle: University of Washington Institute for the Study of Ethnicity, Race and Sexuality, 2010).

Although most true believers disagreed with the statement that "government can detain people as long as they wish without trial," substantially fewer true believers (54 percent) disagreed than skeptics (90 percent).

Tea Party true believers tended to be anti-immigration. They were more likely to see immigrants taking jobs from people already here (56 percent) than skeptics (only 31 percent). Moreover, 54 percent supported decreasing the number of foreign immigrants into the United States, compared to only 34 percent of Tea Party skeptics.

Racial animus has also been documented in an extensive study of the racial attitudes characterizing the Tea Party movement conducted by the Institute for Research and Education on Human Rights (IREHR). Some of the rage that fueled the Tea Party movement emerged with the election of President Obama. This Obama rage has been expressed in the movement's obsession with the president and in the display of many racist images of him and his family, as described in earlier chapters.[51]

According to the IREHR study, another indication of racial animus in the movement has been the attack on members of the Congressional Black Caucus and liberal Democrats. On March 10, 2010, Tea Party protestors outside Congress screamed at members of Congress, calling Barney Frank a "faggot" and John Lewis a "n__ger" and spitting on members of the Congressional Black Caucus.[52]

The IREHR study notes that, although the Tea Party movement might not be inherently racist, it was a magnet for racist groups. It attracted activists in some of the most racist, anti-immigrant, anti-Semitic organizations in the nation including the Minutemen, the militia movement, the KKK, and the neo-Nazis. The IREHR study provides detailed examples of these connections between local Tea Party organizations and racist groups. One such example is the Wood County, Texas, Tea Party, formed in 2009, whose website states that the organization is committed to the constitution, fiscal responsibility, limited government, and a free market society. It notes its affiliation with the Tea Party and Freedom Works.[53] The Wood County Tea Party was founded by Karen Pack, who describes herself as a Christian, a Tea Party member, a constitutionalist, and a patriot. The study explains,

> Missing from that description, however, is Karen Pack's history with the Ku Klux Klan. Documents obtained by IREHR show that Karen Pack of Winnsboro, subscribed to the White Patriot tabloid, and that Thom Robb's Knights of the Ku Klux Klan listed her as an "official supporter." Founded by David Duke in the mid-1970s, the Knights of the Ku Klux Klan fell into Robb's hands after a series of factional disputes . . . over the decades. By the 1990s, Robb attempted to steer his Klan closer to a more mid-stream "Christian-patriot" position. It was still a Klan, however, an inheritor of the violent tradition associated with white supremacist organizations of that type. Pack's association with Robb's Klan in 1996 should not be read as an indication that the entire Tea Party movement is like the KKK.[54]

Another Tea Party faction that had connections with racist groups is the Tea Party Express, which was associated with the Free Republic. The IREHR describes the Free Republic as follows:

> It is an important space for the birthers and racist. One of those posting material on Free Republic claiming that President Obama had no birth certificate was James von Brunn, the white supremacist who killed the guard at the holocaust Museum in Washington, D.C., on June 10, 2009. This website has also posted racist attacks on the Obama family. In July 2009, after Obama's eleven-year-old daughter Malia was photo graphed wearing a t-shirt with the peace symbol, a Free Republic thread featured racially charged comments about President Obama's wife and children, using racist epithets and terms like "Ghetto street trash." The thread was accompanied by a photo of Michelle Obama speaking to Malia that featured the caption, "To entertain her daughter, Michelle Obama loves to make Monkey sounds."[55]

Racism in the Tea Party movement is shown further by an incident that occurred at the Conservative Political Action Conference (CPAC) in March 2013. The Tea Party sponsored a breakout session "Trump the Race Card," the purpose of which was to teach members how to effectively defend themselves against the charge of racism. The session was conducted by K. Carl Smith, a black motivational speaker, author, and Tea Party activist. During the session, Smith was interrupted by a black woman who objected to the Democratic Party being portrayed as the party of slavery and the KKK. She also asked Smith how many black women were at the Women's Rights Convention in 1848. The woman was shouted down by the audience and told that she was not welcome there. Smith was later interrupted by Scott Terry who claimed that he was proud of his white Southern heritage and that whites were disenfranchised. Smith tried to put the session back on track by insisting that Tea Party Republicans refer to themselves as Frederick Douglass Republicans, noting that Douglass wrote his former master a letter saying that he forgave him. Terry interrupted again, claiming that Douglass had nothing to forgive his former master for because his master had provided him with shelter and food. Smith then asked why they could not be Booker T. Washington Republicans and advocate segregation, being as separate as the fingers but part of the same hand.[56] This incident illustrates the fact that the Tea Party movement attracts racists and that its members deny the persistence and prevalence of racism.

In their recent book on the Tea Party movement, Parker and Barreto conclude that despite strong arguments that the movement promotes traditional conservative values, all the evidence suggests that it is a reactionary movement with racist overtones. The movement emerged in reaction to Obama's election to the presidency, to the perception that they are losing control of their country, to fear of Mexican immigrants, to the growth of government programs.[57]

The Tea Party movement along with other ideological organizations, political leaders, and pundits have pushed the Republican Party to the extreme right. As Jacob Hacker and Paul Pierson note,

> Exhibit A for the rightward shift of Republicans has to be South Carolina Senator Jim DeMint. Within the shrunken GOP caucus, DeMint anchors the right wing. Yet in the early days of the Obama administration, he emerged as a prominent, if shrill, voice on economic issues. In a January 2009 speech to the Heritage Foundation, DeMint outlined a Republican alternative to the administration's economic stimulus plan. Introducing his own version of historical perspective, he denounced the Obama proposal as "the worst piece of economic legislation Congress has considered in a hundred years." He then identified the infamous bill he had in mind—the 1909 passage of the Sixteenth Amendment, which had cleared the way for a federal income tax.
>
> DeMint's identification of 1909 as the year everything began to go wrong provided a pretty good clue for where he was heading. . . . With his potshots at insufficiently pure Republicans and his ominous perplexing warnings that Obama's Washington resembled "Germany . . . before World War II," DeMint is an easy target. Yet when it came to the floor for a vote, DeMint's American Option received the support of all but four GOP senators.[58]

DeMint's American Option plan would have made the George W. Bush tax cuts permanent and cost over $3 trillion in lost revenue over a ten-year period.[59]

DeMint not only shows the extreme position of the new Republicans, but also the central role of Tea Party members in the Republican coalition and among Republican political leaders. Other extreme positions became a common feature in the 2012 Republican presidential primary. Gingrich proposed to repeal the Child Labor Law to allow poor children to work as janitors in their schools to save public spending in education; Rick Perry called social security "a Ponzi scheme" and "a monstrous lie"; and Herman Cain referred to social security as "immoral and oppressive" and income taxes as "involuntary slavery." Michele Bachmann and Rick Santorum signed a pledge to support marriage that contained a statement claiming that black families were better off under slavery than under President Obama: "Slavery had a disastrous impact on African-American families, yet sadly a child born into slavery in 1860 was more likely to be raised by his mother and father in a two-parent household than was an African-American baby born after the election of the USA's first African-American President."[60] After the political outcry over the pledge, Family Leader officials apologized and deleted it. Bachmann's campaign issued this retraction: "In no uncertain terms, Congresswoman Bachmann believes that slavery was horrible and economic enslavement is also horrible." If Bachmann's concept of economic enslavement is anywhere similar to Cain's, then social security, federal income taxes, and any federal program that assists the poor (particularly poor blacks) is a form of economic slavery, just as horrible as plantation slavery prior to the Civil War. Political statements that were once considered extreme and on the fringe have now moved to center stage.

A number of new organizations associated with the Tea Party movement have emerged as part of the corporate-centered conservative coalition. One is the Faith and Freedom Coalition founded by Reed, former CEO of the Christian Coalition, who claims that his organization connects the evangelical movement to the Tea Party movement. The mission of this organization is to tie together the Christian right, the Tea Party, and the corporate right. The written mission states, "Respect for the sanctity and dignity of life, family and marriage as the foundation of a free society." The organization's website expresses a commitment to "limited government, lower taxes and fiscal responsibility to unleash the creative energies."[61]

Other such organizations include Freedom Works, Americans for Prosperity, Americans for Tax Reform, ALEC, and the Club for Growth. All of these except the Club for Growth, which was established in 1999, have been discussed earlier in the chapter. According to its website, the Club for Growth has been committed to a range of conservative issues including reducing the income tax rate, repealing the death tax, promoting school choice, and reducing the size of government. Most recently it has been adamant about repealing the Affordable Care Act and reducing the deficit by cutting spending. It has also been committed to cutting taxes.[62] *The Economist* quoted Stephen More, founder and former head of this organization, stating, "We want to be seen as the tax cut enforcer for the [Republican] party."[63] The Club for Growth pressured House Republicans to oppose the emergency relief bill for Hurricane Sandy victims at the beginning of 2013.[64] Even though the House relief bill had stripped the Senate bill of riders that had nothing to do with helping the victims, the Club for Growth continued to lobby against the bill because it required an increase in government spending.[65]

There have been some recent divisions in the movement, especially between the new Tea Party Republicans, Freedom Works and traditional conservatives. The main divisions have been between the ideological purist and the politically practical. In the House of Representatives, the division has been between the Tea Party purists and traditional Republican leaders, like John Boehner. This division became most evident in the summer of 2014 after the defeat of House Republican Majority Leader Eric Cantor by Tea Party purist David Brat.[66]

The Democratic Party's Shift to the Right
and the Disintegration of the Left

Some conservative commentators have asserted that the Democratic Party has moved to the left and become more liberal, just as the Republican Party has moved to the right and become more conservative. The Democratic Party has remained a defender of civil rights, women's rights, LGBT rights, and reproductive rights. It is committed to promoting clean air, clean water, and fair competition. It is also committed to preserving the social safety net. As noted in Chapter 1, the Dixiecrats have left the Democratic Party and joined the Republican Party. However, contrary to this portrait, there are several indicators that the Democratic Party, like the Republican Party, has also moved to the right and has become more conservative, although not as extremely conservative as the Republican Party. Several factors have pushed the Democratic Party to the right: the party itself, the emergence of the conservative coalition, and the decline of the egalitarian coalition.

With the rise of a powerful corporate-centered conservative coalition, the entire political spectrum has shifted to the right. Whereas the Republican Party has moved to the far right, contrary to conventional wisdom the Democratic Party has not shifted to the left. With the exception of its support for LGBT rights issues, the Democratic Party has moved to the right.

Having lost every presidential election except one from 1968 to 1988, the Democratic Party deliberately shifted to the right. By the 1990s, the party had become more hawkish on foreign policy, more hostile to civil liberties, tougher on crime, more supportive of deregulation, more pro-business, more hostile to welfare, and more committed to balancing the budget than the Democratic Party of the past. With the exception of its support for LGBT rights and its moderate position on civil rights and reproductive rights, the Democratic Party has clearly moved to the right.

The Democratic Party moved to the right in part because of a growing dependency on corporate contributions and partly because the New Deal coalition was unraveling. White working-class, union, and Southern voters were shifting to the Republican Party. This shift became clear just after the disastrous defeat of Walter Mondale by Reagan in 1984.[67]

A year later in 1985, a number of centrist Democrats formed the Democratic Leadership Council (DLC). The purpose of this council was to change the image of the party and respond to the loss of Reagan Democrats and the breaking up of the New Deal coalition. The council was concerned with countering the image of Democrats as too generous on social welfare; too soft on crime; too obsessively concerned about minority rights; too weak on foreign policy; and too strongly associated with big government, big spending, and high taxes. Francis Fox Piven, Lorraine C. Minnite, and Margaret Groarke describe the rise of the DLC:

The disastrous election of 1988—the third straight defeat of the Democrats' presidential candidates—was a boon to the DLC, vindicating its criticism of the party as out of touch with the mainstream of American political life. The DLC became a bigger organization and proclaimed itself an "ideas movement" dedicated to rebuilding the Democratic Party. It expanded its donor base, attracted new membership, attempted to establish a grassroots network of state and local Democratic elected officials, and founded a think tank to develop its centrist policy agenda. The Dukakis drubbing "paved the way for the DLC's policy ideas to get a hearing inside the party." An influential DLC policy paper by political scientists William Galson and Elaine Kamarck argued that "since the late 1960s, the public has come to associate liberalism with tax and spend policies that contradict the interests of average families; with welfare policies that foster dependence rather than self-reliance; with softness toward the perpetrators of crime and indifference toward its victims; with ambivalence toward the assertion of American values and interest abroad; and with the adversarial stance toward mainstream moral and cultural values."[68]

Bill Clinton chaired the DLC in 1990 and 1991, then ran for and won the presidency in 1992. He took the advice of the DLC and ran on a conservative platform. He epitomized the new Democrat: he was a fiscal conservative who advocated smaller government, tax cuts, deregulation, welfare reform, a balanced budget, and free trade. He was so tough on crime that he stopped in the middle of his campaign to return to Arkansas and preside over an execution.

President Clinton and the new Democratic Party operated to neutralize liberal issues. Clinton dropped the party's commitment to antipoverty programs. He supported the Republican Party's welfare reform proposal, although his reform proposal was not as extreme as the Republican one. He avoided special rights issues such as abortion, LGBT rights, and affirmative action. He claimed that abortions should be rare and safe. He supported the "Don't ask, Don't tell" military policy. He opposed set-asides. He promoted the Democratic Party as the party of the middle class. With the exception of promoting health care reform and expanding health care benefits for children, Clinton promoted a distinctively conservative business agenda. He was able to get welfare reform, NAFTA, and deregulation of the finance sector passed in Congress.

Democrats in Congress, including those with reputations as liberals, have pursued a pro-business agenda. Hacker and Pierson provide several examples of the role of Democrats, including Chuck Schumer and John Kerry, in supporting policies that benefited both Wall Street and corporate CEOs:

Schumer quickly established himself as an aggressive and extremely adept fund-raiser. . . . As he rose through the ranks in the House, he played a critical role in helping Democrats build strong ties to the financial industry. In the

words of a detailed New York Times profile, "Mr. Schumer became a magnet for campaign donations from wealthy industry executives, including
Jamie Dimon, now the chief executive of JP Morgan Chase; John J. Mack,
the chief executive at Morgan Stanley; and Charles O. Prince III, the former
chief executive of Citigroup. And he was not at all reluctant to ask them for
more. . . ." From 1999–2000 through 2005–2006, only one member of Congress raised more money from securities and investment firms than
Schumer's $3.7 million. That was John Kerry, whose presidential run doubt-
less boosted his totals just a wee bit.
    Strikingly, while Kerry and Schumer ran first and second, numbers three,
four, and five were all Democrats as well—Joe Lieberman, Hillary Clinton,
and Chris Dodd. . . .
    Schumer was the perfect person to broker the strengthening relationship
between Democrats and Wall Street.[69]

The point is that the entire Democratic Party has become deferential to business interests.

The Weakening of the Egalitarian Coalition

This shift of the Democratic Party to the right is consistent with the view
that the egalitarian coalition is weakening, equal opportunity programs are
eroding, and the major political conflict of twenty-first century US politics
is between the centrist egalitarian coalition holding on to what is left of
these programs and a far right conservative coalition engaging in a relentless assault on these programs. The consequences of this assault, which
will be demonstrated in the next few chapters, are higher levels of racial
inequality.

    There are many signs of the weakening of the egalitarian coalition: the
disintegration of the extreme left, the decimation of the antipoverty movement, the decline of labor, and splits in the civil rights coalition. Most
extreme leftist organizations had disappeared by the 1990s. Gone are the
American Socialist Party, the American Communist Party, Students for a
Democratic Society (SDS), and the Weathermen. The Black Panther Party,
a black Marxist organization established in the mid-1960s, which held
alliances with other radical organizations such as the SDS and had chapters
and community programs in most cities and a national newspaper, had dis-
solved by the early 1980s. A new Black Panther Party just emerged, but it
has no connection and little resemblance to the original party. Moreover,
this tiny, fringe organization has been designated a hate group by the Southern Poverty Law Center.[70]

    There are still a few active leftist organizations, but they are weaken-
ing. The two most notable include Occupy Wall Street (OWS) and the
Green Party. The Green Party emerged out of the US Greens organization,

established in 1984 to promote progressive environmental policies, diversity, peace, and social justice; the party was formed in the early 1990s. Consumer advocate, Ralph Nader, ran for president on the Green Party ticket in 1996 and 2000. In the 1996 election, he captured 685,297 votes. In 2000, he earned 2,883,105 votes or 2.7 percent of the votes cast. Since then, the party has gotten less than 1 percent of the vote or less than 500,000 votes. There are no Green Party members in Congress.[71]

Occupy Wall Street made its official debut on September 17, 2011, when a few bloggers initiated a demonstration in Liberty Square in Manhattan's Financial District. Since the initial Wall Street protest, OWS demonstrations sprang up in more than one hundred US cities. The demonstrators protested the growth of extreme inequality in the United States and the irresponsible and risky speculation on Wall Street, which led to the near collapse of the banking industry and the need for the federal bailout in 2008. Protesters claimed that they spoke for the bottom 99 percent of the population, while Wall Street represented the 1 percent of the population that had virtually monopolized the wealth increases of the last decades. The OWS protests lasted for about two years. However, as a political movement it had little organization, little direction, and few policy proposals.[72]

Antipoverty organizations have weakened. A few of these organizations have died. One of the most powerful advocacy groups for welfare rights, the National Welfare Rights Organization, started in the mid-1960s. It peaked in membership with close to 25,000 paying members, but by 1975 had died.[73]

Another powerful community-based organization, ACORN died recently. ACORN, the organization that fought to protect the Community Reinvestment Act, that campaigned for a living wage, that pushed for affordable homes, and that engaged in voter registration drives was decimated by a scandal in 2009. Posing as a prostitute and a pimp, two amateur investigative journalists asked an ACORN official to help them avoid paying taxes on their business that engaged in human trafficking and child prostitution. The couple videotaped the encounter and Fox News played parts of it on the air. The video effectively discredited the organization. Congress responded by passing a special bill to defund the agency, and ACORN disintegrated shortly afterward.[74]

A few antipoverty organizations remain active, but with a narrow focus. These include the Children's Defense Fund and the National Coalition for the Homeless. The Children's Defense Fund, founded by Marian Wright Edelman in 1973, has been effective in advocating for children. It has lobbied for the expansion of health care, child nutrition, and child care programs. However, it has been silent on welfare rights issues.[75]

The National Coalition for the Homeless founded in the early 1980s by Robert Hayes was effective in securing the passage of the Homeless Assistance Act of 1987. It is committed to promoting affordable housing. In the past thirty years it has been more successful in getting local governments to respond to the problem of homelessness than securing an expanded federal role.[76]

Another sign of the weakening of the egalitarian coalition is the weakening of the alliance between civil rights and antipoverty organizations. At one time during the 1960s, there was a much stronger alliance between these two groups. This alliance was exemplified by the subtitle of the 1963 March on Washington, "For Jobs and Freedom"; by Martin Luther King Jr.'s support for the Memphis sanitation workers in 1968 just before he was assassinated; and by King's establishment of a Poor People's campaign and Operation Breadbasket (affiliated with the Southern Christian Leadership Conference, created to respond to poverty related issues).[77] King's Poor People's campaign died shortly after his assassination in 1968. Operation Breadbasket fell apart after Jesse Jackson broke from this organization to form the People United to Save Humanity (PUSH) and the Rainbow Coalition. These organizations began to wane when Jackson ran for president in the 1980s. This alliance between antipoverty and civil rights organizations failed in the mid-1990s, as the voices of the poor and their supporters were silent during congressional hearings over the Personal Responsibility and Work Opportunity Act of 1996.[78]

The decline of organized labor is another sign of the weakening of the egalitarian coalition. Organized labor has historically been the bedrock of the New Deal coalition. It played a major role in the civil rights movement and supported equal opportunity policies. Labor power has historically balanced corporate/business power. The decline of labor is indicated by the dramatic decline of workers belonging to unions. At the peak of organized labor in 1954, 34.8 percent of all US wage and salary workers were members of a labor union. This figure declined to 20.1 percent in 1983 and to 11.3 percent in 2013.[79]

Evidence of splits within the civil rights coalition is another sign of the weakening of the egalitarian coalition. Tensions have emerged within the civil rights coalition over moral issues such as same-sex marriage and LGBT rights. These tensions were evident when the national office of the Southern Christian Leadership Conference threatened to fire Los Angeles chapter president Eric Lee because of his opposition to Proposition 8, the state of California's constitutional initiate that banned same-sex marriage. These tensions appeared again in the summer of 2012 just before the reelection of President Obama. Reverend William Owens, head of the Coalition of African American Pastors, headed an organization of more than 3,700 black ministers who opposed President Obama because of his support for same-sex marriage.[80]

The disintegration of the far left, the weakness of the left, the dissolution of antipoverty organizations, the weakening of organized labor, and splits within the civil rights coalition are all signs of the weakening of the egalitarian coalition. Moreover, the weakening of the left, the growing power of the business/corporate sector, and the increasing dependence of Democratic Party candidates on corporate contributions have added to a drift of this coalition to the right.

Conclusion

During the 1970s, the business and corporate sector emerged with a vengeance in reaction to several social movements that created the egalitarian coalition and the equal opportunity regime. The business and corporate sector formed alliances with the Christian fundamentalist groups to form a powerful conservative coalition. This coalition launched an assault on the equal opportunity regime in the 1980s. It continued its assault over the next two decades, hacking away at the public policies produced by the regime that had ameliorated racial oppression and reduced racial inequalities.

The egalitarian coalition struggled to sustain its regime, a struggle that continued into the twenty-first century and was a paradox of progress and regression. With the election of this nation's first black president, opposition to the egalitarian regime intensified. The conservative coalition pushed both political parties to the right. The Republican Party purged itself of its moderates and became more ideologically pure and more uncompromising. The Tea Party movement emerged and joined forces with the conservative coalition, making the reactionary movement more aggressive and relentless in its assault on equal opportunity programs and producing reactionary policy changes across a wide spectrum. As Chapters 5 and 6 will demonstrate, these changes began to reverse the progress of the 1960s and 1970s. They contributed to the rise of inequality; the growth in the black/white gap in wealth, income, and education; the formation of a less supportive and more exploitive welfare system; the establishment of a racially repressive criminal justice system; and the ascension of the minority voter suppression movement. These policy changes will be explored in the next few chapters.

Notes

1. For a good discussion of the conflict between the corporate/business sector and regulatory agencies during the late 1970s and early 1980s, see Susan Tolchin and Martin Tolchin, *Dismantling America: The Rush to Deregulate* (New York: Oxford University Press, 1983).

2. See Frank Baumgartner and Bryan Jones, *Agendas and Instability in American Politics* (Chicago: University of Chicago Press, 2009); Roger Cobb and Charles Elder, *Participation in American Politics: The Dynamics of Agenda Building* (Bal-

timore: Johns Hopkins University Press, 1983); Robert Dahl, *Who Governs? Democracy and Power in an American City* (New Haven: Yale University Press, 2005).

3. Elmer Schattschneider, *The Semi-sovereign People: A Realist's View of Democracy in America* (Forth Worth, TX: Harcourt Brace and Jovanovich College, 1975).

4. David Vogal, *Fluctuating Fortunes: The Political Power of Business in America* (New York: Basic Books, 1989); Hedrick Smith, *Who Stole the American Dream* (New York: Random House, 2012); Ian Lopez, *Dog Whistle Politics: How Coded Racial Appeals Have Reinvented Racism and Wrecked the Middle Class* (Oxford: Oxford University Press, 2014), pp. 64–65. Lopez provides an excellent discussion of the role of Louis Powell's memo to the US Chamber of Commerce in influencing the organization and political activism of the business sector, and the role of corporate leaders and corporate sponsored think tanks in setting the national policy agenda. He notes the impact of The Heritage Foundation's's *Mandate for Leadership,* a twenty-volume, 3,000 page report, setting the agenda for the Reagan administration. See *Mandate for Leadership*, Vol. 1 (Washington, DC: The Heritage Foundation, 1981).

5. Lopez, *Dog Whistle Politics.*

6. Thomas Edsall, *The New Politics of Inequality* (New York: W. W. Norton, 1984), p. 128.

7. *National Federation of Independent Business v. Sebelius,* Secretary of Health and Human Services 567 U.S. (2012), 132 S. Ct. 2566.

8. David Harvey, *A Brief History of Neoliberalism* (New York: Oxford University Press, 2007).

9. See the ALEC Exposed website for links to articles exposing ALEC, http://www.alecexposed.org/wiki/ALEC_Exposed. See also, Lisa Graves, "A CMD Special Report on ALEC's Funding and Spending," *PRWatch,* http://www.prwatch .org/news/2011/07/10887/cmd-special-report-alecs-funding-and-spending. For a list of corporate members and contributors, see ALEC Corporations, http://www.source watch.org/index.php?title=ALEC_Corporations.

10. Mary Bottari, "A Field Guide to the Koch O'Nut's Behind the Near Government Default," *PR Watch,* October 21, 2013, http://truth-out.org/news/item/1954-a -field-guide-to-the-koch-o-nuts-behind-the-near-government-default.

11. Robert Reich, *Super Capitalism: The Transformation of Business, Democracy, and Everyday Life* (New York: Vintage Books, 2008), p. 134.

12. Ibid., pp. 135–136.

13. Andy Kroll, "You Need to See These 5 Shocking Facts About the Money in the 2012 Election," *Mother Jones,* January 2013, http:/motherjones.com/mojo/2013 /01/2012.

14. Adam Lioz and Blair Bowie, "Billion-Dollar Democracy: The Unprecedented Role of Money in the 2012 Election" (New York: Demos/US PIRG, January 2013). www.demos.org/sites/default/files/publications/BillionDollarDemocracy_Demos.pdf.

15. William Hudson, *American Democracy in Peril: Seven Challenges to America's Future* (Chatham, NJ: Chatham House, 1995), p. 191.

16. Antonia Juhasz, *The Tyranny of Oil: The World's Most Powerful Industry— and What We Must Do to Stop It* (New York: HarperCollins, 2008), p. 280.

17. David Ricci, *The Transformation of American Politics: The New Washington and the Rise of Think Tank Politics* (New Haven: Yale University Press, 1993), p. 160.

18. William Greider, *Who Will Tell the People: The Betrayal of American Democracy* (New York: Touchstone, 1993), p. 48.

19. Richard Herrnstein and Charles Murray, *The Bell Curve: Intelligence and Class Structure in American Life* (New York: Simon and Schuster, 1996).

20. Charles Murray, *Losing Ground: American Social Policy, 1950–1980* (New York: New York University Press, 2003 [1984]).

21. Williamson Evers, *Victims' Rights, Restitution and Retribution* (Oakland, CA: Independent Institute, 1996).

22. Murray, *Losing Ground*; Gilder, *Wealth and Poverty*.

23. David Brock, *The Republican Noise Machine: Right-Wing Media and How It Corrupts Democracy* (New York: Crown, 2004), p. 174.

24. Ibid.

25. *Roe v. Wade* 410 U.S. 113.

26. Haynes Johnson, *Sleepwalking Through History: America in the Reagan Years* (New York: Anchor Books, 1992).

27. Thomas Edsall and Mary Edsall, *Chain Reaction: The Impact of Race, Rights, and Taxes on American Politics* (New York: W. W. Norton, 1992), pp. 131–132.

28. There are different versions of the story of the formation of the Moral Majority. Robert Billings formed the National Christian Action Coalition in 1978 in response to the IRS's attempt to revoke the tax-exempt status of Christian schools formed to promote racially segregated schools. Jerry Falwell, Paul Weyrich, and other conservative religious leaders, including Robert Billings, formed the Moral Majority in 1979. The Moral Majority consisted of four organizations: Moral Majority, Inc., Moral Majority Foundation, Moral Majority Legal Defense Fund, and Moral Majority Political Action Committee. See Robert Liebman and Robert Wuthnow, *The New Christian Right* (New York: Aldine Publishing Company, 1983). These organizations had disappeared by the end of the 1980s.

29. David Harvey, *A Brief History of Neoliberalism* (New York: Oxford University Press, 2007), p. 84.

30. Esther Kaplan, *With God on Their Side: George W. Bush and the Christian Right* (New York: New Press, 2004), p. 249.

31. Ibid., p. 86.

32. Ralph Reed, "Casting a Wider Net," *Policy Review* (Summer 1993): 31, quoted in Leonard Zeskind, *Blood and Politics: The History of the White National-ist Movement from the Margins to the Mainstream* (New York: Farrar, Straus and Giroux, 2009).

33. See Leonard Zeskind, *Blood and Politics*; Edsall and Edsall, *Chain Reaction*; and Chapter 1 in this volume.

34. Stanley Greenberg, Report on Democratic Defection (Washington, D.C.: The Analysis Group, April 15, 1985) pp. 13–18, 28. Quoted in Edsall and Edsall, *Chain Reaction*, p. 182.

35. Ibid, pp. 182–183.

36. Theda Skocpol and Vanessa Williamson, *The Tea Party and the Remaking of Republican Conservatism* (New York: Oxford University Press, 2012).

37. Christopher Parker and Matt Barreto, *Change They Can't Believe In: The Tea Party and Reactionary Politics* (Princeton: Prenceton University Press, 2013).

38. Ibid.

39. Skocpol and Williamson, *The Tea Party and the Remaking of Republican Conservatism*, p. 121.

40. Ibid.

41. Ibid.

42. Ibid.

43. Ibid., p. 103.

44. Ibid., pp. 104–105.

45. Information on ALEC's States and Nation Policy Summit can be found on its website, http://www.alec.org/snps/.

46. Lopez, *Dog Whistle Politics*; Parker and Barretto, *Change They Can't Believe In*; Skocpol and Williamson, *The Tea Party and the Remaking of Republican Conservatism*.

47. Ibid.

48. Ibid.

49. Christopher Parker, "WISE Multi-state survey of Race and Politics," University of Washington Institute for the Study of Ethnicity, Race and Sexuality, 2010, http://depts.washington.edu/uwiser/racepolitics.html.

50. Ibid.

51. Institute for Research and Education on Human Rights (IREHR), "Tea Party Nationalism: A Critical Examination of the Tea Party Movement and the Size, Scope and Focus of Its National Factions" (Kansas City, MO: IREHR, 2010).

52. Ibid.

53. Ibid.

54. Ibid., pp. 44–45.

55. Ibid.

56. Adam Gabbatt and Paul Harris, "Race Debate at CPAC Descends into Chaos After Slavery Slur: Panel Designed to Offer Ways for GOP to Connect with Minority Voters Falls Apart After Provocative Remarks from Attendee," *The Guardian* (March 15, 2013). http://www.theguardian.com/world/2013/mar/15/race-debate -cpac-slavery-slur.

57. Parker and Barreto, *Change They Can't Believe In*.

58. Jacob Hacker and Paul Pierson, *Winner-Take-All Politics: How Washington Made the Rich Richer and Turned Its Back on the Middle Class* (New York: Simon and Schuster, 2011), pp. 266–267.

59. Ibid.

60. Zack Ford, "The Family Leader's Marriage Pledge Says Unwed Slaves Preferable Parents for African-Americans," *ThinkProgress,* July 8, 2011. http://think progress.org/politics/2011/07/08/264264/the-family-leaders-marriage-pledge-says -unwed-slaves-preferable-parents-for-african-americans/.

61. See the Faith and Freedom Coalition website, http://ffcoalition.com.

62. See the Club for Growth website, http://www.clubforgrowth.org/about.

63. Quoted in Peter Peterson, *Running on Empty: How the Democratic and Republican Parties Are Bankrupting Our Future and What Americans Can Do About It* (New York: Picador, 2005).

64.Travis Waldron," Conservative Group Tells Republicans to Hold Hurricane Sandy Relief Package Hostage," *ThinkProgress*, December 17, 2012. http://think progress.org/economy/2012/12/17/1347781/club-for-growth-sandy-relief/.

65. Ibid.

66. Jonathan Martin, "Eric Cantor Defeated by David Brat, Tea Party Challenger, in G.O.P. Primary Upset," *New York Times*, June 10, 2014. http://www .nytimes.com/2014/06/11/politics/eric-cantor-loses-gop-primary.html.

67. Edsall and Edsall, *Chain Reaction*; Hacker and Pierson, *Winner-Take-All Politics;* Mike Lofgren, *The Party Is Over: How Republicans Went Crazy, Democrats Became Useless, and the Middle Class Got Shafted* (New York: Viking, 2011).

68. Francis Fox Piven, Lorraine C. Minnite, and Margaret Groarke, *Keeping Down the Black Vote: Race and the Demobilization of American Voters* (New York: New Press, W. W. Norton, 2009), p. 132.

69. Hacker and Pierson, *Winner-Take-All Politics*, pp. 226–227.

70. Gene Demby, "New Black Panther Party Leader Says Blacks are Under Siege in Tampa Before Republican Convention," *Huffington Post*, August 22, 2012. http://www.huffingtonpost.com/2012/08/22new-black-panther-party-a_n _1822132.html.

71. Mike Feinstein, "From the Birth of the U.S. Greens to the Birth of the Green Party in the U.S." Green Party website, http//:www.gp.org/birth-of-US-greens.

72. Occupy Wall Street website, http://www.occupywallst.org/about/.

73. Frances Fox Piven and Richard Cloward, *Poor People's Movements: Why They Succeed, How They Fail* (New York: Vintage Books, 1979), p. 296. Also see the "Black Past" website, blackpast.org/aah/national-welfare-rights-organization -1966-1975.

74. Darryl Fears and Carol Leonnig, "Duo in ACORN Video Say Effort Was Independent," *Washington Post*, September 18, 2009. http:www.washingtonpost .com/wp-dyn/content/article/2009/09/17 AR2009091704805.html.

75. From the Children's Defense Fund website, http://www.childrensdefense .org/about-us/our-history.

76. From the National Coalition for the Homeless website, http://national homeless.org/about-us/who-we-are.

77. Harvard Sitkoff, *The Struggle for Black Equality, 1954–1992* (New York: HarperCollins, 1993 [1981]).

78. Carter Wilson, "Policy Regimes and Policy Change," *Journal of Public Policy* 20, no. 3 (2000): 247–274.

79. Drew Desilver, "American Unions Membership Declines as Public Support Fluctuates," Pew Research Center, February 20, 2014. http://www.pewresearch .org/fat-tank/2014/02/20/for-american-unions-membership-trails. Data from the Congressional Research Service, http://digitalcommons.ilr.cornell.edu/cgi/viewcontent.cgi?; and the Bureau of Labor Statistics, http://bls.gov/news.release/union2 .nro.htm.

80. Penny Starr, "Black Pastors Oppose Gay 'Marriage' Warn Obama: We Will Not Stand with You," CNS News, July 31, 2012. http://www.cnsnews.com/news /article/black-pastors-oppose-gay-marriage-warn-obama-we-will-not-stand-with -you.

5

The Growth of Inequality

The ascension of the New Deal coalition in the 1930s, the rise of
the egalitarian coalition during the 1960s, and the dominance of a progressive political culture produced changes in public policies that reduced
inequalities, ameliorated racial oppression, and enhanced equal opportunities. The New Deal programs of the 1930s and the Great Society programs
of the 1960s helped all people, especially those most vulnerable: people
who were unemployed, people who were underemployed, people who were
older, people with disabilities, people who were homeless, and people who
were outcast. President Lyndon Johnson as well as the leaders of the civil
rights movement saw the War on Poverty as an effort to eliminate racism.

In the late 1970s and early 1980s, the conservative coalition began to
emerge and attack these programs. As the attack weakened these programs,
the rich got richer and the poor got poorer. Upward social mobility stagnated. Inequality of income and wealth increased, both within and between
racial groups. The black/white gap in wealth, income, and education, which
shrank during the 1970s, stagnated in the 1980s and increased in the first
decade of the twenty-first century, as the conservative coalition engaged in
an all-out attack on these programs.

Conservative critics insisted that New Deal programs had overregu-
lated banking and financial institutions, given labor unions too much
power, and created a welfare state that had done more harm than good and
that now threatened to bankrupt the federal government. These critics maintained that the Great Society programs of the 1960s destroyed families,
sapped individual initiatives, facilitated lifelong and intergenerational
dependency, and wasted billions of dollars by throwing money at poverty
with few results. Others claimed that inequality is the result of impersonal
global markets and markets that distribute wealth and income on the basis

125

of merit, hard work, initiative, talent, and education. By the twenty-first century, this criticism had become more strident and more alarmist. Black conservatives joined the chorus of critics who claimed that social programs constituted a new form of slavery and that young black men were more of a threat to themselves than racism is to them.

Like the Redeemer movement's attack on the Reconstruction programs, the attack on the New Deal and Great Society programs exaggerated their failures and ignored their successes. Indeed, the New Deal and Great Society programs alleviated poverty, reduced inequality, and expanded the middle class. These programs substantially ameliorated racial oppression. Whereas a great deal of the advancement of African Americans resulted from nongovernment factors such as the migration from rural areas and sharecropping work to urban areas and industrial jobs, the role of these public programs has been understated by the left and maligned by the right. New Deal programs raised the standard of living for blacks and whites. These policies instituted a minimum livable wage for black and white workers, allowed black and white workers to engage in collective bargaining for higher wages and better benefits, provided public jobs for blacks and whites, and established a social safety net with social insurance and social welfare programs. The Great Society programs reduced class and racial disparities in income, poverty, health care, employment, education, and housing. These programs provided fair treatment in criminal justice, expanded voting rights, and promoted equal opportunities in employment. These policies mattered for all classes and all racial groups, but they mattered most for the most vulnerable and disadvantaged in society. Public policies that prohibit racial discrimination in employment, housing, finance, education, and other areas contributed to improvements in the economic conditions of minorities. These policies gave racial minorities the opportunity to attain jobs commensurable with their skills and level of education and allowed them to obtain bank loans commensurate with their credit rating to purchase homes, remodel their property, or establish or expand their businesses. These policies improved the economic conditions of racial minorities.

New Deal programs strengthened and expanded the middle class, and redistributed wealth and income in a more equitable manner. Despite some failures, some waste, and some mismanagement, the equal opportunity policies of the 1960s lessened the severity of poverty, improved the economic conditions of those at the bottom, ameliorated racial oppression, and created equal opportunities.

The corporate-centered conservative coalition's attack on New Deal and equal opportunity programs contributed directly to the rise of inequality in general and of black/white inequality in particular. The deregulation in the financial sector, the rise of predatory lending, the recession of 2008, and the erosion of civil rights protections contributed to rising black/white gaps in income and wealth.

In this chapter, I summarize data and research on the growth of inequality. I first document the growth in inequality among all groups: between and among blacks, whites, and Hispanics. I then identify specific public policies associated with this growth. Finally, I investigate select public policies and examine the manner in which they have changed in ways that contributed to this growing inequality. In Chapter 6, I continue this discussion with an analysis of changes in social welfare, employment, and education programs.

Research on the Growth of Inequality

The Two Major Periods in the Growth of Inequality

Research on the growth of inequality in the United States identifies two major periods: the Great Compression, a period of shrinking inequality; and the Great Divergence, a period of growing inequality. Whereas economists differ on the precise timing of these periods, the Great Compression occurred roughly from 1941 to about 1979, which includes the era of the New Deal and equal opportunity policies. The Great Diversion occurred roughly from 1980 to the present. Robert Kuttner describes these two periods: "Between 1947 and 1973, the economy grew at an average annual rate of nearly 4 percent and became more equal in the process. In what the economist Claudia Goldin termed 'the Great Compression,' the incomes of the lowest fifth increased by 116 percent, while those of the top fifth grew by 85 percent; the middle also gained more than the top. But then, in a fundamental shift, the economy steadily became more unequal."[1] Kuttner points out the sharp contrast in median family income between the periods:

> The experience of the two postwar eras is a story of two entirely different societies. The first era was one of broadly shared gains. Between 1947 and 1973, productivity rose by 103.5 percent and median family income rose by almost exactly the same amount, 103.9 percent. But between 1973 and 2003 productivity rose by 71.3 percent, while median family income rose by just 21.0 percent. Factor out the extra hours worked by wives, and median family income rose scarcely at all.[2]

The common cliché that "the rising tide of the economy lifts all boats" was true for the period from 1947 to 1973. That is, when the economy expanded

Table 5.1 Percentage Change in Real Family Income, 1947–1979 and 1979–2009 (by quintile and top 5 percent)

Quintile	1947–1979	1979–2009
Top 5% ($200,000+)	+86	+72.7
Top 20% ($112,540+)	+99	+49.0
Fourth 20% ($73,338–$112,540)	+114	+2.7
Middle 20% ($47,914–$73,338)	+111	+11.3
Second 20% ($26,934–$47,914)	+100	+3.8
Bottom 20% (>$26,934)	+116	−7.4

Sources: Economic Policy Institute, US Census Bureau, "Historical Income Tables Families," table F-3 (income changes) and table F-1 (income ranges for 1979–2009); Economic Policy Institute, *The State of Working America 1994–95* (Armonk, NY: M. E. Sharpe, 1994), p. 37.

between 1947 and 1973, the incomes of all families increased. Table 5.1 shows that from 1947 to 1979, all five quintiles of income earners enjoyed more than a 99 percent increase in their incomes and that those of the lowest quintile experienced the largest gains of about 116 percent. However, this pattern of income distribution changed after 1979. As the economy expanded in the last two decades of the twentieth century and the first decade of the twenty-first century, the top 5 percent of income earners experienced the most dramatic increases in income. Indeed, the contrast between the top 5 percent and the bottom 20 percent best illustrates the extent of the growth of inequality. Between 1979 and 2009, the top 5 percent experienced a gain in income of 72.7 percent. The bottom 20 percent suffered a 7.4 percent decline in income. The rich got richer and the poor got poorer. By the end of the first decade of the twenty-first century, the common cliché about rising tides had become a common myth.

Figure 5.1 offers a clear and dramatic visual image of the growth of inequality in the United States. Inequality was high from 1917 to 1942, as measured by the share of income going to the top 10 percent of income earners. Just before the 1929 stock market crash, close to 50 percent of all income, including income from capital gains, went to the top 10 percent. From 1929 to 1941, the period of the Great Depression, income going to this group hovered between 43 percent and 49 percent. But as shown in Figure 5.1, the years from 1941 to 1979 marked the Great Compression. The share of income (including or excluding capital gains) going to the top

Figure 5.1 The Top 10 Percent Income Share, 1917–2008

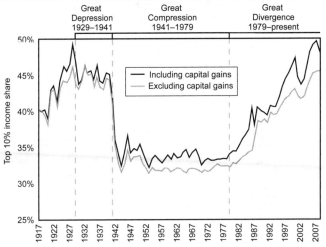

Sources: Emmanuel Saez, "Striking It Richer: The Evolution of Top Incomes in the United States," http://eml.berkeley.edu/~saez-ustopincomes-2008.pdf. Reprinted in Timothy Noah, "The Great Divergence, Part One: Introducing the Great Divergence," *Slate*, http://img.slate.com/media /3/100914/_NoahT_GreatDivergence.pdf.

10 percent plummeted to below 40 percent and stayed below 35 percent from 1950 to 1980. Inequality began to increase sharply during the 1980s. From 1987 to 1992, the percentage of income going to the top 10 percent increased from about 35 percent to 40 percent. This figure increased to around 45 percent by 1997. By 2006 and 2007, close to 50 percent of income earned went to the top 10 percent of income earners.

The Gini Coefficient

Social scientists and economists use a statistical index or figure called the Gini coefficient, index, or ratio to measure the degree of inequality in a society. This figure was developed by Italian statistician and sociologist, Corrado Gini. It is generally a number between zero and one. Zero represents perfect equality. That is, when the index is zero, then income will be equally distributed to everyone in society. An index of one represents absolute inequality. That is, when the index is one, then income would be totally concentrated in one person. That is, one person will get all of the income in society. Since perfect equality and absolute inequality do not exist in reality, the index would be somewhere between zero and one. Most societies or countries in the world have Gini coefficients somewhere between .22 and .65.

Table 5.2 Gini Ratios for All US Families, 1947–2011

Year	Gini Ratio
1947	.376
1952	.368
1957	.351
1962	.362
1967	.358
1972	.359
1977	.363
1982	.383
1987	.393
1992	.404
1997	.429
2002	.434
2005	.440
2006	.444
2007	.432
2008	.438
2009	.443
2010	.440
2011	.450

Source: US Census Bureau, *Current Population Survey, Annual Social and Economic Supplement* (Washington, DC: Government Printing Office, 2012).

US Gini coefficients from 1947 to 2011 are shown in Table 5.2. This summary corresponds to Figure 5.1. That is, the Gini coefficients illustrate a low level of inequality from 1947 to 1977, the period of the Great Compression, and a high level of inequality from 1982 to 2011, the era of the Great Divergence. The Gini coefficient was less than .379 from 1947 to 1977. It began to climb during the 1980s. It increased from .383 in 1982 to .404 by 1992. It increased every year up to 2006, where it reached .444. It fluctuated up and down over the next four years, and reached an all-time high of .450 by 2011.

The severity of this inequality is best seen within an international perspective. Gini coefficients for select countries are shown in Table 5.3. This table indicates that inequality varies widely among the countries of the world. Moreover, according to the 2014 Central Intelligence Agency's *World Factbook,* out of 141 countries, the United States is ranked forty-first.[3] Only forty countries have higher levels of inequality than the United States. All of these countries are developing nations with extreme levels of inequality.

Thus, inequality in the United States has reached a critical level: a level higher than any other developed nation, a level characteristic of politically

Table 5.3 Gini Coefficients for Select Countries, 2011

Country	Gini Coefficient
South Africa	.650
Brazil	.567
Mexico	.482
United States	.450
Russia	.422
China	.415
Japan	.376
France	.327
Canada	.321
Italy	.320
Spain	.320
Romania	.320
European Union	.304
Ireland	.293
Denmark	.290
Belgium	.280
Iceland	.280
Germany	.270
Finland	.267
Austria	.260
Czech Republic	.260
Norway	.250
Hungary	.247
Sweden	.230

Source: CIA, *World Factbook,* https://www.cia.gov/library/publications/the-world-factbook/.

polarized and unstable third world nations, and a level with severe consequences. Nobel Prize–winning economist Joseph Stiglitz explains some of the reasons for these consequences:

(c) And those at the bottom and in the middle are actually worse-off today than they were at the beginning of the century.

(d) Inequalities in wealth are even greater than inequalities in income.

(e) Inequalities are apparent not just in income but in a variety of other variables that reflect standards of living, such as insecurity and health.

(f) Life is particularly harsh at the bottom—and the recession made it much worse.

(g) There has been a hollowing out of the middle class.

(h) There is little income mobility—the notion of America as a land of opportunity is a myth.

(i) And America has more inequality than any other advanced industrialized country, it does less to correct these inequalities, and inequality is growing more than in many other countries.[4]

Metaracism and the Masking of Inequality

Stiglitz notes that the United States has the highest level of inequality of any developed industrialized country in the world, that the level of inequality in the United States is growing, and that the United States does little to ameliorate inequality and much to enable and facilitate it.[5] Moreover, this inequality has severe consequences. It diminishes the quality of the lives of people at the bottom and reduces their life chances. It erodes the middle class, and it obstructs social mobility.

Timothy Noah illustrates the disconnection between the reality of inequality and the perceptions of people in the United States:

> Economic inequality is less troubling if you live in a country where any child, no matter how humble his or her origins, can grow up to be president. In a survey of 27 nations conducted from 1998 and 2001, the country where the highest proportion agreed with the statement "people are rewarded for intelligence and skill" was, of course, the United States (69 percent). But when it comes to real as opposed to imagined social mobility, surveys find less in the United States than in much of (what we consider) the class-bound Old World. France, Germany, Sweden, Denmark, Spain—not to mention some newer nations like Canada and Australia—are all places where your chances of rising from the bottom are better than they are in the land of Horatio Alger's Ragged Dick.[6]

Racism has always functioned to mask extreme inequality; metaracism is no different in this regard. Metaracism masks the current extreme inequality three ways. First, like earlier forms of racism, metaracism racializes those at the bottom. Racism has done this since the time of slavery. Making slaves of blacks and constructing a racist culture that dehumanized slaves not only desensitized people to the suffering of the slaves, but it blinded them to extreme inequality. Racism served the same function in the South during the Jim Crow era as metaracism does today.

Second, metaracism shifts attention from inequality to racial minorities. Because of the prevalence of racial thinking in US culture, when the subject of inequality is raised people instinctively think about race. Nancy DiTomaso illustrates this point in her findings on the attitudes of white voters:

> Democratic Party talk about fairness, inequality, and expansion of opportunity is interpreted by many white voters as support for policies that benefit blacks at whites' expense. Republican Party talk about responsibility, getting government out of our lives or off our backs, and reducing taxes so that people can "keep their own money" is translated by many white voters into opposition to policies that are thought to benefit blacks. Politicians do not have to mention race explicitly. They can frame their messages in terms of value differences or morality.[7]

Third, the racial myth plays a part in this disconnection from the reality of inequality. This myth assumes that the United States is an open society and that anyone who works hard and acquires enough education can make his or her way up to the top. Indeed, anyone can become president of the United States, including a black child from a single-parent household. The corollary of this myth is that those at the bottom are generally racial minorities who do not work as hard, who do not value education, who expect stuff from the government, and who believe they are entitled to preferential treatment. Through the lens of this myth, inequality is not the problem; the culture of poverty and minority subcultures is presumed to be the problem. This racial myth defines the new metaracism. It assumes that inequality has driven the increase in black and Hispanic poverty. The presence of this myth makes it more difficult for people to see the growth of inequality or see it as a problem impacting everyone.

A careful examination of data presented in Tables 5.4, 5.5, and 5.6 explodes the racist myth and paints a more complex picture. Inequality impacts everyone in this country. Table 5.4 demonstrates that inequality has increased among whites, blacks, and Hispanics. Table 5.5 indicates that although poverty rates decreased among blacks from 1960 to 2000, these rates increased for both blacks and whites after 2000. Table 5.6 shows that between 1950 and 1975, the median income of blacks as a percentage of the median income of whites increased.

Inequality Has Increased Among Whites, Blacks, and Hispanics

Table 5.4 demonstrates quite clearly that as inequality was increasing for the nation as a whole, it was also increasing within each racial group, particularly among whites, blacks, and Hispanics. What is most striking about this table is that the level of inequality is higher among blacks and Hispanics than among whites. This high Gini coefficient is consistent with the view of growing class divisions among blacks.

Race and Poverty

Table 5.5 presents a summary of white, black, Hispanic, and total poverty rates from 1960 to 2011. It indicates that poverty rates declined substantially for all groups from 1960 to 1975. During this period, poverty rates for whites declined from 17.5 percent to 9.7 percent. For blacks, these rates declined from 53.5 percent to 31.3 percent.

This decline in poverty had ceased by 1975. Poverty rates increased for blacks and whites from 1975 to 1980. The rates went up and down throughout the 1980s, and continued to fluctuate during the 1990s. As shown in Table 5.5, between 1990 and 1995, poverty rates for whites increased from

Table 5.4 Gini Ratios for White, Black, and Hispanic Families

Year	White Ratio	Black Ratio	Hispanic Ratio
1965	.346	n/a	n/a
1970	.345	.388	n/a
1975	.349	.386	.371
1980	.353	.410	.386
1985	.378	.430	.406
1990	.384	.445	.416
1995	.409	.457	.439
2000	.425	.442	.444
2005	.430	.470	.427
2006	.434	.473	.439
2007	.422	.465	.435
2008	.428	.460	.447
2009	.431	.469	.457
2010	.430	.463	.455

Source: US Census Bureau, *Current Population Survey, Annual Social and Economic Supplement* (Washington, DC: Government Printing Office, 2012), www.census.gov/.
Note: n/a = data not available.

Table 5.5 Persons Below the Poverty Level by Race and Ethnicity, 1980–2011 (in percentage)

Year	All	Whites	Blacks	Hispanics
1960	22.2	17.5[a]	53.5[a]	n/a
1965	17.3	13.4[a]	43.0[a]	n/a
1970	12.6	9.9	33.5	n/a
1975	12.3	9.7	31.3	26.9
1980	13.0	10.2	32.5	25.7
1985	14.0	11.4	31.3	29.0
1990	13.5	10.7	31.9	28.1
1995	13.8	11.2	29.3	30.3
2000	11.3	9.5	22.5	21.5
2005	12.6	10.6	24.9	21.8
2006	12.3	10.3	24.3	20.6
2007	12.5	10.5	24.5	21.5
2008	13.2	11.2	24.7	23.2
2009	14.3	12.3	25.8	25.3
2010	15.1	13.0	27.4	26.5
2011	15.0	12.8	27.6	n/a

Source: US Census Bureau, *Current Population Survey, Annual Social and Economic Supplement 2012.*
Notes: a. Estimates.
n/a = data not available.

10.7 percent to 11.2 percent whereas these rates declined for blacks from 31.9 percent to 29.3 percent. From 1995 to 2000, poverty rates declined to a historic low of 9.5 percent for whites and an all-time low for blacks of 22.5 percent.

Throughout the first decade of the twenty-first century, poverty rates increased for whites, blacks, and Hispanics. This increase began before the recession. According to Table 5.5, white rates increased to 10.6 percent by 2005 and to a high of 13.0 percent by 2010. Black rates increased to 24.9 percent by 2005 and to 27.4 percent by 2010.

Race and Median Family Income

Black and white median family income from 1950 to 2009 and black family income as a percentage of white family income are shown in Tables 5.6 and 5.7. In terms of median family income, several trends emerge from these tables. First, black and white incomes nearly double over a twenty-year period from 1950 to 1970. This was an era of low inequality. However, between 1960 and 1965, whites gained at a marginally faster rate than blacks. Consequently, the black median income as a percentage of white median income declined slightly. However, the incomes of both blacks and whites increased dramatically between 1965 and 1970. Black median income increased from $18,317 to $23,384; white median income increased

Table 5.6 Black and White Median Family Income, 1950–1990 (in constant 1993 dollars)

Year	White Median Family Income	Black Median Family Income	Black Median Income as a % of White Income
1950	$20,656	$11,206	54.25
1960	$28,485	$15,768	55.36
1965	$33,263	$18,317	55.07
1970	$38,121	$23,384	61.34
1975	$38,322	$23,579	61.53
1980	$38,412	$22,226	57.86
1985	$39,149	$22,543	57.58
1990	$40,813	$23,685	58.03

Sources: Data from US Department of Commerce, Census Bureau, *Current Population Report,* Series P-60, "Money Income of Families and Persons in the United States," nos. 105 and 157, "Money Income of Households, Families, and Persons in the United States," nos. 162, 174, and 180, and "Money Income and Poverty Status in the United States," nos. 166 and 168; "Income, Poverty, and Valuation of Non-cash Benefits," no. 188. US Department of Labor, Bureau of Labor Statistics, Consumer Price Index; US Census Bureau, *Statistical Abstract of the United States: Net Median Household Worth by Race and Nationality* (Washington, DC: US Census Bureau).

Table 5.7 Black and White Median Family Income, 1990–2009 (in constant 2009 dollars)

Year	White Median Family Income	Black Median Family Income	Black Median Income as a % of White Income
1990	$56,771	$32,946	58.03
2000	$63,849	$40,547	63.50
2008	$65,000	$39,879	61.35
2009	$62,545	$38,409	61.41

Source: US Census Bureau, *Statistical Abstract of the United States: 2012* (Washington, DC: US Census Bureau, 2013).

from $33,263 to $38,121. Black median income increased marginally faster than white median income. Consequently, black median income as a percentage of white median income increased from 55.07 percent to 61.34 percent. Incidentally, this was the period of the height of the war on poverty. No doubt these programs played a role in increasing racial equality. The increase in incomes began to slow by the mid-1970s. Blacks began to lose ground by the late 1970s and early 1980s. Black median income as a percentage of white median income peaked in 1975 at 61.53 percent and declined to 57.58 percent by 1985. Blacks gained ground from 1990 to 2000 when black median family income increased from 58.03 percent to 63.5 percent. This progress was followed by another decade of stagnation. By 2008, black family income had fallen to 61.35 percent of white family income. Whereas this percentage represented an advancement over 1980, it fell below the 1975 percentage.

A summary of median net household worth by race for select years from 1984 to 2009 is shown in Table 5.8. The right column provides a ratio of white household worth to black household worth. That is, a ratio of 10 indicates that white worth is ten times black worth. The period from 1984 to 1995 indicates tremendous progress as the black/white gap in net worth declined. In 1984, white worth was twelve times black worth. By 1995 it was only seven times black worth. The recession of 2008 had a devastating impact on black household worth, as white median household worth jumped up to nineteen times black median household worth, a historic high.

Explaining Inequality

In addition to the racist myth, there are two other mistaken assumptions about the origins of the growth of inequality in the United States. The first is the assumption that inequality is the result of a trade-off between equality

Table 5.8 Median Net Worth of Households by Race and Nationality, 1984–2009 (in 2009 dollars)

Year	Median Net Worth			Ratio	
	White	Black	Hispanic	White:Black	White:Hispanic
1984	$76,951	$6,679	$9,660	12	8
1988	$75,403	$7,263	$9,624	10	8
1991	$68,203	$7,071	$8,209	10	8
1993	$67,327	$6,503	$6,853	10	10
1995	$68,520	$9,885	$10,139	7	7
2004	$111,313	$9,823	$15,188	11	7
2009	$92,000	$4,900	$6,325	19	15

Sources: Pew Research Center, *Wealth Gaps Rise to Record Highs Between Whites, Blacks, and Hispanics,* July 26, 2011, p. 29. For 2009, Pew Research Center, "Survey of Income and Program Participation," 2008 panel. For 1984–2004, US Census Bureau, *Current Population Reports* (Washington, DC: US Census Bureau).

and productivity. The second is the belief that inequality is the inevitable result of global economic forces over which no one has any control.

Contrary to the trade-off assumption, in the United States greater equality has been associated with more economic expansion and higher levels of productivity. From 1947 to 1973, productivity rose by 103.5 percent and family income increased by about 103.9 percent. The income of the lowest fifth increased the most (by about 116 percent) while the income of the top fifth increased by only 85 percent. In contrast, during the period from 1973 to 2003, productivity increased by only 71.3 percent and family income rose by only 21.9 percent.[8] The era of expanding equality was a period of higher productivity. The era of increasing inequality was a period of lower productivity. Contrary to the impersonal global economic forces belief, during the late 1970s industries in the more developed countries all over the world faced the same problems of increasing energy costs, inflation, and global competition but they responded differently. Countries like France, Germany, and Sweden and other Scandinavian countries responded to the crisis with policies that protected their working class and that created far less inequality than did the United States. Countries other than the United States responded to the crisis in ways that produced more equality without reducing productivity. Indeed, the United States—the industrial sector in conjunction with the state—responded to the economic crisis of the late 1970s in ways that produced far greater inequality. Timothy Noah argues that "Rust Belt manufacturers did face increased foreign competition. But they [economists] argue that the policies embraced, and the increased income inequality that resulted, were not inevitable. The proof, they argue, lies in the fact that other industrialized nations faced similar pressures but often embraced different policies, resulting in far less income inequality." [9]

Thomas Geoghegan makes this point largely by looking at Germany. He writes that German firms

> don't have the illusion that they can bust the unions, in the U.S. manner, as the prime way of competing with China and other countries. It's no accident that the social democracies Sweden, France, and Germany, which kept on paying high wages, now have more industry than the U.S. or the UK. . . . [T]hat's what the U.S. and the UK did: they smashed the unions, in the belief that they had to compete on cost. The result? They quickly ended up wrecking their industrial base. [10]

The growth of inequality in the United States has been strongly associated with Republican presidents, according to Larry Bartel:

> The narrowly economic focus of most previous studies of inequality has caused them to miss what may be the most important single influence on the changing U.S. income distribution over the past half-century—the contrasting policy choices of Democratic and Republican presidents. Under Republican administrations, real income growth for the lower- and middle-classes has consistently lagged well behind the income growth rate for the rich—and well behind the income growth rate for the lower and middle classes themselves under democratic administrations. [11]

Bartel provides a summary of the average annual pretax growth in income (accounting for inflation) from 1948 to 2005 under Democratic and Republican presidential administrations. Table 5.9 summarizes his findings. What is clear from this table is that all income groups experienced both higher annual income growth and greater equality under Democratic administrations than under Republican administrations. Under Democratic administrations, the 20th percentile group (the lower and lower middle) experienced an annual income growth of 2.64 percent, compared to an annual growth of only 0.43 percent under Republican administrations. Under Democratic administrations, the annual income growth of those in the 20th percentile was slightly higher than the annual income growth of those in the 95th percentile. In contrast and most strikingly, Table 5.9 indicates that under Republican administrations the annual income growth of the top 95th percentile was 1.90 percent annually, 4.4 times the annual income growth of the bottom 20th percentile of .43 percent.

Nobel Prize–winning economist Paul Krugman argues that contrary to conventional wisdom, the market did not produce the middle class. Instead, the middle class was produced by public policies that emerged during the Progressive period of the early twentieth century and the New Deal era of the 1930s. Krugman suggests that the current assault on these policies has

Table 5.9 Real Income Growth Rates by Income Level and Presidential Partisanship, 1948–2005

	All Presidents	Democratic Presidents	Republican Presidents	Partisan Differences
20th Percentile	1.42 (.50)	2.64 (.77)	0.43 (.61)	2.21 (.97)
40th Percentile	1.54 (.39)	2.46 (.58)	0.80 (.49)	1.67 (.75)
60th Percentile	1.73 (.34)	2.47 (.52)	1.13 (.43)	1.33 (.67)
80th Percentile	1.84 (.33)	2.38 (.50)	1.39 (.42)	0.99 (.65)
95th Percentile	2.00 (.38)	2.12 (.65)	1.90 (.46)	0.22 (.77)
N	58	26	32	58

Source: Timothy Noah, "The Great Divergence," *Slate,* September 2010, http://www.slate.com/media/3/100914_NoahT_GreatDivergence.pdf.

been an attack on the middle class. He notes that, in the past, industrial leaders were accountable to stockholders and governing boards. Today, they are driven by greed and there is no accountability to stockholders or boards. Corporate leaders have increased their earnings to outrageous levels, and the public has tolerated the increase. According to Krugman, the only thing that limits executive pay is the "outrage factor," "the concern that very high executive compensation will create a backlash from usually quiescent shareholders, workers, politicians, or the general public."[12] However, this outrage is gone. It was swept aside by a new political culture that suggests that greed is good and that inequality benefits all. Krugman explains,

> To the extent that this view is correct, soaring incomes at the top can be seen as a social and political, rather than narrowly economic phenomenon: high incomes shot up not because of an increased demand for talent but because a variety of factors caused the death of outrage. News organizations that might once have condemned lavishly paid executives lauded their business genius instead; politicians who might once have led populist denunciations of corporate fat cats sought to flatter the people who provide campaign contributions; unions that might once have walked out to protest giant executive bonuses had been crushed by years of union busting.[13]

The growth of inequality has been produced by major shifts in public policy. Jacob Hacker and Paul Pierson attribute the growth of inequality to the dramatic rise of corporate lobbyists and the drowning out of voices from the middle and lower middle classes.[14] Bartel explains the inequality in terms of institutional changes accompanying partisan shifts. Stiglitz identifies a number of specific changes in public policies and ideas that have contributed to the growth of inequality.[15] These changes have been occurring in a number of specific public policy areas that have had a devastating impact on both the middle class and racial minorities. Such policy areas include attacks on labor, shifts from Keynesian economics to supply-side economics, deregulation in the finance sector, and erosion of anti–employment discrimination regulations.

Public policy shifts in the areas of labor, economic, finance, employment, welfare, and education policy have contributed to the increase in nationwide and racial inequality. The following is a short summary of a few select policy shifts that help explain the growth in both inequality and racial inequality: labor, economic, financial, and employment policy. The next chapter will cover changes in welfare and education policy.

Labor Policy

The New Deal labor policies and the Treaty of Detroit contributed tremendously to the Great Compression. Labor policy and unionization had a ripple effect. Unionization among unskilled workers dramatically increased their wages and benefits and pushed them into the middle class. The wage increases among union workers impacted nonunion workers as well. Employers fearful of expanding unions raised wages to preempt unionization. The social norm that accompanied the Great Compression was that employers were expected to negotiate with employees, pay a decent wage, and treat them fairly. At the same time, employers were to maintain management prerogatives and control over business operations and organization. Public policies played a role in ensuring an equitable distribution of income by protecting workers' rights to organize and engage in collective bargaining, by enforcing fair labor practices, and by maintaining a decent and livable minimum wage during this period.

New Deal labor policies began to unraveled by 1981, the beginning of the Great Divergence. The groundwork for the unraveling was laid by the passage of the Taft-Hartley Act of 1947, which outlawed a number of practices that had made unions powerful during the 1930s: spontaneous or wildcat strikes, secondary boycotts, and common situs picketing. It banned closed shops, which was the practice of requiring union membership to qualify for a job. It prohibited strikes during the duration of a contract. After the contract expired, it required unions to give an eighty-day notice before going on strike. It forbade secondary and common situs strikes. That is, it prohibited union workers from boycotting an entire construction site because of a strike against one of the subcontracting companies, and it banned the practice of union workers refusing to cross a picket line to provide goods or services to an unaffiliated business that was the target of a strike from another union.

It allowed individual states to pass so-called right-to-work laws. These laws became popular in in the former Confederate states of the Deep South. Supporters claim that these laws protect the rights of workers, defend them against oppressive unions, and expand their individual liberties and freedoms, particularly the freedom to enter into individual contracts with employers. Opponents claim that the right to work is a form of double-speak, and that these laws do not guarantee jobs to workers who want to work. In the name of individual freedom and individual rights, these laws take away the rights of workers to engage in collective bargaining where, as an organization and more powerful than a single individual, they can demand higher wages, more benefits, and better working conditions or collectively go on strike and close the business down. Right-to-work laws allow employers to give individual workers a choice between lower wages, no benefits, and deplorable working conditions or no job at all. Right-to-work states have been successful in keeping unions out, wages low, workers weak, and poverty high.

In the late twentieth century, right-to-work states and antilabor countries aided manufacturing firms in launching an assault on unions. These firms engaged in a large movement to relocate production facilities to low-wage and antiunion areas, particularly in the Southern right-to-work states and in countries that have outlawed and suppressed labor unions. This movement decimated unions and depressed wages. It did much to expand poverty among low-skilled workers. The South remained a low-wage and high-poverty region, even though jobs grew.

Manufacturing firms have engaged in other tactics that have had the impact of weakening labor unions and reducing wages and benefits. For example, automobile manufacturers have relied more on outsourcing and a two-track personnel program. Outsourcing involves the use of smaller, nonunion, lower-wage companies to produce parts for the major automobile companies. A two-track personnel program entails collective bargaining agreements between the automobile companies and the United Automobile Workers (UAW), with a lower entry pay and job title for all new workers hired under the new contract.

The mass movement of manufacturing jobs out of the Rust Belt decimated Northern cities with the loss of millions of jobs in the apparel industry in New York state; in the automobile industry in Detroit and Flint, Michigan; and in the steel industry in Youngstown and Cleveland, Ohio, Gary, Indiana, and Pittsburgh, Pennsylvania. The exodus of manufacturing jobs contributed to the decline of the US manufacturing sector.

The federal government joined the assault on unions. Ronald Reagan, a former president of the Screen Actors Guild, had already earned a reputation for his hostility to unions during his term as governor of California. He promoted legislation to outlaw union organizing among California farmworkers. He enhanced his antiunion reputation as president by firing striking Professional Air Traffic Controller Organization (PATCO) workers; his administration decertified the PATCO union. Reagan appointed officials with antiunion track records to serve in labor policy positions in his administration such as Donald Dotson, a former labor relations specialist for Wheeling Pittsburgh Steel, a steel company with a reputation for firing union activists.

The assault on labor unions intensified with the recent expansion of right-to-work states and with the attack on public service unions. Indeed, Michigan, Ohio, Wisconsin, Florida, and a few other states have passed laws to restrict collective bargaining among public service workers. The governor of Wisconsin, Scott Walker, was caught on camera claiming that the law was enacted to deliberately divide public service unions from private sector unions and to eventually crush labor unions. The Wisconsin anti–public service union law was struck down by the state court. Unions mobilized in Ohio and were successful in getting that state's anti–public service union law. Michigan recently passed a right-to-work law, which has survived a court challenge. This law prohibits employers from deducting union dues and collective bargaining fees as a condition of employment.

Whereas most people would have been appalled by the assault on unions in the 1960s, most accept this assault today. Indeed, even during the 1970s, there was bipartisan support for the collective rights of workers. Richard Nixon campaigned for the support of labor unions. But this bipartisan support for labor ended with Reagan. This change in attitude is a function of the shift in the dominant political culture from one that accepted collective bargaining rights and freedom to one that defines the use of state power to suppress these rights as the new freedom and the new individualism.

Erosion of the Minimum Wage

The assault on labor includes an attack on minimum wages. The real value of the federal minimum wage has declined since the era of the Great Compression. Table 5.10 provides a summary of the minimum wage in current dollars and in constant dollars (1996 dollars, controlling for increases in the Consumer Price Index). The constant dollar figure indicates the real value of the minimum wage. As Table 5.10 indicates, throughout the decades of the 1950s, 1960s, and 1970s, the period of the Great Compression, the real value remained well above $5.00. Indeed, from 1964 to 1978, it remained above $6.30. Its peak constant value was $7.21 in 1968.

The real value of the minimum wage began to fall at the beginning of the Great Divergence period. As shown in Table 5.10 it fell steadily, from $6.38 in 1978 to $5.90 in 1980. By the end of Reagan's first term in 1984, it had fall to $5.06; by the end of his second term in 1988, it had reached an all-time low of $4.44. The real value of the minimum wage remained well below $5.00 from 1988 to 2008. The current value of the minimum wage

Table 5.10 Minimum Wage, 1956–2012 (1996 dollars)

Year	Current Dollars	Constant Dollars
1956	1.00	5.77
1958	1.00	5.43
1960	1.00	5.30
1962	1.15	5.97
1964	1.25	6.33
1966	1.25	6.05
1968	1.60	7.21
1970	1.60	6.47
1972	1.60	6.01
1974	2.00	6.37
1976	2.30	6.34
1978	2.65	6.38
1980	3.10	5.90
1982	3.35	5.78
1984	3.35	5.06
1986	3.35	4.80
1988	3.35	4.44
1990	3.80	4.56
1992	4.25	4.75
1994	4.25	4.50
1996	4.75	4.75
1998	5.15	4.96
2000	5.15	4.69
2002	5.15	4.49
2004	5.15	4.28
2006	5.15	4.04
2008	6.55	4.77
2010	7.25	5.22
2012	7.25	4.97

Source: US Department of Labor, http//www.dol.gov/esa/whd/flsa/; Information Please Database, Pearson Education, 2012, http://www.infoplease.com/ipa/A0774473.html.

was raised to $7.25 by 2010; in 1996 dollars, the real value of this minimum wage would be $5.22. But by 2012, the real value of the minimum wage had fallen to $4.97. President Barack Obama has been campaigning to increase the minimum wage.

The low minimum wage has been strongly associated with high levels of inequality and high percentages of the working poor. Opponents of raising the minimum wage claim that it is a job killer. Nevertheless, considerable research refutes this notion. If anything, raising the minimum wage lowers inequality and poverty. However, the idea that it kills jobs has become increasingly popular in the age of the Great Divergence.

The Shift from Keynesian to Neoliberal Economic Policy

Both Republican and Democratic presidents during the Great Compression supported Keynesian economic policies. Keynesian economic theory emerged in response to the Great Depression. John Maynard Keynes claimed that direct government transfer payments to individuals had a multiplier effect; that is, it has a much more profound economic stimulus effect than tax cuts. He believed that budget cuts retard the expansion of the economy. Keynes advocated expanding government spending during recessions, any spending to get money into the hands of potential consumers. When consumers get more money, they spend more money. When they spend more money, retail companies sell more goods. As these companies sell more goods, they hire more people. As they hire more people, more people work and spend more money to buy more things. As people buy more and as retailers sell more, manufacturers produce more goods. As manufacturers produce more, they hire more people. Thus, the increase in government spending stimulates the economy.[16]

Whereas Keynes claimed that it did not make any difference how the government got money in the hands of consumers, more constructive ways include spending on infrastructure and services. Spending on infrastructure means hiring people to repair deteriorating streets, sewers, bridges, levies, and highways. Spending money on services means allocating more money to state and local governments to hire more teachers, teacher aides, firefighters, police officers, and others.[17]

The Keynesian approach to economic policy came under assault during the 1980s when Reagan campaigned on an anti-Keynesian platform. Whereas Keynes advocated increasing federal spending during a recession, Reagan was committed to decreasing spending and advocated a supply-side approach that called for reduced taxes and less regulations. Today, most Republican politicians are anti-Keynesians insofar as they advocate cutting budgets during recessions. Rather than advocating increased spending, they advocate tax cuts with the expectation of cutting more spending.

The Keynesian approach to economic policies contributes to more equitable patterns of distributing incomes. The supply-side approach contributes to greater inequality. Today, most pundits and political leaders strongly advocate a balance between budget cuts and tax increases, an anti-Keynesian approach. Republican leaders speak loudly and convincingly about how tax cuts and balanced budgets will stimulate the economy.

Rules of the Market and Rent Seeking

A number of economists have explained the increase in inequality in terms of changes in the rules of the market. Many suggest that there is no such thing as anarchy in the market or a market free of government rules. Governments provide rules for fair competition that allow the open market to work. Changing these rules have distributional consequences. For example, changing rules to allow for the formation of monopolies undermines competitive markets and allows for price gouging, which shifts more money and wealth from consumers to the monopolistic firm. In Chapter 3, I mentioned some of these rule changes in the discussion of neoliberalism. Stiglitz refers to changes in rules or policies that help the rich get richer at the expense of everyone else as "rent seeking."[18] There are countless examples of rent seeking: changes in bankruptcy laws that protect the financial sector and creditors, but allow for the liquidation of retirement funds and the dissolution of labor unions; multi-billion-dollar subsidies to major corporations in the forms of free land, tax breaks, and grants; intellectual property laws that favor corporations at the expense of inventors; regulations of corporate governance that allow CEOs to select their own boards, unilaterally raise their own salaries, and cut workers' pay without regard to performance; no-risk student loans with interest rates higher than market value that favor finance corporations and disadvantage college students; and many others. David Cay Johnston explains how the increased political activism of the business and corporate sector contributed to the types of changes in public policies and the rules of the market that shifted income and wealth from the 99 percent to the 1 percent:

> To business owners and executives, the cost of campaign contributions is chump change compared to the benefits of shortchanging pension plans. . . .
> Stock options are just one part of a bigger scandal about how executives of publicly traded companies are paid. Congress and the courts have made it harder and harder for unions to organize, which inherently reduces the bargaining power of workers to get more for their labor. But Congress and agencies like the SEC [Securities and Exchange Commission] have allowed the compensation of executives to become a rigged game. Among other abuses, directors who sit on the committees that decide how much to pay a chief executive often have indirect interests. And, of course, they have a direct interest in keeping their seat on the board.
> Because of law rules, the very top executives at companies are now paid with little regard for their performance. Just look at the mediocre to disastrous performances put in by the top acolytes of Jack Welch, the retired chairman of General Electric, when they moved to other companies. The poster boy for being overpaid for negative performance is Bob Nardelli. He left GE for Home Depot, which turned out to be the best thing that could have happened for its major competitor, Lowe's.
> Nardelli, like many executives, paid attention to numbers, not people. For a while the numbers like the total sales and profits improved, but that is not sustainable without good people. Those helpful Home Depot workers who can show you tricks, and warn you about do-it-yourself mistakes that can ruin your new fixture. . . . To make the bottom line look better, Nardelli cut many of them from full-time to part-time. The best of them migrated over to the competition.[19]

Deregulation of the Finance Sector and Growth of Inequality

Deregulation played a direct and major role in the near collapse of the financial sector, in making the rich richer and the poor poorer, and in precipitating the explosion in the black/white gap in wealth. The explanation for this is simple. The regulations that were put in place to prevent the collapse of the finance sector, to ensure fair and equitable treatment of consumers, and to prevent racial discrimination were either weakened or dismantled.

What made the connection between deregulation and inequality complicated was the fact that there were two sets of regulations: the New Deal regulations and the equal opportunity regulations. Some of the New Deal regulations were dismantled first while the equal opportunity regulations were strengthened during the 1990s. The strengthening of the equal opportunity regulations explains why the black/white wealth gap declined during that decade. These regulations weakened during the first decade of the twenty-first century. The weakening of these regulations and the collapse of the housing market explain why the black/white wealth gap expanded.

The first set of regulations emerged out of the New Deal era. They included banking regulations such as the Glass-Steagall Act of 1933, which mandated the separation of commercial banks from financial institutions. Because commercial banks held family savings deposits guaranteed by the Federal Depository Insurance Corporation (FDIC), these banks could not engage in the wild and risky types of investment practices of financial institutions. There were a host of other banking restrictions: restrictions that prohibited the merging of banks and insurance companies, and that prevented the emergence of superbanks too big to fail. The Federal Reserve Board restricted the amount of money that banks could use for loans or investments.

The New Deal regulations were dismantled through legislative and administrative changes. Congress passed the Gramm-Leah Act of 1999 which repealed the Glass-Steagall Act and allowed the merger of commercial banks, financial institutions, and insurance companies. Congress enacted the Commodity Futures Modernization Act of 2000, which deregulated commodity trading. The Federal Reserve Board under the leadership of Alan Greenspan was committed to further relaxing of banking regulations, particularly the restrictions on the amount of money available for loans and investments. Nomi Prins documents how the deregulation of commodity trading and banking stimulated a dramatic rise in mortgage-backed securities (MBS) and collateralized debt obligations (CDOs)—the bundling of loans, particularly mortgage and credit card loans, and the buying and trading of these bundles. The trading of CDOs went from a billion-dollar enterprise to a multitrillion-dollar enterprise that brought the banking industry to the brink of collapse.[20]

The Community Reinvestment Act of 1977

The other set of regulations were antidiscrimination and consumer protection laws. They included the Community Reinvestment Act of 1977, which prohibited redlining, required banks to make annual reports, and encouraged them to act responsibly. Redlining involved the banking practice of drawing a red line around a black neighborhood and refusing to grant loans to the residents who ordinarily would qualify for a loan. It was racial discrimination pure and simple, as individuals with good credit ratings were denied loans for the simple reason that they lived in a black neighborhood. Redlining was considered a serious problem not just because it discriminated against blacks, but because it contributed to the decline of entire black communities and increased the black/white gap in homeownership.

When banks took deposits from families in black neighborhoods and invested in suburban neighborhoods, the banks were exploiting black communities. They were using the wealth from the black community to enhance property values in suburban communities. At the same time, by denying inner-city communities rehabilitation loans, the banks were accelerating the decline of these communities. When banks refused to grant loans for purchasing or renovating homes in black communities, they contributed to the decline in housing values and the increase black/white gap in homeownership.

The Community Reinvestment Act did not require banks to make high-risk loans or to grant loans to blacks with weak credit ratings. It simply prohibited banks from engaging in racial discrimination. It encouraged banks to act responsibly and to reinvest where feasible in the neighborhoods in which they were chartered. Loans made under the act had a low default rate. Community Reinvestment Act regulations were strengthened under the Bill Clinton administration during the 1990s. According to the Financial Crisis Inquiry Commission,

> In 1993, President Bill Clinton asked regulators to improve banks' CRA (Community Reinvestment Act) performance while responding to industry complaints that the regulatory review process for compliance was too burdensome and too subjective. In 1995, the Federal Office of Thrift Supervision . . . , Office of Comptroller of Currency . . . , and Federal Deposit Insurance Corporation . . . issued regulations shift[ing] focus from the efforts that banks made to comply with the CRA to their actual results. Regulators and community advocates could now point to objective, observable numbers that measured banks' compliance with the law.[21]

In other words, the Clinton administration relaxed regulations in financial areas, but increased regulations to prevent racial discrimination in finance. It appears that these antidiscrimination regulations had real impacts. The implementation of the Community Reinvestment Act was having a positive impact on black communities at little cost to the banks, although many banks continued to complain about the reporting requirements.

Predatory Lending Practices

Concerns emerged over predatory lending practices during the 1990s. Whereas there is no established definition of *predatory lending,* the Government Accountability Office (GAO) offers this definition:

> Predatory lending is an umbrella term that is generally used to describe cases in which a broker or originating lender takes unfair advantage of a borrower, often through deception, fraud, or manipulation to make a loan that contains terms that are disadvantageous to the borrower. While there is no universally accepted definition, predatory lending is associated with the following loan characteristics and lending practices:
>
> *Excessive fees.* Abusive loans may include fees that greatly exceed the amounts justified by the costs of the services provided and the credit and interest rate risks involved. Lenders may add these fees to the loan amounts rather than requiring payment up front, so the borrowers may not know the exact amount of the fees they are paying.
>
> *Excessive interests rates.* Mortgage interest rates can legitimately vary based on the characteristics of borrowers (such as creditworthiness) and of the loans themselves. However, in some cases, lenders may charge interest rates that far exceed what would be justified by any risk-based pricing calculation, or lenders may "steer" a borrower with an excellent credit record to a higher-rate loan intended for borrowers with poor credit histories.
>
> *Single-premium credit insurance.* Credit insurance is a loan product that repays the lender should the borrower die or become disabled. In the case of single-premium credit insurance, the full premium is paid all at once—by being added to the amount financed in the loan—rather than on a monthly basis. . . .
>
> *Lending without regard to ability to repay.* Loans may be made without regard to a borrower's ability to repay the loan. In these cases, the loan is approved based on the value of the asset (the home) that is used as collateral. In particularly egregious cases, monthly loan payments have equaled or exceeded the borrower's total monthly income. Such lending can quickly lead to foreclosure of the property.
>
> *Loan flipping.* Mortgage originators may refinance borrowers' loans repeatedly in a short period of time without any economic gain for the borrower. With each successive refinancing, these originators charge high fees that "strip" borrowers' equity in their homes.
>
> *Fraud and deception.* Predatory lenders may perpetrate outright fraud through actions such as inflating property appraisals and doctoring loan applications and settlement documents. Lenders may also deceive borrowers by using "bait and switch" tactics that mislead borrowers about the terms of their loan. Unscrupulous lenders may fail to disclose items as required by law or in other ways may take advantage of borrowers' lack of financial sophistication.

Repayment penalties. Penalties for prepaying a loan are not necessarily abusive, but predatory lenders may use them to trap borrowers in high-cost loans.

Balloon payments. Loans with balloon payments are structured so that monthly payments are lower but one large payment (the balloon payment) is due when the loan matures. Predatory loans may contain a balloon payment that the borrower is unlikely to be able to afford, resulting in foreclosure or refinancing with additional high costs and fees. Sometimes, lenders market a low monthly payment without adequate disclosure of the balloon payment.[22]

Steering, the practice of pushing high-interest subprime loans of borrowers who qualify for prime-interest loans, has been a major problem with predatory lending that has attracted little public attention. Summarizing this problem, Lisa Keyfetz says: "In particular several studies indicate that about 50% of all subprime borrowers could have obtained loans in the prime market based on their credit status, but were steered toward higher interest rate loans by deceptive [lenders]."[23]

After conducting a series of hearings, the US Department of Housing and Urban Development published a report on predatory lending in 1998. The report documented testimony from borrowers and consumer protection organizations. Many of the cases were particularly egregious and disturbing. In one case a 72-year-old homeowner "paid $23,000 in upfront finance charges on a $150,000 second mortgage."

In response to cases of predatory lending Congress passed the Home Ownership and Equity Protection Act of 1994. This law amended the Truth in Lending Act of 1968 and applied it to mortgage institutions. It set limits on interests and fees on secondary mortgages and prohibited fraudulent and deceptive practices in the subprime lending market. It left enforcement up to the Federal Reserve Board, Federal Trade Commission, and state attorneys general. This law was ineffective in preventing predatory lending because the Federal Reserve Board under Greenspan was reluctant to engage in aggressive enforcement. Some action was taken by attorneys general from several states who worked together. The Federal Trade Commission and Justice Department targeted a couple of the most egregious violators. However, the fines and penalties were so small that they had little impact on curbing predatory lending. Moreover, the involvement of Wall Street firms like Lehman Brothers made predatory lending enormously profitable with little risk.

A Predatory Lending Feeding Frenzy

Predatory lending emerged with a vengeance during the first decade of the twenty-first century. A 2004 GAO report notes that enforcement agencies had prosecuted some companies during the 1990s. The Federal Trade Commission had prosecuted several companies for engaging in fraud and deceptive trade practices and violating the Truth in Lending Act and the Home Ownership and Equity Protection Act, and the Justice Department prosecuted a company for deliberately targeting black communities. State attorneys general from several states worked together to prosecute several businesses that engaged in substantial predatory lending. Also noted by the GAO were many cases of predatory lending during the 1990s and many prosecutions, but these cases did not involve the banks and were probably exceptional.

Investigative journalist Michael Hudson portrays a different picture—one based on a thorough review of documents and reports and extensive interviews of victims, perpetrators, and prosecutors. He demonstrates that predatory lending was not incidental or disconnected from Wall Street. It was institutionalized and well connected to Wall Street. The few prosecutions of the 1990s involved such minor penalties that, rather than discouraging predatory lending, they encouraged it.[24]

By the twenty-first century, predatory lending rose to a level that can best be described as massive and systematic. Predatory lending institutions targeted minority communities in a feeding frenzy, like piranhas of the Amazon target fresh meat in the river. Company presidents and CEOs did not encourage predatory lending. They created organizational cultures that promoted predatory lending. They hired young inexperienced salespeople and trained them in a culture where making money—as much money as possible—was the only thing that mattered; where ethics, principles, and compassion had no place. According to Hudson, all aspects of predatory lending thrived in this culture:

> In the first years of the twenty-first century, AmeriQuest Mortgage unleashed an army of salespeople on America. They numbered in the thousands. They were young, hungry, and relentless in their drive to sell loans and earn big commissions. One AmeriQuest manager summed things up in an e-mail to his sales force: "We are all here to make as much . . . money as possible. Bottom line. Nothing else Matters."[25]

Hudson demonstrates that predatory lending involved all of the practices mentioned in the GAO report and more: that it was financed by Wall Street; that it was enabled by trivial government fines, weak enforcement of the law, and the deregulatory movement; that loan companies deliberately and systematically targeted minority communities in a substantial way; and that it was a multitrillion-dollar enterprise driven by greed. Loan officers and salespeople were driven to make as much money as possible. They were required by their superiors to engage in predatory lending. They made their money, not by helping people purchases homes, but by campaigning to get as many people to take out as many loans for as much money as they could and by charging the highest interest rates they could get away with. In their frenzy to make money, they operated with few restraints and few scruples. They engaged in fraudulent and deceptive behavior. Sometimes they forged borrowers' signatures; other times they added pages to the loan documents with conditions borrowers never agreed to or signed off on. They routinely told customers to ignore truth in lending summaries and routinely lied about fees and interest rates. They steered people with high credit ratings—people who ordinarily would qualify for prime loans—into subprime loans because the salespeople could make more money off the subprime loans that had higher fees and higher interests. They promoted home equity loans. They claimed that people could get easy loans to pay off credit card debts, make home repairs, or consolidate bills. They charged exorbitant fees and excessively high interest rates. They commonly made false claims that refinancing the second time would lower interest rates and monthly payments. It generally led to higher loan fees, higher interest rates, and higher monthly payments. Loan companies made enough money from the loan fees and interest rates to compensate for any losses from defaults.

Wall Street played a major role in predatory lending. Because loan companies could bundle the loans into mortgage-based securities, they could sell the loans on Wall Street. By purchasing the mortgages, Wall Street provided the mortgage and finance companies with an endless supply of money to make the loans. Both Wall Street and the loan companies profited. Hudson explains,

> Wall Street bankers and investors flocked to the loans produced by BNC, AmeriQuest, and other subprime operators; the steep fees and interest rates extracted from borrowers allowed the bankers to charge fat commissions for packaging the securities and provided generous yields for investors who purchased them. Up-front fees on subprime loans totaled thousands of dollars. Interest rates often started out deceptively low—perhaps at 7 or 8 percent—but they almost always adjusted upward, rising to 10 percent, 12 percent, and beyond. When their rates spiked, borrowers' monthly payments increased, too, often climbing by hundreds of dollars. Borrowers who tried to escape overpriced loans by refinancing into another mortgage usually found themselves paying thousands of dollars more in backend fees—"prepayment penalties" that punished them for paying off their loans early.[26]

Hudson recounts several examples of high fees and high interest rates. One story involved Carolyn Pittman who in 1993 purchased a home with her husband in Jacksonville, Florida, through a Federal Housing Administration (FHA) loan with notes of $500 a month. Her husband died in 1998 and, after she had a heart attack a few years later,

> a salesman from AmeriQuest Mortgage's Coral Springs office caught her on the phone and assured her he could ease her worries. He said AmeriQuest would help her out by lowering her interest rate and her monthly payments. She signed the papers in August 2001. Only later did she discover that the

loan wasn't what she'd been promised. Her interest rate jumped from a fixed 8.43 percent on the FHA loan to a variable rate that started at nearly 11 percent and could climb much higher. The loan also was packed with more than $7,000 in up-front fees, roughly 10 percent of the loan amount.[27]

Another case involved Bernae Gunderson, a paralegal in Saint Paul, Minnesota, who paid $13,000 in upfront fees on a $46,172 loan. Gunderson recorded her conversation with the branch manager of the loan company when she called for an explanation about the fees. Hudson describes that telephone conversation:

> When Bernae saw the $13,000 figure on the loan documents, she had called FAMCO [Fiduciary Asset Management Company] to figure out what it meant. She asked the manager to confirm that they'd borrowed just under $47,000.
> "Right, your amount financed is $46,172," the manager assured her. "That doesn't change."
> "Right, right," she continued. "And then the thirteen thousand goes on top of that? And then interest is charged?"
> "No, no, no," he said.
> His answer . . . should have been "yes, yes, yes." The $13,000 was paid on top of the $46,172, bringing the Gundersons' mortgage debt to around $60,000 and requiring them to pay interest on the fees each year for the life of the loan. The fees accounted for roughly 22 percent of the couple's house note.[28]

Hudson points out that predatory lending was never about assisting young minority couples with low credit ratings to secure a loan to purchase their first home. It was about loan officers targeting vulnerable minorities and engaging in deception, false advertisement, and outright lies to get them to take out home equity loans:

> Loan officers focused on selling refinancing to people who were already Long Beach customers or especially, folks who had mortgages with consumer-finance companies. Geographically, Rouch and his fellow loan officers at the Long Beach Boulevard branch in downtown Long Beach targeted South Central Los Angeles—Compton, Bell Gardens, Lawndale, Inglewood, and other communities where home owners tended to be elderly, African American, and Hispanic.[29]

Hudson insists that the targeting of minority communities was massive and systematic:

> The Justice Department's statistical analysis exposed a pattern: minorities, women, and older borrowers were indeed more likely to pay higher prices, even when compared to whites, men, and younger borrowers with similar credit histories. African-American women over the age of fifty-five who borrowed directly from Long Beach were 2.6 times more likely than younger

white men to receive loans with up-front fees and points totaling 6 percent or more of their loan amount. Older black women who got a Long Beach loan through an outside mortgage broker were nearly four times more likely than younger white men to pay higher points and fees. . . . "When you've got an elderly black woman, you can pretty much sell them anything you want."[30]

Long Beach officials deliberately targeted minority neighborhoods and elderly black women because they believed they could get away with charging higher prices for their loans without question. Long Beach loan officers deliberately led borrowers to believe they were getting a better deal than they would with a conventional loan. These loan officers focused on monthly payments and avoided discussions on points, fees, and interest rates.[31]

Predatory lending and the recession of 2008 decimated black communities. Because a large proportion of black wealth was in homeownership, the collapse of the housing market and massive foreclosures also had a tremendous impact on black communities. Thus, predatory lending, the recession of 2008, and the collapse of the housing market contributed directly to the explosion of the black/white wealth and income gaps. The recession also contributed to the rise of poverty.

Contrary to conservative political leaders, the Community Reinvestment Act of 1977 did not contribute to the rise of the foreclosures. This common conservative talking point was another myth. The act was effective in preventing racial discrimination in the bank home loan industry. The aggressive enforcement of this act during the 1990s under the Clinton administration contributed to the closing of the black/white gap in wealth. Indeed, variations in the promotion of antidiscrimination laws played a major role in explaining why economic conditions of minorities continued to improve during the 1990s, but reversed during the 2000s.

The growth of the black/white gap in wealth in the first decade of the twenty-first century was not a function of impersonal economic trends. It was the result of the systematic and deliberate targeting of black communities for predatory lending practices. These practices included excessive loan fees and interest rates, balloon payments, fraud, and loan flipping.

The storm of mass foreclosures and predatory lending has subsided. The end of the recession, the expansion of jobs, and the scarcity of money from Wall Street that fed this storm all helped to calm it. Congress played a role as well by passing the Dodd-Frank Wall Street Reform and Consumer Protection Act of 2010. Title XIV of this act, Mortgage Reform and Anti-Predatory Lending, addresses the problem of predatory lending. This title does not outlaw predatory lending. Rather, it contains provisions that restrict select aspects of predatory lending. The act allows loan officers to earn money based on the size of loans, but not on the size of the fees for the loan. It prohibits repayment penalties, balloon payments, and lending without ability to pay. It also strengthens the enforcement of laws already in place like truth in lending, limits on excessive interest rates, and fraud.

The Erosion of Anti–Employment Discrimination Protection

At first glance, it seems that conditions improved for blacks during both eras: the Great Compression and the Great Divergence. Indeed, some conservatives insist that as inequality expanded during the Great Divergence, conditions improved for blacks. However, a more careful analysis of the Great Divergence period indicates that blacks experienced ups and downs: stagnation during the 1980s, progress during the 1990s, and regression during the 2000s. These ups and downs are consistent with variations in civil rights policies. Indeed, anti–employment discrimination policies expanded from 1965–1978, stagnated during the 1980s, expanded during the 1990s, and regressed during the 2000s.

Creation of the Equal Employment Opportunity Commission and expansion in the 1965–1978 period. Anti–employment discrimination policies were established in 1964 with the enactment of Title VII of the Civil Rights Act and the creation of the Equal Employment Opportunity Commission (EEOC). In its first few years of operation, the EEOC pursued racial discrimination in employment on a case-by-case basis, but this approach was inefficient and ineffective. The agency quickly became overwhelmed by the volume of complaints. Initially, it ignored institutionalized practices that had profound racially discriminatory impacts such as the use of personality tests based on preference that had nothing to do with the job but excluded minorities and the recruitment of the friends, neighbors, and relatives of those already employed. These practices excluded minorities and reproduced racially and ethnically homogenous workplaces. In the 1970s, the EEOC issued regulations requiring firms to advertise in both local and minority newspapers and to state that they are an affirmative action/equal opportunity employer and encourage minorities and women to apply. The commission became more aggressive and targeted entire industries. It began pursuing class action suits. The Supreme Court enhanced the EEOC's powers in *Griggs v. Duke Power Company* by acknowledging institutional discrimination and by establishing the Griggs principle: if a hiring standard or practice has a discriminatory impact, then the company must demonstrate that the standard or practice is related to job performance.[32] If the standard has a discriminatory impact and is unrelated to job performance, then it violates the law. By the early 1970s, discriminatory practices had declined. Private companies became more aggressive in hiring minorities. Business, universities, and the federal government expanded affirmative action programs.

As mentioned earlier in the book, President Nixon established the Philadelphia Plan, which was conceived to stimulate economic development in the black community. This plan became law when Congress passed the Public Works Act of 1976, which set aside 10 percent of the dollar value of federal contracts for minority contractors. State and local governments followed suit in the early 1980s. As more aggressive affirmative action practices emerged during this period, the economic position of blacks improved immensely. The black/white gap in income declined.

EEOC policy in the 1980s. Minority progress stagnated during the 1980s and into the early 1990s. The black/white gap in income increased. The Reagan administration weakened antidiscrimination and civil rights programs, and the Supreme Court weakened affirmative action and civil rights programs in a number of cases.

President Reagan had a reputation for his opposition to civil rights, and had opposed the Civil Rights Act of 1964 and the Voting Rights Act of 1965. Although he had signed the Voting Rights Act of 1982, he vetoed the Civil Rights Restoration Act of 1988, which was passed over his veto.

Reagan appointed Clarence Thomas, who later became a Supreme Court justice, to serve as director of the EEOC from 1982 to 1990. Because of budget cuts, the EEOC lost personnel during the 1980s. This loss of personnel weakened the ability of the EEOC to pursue antidiscrimination cases. As Table 5.11 indicates, the number of staff members declined measurably, from a high of 3,390 in 1980 to 2,853 in 1990. The EEOC staff continued to decline until 1992.

The Supreme Court hacked away at affirmative action. In the 1978 *University of California Board of Regents v. Bakke* decision, the Court struck down the affirmative action plan for the University of California Medical School at Davis.[33] This plan had set aside 16 out of 100 seats for special admission students who were not admitted through the regular admissions process. Whereas the Court struck down this plan as too expansive and harmful to nonminorities, it used the Harvard Law School plan as a model affirmative action plan. According to the Harvard University affirmative action plan, the admission board never set aside any seats for minorities. Instead, the board looked at the file of each applicant and considered a wide range of factors in making an admission decision, which included test scores and grade point averages. They would also include subjective factors, such as the applicant's interest in medicine, the region, and economic state of the areas from which the applicant came and the area in which the applicant planned to practice. Because the Harvard plan was committed to producing a diverse medical class, admission boards would also consider the race and gender of the applicant. The Bakke decision both weakened and reaffirmed the legality of affirmative action. In the 1989 *City*

Table 5.11 Equal Employment Opportunity Commission Staffing History, 1980–2012

Year	Staff
1980	3,390
1981	3,358
1982	3,166
1983	3,084
1984	3,044
1985	3,097
1986	3,017
1987	2,941
1988	3,168
1989	2,970
1990	2,853
1991	2,796
1992	2,791
1993	2,831
1994	2,832
1995	2,813
1996	2,676
1997	2,586
1998	2,544
1999	2,593
2000	2,852
2001	2,704
2002	2,783
2003	2,617
2004	2,462
2005	2,441
2006	2,246
2007	2,158
2008	2,176
2009	2,192
2010	2,385
2011	2,505
2012	2,346

Source: US Equal Employment Opportunity Commissions, http://www1.eeoc.gov/eeoc/plan /budgetandstaffing.cfm.

of Richmond v. J.A. Croson decision, the Court struck down the minority business enterprise set-aside program of the city of Richmond, Virginia.[34] Richmond required prime contractors to set-aside 30 percent of the dollar value of a city construction contract for minority businesses. This plan was enacted in response to the fact that less than one-half of 1 percent of city contracts went to minority contractors, even though half of the city population was black. The Court decided that the fact that few city contracts were going to minority contractors was not proof of discrimination. Cities needed to collect relevant data on the types of minority businesses operating in the city, on whether those businesses had the capacity to handle city contracts, and on whether there was evidence of past discrimination. In the same year in *Ward Cove v. Atonio,* the Supreme Court struck down the Griggs principle.[35] And in the 1995 *Adarand v. Pena* decision, the Court ended the federal set-aside program.[36]

EEOC policy in the 1990s. The 1990s saw both more aggressive EEOC enforcement and improvements in the economic status of blacks. Three factors contributed to changes in enforcement: the passage of the Civil Rights Act of 1991, the expansion of EEOC staff, and the commitment of Clinton administration. George H. W. Bush had initially vetoed the Civil Rights Act and called it a quota bill. He signed the bill after Congress included language that expressly prohibited the use of quotas. The act expanded civil rights protections and responded to several Supreme Court decisions that had eroded these protections, most notably *Ward Cove v. Atonio,* which had struck down the Griggs principle. The bill restored the Griggs principle. As shown in Table 5.11, the EEOC staff expanded from 2,791 in 1992 to 2,852 by 2000.

EEOC policy in the 2000s to present. Both the president and the Supreme Court were hostile to civil rights policies in the first decade of the twenty-first century. President George W. Bush publicly opposed affirmative action and appointed officials that had defended corporations against EEOC suits. As can be seen in Table 5.11, staffing for the EEOC continued to decline from 2,852 in 2000 to 2,158 in 2007. The EEOC had a staff of 2,176 by the end of his second term in 2008.

Conditions improved somewhat under the Obama administration. The EEOC staff increased gradually, from 2,176 in 2008 to about 2,505 in 2011, but declined to 2,346 in 2012. Nevertheless, the EEOC began to challenge business decisions that excluded people with police records because this exclusion had a substantial impact on black employment because black men tend to have higher arrest and conviction rates.

Persisting Discrimination

Racial discrimination in the job market never disappeared. It persisted, as shown by studies such as the one conducted by Joleen Kirschenman and Kathryn Neckerman, which is based on 185 extensive interviews with employers in the Chicago area. Their findings revealed evidence of continuing racial discrimination in the Chicago job market. However, there was less discrimination involving jobs that required higher levels of skills, training, or education. In the higher-skilled or professional job areas, employers hired the best qualified candidates regardless of race or gender. In the lower-skilled areas, some employers considered homogeneous workplaces more manageable. In some cases, employers preferred job candidates from the suburbs over candidates from the inner city. They were more likely to use race, class, or residency as a surrogate measure of work ethics.[37] Overall, a few employers admitted to having engaged in direct discrimination. Discrimination varied within the job market. Employers of low-skilled production facilities or warehouses tended to prefer white workers because they felt there would be less conflict among workers. Employers in higher-skilled more professional areas tended to be more committed to diversity and there was little evidence of direct discrimination in these areas.

For example, Kirschenman and Neckerman found evidence of consumer discrimination that impacted employment discrimination in suburban restaurants. In other words, there were cases of racial discrimination among restaurant owners who believed that their customers preferred all white waitresses, such as one who commented: "I have all white waitresses for a very basic reason. My clientele is 95 percent white. I simply wouldn't last very long if I had some black waitresses out there."[38]

A study conducted by the Urban Institute also found some degree of racial discrimination in the Washington, DC, area. The institute hired black and white college students and trained them to conduct interviews for the study. They paired each team of black and white students so that everything matched in terms of their resume and qualifications, except their race. The study found a small degree of discrimination at the interview stage: black men were slightly less likely to be called back and hired.[39]

Devah Prager conducted a study of the resumes of black and white volunteers applying for entry-level jobs. Black and white applicants claimed to have had the same level of education and experience. The only difference was that white applicants claimed to have served eighteen months in prison for felony possession of cocaine and black applicants had clean police records. Prager was surprised when more white "criminals" were offered jobs than African American men who'd stayed on the straight and narrow.[40] Prager concluded that racial stereotypes and assumptions about black males was a stronger factor in determining hiring decisions than criminal records.

Critics of Prager's study claim that the white applicants with admitted felony convictions may have been more charismatic and impressive than the black applicants during the interview stage. Economist Joshua Holland cited a study by Marianne Bertrand and Sendhil Mullainathan that tested this hypothesis. They matched hundreds of resumes in terms of experience, education, and quality. They assigned white- and black-sounding names to the resumes. Among the matched resumes, the only difference was the sound of the name. Resumes with white-sounding names were more likely to get calls than resumes with black-sounding names. Among the resumes with higher levels of education and experience, "applicants who sounded white were 30 percent more likely to elicit a callback, but those whose names sounded black were only 9 percent more likely to get a response."[41]

The data on education and unemployment presented in Table 5.12 indicate two points. First, the unemployment rate among blacks is almost double the unemployment rate for whites. The 2010 white unemployment rate was 7.5 compared to a black rate of 13.4. Second, black unemployment rates remain higher than white rates even when education rates are taken into consideration. In fact, the unemployment rate of blacks with a high school diploma is higher than the unemployment rate of whites who never completed high school. The 2010 unemployment rate for blacks with a high school diploma was 15.8 compared to an unemployment rate of 13.9 for whites with less than a high school degree. Moreover, the unemployment rate for blacks with some college is higher than the unemployment rates for whites with only a high school degree. For this same year, the unemployment rate for blacks with some college was 12.4, substantially higher than the unemployment rate of 9.5 for whites with just a high school degree.

Table 5.12 Unemployment Rates by Race and Education, 2000–2010

		Whites			
Year	Total	Less than High School	High School	Some College	More than Bachelor's Degree
2000	2.6	5.6	2.9	2.4	1.6
2005	3.5	6.5	4.0	3.4	2.1
2010	7.5	13.9	9.5	7.6	4.3

		Blacks			
Year	Total	Less than High School	High School	Some College	More than Bachelor's Degree
2000	5.4	10.7	6.4	4.0	2.5
2005	7.5	14.4	8.5	6.9	3.5
2010	13.4	22.5	15.8	12.4	7.9

Source: US Census Bureau, *Statistical Abstracts of the United States: 2012* (Washington, DC: US Census Bureau, 2013).

Conclusion

Within the past few years, inequality increased, the black/white gap in income and wealth expanded, and the economic conditions of minorities deteriorated. These changes corresponded to shifts in power, the dominant ideology, and public policies. They correlated with the rise of the corporate-centered conservative coalition and the resurgence of neoliberalism and neoconservatism. These power and ideological shifts were associated with changes in labor, economic, financial, and employment policies.

As noted in Chapter 2, many manufacturing corporations moved their production facilities to areas of low wages and no unions. This movement contributed to the decline of unions and the decline of the incomes of work-ers in the manufacturing sector. And these changes contributed to the rise of inequality in the United States. Also noted in Chapter 2, the out-migration of the black middle class from inner city areas combined with the decline in the manufacturing sector in the United States contributed to the increase in concentrated urban poverty.

Public policy changes also contributed to the increase in inequality. Deregulation of the finance sector enabled the rise of predatory lending, which disproportionately impacted black communities (these communities were targeted). Predatory lending, the collapse of the housing bubble, and the weakening of the economy in 2008 contributed to massive housing foreclosures. These foreclosures had a devastating impact on black wealth, contributing to increases in racial disparities in wealth. The weakening of antidiscrimination laws enabled the rise in labor market discrimination. No doubt this discrimination partially explains the disparities in unemployment rates even when education is taken in consideration. Higher black unem-ployment rates are also related to the isolation of blacks in inner cities. Deregulation of the finance sector allowed for the rise of predatory lending, which decimated black communities and contributed to the increase in the black/white gap in wealth. The reduction of the EEOC staff weakened the enforcement of antidiscrimination laws.

There was nothing good or natural about the growth of inequality in the United States. It had nothing to do with merit. It did not produce a healthier economy. It did not benefit blacks. It benefited only the dominant class. It contributed to the expansion of concentrated poverty, both black and white.

This has become the reality of the new metaracism. Although the black middle class has expanded, the real value of wages has declined, inequal-ity has become more extreme, poverty has become more concentrated, and racial disparities in wealth and income have increased. Racial discrimina-tion in labor markets has persisted. The rules of the market and public poli-cies have changed to favor the dominant class. Nevertheless, this society, led by the conservative coalition, has racialized the poor and the lower classes and changed political rhetoric in ways that have normalized extreme inequality, desensitized Americans to poverty, and convinced most American that we live in a postracial/post–civil rights society.

Metaracism did not produce the inequality. However, like earlier forms of racism, it played a role in normalizing and legitimizing inequality. As a result of the presence of metaracism, most people in the United States associate discussions of inequality with discussions of race and poverty. As a result of the success of the conservative coalition and reactionary political culture, public policies that built the middle class have weakened and the real earning power of the majority of workers has declined. People have responded to this decline in earning power by working longer hours, by having more family members who work, and by borrowing more money. Indeed, personal debt has skyrocketed within the past two decades. Despite the fact that the rise of inequality impacts the majority of people negatively, it remains a marginal issue precisely because of two myths.

The first myth is that extreme inequality is the result of an economic system that distributes income and wealth on the basis of merit, giving more to those who have higher levels of education, who work harder, who are more innovative, and who take greater risks. This myth is belied by the fact that members of the top 1 percent have not experienced an increase in education, hard work, innovation, or risk taking commensurate with their increase in wealth and income.

The second myth is that those at the bottom and those who complain the most about inequality are those who have less education, who work less, and who contribute less to society. They are likely to be people of color. This myth is belied by the fact that members of the bottom 99 percent have indeed worked longer hours and attained higher levels of education without the commensurate increases in earning power. Moreover, most are not people of color.

Metaracism had its most devastating impact in the areas of antipoverty policies. As Chapter 6 will demonstrate, metaracism played a major role in racializing antipoverty programs, desensitizing society to the plight of the poor, and generating hostility toward programs to assist poor women with children. As the conservative coalition attacked these programs, metaracism acted as an accelerant, enlarging the fire of opposition to welfare programs, especially when these programs were defined as benefiting primarily black recipients.

Notes

1. Robert Kuttner, *The Squandering of America: How the Failure of Our Politics Undermines Our Prosperity* (New York: Alfred A. Knopf, 2007), p. 16.

2. Ibid.

3. Central Intelligence Agency, "Country Comparison: Distribution of Family Income—Gini Index," in *The World FactBook.* https://www.cia.gov/library/publications/the-world-factbook/rankorder/2172rank.html.

4. Joseph Stiglitz, *The Price of Inequality* (New York: W. W. Norton, 2012), p. 4.

5. Ibid.

6. Timothy Noah, "The Great Divergence: What's Causing America's Growing Inequality," *Slate,* September 2010. http://www.slate.com/media/3/100914 _NoahT_GreatDivergence.pdf. See also Timothy Noah, *The Great Divergence: America's Growing Inequality Crisis and What We Can Do About It* (New York: Bloomsbury, 2012).

7. Nancy DiTomaso, *The American Non-Dilemma: Racial Equality Without Racism* (New York: Russell Sage Foundation, 2013), p. 307.

8. Robert Kuttner, *The Squandering of America: How the Failure of Our Politics Undermines Our Prosperity* (New York: Alfred A. Knopf, 2007), p. 21.

9. Noah, "The Great Divergence." See also Robert Kuttner, *Economic Illusions: False Choices Between Prosperity and Social Justice* (Boston: Houghton, Mifflin, 1987).

10. Thomas Geoghegan, *Were You Born On the Wrong Continent? How the European Model Can Help You Get A Life* (New York: New Press, 2010).

11. Larry Bartel, *Unequal Democracy: The Political Economy of the New Gilded Age* (Princeton: Princeton University Press, 2008).

12. Paul Krugman, *The Conscience of a Libe*ral (New York: W. W. Norton, 2007), p. 145.

13. Ibid.

14. Jacob Hacker and Paul Pierson. *Winner-Take-All: How Washington Made the Rich Richer and Turned Its Back on the Middle Class* (New York: Simon and Schuster, 2011).

15. Stiglitz, *The Price of Inequality.*

16. John Maynard Keynes, *General Theory of Employment, Interest and Money* (New York: Harcourt, Brace and World, 1962).

17. Ibid.; Robert Lekachman, *The Age of Keynes* (New York: Vintage Books, 1968).

18. Stiglitz, *The Price of Inequality,* p. 39.

19. David Cay Johnston, *Free Lunch: How the Wealthiest Americans Enrich Themselves at the Government's Expense (And Stick You with the Bill)* (New York: Penguin Books, 2007), p. 269.

20. Nomi Prins, *It Takes a Pillage: Behind the Bailouts, Bonuses and Backroom Deals from Washington to Wall Street* (Hoboken, NJ: John Wiley, 2009).

21. Financial Crisis Inquiry Commission, *The Financial Crisis Inquiry Report: Final Report of the National Commission on the Causes of the Financial and Economic Crisis in the United States* (Seattle: Pacific Publishing Studio, 2011), p. 73.

22. Government Accountability Office (GAO), *Consumer Protection: Federal and State Agencies Face Challenges in Combating Predatory Lending* (Washington, DC: Government Printing Office, 2004), p. 19.

23. Lisa Keyfetz, "Home Ownership and Equity Protection Act of 1994: Extending Liability for Predatory Subprime Loans to Secondary Mortgage Market Participants," 2005. http://www.kttlaw.com/images/news/keyfetz_home_ownership_equity _protection.pdf.

24. Michael Hudson, *The Monster: How a Gang of Predatory Lenders and Wall Street Bankers Fleeced America and Spawned a Global Crisis* (New York: Times Books, Henry Holt, 2010).

25. Ibid., p. 7.

26. Ibid., p. 9.

27. Ibid., p. 4

28. Ibid., p. 139.

29. Ibid.

30. Ibid., p. 88.

31. Ibid.

32. *Griggs v. Duke Power Company,* 401 U.S. 424 (1971)

33. *University of California Board of Regents v. Bakke,* 438 U.S. 265 (1978).

34. *Richmond, Virginia v. J.A. Croson Co.,* 488 U.S. 469 (1989).

35. *Ward Cove v. Atonio,* 490 U.S. 642 (1989).

36. *Adarand v. Pena,* 515 U.S. 200 (1995).

37. Joleen Kirschenman and Kathryn Neckerman, "We'd Love to Hire Them, But . . . : The Meaning of Race for Employers," in Paul Peterson and Christopher Jencks, eds., *The Urban Underclass* (Washington, DC: Brookings Institution, 1991).

38. Ibid., p. 220.

39. Arch Parsons, "Racial Bias Widespread in Study of Job Applicants," *Baltimore Sun,* May 15, 1991. http://articles.baltimoresun.com/1991-05-15/news/1991 135075_1job-applicants-study-of-job-black-job.

40. Devah Prager, *Marked: Race, Crime, and Finding Work in an Era of Mass Incarceration* (Chicago: University of Chicago Press, 2007).

41. Joshua Holland, *The Fifteen Biggest Lies About the Economy: And Everything Else the Right Doesn't Want You to Know About Taxes* (Hoboken, NJ: John Wiley, 2010), p. 223. The study was reported by Bootie Cosgrove-Mather, "Black Names and Resume Burden?" CBS News, September 29, 2003.

6

The Assault on Social Welfare and Education Policies

In Chapter 5, I examined the emergence of both general and racial inequality and illustrated the role of public policy changes in producing both forms of inequality. I continue that discussion in this chapter by examining changes in social welfare and education policies that exacerbated racial inequality. I focus on the role of metaracism and the conservative coalition in producing and enabling these policy changes.

Federal social welfare programs emerged in the United States with the passage of the Social Security Act of 1935 and as part of the New Deal. They expanded with the War on Poverty and Great Society era during the 1960s. Social welfare programs have functioned as a safety net; lessened the severity of poverty; reduced the number of cases of hunger, malnutrition, and disease related to poverty; and stabilized the economy by putting money and in-kind benefits (e.g., health care, energy assistance, food stamps, housing assistance) in the hands of people who are unemployed, who are older, who have disabilities, who are poor, or who are the working poor. These programs have operated as part of a system that raised the bargaining power of labor by reducing the desperation of the unemployed and by allowing people to choose better jobs, with better wages and less abusive bosses. All of this has helped to improve the quality of life in the United States.

As these programs expanded to include racial minorities, they functioned to ameliorate racial oppression. They expanded opportunities, contributed to the rise of upward mobility, improved the quality of the lives of poor children, reduced the number of cases of cognitive impairment resulting from malnutrition (which substantially reduced the number of cases of long-term dependency on government programs), and helped poor children move out of poverty.

Despite the criticism of welfare, these programs were never overly generous. Compared to programs in other developed countries, the United States has a minimalist welfare state. In fact, programs in the United States have lifted a smaller percentage of its poor out of poverty than programs of other developed countries: less than 30 percent of poor children have been brought out of poverty in the United States compared to well above 50 percent in Canada and Great Britain; over 60 percent in Ireland, Italy, and Spain; and more than 70 percent in the Scandinavian countries.[1]

Political scientists have historically explained this minimalist welfare state in terms of American exceptionalism: the strong commitment to limited government and individualism that emerged out of the American Revolution and the absence of a feudal past, which allegedly precluded the formation of a strong national bureaucracy required for a comprehensive welfare state.[2] However, the use of federal powers to implement the Alien and Sedition Acts of 1798; the building of the transcontinental railroad during the 1860s with the use of federal engineers, federal bonds, federal land grants, and federal planning; the formation of a strong veterans' pension program after the Civil War; and the creation of federal departments such as interior and agriculture all belie the exceptionalism argument.

A number of other scholars completely reject this notion of US exceptionalism. They place the blame for the minimalist welfare state squarely on the persistence of racism. Jill Quadagno points to the persistence of racial prejudices as the strongest obstacle to the construction of a comprehensive social welfare state:

> Among the distinctive features of American state formation, none is more salient than the failure to extend full citizenship to African Americans. It is this characteristic, more than any other, that has influenced the development of the welfare state. The battle over racial equality delayed national welfare programs, limited the reach of the federal bureaucracy, and shaped the structure of the programs that were developed in the two key periods—the New Deal and the War on Poverty.[3]

Other scholars point to the role of controlling images, racist-sexist-classist stereotypes, demeaning portrayals, and negative narratives that apply almost exclusively to African American women as factors that have obstructed the development of a more comprehensive, European-style welfare system in the United States.[4] Four controlling images or racist-sexist stereotypes stand out in the welfare literature. The first stereotype is that of the black woman matriarch. This image emerged as part of the backlash of the civil rights movement.[5] It characterizes the black woman as loud, overly aggressive, domineering, emasculating, overly dependent, and irresponsible. The second stereotype is the Jezebel/hoochie-mama, a hypersexual, sexually aggressive, promiscuous, calculating, conniving, manipulative, and materialistic woman. The teenage version of this stereotype is the young black woman who has babies to get welfare money. The third image is the welfare queen, discussed in earlier chapters. This is the image of the large black woman who drives a Cadillac, has several fake names, and receives multiple welfare checks.[6] The fourth stereotype is that of the crack addict—a wild, hyperactive, erratic addict who would do anything for crack cocaine, including providing sexual favors. These racist-sexist images of black women provoke moral outrage, disgust, and hostility. They contributed to the political movement to criminalize the poor and welfare recipients and to dismantle the welfare system or replace it with a more controlling and punitive system designed to change the bad values of women dependent on welfare.[7] These stereotypes explain the minimalist US welfare state. They also contributed to the criminalization of the poor.

In her book *Killing the Black Body*, Dorothy Roberts presents many legal case studies involving efforts to criminalize and prosecute poor women based on the image of the black crack addict. She demonstrates that although alcohol abuse was more prevalent among middle class women and did far more damage to the brains of unborn children, prosecutors in several states engaged in a campaign to target poor pregnant women entering state hospitals to deliver their babies. These hospitals tested women for cocaine and contacted the local policy to report women who tested positive. She documented several cases in which police arrested mothers while they were still in the hospital and social services took newborn infants from their mothers. Most of these mothers were charged with and convicted of child endangerment for exposing their infants to cocaine.[8] Many of these convictions were overturned on grounds that state legislators never intended for child endangerment laws to be applied to mothers in this manner. A more recent article by Ana Ortiz and Laura Briggs demonstrates how these racist-sexist images of crack-addicted mothers continue to shape and drive the formation and administration of welfare and child welfare policies.[9] They point out that these images influenced agencies to engage in a more punitive approach to child welfare, becoming more aggressive in taking black children out of poor black families and placing them in foster care.

This tendency of social welfare agencies to criminalize the black poor and engage in excessive exercises of police powers contradicts the notion of a US exceptionalism supporting limited government. This tendency is more consistent with policies shaped by racial and sexist stereotypes. It is also consistent with the persistence of a racialized political culture that not only defines blacks as binary opposites of whites, but defines citizenship, national identity, and political community in racially exclusionary ways. Indeed, this is precisely the point made by Roberts in a review of two major books on the history of social welfare programs:

From the Founding of the nation, the meaning of American citizenship has rested on the denial of citizenship to Blacks living within its borders. Citizenship had to be defined so as to account for the anomaly of slavery existing in a republic founded on a radical commitment to liberty, equality, and natural rights. . . . The development of a republican conception of citizenship corresponded with the Founders' insistence on a white national identity. Republicanism defined the requirements for citizenship in opposition to the traits whites attributed to Blacks. Whites rationalized Blacks exclusion from citizenship by claiming that Blacks lacked the capacity for rational thought, independence, and self-control that was essential for self-governance.[10]

Roberts insists that throughout US history, African Americans struggled to be included as citizens and were treated like subjects. She argues that a social welfare system for citizens would focus on the defects in the economy, whereas a social welfare system for subjects focuses on the imagined defects of the recipients.[11] Such a system would put more resources into controlling, regulating, and changing the behavior of recipients. She notes that prior to the establishment of a federal welfare program for mothers, state-level government programs were created for mothers. "Black single mothers, on the other hand, were simply excluded. The first maternalist welfare legislation was intended for white mothers only: Administrators either failed to establish programs in locations with large black populations or distributed benefits according to standards that disqualified black mothers."[12] The exclusion of blacks from the initial state-level welfare system was consistent with blacks exclusion from the political community and their status as second-class citizens. When the national system was established, this exclusion continued. The welfare system for mothers was restricted to prevent blacks from benefitting from the program. The exclusion of blacks from the welfare system tended to enhance the social status and privileges of whites. Roberts concludes:

Our deficient welfare state is "the price the nation still pays for failing to fully incorporate African Americans into the national community." Privileged racial identity gives whites a powerful incentive to leave the existing social order intact. White Americans therefore have been unwilling to create social programs that will facilitate Blacks' full citizenship, even when those programs would benefit whites. Even white workers' and feminist movements have compromised their most radical dreams in order to strike political bargains that sacrifice the rights of Blacks.[13]

Roberts also notes that state benefit programs for widows, the precursor for Aid to Families with Dependent Children (AFDC), now Temporary Assistance for Needy Families (TANF), routinely excluded black women.[14]

The Social Security Act of 1935 excluded agricultural and domestic laborers from social security and Aid to Dependent Children. In 1935, "about 65 percent of gainfully employed African Americans worked in the agricultural or domestic sectors of the economy,"[15] and were thus excluded from these programs. In parts of the Deep South, the rate of exclusion was between 70 percent and 80 percent.[16] Reporting on her study of the rise of welfare, Linda Gordon claims, "These exclusions were deliberate and mainly racially motivated, as Congress was then controlled by wealthy southern Democrats who were determined to block the possibility of a welfare system allowing blacks freedom to reject extremely low-wage and exploitive jobs as agricultural laborers and domestic servants."[17]

Racial barriers to AFDC were removed by the end of the 1960s. These barriers were broken down by the passage of the Civil Rights Act of 1964, which prohibited racial discrimination in federal programs by liberalizing administrative changes in the program and by Supreme Court decisions that struck down restrictive administrative rules such as the "man in the house" rule.[18] The number of needy black families receiving AFDC benefits increased as a result of the removal of these racial barriers.

Escalation of the Attack on AFDC

The attack on social welfare programs escalated after the passage of the Civil Rights Act of 1964, after the urban riots of the late 1960s, and with the growth of concentrated poverty in the late 1970s and 1980s. But the attack intensified during the 1990s.

Throughout the 1980s, Ronald Reagan campaigned against welfare. He called for substantial cuts in funding and for shifting responsibilities over AFDC to the states. As described earlier in the book, Reagan used coded racist language and stories to capture public support in his campaign against welfare. Although he avoided the direct use of the words "race" and "blacks," the expressions of welfare queen and strapping young buck that he used in his stories conjured up clear racial images.

While spending for AFDC was not cut under Reagan, it was capped. As the cost of living increased, the real value of benefits declined. Reagan gave the states a little more discretion over AFDC, encouraging them to increase the regulation of recipients and to become more aggressive in going after fraud. But Reagan's assault on welfare had minimum impacts for a three reasons: (1) the egalitarian coalition and the Democratic Party defended social welfare programs; (2) there was still some interest group support for the programs; and (3) the public was some somewhat ambiguous because they hated welfare, but had some sympathy for the poor.

The assault on welfare broke out into an all-out war on AFDC during the mid-1990s. With the passage of the Personal Responsibility and Work Opportunity Reconciliation Act of 1996 (hereafter, the welfare reform law), AFDC was replaced with the new TANF. This act contained several major provisions: time limits, mandatory work requirements, block grants, and sanctions. TANF offered short-term temporary assistance for families with children. It set time limits for participating in the program: a lifetime limit of five years and a limit of two consecutive years. It imposed a mandatory requirement that recipients obtain jobs within a short period of time. Long-term dependency ended with the five-year maximum lifetime limit for getting benefits. The reform also turned AFDC into a block grant, with a fixed amount of federal money allocated to each state. State governments would no longer get more money when more families became eligible for the program. However, the new program provided some additional money to assist recipients with day care.

Within the context of conservative rhetoric, these reforms were said to be race neutral and based on common sense. They were designed to reduce welfare dependency, encourage and incentivize work, move women with children from a state of dependency on the government to a state of independence and freedom, promote two-parent families, and enforce individual responsibility.

The Left Shifts to the Right

The weakening of the left and the shift of the Democratic Party to the right contributed to the demise of AFDC. By 1992, the new Democratic Leadership Council had joined the attack on welfare. Indeed, Bill Clinton campaigned on a promise to end welfare as we know it. Of course, in 1994 under the leadership of Newt Gingrich and Dick Armey, the Republican Party produced the Contract with America, a campaign platform with a list of public policy programs that Republicans advocated. The welfare reform law was part of this platform. However, the Republican proposal was more draconian than Clinton's. The Republican proposal called for much deeper budget cuts, prohibited support to mothers younger than eighteen years old, excluded legal immigrants, allowed a maximum lifetime limit of five years, and enforced a limit of only two consecutive years. Clinton had vetoed the original Republican bill. The bill that passed was the result of compromise. The final bill did not contain the deep cuts in the program, which were the prohibition of teenaged mothers and the exclusion of legal immigrants.

The congressional hearings over the original bill were revealing. Voices advocating for women and the poor were conspicuously absent from the hearings. Middle-class feminist, civil rights, and civil libertarian organizations provided little support. These hearings were dominated by organizations representing the conservative coalition: organizations from the business and corporate sector, conservative think tanks, and the Christian right.

The Conservative Coalition

Business organizations, including the US Chamber of Commerce and the Business Roundtable, played a key role in the assault on welfare. They were well represented in the congressional hearings over welfare reform in the early 1990s. Business organizations strongly supported the work requirement and the time limits for participating in the program.

Christian fundamentalist groups weighed in on the debate. Their main concern was in maintaining traditional male-dominated two-parent families and fighting immorality. They believed welfare encouraged teen pregnancy, illegitimacy, and the breakdown of traditional families. These Christian organizations included the Traditional Values Coalition headed by Reverend Louis Sheldon and the Christian Coalition headed by Ralph Reed.

The Neoconservatives

Neoconservative scholars supported by conservative think tanks played a critical role in the intellectual assault on welfare. (See Chapter 3 for a discussion of neoconservatives' contributions to the poverty literature.) Some of these scholars include Michael Tanner of the Cato Institute, Charles Murray of the American Enterprise Institute, and Lawrence Mead and Thomas Sowell of the Hoover Institution.

As noted in Chapter 3, neoconservatives imagined a range of social and moral problems associated with welfare. They saw welfare as producing female-headed households that consequently contributed to a range of urban social problems: social disorganization, juvenile delinquency, long-term intergenerational welfare dependency, promiscuity, teen pregnancy, job aversion, laziness, hostility to education, drug abuse, welfare fraud, street crime, and all of the other problems associated the urban underclass.[19]

Tanner insists that prior to the New Deal welfare was provided by private charitable religious organizations that exposed recipients to religious messages and moral values.[20] He argues that federal welfare programs undermined these efforts and provided incentives not to work. Tanner also claims that the value of welfare benefits far exceeded the earnings of minimum wage workers.[21] He argues for ending government welfare and returning to private charities.

Murray attacks the welfare program in his book *Losing Ground*.[22] He argues that it was wrong to take money from hardworking industrious people and give it to lazy irresponsible people, and that it was wrong to offer teenaged girls money to have babies and to foreclose on their futures. As noted in Chapter 3, Murray blames social problems in black communities on welfare programs.

Murray claims that white liberals were part of the problem. They were so overwhelmed with guilt and concerned with negative prejudices toward blacks that they became overly generous in welfare benefits and obsessed with not blaming blacks for their bad values and self-destructive behavior. They shifted the blame for poverty from the self-destructive behavior of the poor and placed the blame on society and the economy.

Murray argues that "Whites began to tolerate and make excuses for behavior among blacks that whites would disdain in themselves or their children."[23] Murray adds that, when black crime rates increased, whites blamed society and favored rights for the accused; when black illegitimate birth rates increased, whites applauded blacks for having a much broader conception of family that includes aunts and grandmothers.

Mead emphasizes the need to change the values and behavior of welfare recipients. Like Murray he saw the problem of poverty arising from the breakdown of public authority and the irresponsible behavior of the poor. But he was more forceful in arguing for a paternalistic and authoritarian approach to social welfare. Although he maintains that people in the United States value freedom and equality, Mead questions whether there can be true equality in a society where the majority of citizens are independent and a minority are dependent and engage in irresponsible behavior.[24]

Black conservative scholars like Thomas Sowell joined the attack on welfare. Sowell, a senior Hoover Institution scholar, believes that welfare benefits led "to worsening behavior by the recipients."[25] He insists that welfare hurt the poor, but helped liberal politicians. He argues that the poor are fairly well off in the United States; that they have cars, cell phones, microwaves, and televisions. He suggests that welfare programs are overly generous: they hurt the poor by providing disincentives to work, by breaking up families, and by making recipients dependent on government. Because these programs give away government money, they earn votes for the liberal politicians that promote them. Sowell refers to welfare recipients as hostile and ungrateful parasites: "In politics, few talents are as richly rewarded as the ability to convince parasites that they are victims. Welfare states on both sides of the Atlantic have discovered that largesse to losers does not reduce their hostility to society, but only increases it. Far from producing gratitude, generosity is seen as an admission of guilt, and the reparations as inadequate compensation for injuries—leading to worsening behavior by the recipients."[26]

Ange-Marie Hancock, refers to the politics surrounding welfare reform policy as the "politics of disgust."[27] She examines the racist discourse and images surrounding welfare reform and identifies a series of adjectives associated with welfare recipients, including: overly fertile, don't work, lazy, cross-generational dependency, single-parent family, drug user, crime, teen mothers, culture of poverty, system abusers, and inner-city resident.

She believed these adjectives were part of the social construction of welfare recipients, which involved a series of racial, gender, and class stereotypes. Promoted in the academic literature, in the media, and by political leaders, these stereotypes impacted public opinion and shaped changes in welfare policy.[28]

Welfare as Slavery

Black conservatives have been more visible and passionate in the conservative assault on welfare. Several of them appeared in a 2013 documentary entitled *Runaway Slave,* which was sponsored by Freedom Works.[29] Narrated by Reverend C. L. Bryant, the documentary featured black conservative political leaders such as Allen West and Herman Cain; black conservative scholars such as Sowell; and black conservative religious leaders such as Alveda King, niece of Reverend Martin Luther King Jr. The theme of the documentary was that welfare and entitlement programs are the modern equivalent of slavery. They produce slavelike dependency on the government. As narrator, Bryant explains how dependency on the government for food, shelter, and clothing is strikingly similar to black dependency on food, shelter, and clothing provided by the slave master. He likens himself to Harriet Tubman, helping blacks to escape from slavery. He calls on blacks to run way from these government programs and from the political leaders who promote them just as slaves would run away from slavery.

The documentary condemns welfare for destroying black families. It insists that welfare provided incentives for fathers to leave their families and that broken families caused the rise of black crime and incarceration. It blames black civil rights leaders for misinforming and misleading the people.

Metaracism and the Changes from AFDC to TANF

More so than any other welfare program changes in the past twenty years, the changes from AFDC to TANF were driven by the racialization of the poor and program recipients and by racist stereotypes, images, and narratives that reinforced neoconservative and neoliberal policy arguments for imposing deep funding cuts and paternalistic controls on recipients. The racialization of the poor and of welfare recipients took place in full view of the public. It defied reality.[30]

Despite the fact that the overwhelming majority of poor people in this nation are white, public portrayals of poor people changed from images of whites to those of people of color. Despite the fact that blacks have never constituted more than 40 percent of welfare recipients, the majority of people depicted to be on welfare have been black. Portraying the poor and welfare recipients as people of color constitutes the racialization of the poor and of welfare.[31]

Without explicitly defining welfare as a black issue, the conservative media paraded in front of the public negative stories about welfare that featured mostly black recipients: black welfare queens, welfare Cadillac cars, calculating teenaged women who had babies to get welfare money, irresponsible women on welfare who had multiple sex partners and ended up with several babies, and women who continued intergenerational welfare dependency.

The discussion of welfare shifted public attention from the issue of poverty to the issue of welfare. Welfare became the problem—a moral and social order problem. Welfare became a sickness, a pathological and unhealthy way of life perpetuated by the government.[32]

The racist images of women on welfare were tied into the racist discourse on the urban underclass and the irresponsible behavior of inner-city residents. To the conservative media, the problem was twofold: (1) the overly generous government programs that produced the pathological dependency, family breakdown, social disorganization, and a new form of slavery; and (2) the irresponsible and defiant behavior of poor people.

Although the language was coded and subtle, the accumulated impacts of the words, the images, the ideas, and the narratives were not—they were substantial. Like the old forms of racism, the racialization and the racial innuendos of metaracism were accepted as factual, as reality. Metaracism not only desensitized society to the problems of the poor, but these racist insinuations provoked outright hostility, disgust, and contempt for welfare and for welfare recipients.

In his analysis of print and broadcast media, Martin Gilens presents extensive data based on a review of thousands of magazine articles and hundreds of hours of television news presentations from 1952 to 1992.[33] He supplements his media analysis with public opinion survey data. His research demonstrates a clear and striking pattern involving the racialization of the poor and racist constructions of welfare recipients. Prior to 1964, news coverage of poverty was rare; fewer than 15 percent of the photographs of poor people were black. By 1964 this figure had jumped to about 27 percent, which more accurately reflected the actual percentages of poor people who were black.

After 1964, this pattern changed in three important ways.[34] First, the percentage of poverty stories increased noticeably. Second, the media presented poor people as being predominantly black people, thus racializing the poor. Third, the media presented a series of negative stories of welfare fraud and abuse committed primarily by black recipients.[35] According to Gilens, "From the beginning of this study through 1964, poor people were portrayed as predominantly white. But starting in 1965 the complexion of the poor turned decidedly darker. From only 27 percent in 1964, the proportion of African Americans in pictures of the poor increased to 49 percent and 53 percent in 1965 and 1966, and then to 72 percent in 1967."[36] He suggests that as the color of welfare recipients darkened, the tone of welfare stories became more negative.[37] Whereas blacks constituted less than 30 percent of poor people and less than 40 percent of AFDC recipients, "blacks comprised 70 percent of the poor people pictured in stories indexed under poverty and 75 percent of those pictured in stories on welfare."[38] Gilens found the same pattern in ABC, NBC, and CBS nightly news coverage of poverty and welfare stories from 1969 to 1992. Television news exaggerated the percentage of blacks among both the poor and welfare recipients. The media practice of portraying the majority of welfare recipients as black continued into the twenty-first century.[39]

Using public opinion surveys, Gilens confirmed that opposition to welfare is primarily a function of negative attitudes toward blacks. In his analysis, he accounts for the influence of education, party affiliation, and ideology. He concludes that, although ideology plays a role, the perception that blacks are lazy is the strongest factor explaining opposition to welfare.[40] Gilens explains, "Among respondents with the same demographic characteristics, ideology, party identification, and attitudes toward individualism, those who hold the most extreme views of blacks as lazy score 40 points higher in opposition to welfare than those who view blacks as hard working."[41]

Gilens also examined media racialized urban problems. Gilens notes that, during the 1990s, over 80 percent of the people featured in magazine articles on urban problems were black. In stories featuring the urban underclass, 100 percent of the people featured were black. Gilens draws this conclusion:

> Although the underclass lacks any consistent definition in either popular or academic discourse, it is most often associated with intergeneration poverty, chronic unemployment, out-of-wedlock births, crime, drugs, and welfare dependency as a way of life. In fact, blacks do compose a large proportion of the American underclass, the exact proportion depending on how the underclass is defined. But even those definitions that result in the highest percentages of African Americans consider the underclass to include at least 40 percent nonblacks, in contrast to the magazine portrayals of the underclass as 100 percent black.[42]

Gilens demonstrates that the mass media promoted negative and racialized images of the urban underclass, welfare, and antipoverty programs. This racialization of welfare contributed to both the metaracism and the current assault on social welfare.

Joe Soss, Richard Fording, and Sanford Schram provide a more recent and comprehensive survey of the association between values or attitudes and welfare policy preferences.[43] They draw from several data sets: the American National Election Study, the National Survey on Poverty Policy, the Symbolic Racism 2000 Scale, and surveys of four core values: individualism, egalitarianism, humanitarianism, and authoritarianism. They looked at two sets of welfare policy preferences: spending (whether to cut or increasing spending) and paternalism (support for or opposition to the following 7 policies),"(1) mandatory drug testing; (2) unannounced home visits to check for rule violations; (3) sanctions for noncompliance; (4) a family cap denying benefits to children born to current recipients; (5) a 'man in the house' rule barring nonsupportive male residents; (6) mandatory classes on sex, marriage, and parenting; and (7) a suspension of rights to privacy in one's home."[44] They also included surveys of perceptions of race, gender, and sexual irresponsibility.

Soss, Fording, and Schram's findings about racial attitudes and welfare policy preferences confirm Gilens's findings. Symbolic racism was the strongest independent predictor of support for cutting welfare spending (.478) and support for welfare paternalism (.504). Individualism was a modest predictor of support for cuts in welfare spending (.324).[45] There was no association between individualism and opposition to or support for welfare paternalism, even though those who value individualism generally prefer less government intrusion into the lives of individuals. Their strongest association was between symbolic racism and welfare paternalism (.504).[46] Soss and colleagues also found that, of all of the racist stereotypes driving changes in welfare policy, the image of the irresponsible sexual behavior of black women was the strongest.[47]

In other words, despite the strong contention of conservative leaders that support for cuts in welfare spending and welfare paternalism or greater regulation of the behavior of welfare recipients is race neutral and has more to do with conservative values of individualism and personal responsibility, Soss and colleagues' findings clearly refute this contention.[48] Racist attitudes and beliefs are the strongest factors driving opposition to welfare, promotion of cuts in welfare spending, and efforts to regulate the behavior of welfare recipients and to impose sanctions of unacceptable behavior.

Children in Poverty

The racial composition of children receiving TANF benefits from 2000 to 2010 is presented in Table 6.1. This table indicates that black children constituted less than 40 percent of the total number of children receiving TANF from 2000 to 2010. Moreover, this percentage declined in recent years. In 2000, the percentage of children receiving TANF was 38.6. By 2010, this figure had declined to 31.9 percent, a change of 6.7 percent. However, dur-

Table 6.1 Percentage of Children Who Receive TANF by Race, 2000–2010

Year	White	Black	Hispanic
2000	31.2	38.6	25.0
2001	30.1	39.0	26.0
2002	31.6	38.3	24.9
2003	31.8	38.0	24.8
2004	32.9	37.6	24.1
2005	32.1	37.1	25.5
2006	33.4	35.7	26.1
2008	31.5	34.2	28.0
2007	32.4	35.5	27.0
2009	31.2	33.3	28.8
2010	31.8	31.9	30.0

Source: US Department of Health and Human Services, Office of Family Assistance, "Characteristics and Financial Circumstances of TANF Recipients, Fiscal Year 2010," August 8, 2012, www.acf.hhs.gov/programs/ofa/resource/character/fy2010/fy2010-chap10-ys-final.
Note: TANF = Temporary Assistance for Needy Families.

ing the same period, the percentage of white recipients varied little. In 2000, the percentage of children receiving TANF was 31.2. By 2010, the percentage was 31.8, a change of only 0.6 percent. The percentage who were Hispanic increased from 25 percent to 30 percent.

Throughout the late twentieth century and the early twenty-first century, welfare recipient mothers were not much different than any other mothers. They had one or two children. They had a work history. Most had ended up in the welfare line because of a loss of a job or a supportive partner, or the experience of a sudden illness. Few were involved in crimes or drugs. Most need temporary assistance. Only about 25 percent of AFDC recipients had fallen into the category of long-term dependent.[49] There were fewer incidents of welfare fraud than incidents of fraud in any other government program. Nancy Rose argues that this common prejudice about welfare fraud led to unfair, but aggressive campaigns against welfare recipients: "Welfare recipients were arrested even if eligibility workers made mistakes in their calculations and paid recipients more than they were entitled to receive. Due to the complexity of applications for AFDC and food stamps, as well as the inferior treatment (too many cases and low wages) of eligibility workers, this was a common occurrence—in fact, it accounted for more than half of all fraud cases in California."[50] The welfare reform law shifted welfare from a program providing cash benefits to poor, unemployed mothers to a program designed to discipline, control, and exploit vulnerable low-income mothers. By the second decade of the twenty-first century, it was clear that TANF no longer responded to increases in the number of children in poverty. Instead, TANF forced women into exploitive, low-wage, and dead-end jobs. It provided no support for education or occupational development. Worse, it contained provisions that targeted poor mothers for control and discipline.

The block grant provision of this new program hurt impoverished children. Under this provision, state governments got a fixed amount of money, regardless of any changes in poverty rates or needs. Under the old program, when child poverty increased, federal and state spending increased to meet the rising poverty needs. Under the new program, when child poverty increased, spending no longer increased.

Table 6.2 corroborates this trend. It presents the percentage of children in poverty who received either AFDC (up to 1996) or TANF (after 1996) benefits. In 1973, 80.5 percent of children in poverty in the United States were recipients of AFDC. This figure was an all-time high, but it did not mean that child poverty had reached an all-time high. Child poverty had declined to its lowest point of the century. What this figure indicates is that 80.5 percent of children in poverty were covered by this program.

Since 1973, the percentage of poor children who became AFDC recipients declined as state governments applied more rigorous eligibility standards and as the federal government imposed penalties on the states for enrolling ineligible recipients.[51] These administrative changes in the programs originated during Richard Nixon's administration, but were carried out in the administrations of Gerald Ford and Jimmy Carter. By 1980, the percentage of poor children covered had declined to about 63.2 percent. This decline continued under the Reagan administration. It reached 54.4 by 1985. It fluctuated in the early 1990s, increasing to 61.5 percent by 1995.

The percentage of poor children covered by these welfare benefits plummeted after the passage of the 1996 welfare reform law. With the passage of this law and the transformation of AFDC into TANF, the percentage of poor children covered by welfare benefits declined even more sharply. The convenient explanation for the decline was that more poor mothers got off welfare and got jobs, a trend attributed to both the success of the program and the expansion of the economy. However, as Table 6.2 indicates, the program simply covered a smaller percentage of children in poverty. In 1997, 50.1 percent of poor children were covered by TANF. This figure declined every year up to 2010, where it fell to 20.3 percent. In other words, as this nation sunk into a recession, and as unemployment and poverty rates soared, the welfare program became less sensitive and less responsive to poor families with children.

As Table 6.3 indicates, with the establishment of TANF, not only did the percentage of poor children covered by welfare decline, but the total number of poor children covered plummeted. In 1995, the number of children covered by AFDC reached a historic high of 9,013,000, even though this represented only 61.5 percent of children in poverty. This figure

Table 6.2 Child Recipients of AFDC and TANF Benefits as a Percentage of Children in Poverty

Year	Percentage
1970	58.5
1971	69.2
1972	75.5
1973	80.5
1974	75.5
1975	71.4
1980	63.2
1985	54.4
1990	57.9
1995	61.5
1996	57.8
1997	50.1
1998	42.9
1999	39.4
2000	36.8
2001	34.0
2002	31.2
2003	28.8
2004	27.6
2005	26.4
2006	24.8
2007	22.5
2008	20.8
2009	20.4
2010	20.3
2011	20.3

Sources: Child Trends Data Bank, www.childrensdatabank.org. For 2000–2011 data, TANF caseload data, Administration for Children and Families, Office of Family Assistance, http://www .acf.hhs.gov/programs/ofa/data-reports/index.htm. Years prior to 2000, Indicators of Welfare Dependence Annual Report to Congress 2008, US Department of Health and Human Services, table TANF2, http://aspe.hhs.gov/hsp/indicators08/apa.shtm.
Note: AFDC = Aid to Families with Dependent Children; TANF = Temporary Assistance for Needy Families.

declined to about 4.26 million by 2000. By 2008, it had declined to 2,922,000, which represented 20.8 percent of children in poverty. By 2010, at the height of the recession, only 3,280,000 children were covered.

The true test of any safety net program is how responsive it is to a recession and an increase in poverty. The worst recession in over fifty years erupted in 2008–2010. Unemployment, poverty, and child poverty rates increased dramatically.[52] Whereas the government responded to the increase in unemployment rates with increased spending and an increase in beneficiaries, it was disturbingly unresponsive to the dramatic increase in

Table 6.3 Number of Child Recipients of AFDC and TANF

Year	Number
1970	6,104,000
1975	7,928,000
1980	7,295,000
1985	7,073,000
1990	7,781,000
1995	9,013,000
2000	4,260,000
2005	3,407,000
2006	3,185,000
2007	3,003,000
2008	2,922,000
2009	3,156,000
2010	3,307,000
2011	3,280,000

Sources: TANF caseload data, Administration for Children and Families, Office of Family Assistance, http://www.acf.hhs.gov/programs/ofa/data-reports/index.htm; Indicators of Welfare Dependence Annual Report to Congress 2008, US Department of Health and Human Services, table TANF2, http://aspe.hhs.gov/hsp/indicators08/apa.shtm.

both poverty and child poverty. Table 6.3 shows that the number of children supported annually by TANF throughout those recession years was less than the number supported in 2005, when child poverty rates were much lower. Welfare reform was no longer a safety net program. It no longer responded to the increase in poverty. Based on this safety net test, it had become insensitive to the rise in child poverty.

Exploitation of Workers

Jane Collins and Victoria Mayer offer an insightful analysis of some of the local administrative changes that occurred with the implementation of the welfare reform bill and the transformation of AFDC into the TANF program. This analysis came from their review of the literature and from extensive interviews of program administrators and TANF recipients in two Wisconsin cities: Racine and Milwaukee.[53] Contrary to the racist stereotypes that drove reform, the majority of the recipients in Collins and Mayer's study had an employment history:

> Contrary to the presuppositions built into TANF, the women we interviewed all had extensive work experience. Nearly three-quarters of them had held onto jobs for a year or more, and some had histories of promotions and responsible managerial positions. As we sat with each woman and mapped out

her employment history, a complex picture of the low-wage economy emerged; Popeyes, Walmart, grocery stores and pharmacies, temp work and stints cleaning hotel rooms.[54]

Collins and Mayer insist that that the change in welfare policy must be understood in the context of the transformation of urban labor markets. Like in most older industrial cities—such as Buffalo, Cleveland, Chicago, Detroit, Flint, Gary, Pittsburgh, and Youngstown (discussed in Chapter 2)— the cities of Milwaukee and Racine experienced massive losses of manufacturing firms and as their labor markets shifted from an industrial base to a service base, with a large number of low-paying, labor-intensive service sector jobs replacing higher-paying industrial jobs. Collins and Mayer add: "This 'spatial fix' for struggling firms devastated Milwaukee and Racine. Between 1979 and 1995 the Milwaukee-Racine metropolitan area lost more than 35 percent of its manufacturing jobs. The story for inner-city Milwaukee was even more dramatic: between 1970 and 2000, 80 percent of manufacturing jobs disappeared."[55]

Collins and Mayer argue that the old welfare system was part of the New Deal and tied to the industrial-based economy. This system not only provided a safety net for poor families, but it was part of a larger system that supported a living wage for all families. That is, it maintained a floor below which wages would not fall. It strengthened the rights and bargaining power of all workers. It provided an alternative to labor market participation. It allowed women to temporarily drop out of the labor force to take care of infant children, to leave abusive men, or to avoid low-paying, exploitive jobs with abusive bosses. This escape option empowered women to leave abusive husbands or bosses.

Collins and Mayer insist that the shift from AFDC to TANF eliminated this escape option and destroyed the bargaining power of workers, in general. This change forced millions of low-skilled women into the labor market to compete with other low-skilled women already in the market for low-paying, low-skilled, dead-end jobs. It lowered the wages of the workers in this market and made them powerless to bargain with their employers. Collins and Mayer cite Patricia Williams's contract theory of economic citizenship to elaborate on this point:

> Williams points to another strategy by which rights may be constrained: when individuals are asked to enter into contracts in which they surrender basic liberties in return for something else. . . . As we shall see in the chapters that follow, new theories of welfare contractualism are premised on the trading of civil rights for aid. By accepting assistance from the state, poor women are asked to relinquish a range of rights and liberties, from the freedom to decide whether to stay home with their children and to maintain ties to the fathers of their children, to the right to choose when and where to work and at what kind of job, to basic labor rights and protections while working at that job.[56]

The change from AFDC to TANF was not a reform. It was a regressive change driven by metaracism and the impulse to discipline the poor. This change operated to discipline the low-wage, low-skilled workforce. It was designed to change the attitudes and behavior of low-skilled women: to lower their expectations about wages, hours of work, working conditions, and opportunities and rights. Collins and Mayer explain, "Like the removal of a wage floor, this training reverberates beyond the lives of the workers directly involved. It demonstrates to others that these conditions are possible, dramatizing, and ultimately normalizing, workplace practices that had been unthinkable since the early twentieth century."[57]

TANF operated as an anemic social safety net. As federal funding increased dramatically in other social programs to meet the challenge of the 2008 recession, funding for TANF barely increased. TANF operated more as an employment agency, with some day care support for working mothers. Almost all TANF recipients received Medicaid and food stamps. About 15 percent received housing subsidies.[58] Nevertheless, compared to other social programs responding to the recession, the TANF response was anemic.

Control and Discipline in the Welfare System

The 1996 welfare reform law introduced a provision that enabled stricter and more punitive regulations of welfare recipients. Whereas the Anti-Drug Abuse Act of 1988 prohibits federal grants, loans, licenses, and contracts from going to persons convicted of felony drug offenses, Section 115 of the welfare reform law expanded this regulation to welfare recipients. The 1996 law prohibits states from providing either TANF or Supplemental Nutrition Assistance Program (SNAP) benefits to persons convicted of felony drug offenses, unless the state passes special legislation to opt out of the ban.

SNAP provides a food debit card for recipients to purchase food. It replaced the old food stamp program. Table 6.4 provides a summary of states that ban benefits to TANF and SNAP applicants convicted of drug offenses, the states that have opted out, and those states that have modified laws. States with modifications often allowed people with drug convictions to receive SNAP benefits only after they went through drug rehabilitation therapy and submitted to periodic drug tests. As of 2012, nineteen states banned from TANF and SNAP any applicants with felony convictions for drug-related offenses. Michelle Alexander argues that, since blacks have a disproportionately higher drug conviction rate, this policy becomes a de facto way of barring a large proportion of black applicants.[59]

In 1996 under the Clinton administration, the US Department of Housing and Urban Development established a no tolerance "One Strike and You're Out" policy for public housing. The policy allowed local public

Table 6.4 State Policy on the TANF and SNAP Drug Conviction Ban

Bans Drug Felons	Passed Special Legislation Eliminating the Ban	Passed Special Legislation Modifying the Ban
Alabama	Washington, DC	California
Alaska	Iowa	Colorado
Arizona	Kansas	Connecticut
Arkansas	Maine	Delaware
Florida	Massachusetts	Hawaii
Georgia	New Hampshire	Idaho
Guam	New Jersey	Illinois
Indiana	New Mexico	Kentucky
Mississippi	New York	Louisiana
Missouri	Ohio	Maryland
North Dakota	Oklahoma	Michigan
South Carolina	Oregon	Montana
Texas	Pennsylvania	Nebraska
Virgin Islands	Rhode Island	Nevada
West Virginia	South Dakota	North Carolina
	Utah	Tennessee
	Vermont	Virginia
	Washington	Wisconsin
	Wyoming	

Source: Maggie McCarthy, Gene Falk, Randy Aussenberg, and David Carpenter, *Drug Testing and Crime Related Restrictions on TANF, SNAP, and Housing Assistance* (Washington, DC: Congressional Research Service, September 6, 2012).

housing authorities to automatically evict any resident caught with drugs on his or her premise or person. The policy was aggressively pursued throughout the late 1990s and into the twenty-first century. A major Supreme Court decision, *Department of Housing and Urban Development v. Rucker* illustrates the extent to which the policy has been administered.[60] The case originated with the Oakland Housing Authority in California, which had evicted four residents. One resident's daughter was caught three blocks from the housing projects with cocaine in her possession; the grandchildren of two residents were caught smoking marijuana in the parking lot of the projects; and the caretaker of a seventy-five-year-old resident was caught with cocaine on the premises. All four families were evicted, including the seventy-five-year-old resident who was evicted instead of the caretaker being banned from the projects. The Supreme Court ruled that the federal government and housing authorities had a rational basis for the intolerance of drugs policy.[61]

Consistent with this trend of introducing more punitive welfare regulations, in 2013 two states, Florida and Georgia, instituted a drug-testing policy for all TANF applicants.[62] Applicants testing positive for any illicit drugs were barred from the program for a year. The policy has generated a great deal of publicity and opposition. Opponents claim that this policy, like many other welfare reform policies, is driven by racist stereotypes of welfare recipients. Since few applicants are caught with drugs in their system, critics claim the policy is both punitive and wasteful. On average, only about 2.6 percent of applicants test positive, mostly for marijuana. This low rate of drug use among welfare applicants contradicts the stereotype, as the average usage rate of illicit drugs in the general population is about 8.7 percent. The drug tests cost between $25 and $45. In December 2013, a lower federal court struck down this state law.[63]

The welfare reform law introduced another punitive change related to SNAP. The law contained a provision for unemployed adults who had no children and who were not disabled. This provision restricted SNAP benefits for unemployed, childless, able-bodied adults to only three months out of three years, unless they were employed at least twenty hours a week or participated in a state-sponsored workfare or job training program. The provision allowed states to apply for a temporary waiver of this restriction under special circumstances: during recessions or periods of unusually high unemployment rates.[64] About forty-five states applied and received waivers during the 2009 recession. The waivers allowed states to provide SNAP benefits to workers who had lost their jobs as a result of the recession and whose unemployment benefits were running out.[65]

In 2013, Congress targeted SNAP for budget cuts. The Recovery Act of 2009 had increased individual SNAP benefits as a response to the 2009 recession, but these increases expired by November 2013. Congress proposed cutting the SNAP budget by several billion dollars and ending SNAP waivers for able-bodied, long-term unemployed people. In a report for the Center for Budget Priorities, Ed Bolen, Dottie Rosenbaum, and Robert Greenstein estimate that eliminating these waivers would result in the elimination of benefits to 1 million to 2 million people who want to work but are unable to find work:

> To be sure, under current law, many childless adults will lose SNAP in coming years anyway as the economy improves and states thus no longer qualify for these waivers (or qualify for waivers for fewer areas of the state) and reinstate the three-month limit in many areas. Over the next several years, approximately 1 to 2 million people will again become subject to the three-month limit, eventually bringing the number of people cut off benefits solely as a result of the elimination of the waivers to 1 to 2 million. But the proposal could immediately terminate food assistance to closer to 4 million individuals, including large numbers of jobless people who want to work and are looking for a job but can't find one. And, it would prohibit states from requesting a waiver at any time in the future—

including in future deep recessions and no matter how bleak the unemployment situation is in depressed parts of a state.[66]

Unlike TANF, SNAP and unemployment benefits increased profoundly in response to the substantial rise in unemployment, providing a safety net for those who became victims of the recession. As noted above, though, SNAP is now falling victim to a political movement to weaken the social safety net and increase the regulation and control of welfare recipients.

Race and the Affordable Care Act

The assault on the Affordable Care Act illustrates the dynamics of the new metaracism. Opponents of the act fiercely deny that the attacks or criticisms of this policy have anything to do with race or racism. Arguments against this policy range from credible to incredible. The credible arguments include those that have to do with costs and mandates. Indeed, without getting into the details of projected costs, the concerns that the expansion of federal health care would be costly, would expand the federal budget deficit, and would bloat the national debt are valid. The idea that the federal mandates may be intrusive and difficult to implement are legitimate.[67]

Some of the ideas about the Affordable Care Act strain credibility. These ideas include the notions that it is a form of socialized medicine, that it would control physicians and hospitals, that it would eliminate choices of individuals in their own personal physicians, that it would implant computer chips in all people, that it would constitute a government takeover of the entire health care system, that it would establish a European-style health care system that is more bureaucratized than the current US system, that it would create death panels that would make life-and-death decisions about older patients. Political protests and organized opposition to this act became intense, as described by Jacobs and Skocpol: "Antireform demonstrations were, at times, marked by startling rhetoric—accusing Obama of being a Nazi or a Communist and claiming that health reform would set up 'death panels' to decide on life or death for elderly Americans on Medicare. Vociferous protests coincided with ads attacking health reform from the Chamber of Commerce and other business interest."[68]

A group of scholars from Stanford University conducted extensive surveys of people's level of awareness of the provisions of the Affordable Care Act. There was only one provision that the majority (52 percent) were able to identify with a high degree of certainty: the provision that required family health insurance to cover children up to the age of twenty-six.[69] The study found that most people supported the major provisions of the law, but opposed it because they believed the misrepresentations and lies about the law promoted by conservative opponents. For example, only about 16.8 percent believed with high certainty that the law did not include a provision creating death panels. The study concluded, "If the public had perfect understanding of elements that we examined, the proportion of Americans who favor the bill might increase from the current level of 32% to 70%."[70] The Stanford study demonstrated that misinformation played a major role in people's opposition to the Affordable Care Act.

The most controversial aspect of the debate over the Affordable Care Act is the extent to which race plays a role. Despite the passionate and fierce denial that race has anything to do with the Affordable Care Act, the research suggests otherwise. On the surface, health care policy seems to lack the clear association with race that affirmative action and welfare policies have, as a significant proportion of the beneficiaries of these policies were black. Nevertheless, recent research has shown that race has been a factor in shaping attitudes toward other policies lacking a clear connection to minorities. Through coded language, subliminal references, and masked innuendos, political leaders and media personalities have managed to link race-neutral policies to race. They have framed political messages in ways that have connected with racial attitudes.[71]

Michael Tesler engaged in a large study of the impact of racial attitudes and attitudes toward President Obama on the Affordable Care Act. He relied on two data bases: the American National Election Study, which surveyed thousands of respondents from 1988 to 2009, and the Cooperative Campaign Analysis Project, which surveyed over 3,000 participants. The American National Election Study data surveyed attitudes toward the Affordable Care Act. He was able to control for ideology, partisanship, and concern for medical costs and examine the independent effect of racial animus on support for the act. He concluded that racial animus increased opposition to the act, independent of ideology, partisanship, and anxiety about health care costs. Tesler concludes, "With ideological self-placement and party identification held constant, changing from least to most racially resentful decreased white support for governmental insurance by 20% of the scale's range in September 2009."[72] Tesler also examined the Obama effect, whether opposition to President Obama affected opposition to the act. He demonstrated this effect through time-sensitive surveys and through experimental research. His survey data indicate that racial animus became a stronger predictor of opposition to the act as the president became more involved in campaigning for it. In other words, Obama's support for the Affordable Care Act triggered both racial animus and opposition.[73]

Tesler used an experimental research design to determine the extent of the Obama effect. The experiment involved randomly assigning Cooperative Campaign Analysis Project participants into three groups: neutral, Clinton-frame, and Obama-frame. The participants were presented with the same health care proposals. The only differences in these identical proposals were the names associated with them. That is, the Obama-frame participants were told that the proposals came from President Obama. The Clinton-frame participants were told that the proposals came from President Clinton. The neutral participants were not told the origin of the proposal. This experiment demonstrated the independent impact of Obama in activating racial attitudes and opposition.[74]

President Obama joined the conventional wisdom and popular view that race had absolutely nothing to do with the debate over health care reform. Tesler's data provides strong evidence to refute this wisdom. Obama's association with the Affordable Care Act triggered racial animus and intensified opposition to health care reform. Tesler also presents evidence that opposition to other policies, such as Obama's association with the stimulus package, was related to racial animus.[75]

President Obama's opponents during the 2012 election used racial cues to trigger opposition to him. For example, Gingrich called Obama "the Food Stamp president," which no doubt triggered opposition to SNAP. Mitt Romney's campaign falsely accused the Obama administration of attempting to eliminate the work requirement of TANF. Political leaders not only played a role in racializing these policies, but they associated Obama's name with the policies in ways calculated to generate opposition to both the president and the policies.

Public Education Programs

No discussion of social programs would be complete without a discussion of education programs. Programs like TANF and unemployment provided only temporary relief from a financial crisis. Social programs were not designed to promote social mobility. People moved out of poverty and up the social ladder when they attained more education, acquired specialized skills, and found better-paying jobs, providing that these jobs were available. Blacks moved out of poverty as racially discriminatory barriers were removed, as better-paying jobs became available, as higher education became more accessible, and as educational levels rose.

Just as the Lyndon Johnson administration opened the floodgates for social programs, it moved to establish an equal opportunity regime in the area of public education. But equal opportunity never meant equal outcomes. It simply meant leveling the playing field. Consistent with the ideals of Thomas Paine, it meant that government would use its resources to provide children from economically deprived families and neighborhoods the same opportunities to grow and develop their intellectual potentials as children anywhere. Hence, the Johnson administration established school nutrition programs to respond to children coming to school hungry and to provide adequate nourishment for the development of young brains; the Head Start program for pre-kindergarteners lacking the preschool experience and exposure to early educational materials; compensatory education programs such as ESEA (Elementary and Secondary Education Act of 1965, a precursor to the No Child Left Behind Act) to provide extra support in the areas of math and reading; and the Upward Bound program for students preparing to go to college.

The quest for equal opportunity also precipitated local and state-wide political movements to equalize funding for local public schools and to respond to the problem of poor districts lacking the resources to provide an adequate education for poor children. This movement emerged in the late 1960s and continues today. Liberal writer Jonathan Kozol published a series of books spanning forty years decrying the debilitating effects of inequality in local school funding, which denies equal opportunity to children from poor families and poor areas.[76] Kozol documented the debilitating impact of inequality in school funding, both between school districts and within school districts in Detroit, Chicago, Saint Louis, New York City, and several other cities.[77] In *Savage Inequalities,* he describes a case in Detroit where resources are so inadequate that teachers had to use pictures of key pads because the school could not afford actual computers.[78] In *The Shame of the Nation*, he notes that the "present per-pupil spending level in the New York City schools is $11,700, which may be compared to a per-pupil spending level in excess of $22,000 in the well-to-do suburban district of Manhasset. He argues that the problem of inequality has been exacerbated by the problem of increasing racial segregation. He maintains that public schools in the United States are more racially segregated today than they were before 1968.[79] He concluded that equal opportunity in public education today is undermined by unequal, underfunded, and racially segregated schools.[80]

Despite Kozol's bleak assessment, there has been progress in the struggle for more equitable funding for public education. Most of this progress came from state supreme court decisions.[81] A number of states have made measurable progress in equalizing funding. For example, in the *DeRolph v. Ohio* decision the Ohio Supreme Court ordered the Ohio General Assembly to develop plans for a more equitable distribution of public education funds throughout the state.[82] This decision was primarily in response to extreme disparities between the funding of public schools in the southeastern part of the state near the Appalachian Mountain range and the rest of the state. For another example, in *Abbott v. Burke*, the New Jersey Supreme Court ordered the New Jersey Legislature to develop and implement a plan for more equitable funding of New Jersey public schools.

Despite this progress, the equal opportunity movement in public education suffered setbacks as it was assailed by a counter movement. This counter movement launched assaults that have taken several forms: legal, ideological, and political. The legal assault came from the US Supreme Court. In the 1973 *San Antonio v. Rodriguez* decision, the court upheld the state of Texas' formula for funding its public schools that allocated substantially more money to a well-endowed, wealthy, white school district (Alamo Heights) than to underfunded, predominantly minority (Latino) poor district (Edgewood). The court decided that unequal funding did not violate the equal protection clause of the 14th Amendment because there was no evidence that the decision was based on racial prejudice and because the 14th Amendment does not require equal funding.[83]

Beyond the *San Antonio v. Rodriguez* decision, the equal opportunity regime has been involved in a long ideological and political dispute. This regime has been the target of three ideological arguments: culture of poverty, money does not matter, and market choice is the new equal opportunity. The general theme is that equal opportunity cannot be achieved through equitable funding. The culture of poverty argument was examined in Chapter 3. However, because of its rootedness in metaracism and its impact on education policy, it bears reexamination.

The Culture of Poverty

In Chapter 3, I summarized the neoconservative/culture of poverty perspective. This perspective is directly related to the assault on equal opportunity. It assumes that low black test scores are the results of the culture of poverty, a culture that does not value education and hard work. John Ogbu's perspective extended beyond a culture of poverty as he claimed that even middle-class blacks were not committed to high levels of educational attainment as they believed that working hard to get good grades was acting white.[84] A corollary to this assumption is the conviction that increasing funding for inner city schools would be a waste of money.

Peter Schrag makes this point in his book *Final Test: The Battle for Adequacy in America's Schools*.[85] Schrag suggests that an increase in school funding, especially for minority urban school districts, would not produce increases in student achievement. He insists that equal school funding would not produce equal educational outcomes. Rejecting old-style racism, he maintains that blacks tend to exhibit lower levels of academic performance, not because of their genes or biology, but because of their culture, values, and attitudes:

What's most vexing is that even children of black professionals—lawyers, doctors, teachers—seem to trail their white peers, a factor that Berkeley an-

thropologist John Ogbu, a Nigerian immigrant, attributes to cultural attitudes. The core of these attitudes is the fear of "acting white" and the failure of those students who Ogbu says, look to rappers and other entertainers
as models, to understand how their parents made it. Others, such as psy-
chologist Claude Steele of Stanford, believe the cause is black students' fear
of failure, what he calls "stereotype threat"—the self-fulfilling fear of black
students of being unable to perform as well as whites on tests. But whether
it's family that's destiny, or peers or genes or culture, there's the same implication that schools have only a marginal effect and the negative consequences for educational policy aren't likely to be all that different. As the
percentage of minority students increases, those factors are likely to loom
even larger.[86]

Schrag's argument is largely a restatement of the culture of poverty and
neoconservative perspective discussed earlier. Black children have low test
scores on standardized tests because they have a bad culture, a low value
for education, rappers for role models, and a fear of acting white. Putting
more resources into black schools would have no impact on improving test
scores.

On the surface, the assumptions of this cultural thesis appear to be race
neutral, based on the facts, and grounded in reason. The corollary argument
also seems to be based on common sense: increased funding to schools
does not translate into higher test scores. However, underneath the surface
the dynamics of this thesis are similar to the dynamics of old-style racial
arguments.

The mean scores on standardized tests of blacks have always been lower
than the scores of whites. Prior to the civil rights movement, the common
assumption was that these lower test scores proved that blacks were biologically and genetically predisposed to lower intelligence than whites. However, this assumption was challenged during World War II when Northern
blacks scored higher than Southern whites. Consequently, researchers began
to examine the effects of other variables on test scores such as social class,
region, and educational systems. By the 1960s, the assumption that blacks
were biologically and genetically predisposed to lower intelligence was discredited. However, researchers wed to the race-biology thesis attempted to
salvage the thesis by accounting for social class, but their comparisons were
flawed. For example, Arthur Jensen compared the scores of middle-class
blacks with the scores of middle-class whites and found that whites continued to outscore blacks. However, when other researchers looked at the data,
they found that the incomes of the middle-class blacks were lower than the
incomes of middle-class whites. This false comparison invalidated the
research. Philip Green has this assessment of Jensen:

> In fact, however, none of the six studies Jensen refers to support this claim.
> . . . Suffice it here to say that on . . . evidence most of those studies were not

remotely comparing "upper-status" blacks with "lower-status" whites, but when they were, the average IQ differentials turned out to be minimal or non-existent. . . .

In sum, Jensen wrote, and was well rewarded for writing, hundreds of pages of tendentious theorizing to "explain," a set of "facts" that did not exist and thus neither required nor supported his explanations. . . .

On first consideration it is incomprehensible that Jensen can have failed to see this, since he himself states that "15 percent of the Negro population exceeds the white "average"—a figure that, to repeat, is just about what we would have predicted on the basis of a totally environmentalist and egalitarian theory of the differences in measured intelligence among racial and ethnic groups.[87]

The point here is that race is now and has always been a spurious variable. There has always been a strong association between standardized test scores and income. Summarizing the research on family income, ethnicity, and test scores, Donald Orlich and Glenn Gufford conclude, "For the SAT, 97% of the variance (r = .97; p < .001) in test scores may be explained by family income of test takers."[88] The lower test scores among school-aged African Americans is explained by their lower family incomes, higher poverty rates, residency in concentrated poverty areas, and attendance in schools that are underfunded schools and that have higher teacher turnover rates—not by a low value on education and hard work.[89]

As Stephen Jay Gould outlines in his book *The Mismeasure of Man,* racist cultures have had a distorting effect on the paradigms and perceptions of scientists from the craniologists who mistakenly saw blacks with smaller brains, to biologists and geneticists who mistakenly believed that blacks were biologically and genetically predisposed to lower intelligence, to the current cultural determinists who see bad behavior, but have difficulty seeing unequal opportunities and unfair privileges.[90] Even today, metaracist culture distorts perceptions of issues of race and education, and plays a role in undermining efforts toward maintaining the equal opportunity regime.

Funding Does Not Matter

A corollary to this assumption that low black test scores are associated with bad black culture is the assumption that increasing funding for education would be a waste of money. This assumption is a growing battle against the equal opportunity regime and a major feature in the school funding debate. Here I summarize the debate.

Conservatives oppose equal funding for three reasons. First, they point to research demonstrating that increasing funding does not translate into increased academic performance.[91] There are examples in which school districts have dramatically increased spending, but suffered declining academic

performance. Second, this nation has increased educational spending exponentially over the past forty years, with little results. In fact, SAT and ACT
scores have been declining, and the nation has lost its competitive advantage
over other nations in the area of education. Finally, what is needed in education today is not more money, but more accountability and choice in education. Teachers, parents, and students need to be held accountable for the
academic performance of students. Most importantly, minority students need
to change their values and attitudes and acquire a higher value for education
and greater regard for hard work. Conservatives are increasingly redefining
equal opportunity, not as a level playing field, but as enhanced choice:
vouchers that allow poor families to send their children to parochial schools
and charter schools that provide alternatives to public schools.

Liberals agree that more money does not necessarily translate into better academic performance, but they insist that the research is contrary to the
conservative view that focusing more resources on academics contributes to
better academic performance.[92] Moreover, a more careful examination of
the research and data demonstrates that increases in educational spending
over the past forty years contributed to measurable increases in academic
performance, particularly for minority students from high poverty neighborhoods.[93] If SAT and ACT scores look like they are declining, it is only
because higher education is no longer the exclusive domain of the economic elite and a much larger proportion of children from working and
poverty households are taking these tests because of increased spending in
equal education programs.[94] Neoconservatives use the works of James
Coleman to support their contention that money does not matter. In the
1960s, Coleman surveyed thousands of schools and about 600,000 students
and teachers. He concludes that the strongest factors determining educational outcomes were family background and peer groups: "Schools bring
little influence to bear on a child's achievement that is independent of background and general social context."[95]

Expanding on the works of Coleman, conservative economist and former student of Moynihan, Eric Hanushek, has published a number studies
on the impact of school funding. He too concludes that school funding had
little impact on student achievement. Hanushek insists, "Detailed research
spanning two decades and observing performance in many different educational settings provides strong and consistent evidence that expenditures are
not systematically related to student achievement."[96] Peter Schrag describes
Hanushek's work:

> For Hanushek and, indeed, for many other educational researchers, class size
> reduction, one of the largest items on that list of increased expenditures—and
> one perhaps the most popular school reform of the past decade among both
> teachers and parents—is particularly suspect. In California, which, beginning
> in the mid-1990s, has thrown over $1.5 billion a year into across-the-board

class size reduction (a maximum of twenty to one) in the primary (K–3) grades, a major four-year study found lots of parents and teacher enthusiasm but few measurable benefits in educational outcomes that could be traced to class size reduction—and very possibly, considerable damage to urban schools forced to hire thousands of unqualified teachers both for all those new classes and to replace the better teachers who suddenly found more attractive offers in neighboring districts. Nationally, Hanushek argues, as class size has gone down across the country—and gone down significantly, from an average teacher-pupil ration of about twenty-seven to one in 1949–1950 to seventeen to one in 1993–1994—student test scores on measures such as the National Assessment of Educational Progress (NAEP), which began testing samples of American students in the early 1970s, hasn't shown any corresponding increase. Thus, "while policies to reduce class size may enjoy popular political appeal, such policies are very expensive and, according to the evidence, quite ineffective."[97]

The conclusion is that no amount of increases in school funding is going to make a difference.

Bruce Biddle and David Berliner challenge the works of Coleman. These scholars have conducted a large amount of research on the school funding issue from a non-neoliberal and non-neoconservative perspective. They reexamined James Coleman's original research, the debate that it precipitated, and subsequent research on school funding. They found serious methodological errors in Coleman's initial research:

> The Coleman report was lengthy, its procedures and statistics were complex, and its text was murky—and as a result, almost nobody read it. The press, however, widely trumpeted its surprising conclusion about the ineffectiveness of school factors. Thus, the public was led to believe that research had "proven" that schools (and their funding) had little effect, and the fat was in the fire. Conservative forces hostile to the public sector rejoiced because their negative opinions about public schools had been vindicated. . . .
>
> Somehow, at the time, almost nobody noticed that the report contained major errors likely to have reduced the size of its estimates for school effects on students' achievements. Among other problems, the report's authors had failed to use available scaling techniques to validate their procedures, had made serious mistakes when assigning indicators to major variables, and had failed to measure crucial variables now known to be associated with school effects. In addition, the report had used non-standard procedures for statistical analyses, which generated falsely deflated estimates of school effects.
>
> To summarize, the Coleman report was badly flawed, although its flaws were not widely understood at the time. Its findings were vigorously promoted, however, and its suspect conclusion that level of school funding has little impact on student achievement passed into the public domain as a confirmed fact.[98]

Biddle and Berliner suggest that the quality of studies on the impact of school funding varies. They insist that high-quality studies use large samples and statistical controls for family income, and examine effects associated with only one level of analysis such as the classroom, the school building, the school district, or the state. High-quality studies break down the school funding variable into specific funding factors likely to impact educational outcomes such as class size.

Researchers have found impressive and substantial increases in the academic performance of minority students in high-poverty areas after reducing class size in the early grades. Some researchers not only have recorded increases in academic performance, they have developed theories to explain why reducing class size improves academic performance. For example, Frederick Mosteller offers this theory:

> Reducing [the size of classes in the early grades] reduces the distractions in the room and gives the teacher more time to devote to each child. . . . When children first come to school, they are confronted with many changes and much confusion. They come into this new setting from a variety of homes and circumstances. Many need training in paying attention, carrying out tasks, and interacting with others in a working situation. In other words, when children start school, they need to learn to cooperate with others, to learn to learn, and generally to get oriented to being students.[99]

Biddle and Berliner argue that students gain more than increased academic performance as a result of smaller classes.[100] With smaller classes in the primary grades, students not only learn grade-level skills, but they also learn how to learn by acquiring better learning habits and skills. With smaller classes, students learn in a more supportive environment, an environment that forms more positive self-concepts that students carry with them into the higher grades.[101] Thus, the benefits of smaller classes in the primary grades carry over into high school and college. The cumulative research demonstrates that these students were more likely to achieve higher grades in high school, less likely to drop out of school, and more likely to go to college.

Biddle and Berliner have taken strong exception to researchers who use the California classroom reduction experiment as proof that reducing class size have no beneficial impact. In 1996, the state of Californian enacted an extensive and expensive program to reduce class sizes to twenty or fewer students. Initial evaluations suggested that the reductions had little impact. Biddle and Berliner claim that the California experiment was the worse example of reducing class size to improve academic performance: "In many ways, the California initiative has provided a near-textbook case of how not to reduce class size within a specific state."[102] California's definition of a small class was another state's definition of a large class. California allocated too little money and eliminated too many workable academic programs to finance the course reductions.

Despite these long ideological and political battles over the equal opportunity regime, most programs such as Head Start, school nutrition, and Upward Bound remain in place. Some of the programs, such as No Child Left Behind, have been expanded. Efforts toward equal funding have stopped. However, the entire debate over equal funding has been eclipsed on the policy agenda by the promotion of market models: charter schools and school vouchers. Research demonstrates that these market model programs do little to improve the academic performance of inner-city school children.[103] The whole idea of equal funding for K–12 public education has been taken off the agendas of progressive Democrats. Increasing costs of higher education, the reduction in the level of state subsidies per college student, and the shifting of student loans to the private sector have increased the difficulty of low-income students to go to college.[104]

Conclusion

In this chapter, I examined the role of metaracism—racist and sexist images and narratives and a racialized political culture—and a conservative coalition in racializing welfare programs, criminalizing welfare recipients, and creating an exploitive and punitive welfare system. I reviewed the role of metaracism in growing opposition to the Affordable Care Act, which continue conflicts over the equal opportunity regime in public education. I suggested that metaracism plays a role in national opposition to efforts to equalize school funding. Chapter 7 continues this examination of the role of metaracism in criminalizing and dehumanizing the black poor. It shifts this examination to the criminal justice policy area and demonstrates how metaracism and the conservative coalition contributed to the formation of one of the most punitive criminal justice systems in US history.

Notes

1. Martin Gilens, *Why Americans Hate Welfare: Race, Media, and the Politics of Antipoverty Policy* (Chicago: University of Chicago Press, 1999).

2. Seymour Martin Lipset, *American Exceptionalism: A Double-edged Sword* (New York: W. W. Norton, 1996). This literature is broad and contentious, as noted in Chapter 1. However, Lipset provides one of the best representations of American exceptionalism as an explanation for the lack of a European-style welfare system.

3. Jill Quadagno, *The Color of Welfare: How Racism Undermined the War on Poverty* (New York: Oxford University Press, 1994), p. 191.

4. See for example Patricia Hill-Collins, *Black Feminist Thought: Knowledge Construction and the Politics of Empowerment* (New York: Routledge, 1990); Kenneth Neubeck and Noel Cazenave, *Welfare Racism: Playing the Race Card Against*

America's Poor (New York: Routledge, 2001); Sanford Schram, Joe Soss, and Richard Fording, eds., *Race and the Politics of Welfare Reform* (Ann Arbor: University of Michigan Press, 2003); Holloway Sparks, "Queens, Teens, and Model Mothers: Race, Gender, and the Discourse of Welfare Reform," in Schram, Soss, and Fording, eds., *Race and the Politics of Welfare Reform*; Frances Fox Piven, "Why Welfare Is Racist," in Schram, Soss, and Fording, eds., *Race and the Politics of Welfare Reform*; Shannon Monnat, "Toward a Critical Understanding of Gendered Color-Blind Racism Within the U.S. Welfare Institution," *Journal of Black Studies* 40, no. 4 (2010): 637–652.

5. Neubeck and Cazenave, *Welfare Racism*.

6. Neubeck and Cazenave, *Welfare Racism*; Ian Lopez, *Dog Whistle Politics: How Coded Racial Appeals Have Reinvented Racism and Wrecked the Middle Class* (Oxford: Oxford University Press, 2014); Schram, Soss, and Fording, eds., *Race and the Politics of Welfare Reform*.

7. Dorothy Roberts, *Killing the Black Body: Race, Reproduction, and the Meaning of Liberty* (New York: Vintage Books, 1997).

8. Ibid. Roberts documents these cases in chapter 4 of *Killing the Body*, "Making Reproduction a Crime." She states, "In fact, scores of women across the country arrested for smoking crack while pregnant had similarly pled guilty to charges of child abuse, distribution of drugs to a minor, or lesser offenses," p. 150.

9. Ana Ortiz and Laura Briggs, "The Culture of Poverty, Crack Babies, and Welfare Cheats: The Making of the Healthy White Baby Crisis," *Social Text* 21, no. 3 (2003): 39–57.

10. Dorothy Roberts, "Welfare and the Problem of Black Citizenship," *Yale Law Journal* 105 (1996): 1574.

11. Ibid., p. 1583.

12. Ibid, p. 1570.

13. Ibid, p. 1573. The quote is taken from Quadago, *The Color of Welfare*, p. 4.

14. Ibid.

15. Linda Gordon, *Pitied but Not Entitled: Single Mothers and the History of Welfare, 1890–1935* (Cambridge: Harvard University Press, 1994), p. 515.

16. Ira Katznelson, *When Affirmative Action Was White: An Untold History of Racial Inequality in Twentieth-Century America* (New York: W. W. Norton, 2005), p. 43.

17. Gordon, *Pitied but Not Entitled*, p. 515.

18. *King v. Smith*, 392 U.S. 309 (1968).

19. George Gilder, *Wealth and Poverty* (New York: Basic Books, 1981).

20. Michael Tanner, *The End of Welfare* (Washington, DC: Cato Institute, 1996).

21. Michael Tanner and Charles Hughes, *The Work Versus Welfare Trade-Off 2013: An Analysis of the Total Level of Welfare Benefits* (Washington, DC: Cato Institute, 2013). Although it is difficult to account for the monetary value of Medicaid and although less than 15 percent of TANF recipients get housing benefits, Tanner and Hughes added the budget allocations for Medicaid, public housing, Section 8 housing subsidies, low income home energy assistants, WIC, and other programs together to calculate the annual earnings of a typical TANF recipient.

22. Charles Murray, *Losing Ground: American Social Policy, 1950–1980* (New York: New York University Press, 2003 [1984]).

23. Ibid., p. 223.

24. Lawrence Mead, *Beyond Entitlement: The Social Obligation of Citizenship* (New York: Free Press, 1986).

25. Thomas Sowell, "Largesse for Losers," National Review Online, April 10, 2012. http://www.nationalreviewdom/articles/295600?/largesse-for-losers-thomas -sowell.

26. Ibid.

27. Ange-Marie Hancock, *The Politics of Disgust: The Public Identity of the Welfare Queen* (New York: New York University Press, 2004).

28. Ibid.

29. Pritchett Cotton, director, *Runaway Slave*, produced by Ground Floor Video (Rocky Mountain Pictures, 2012).

30. Patricia Hill-Collins, *Black Feminist Thought: Knowledge Construction and the Politics of Empowerment*; Neubeck and Cazenave, *Welfare Racism*; Schram, Soss, and Fording, eds., *Race and the Politics of Welfare Reform*; Sparks, "Queens, Teens, and Model Mothers"; Piven, "Why Welfare Is Racist"; Monnat, "Toward a Critical Understanding of Gendered Color-Blind Racism."

31. Gilens, *Why Americans Hate Welfare.*

32. This view of welfare was popular in the neoconservative literature, as discussed above in the works of Gilder, *Wealth and Poverty*; Murray, *Losing Ground*; and Mead, *Beyond Entitlement.*

33. Gilens, *Why Americans Hate Welfare.*

34. Ibid.

35. Ibid.

36. Ibid., p. 114.

37. Ibid., p. 117.

38. Ibid., p. 123.

39. Ibid.

40. Ibid., p. 95.

41. Ibid., p. 92.

42. Ibid., p. 129.

43. Joe Soss, Richard Fording, and Sanford Schram, *Disciplining the Poor: Neoliberal Paternalism and the Persistent Power of Race* (Chicago: University of Chicago Press, 2011).

44. Ibid., p. 71.

45. Ibid., p. 72.

46. Ibid.

47. Ibid., p. 75.

48. Ibid. See also Schram, Soss, and Fording, eds., *Race and the Politics of Welfare Reform.*

49. Ruth Sidel, *Keeping Women and Children Last* (New York: Penguin, 1996). Even neoconservative Gilder, in *Wealth and Poverty,* noted that the long-term dependency rate was 25 percent.

50. Nancy Rose, *Workfare or Fair Work: Women, Welfare, and Government Work Programs* (New Brunswick, NJ: Rutgers University Press, 1995), p. 160.

51. Ron Randall, "Presidential Powers Versus Bureaucratic Intransigence: The Influence of the Nixon Administration on Welfare Policy," *American Political Science Review* 73, no. 3 (1979): 795–810.

52. Jane Collins and Victoria Mayer, *Both Hands Tied: Welfare Reform and the Race to the Bottom of the Low-Wage Labor Market* (Chicago: University of Chicago Press, 2010).

53. Ibid., p. 49.

54. Ibid.

55. Ibid, p. 37. The term *spatial fix* is taken from David Harvey, *The Limits of Capital* (New York: Verso, 1999 [1982]).

56. Collins and Mayer, *Both Hands Tied*, p. 14; Patricia Williams, *The Alchemy of Race and Rights* (Cambridge, MA: Harvard University Press, 1992), p. 226.

57. Collins and Mayer, *Both Hands Tied*, p. 6.

58. Tanner and Hughes, *The Work Versus Welfare Trade-Off 2013*.

59. Michelle Alexander, *The New Jim Crow: Mass Incarceration in the Age of Colorblindness* (New York: New Press, 2010), p. 142.

60. *Department of Housing and Urban Development v. Rucker*, 535 U.S. 125 (2002).

61. Ibid.

62. Jane Suttor, "Florida Law Mandating Drug Tests for Welfare Struck Down by Federal Judge, *Huffington Post*, December 31, 2013. http://www.com/2013/12/31 /florida-law-welfare-drug-tests_n_452534.html.

63. Ibid.

64. Stacy Dean, "Setting the Record Straight on SNAP, Part 2: The Truth about Unemployed Childless Adults" (Washington DC: Center on Budget and Policy Priorities, September 10, 2013). http://offthechartsblog.org/setting-the-record-straight -on-snap-part-2-the-truth-about-unemployed-childless-adults.

65. Ed Bolen, Dottie Rosenbaum, and Robert Greenstein, "House Republicans' Additional SNAP Cuts Would Increase Hardship in Areas with High Unemployment," news release, Center for Budgets and Public Priorities, August 7, 2013. http://www.cbpp.org/cms/index.cfm?fa=view&id=4001.

66. Ed Bolen, Dottie Rosenbaum, and Robert Greenstein, *GOP's Additional SNAP Cuts Would Increase Hardship in Areas with High Unemployment* (Washington, DC: Center for Budget Priorities, August 18, 2013).

67. See Lawrence Jacobs and Theda Skocpol, *Health Care Reform and American Politics: What Everyone Needs to Know* (New York: Oxford University Press, 2012).

68. Ibid, p. 53.

69. Wendy Gross, Tobias Stark, Jon Krosnick, Josh Pasek, Gaurav Sood, Trevor Tompson, Jennifer Agiesta, and Dennis Junius, "Americans' Attitudes Toward the Affordable Care Act: Would Better Public Understanding Increase or Decrease Favorability?" p. 8, unpublished manuscript, 2012. http://web.stanford.edu/dept /communication/faculty/krosnick/docs/2012/Health%20Care%202012%20 -%20knowledge%20and20%Favorability.pdf.

70. Ibid, p. 13.

71. Michael Tesler, "The Spillover of Racialization into Health Care: How President Obama Polarized Public Opinion by Race and Racial Attitudes," *American Journal of Political Science* 56, no. 3 (2012): 690–704.

72. Ibid., p. 695.

73. Ibid., p. 698.

74. Ibid.

75. Ibid., pp. 698–670.

76. Jonathan Kozol, *Death at an Early Age: The Destruction of the Hearts and Minds of Negro Children in Boston* (Boston: Houghton Mifflin, 1967); Jonathan Kozol, *Savage Inequality: Children in America's Schools* (New York: Harper Perennial, 1992); Jonathan Kozol, *The Shame of the Nation: The Restoration of Apartheid Schooling in America* (New York: Crown Publishers, 2005).

77. Kozol, *Savage Inequality*.

78. Ibid.

79. Kozol, *The Shame of the Nation*, p. 19.

80. Kozol, *Savage Inequality*, p. 143.

81. See for example the *De Rolph v. State of Ohio,* 78 Ohio St. 3d 193, 677 NE2d (1998); and *Abbott v. Burke*, 153 New Jersey 480, 710 A 2d 450 (1998).

82. *De Rolph v. State of Ohio.*

83. *San Antonio Independent School District v. Rodriguez,* 411 U.S. 1 (1973).

84. John Ogbu, *Black American Students in an Affluent Suburb: A Study of Academic Disengagement* (Mahwah, NJ: Lawrence Erlbaum, 2003).

85. Peter Schrag, *Final Test: The Battle for Adequacy in America's Schools* (New York: New Press, 2003), pp. 207–208; Ogbu, *Black American Students in an Affluent Suburb.*

86. Schrag, *Final Test*, p. 215.

87. Philip Green, *The Pursuit of Inequality* (New York: Pantheon Book, 1981), pp. 67–68.

88. Donald Orlich and Glenn Gufford, "Test Scores, Poverty, and Ethnicity: The New American Dilemma," paper presented at the Phi Delta Kappa Summit on Public Education, Washington, DC, 2006.

89. Ibid.

90. Stephen Jay Gould, *The Mismeasure of Man* (New York: W. W. Norton, 1996).

91. James Coleman, *Equality of Educational Opportunity* (Washington, DC: Government Printing Office, 1966); Eric Hanushek, "The Impact of Differential Expenditures on School Performance," *Educational Researcher* 18, no. 4 (1989): 49; Schrag, *Final Test.*

92. Bruce Biddle and David Berliner, "A Research Synthesis/Unequal School Funding in the United States," *Educational Leadership* 59, no. 8 (2002): 48–59.

93. Bruce Biddle and David Berliner, *Manufactured Crisis: Myths, Fraud, and the Attack on America's Public Schools* (Reading, MA: Addison-Wesley, 1996); Diane Ravitch, *Reign of Error: The Hoax of the Privatization Movement and the Danger to America's Public Schools* (New York: Alfred A. Knopf, 2013).

94. Biddle and Berliner, *Manufactured Crisis*; Ravitch, *Reign of Error.*

95. James Coleman, *Equality of Educational Opportunity* (Washington, DC: Government Printing Office, 1966), p. 325.

96. Eric Hanushek, "The Impact of Differential Expenditures on School Performance," *Educational Researcher* 18, no. 4 (1989): 49.

97. Schrag, *Final Test*, pp. 207–208; Ogbu, *Black American Students in an Affluent Suburb*; Claude Steel, *Whistling Vivaldi and Other Clues to How Stereotypes Affect Us* (New York: W. W. Norton, 2010).

98. Bruce Biddle and David Berliner, "A Research Synthesis/Unequal School Funding in the United States," *Educational Leadership* 59, no. 8 (2002): 48–59.

99. Frederick Mosteller, "The Tennessee Study of Class Size in the Early School Grades," *The Future of Children* 5, no. 2 (1995): 125.

100. Biddle and Berliner, "A Research Synthesis/Unequal School Funding in the United States."

101. Bruce Biddle and David Berliner, "What Research Says About Small Classes and Their Effects," *Policy Perspectives* (Winter 2002): 13. www.wested.org/online _pubs/small-classes.pdf

102. Ibid.

103. Ravitch, *Reign of Error.*

104. Peter Sacks, *Tearing Down the Gates: Confronting the Class Divide in American Education* (Berkeley: University of California Press, 2007).

7

The Incarceration Crisis

As one of the most racially repressive systems in the world, the US criminal justice system is a profound representation of metaracism. The United States incarcerates a larger proportion of its minority population than any other country in the world. It engages in a war on drugs that operates like a war on its minority population. It is one of the few developed countries that practices capital punishment, even though its criminal justice system is racially biased. It has been repeatedly cited with multiple human rights violations by international human rights organizations that are corroborated by the academic literature.[1] Its criminal justice system is extremely cruel and racially biased, yet there are no visible racists, no hateful bigots, and no public expressions of racism. This repressive system is a product of the reactionary movement and metaracism in the United States. In this chapter, I examine these human rights violations and analyze the role of the reactionary movement and metaracism in normalizing and legitimizing this cruel system.

Racial Repression and Human Rights Violations

These human rights violations appear in annual reports by Amnesty International and Human Rights Watch. These violations have been well documented and analyzed in the criminal justice and sociological literature. They include:

- Extremely high incarceration rates;
- Cruel and excessive sentencing of adult offenders;
- Cruel and excessive sentencing of child offenders;

201

- The death penalty;
- Community targeting and racial profiling; and
- Excessive use of force by police.

Class, Racial Bias, and Extremely High Incarceration Rates

The United States has astronomically high incarceration rates. As Table 7.1 indicates, the number of people in the criminal justice system—in jail (city or county), in prison (state or federal), or on parole or probation—has increased exponentially over the past thirty to forty years. Between 1980 and 1990, the number of people in the system more than doubled, increasing from 1,842,100 to 4,350,300 (jail, prison, parole, or probation). By 1995, there were 5,342,900 people in the system. This figure increased to 6,460,000 by 2000. It peaked in 2010 with 7,079,500 people in the system (4,055,514 on probation, 840,676 on parole, 748,728 in jail, and 1,521,414 in prison). These figures began to recede by 2011 with 6,977,700 people in the system (3,971,319 on probation, 853,852 on parole, 735,601 in jail, and 1,504,150 in prison).[2]

The overwhelming majority of those incarcerated are poor people and people of color:

> Across all racial groups, prisoners are drawn from the poorest sectors of society. A large percentage are unemployed at the time of their arrest or have only sporadic employment. Of those with jobs, many have incomes near or below the poverty level. Seventy-two percent of prison inmates and 60 percent of jail inmates have not completed high school; many are illiterate. . . .
>
> The statistical link between unemployment or underemployment and imprisonment is borne out in the demographic characteristics of prison populations. In 1990, 58.2 percent of all those jailed (about 561,700 people) were

Table 7.1 Number of Persons Under Correctional Supervision, 1980–2011

Year	Probation	Jail	Prison	Parole	Total
1980	1,118,097	183,988	319,598	220,438	1,842,100
1985	1,968,712	256,615	487,593	300,203	3,013,100
1990	2,670,234	405,320	743,382	531,407	4,350,300
1995	3,077,861	507,044	1,078,542	679,421	5,342,900
2000	3,839,532	621,149	1,316,333	725,527	6,460,000
2005	4,162,495	747,529	1,447,942	784,354	7,050,900
2010	4,055,514	748,728	1,521,414	840,676	7,079,500
2011	3,971,319	735,601	1,504,150	853,852	6,977,700

Source: US Department of Justice, *FBI Source Book* (Washington, DC: Government Printing Office, 2013).

unemployed at the time of their arrest. Roughly 68 percent earned less than $15,000 a year. State prison populations reveal a similar link. In Florida, for example, of nearly 30,000 people imprisoned in 1986, barely half (52 percent) were employed full-time at the time of their arrest. Nearly half earned less than $500 a month.[3]

Poor whites and blacks both have high incarceration rates; however, there is a disproportionately higher number of blacks in the system. The incarceration rate for African American men is alarming at 4,789 per 100,000. In 2006 out of a population of 18,262,000 black men, 836,800 black men were in jail or prison.[4] This means that about 4.8 percent of the total black male population in the United States was incarcerated, and about 8 percent was under the control of the criminal justice system. The Sentencing Project notes that by 2013, "for black males in their thirties, 1 in every 10 is in prison or jail on any given day."[5] About a third of the black male population has felony convictions.

Several factors have contributed to these astronomically high incarceration races and the racial and class biases in the system: the war on drugs, biased drug laws, and excessive sentencing laws.

The War on Drugs

The war on drugs initiated under the Ronald Reagan administration played a major role in the construction of a racially repressive criminal justice system. This war targeted black inner-city communities, and it imposed excessively long prison sentences on nonviolent drug offenders. Michelle Alexander demonstrates that incarceration rates increased independent of crime rates and that this increase was largely a function of the war on drugs.[6]

Marc Mauer of the Sentencing Project corroborates Michelle Alexander's research. He notes that drug use had declined substantially in the 1980s before the passage of the more draconian drug laws of the 1990s.[7] He notes too that there was profound racially targeted enforcement. According to Mauer about 0.6 percent of the black population used crack cocaine, compared to 0.2 percent for Hispanics and 0.1 percent for whites in 1995.[8] However, given their much greater proportion of the population, whites constituted 54 percent of crack cocaine users, blacks constituted 34 percent, and Hispanics 12 percent.[9] Whereas blacks constituted 34 percent of crack users—and whites and Hispanics constituted 66 percent of users—of those arrested for crack cocaine offenses, 81.4 percent were black.[10]

The higher arrest and conviction rate of blacks for crack cocaine possession is explained primarily by this racially targeted enforcement. There is a much higher arrest rate in inner cities because drug enforcement targets inner-city areas.[11] Michelle Alexander dismisses the common explanation that this targeting of inner-city areas occurs because drug sales are more frequent and more in the public view in the inner cities.[12] She notes that, contrary to this popular explanation, there are many more cases of open drug sales and drug abuse occurring in suburban areas than in the inner cities. The targeting of inner cities is a function of the common stereotype of the urban underclass and crazed drug addicts.

This racially biased targeting of drug enforcement has been most pronounced with marijuana offenses. According to an American Civil Liberties Union (ACLU) report, despite the fact that blacks and whites have comparable marijuana usage rates, "Black people are 3.7 times more likely to be arrested for marijuana possession than white people."[13] The study notes that these disparities are found all over the country. Although these arrest rates vary, they are not associated with the relative size of the black population. For example, the report states, "In Morgan and Pike Counties, AL, blacks make up just over 12 percent and 37 percent of the population, respectively, but account for 100 percent of the marijuana possession arrests."[14] Blacks made up 72.7 percent of the marijuana possession arrests in Cook County Illinois (which includes Chicago), 87.3 percent in Fulton County (which includes Atlanta), and 91.7 percent of the arrest in Baltimore, Maryland.[15] The total number of people arrested in some of these areas has reached staggering levels. For example, for the year 2010 alone, Cook County Illinois arrested more than 33,000 people for marijuana possession.[16] The director of the ACLU Criminal Law Reform Project, and one of the authors of this report, had this to say about the report: "The war on marijuana has disproportionately been a war on people of color. State and local governments have aggressively enforced marijuana laws selectively against Black people and communities, needlessly ensnaring hundreds of thousands of people in the criminal justice system at tremendous human and financial cost."[17] The report shows that while these disparities were bad ten years ago, they have grown worse.

The marijuana arrest policy has also been costly. The report noted that "states spent an estimated $3.61 billion enforcing marijuana possession laws in 2010 alone. New York and California combined spent over $1 billion."[18] Even though many police departments across the country have made enforcement a priority for the past decade, the aggressive enforcement of marijuana laws has failed to eradicate or even diminish the use of marijuana.[19]

Racially Biased Laws

Crack cocaine laws are biased. For example, the federal Anti-Drug Abuse Act of 1986 imposed a mandatory five-year sentence on anyone convicted of possessing 5 grams of crack cocaine, or of possessing 500 grams of pure cocaine. This law was considered racially discriminatory because blacks were more likely to use crack cocaine, rather than the costlier pure cocaine more commonly found in the suburbs, and because the sentencing for crack cocaine was much more severe than the sentencing for pure cocaine.[20] Recently, Congress passed the Fair Sentencing Act of 2010, which raised the possession requirement for a mandatory sentence of five years from 5 grams to 28 grams (equal to about an ounce) of crack cocaine.

In the 2013 *United States v. Blewett* decision, the Sixth Circuit Federal Appeals Court did not mince words in its condemnation of racially biased crack cocaine laws. The court cited late Harvard criminal law professor William J. Stuntz, who observed that, "persistent bias occurred with respect to the contemporary enforcement of drug laws where, in the 1990s and early 2000s, blacks constituted a minority of regular users of crack cocaine but more than 80 percent of crack defendants."[21] The court added that, prior to the passage of the Fair Sentencing Act, under mandatory minimum federal crack cocaine laws thousands of people were given sentences ranging from five years to life, and more than 80 percent of these federal prisoners were black.[22] In fiscal year 2010, more than 4,000 people, mostly black, received mandatory minimum sentences for crack cocaine. "The racially discriminatory impact of the 100:1 sentencing scheme surfaced early on when statistics showed that nearly one hundred percent of all crack defendants were non-white."[23] Moreover, "from 1988 to 1995, federal prosecutors prosecuted no whites under the crack provisions in 17 states, including major cities such as Boston, Denver, Chicago, Miami, Dallas, and Los Angeles."[24] The court claimed that the enforcement of the Anti-Drug Abuse Act of 1986 was "arbitrary, irrational and racially discriminatory." The court concluded that the Fair Sentencing Act should be applied retroactively and that failure to do so would violate the equal protection clause of the Fifth Amendment. The court added that "the discriminatory nature of prior crack sentences is no longer a point of legitimate debate."[25] It insisted that the racially discriminatory impact of the crack law was indisputable.[26]

The 2012 *Dorsey v. United States* decision arose after Edward Dorsey was arrested in August 2008 for selling 5.5 grams of crack cocaine. In September 2010 he was sentenced to a mandatory term of ten years, the sentence mandated by the Anti-Drug Abuse Act of 1986. He appealed on the grounds that he should have been given a lesser sentence under the Fair Sentencing Act of 2010, which went into effect in August 2010. In a 5 to 4 decision, the Supreme Court agreed.[27] The Fair Sentencing Act of 2010 and the Dorsey decision helped to ameliorate the extreme cases of racially discriminatory impacts in drug enforcement at the federal level. Moreover, in August 2013, Attorney General Eric Holder expressed concern about racial bias in federal drug laws and law enforcement and about federal prisons being overcrowded with nonviolent drug offenders. Holder added that the Justice Department would focus on high-level drug dealers and the more serious drug offenses and would avoid cases involving drug users and lower-level dealers, those with less than 280 grams of crack cocaine.[28]

Nevertheless, these federal policy changes did not eliminate the problem of racial repression in the criminal justice system. The Fair Sentencing Act and the Justice Department changes apply to only the federal criminal justice system. Since most people are incarcerated in state prisons, these changes have just a marginal impact. The racially repressive criminal justice system persists in state laws and state policies The more serious problem is a system that imposes irrational, draconian, and racially discriminatory sentences for nonviolent offenses.

Cruel and Excessive Sentencing of Adult Offenders

In addition to citing the United States for racially biased drug laws and enforcement, international human rights organizations have cited this nation for cruel and excessive sentencing practices.[29] Sentencing problems are found not only in antidrug laws, but also in truth in sentencing, mandatory sentencing, and three- and two-strikes laws.

Truth in sentencing laws address the issue of parole boards releasing prisoners early for good behavior. Whereas a prisoner sentenced to five to ten years could be released in three or four years for good behavior, the truth in sentencing law establishes that the prisoner could not be considered for parole until the fifth year. Mandatory sentences eliminated the discretion of judges. With these laws, judges could no longer consider mitigating circumstances in deciding on the sentence. A mandatory twenty years meant the judge could not impose a sentence of less than twenty years, regardless of the circumstances surrounding the crime of the convict.

The state of Florida provides some recent examples. On October 2012, John Horner was sentenced to a mandatory twenty-five-year minimum prison term for selling his pain pills to a police informant. John, who was married with three children, used prescription pain pills for injuries he sustained in an accident in which he lost his eye. Apparently, the informant told Horner that he had Crohn's disease, but had a choice of paying his rent or purchasing pain pills. Horner sold some of his pills to the informant. Although Horner had no prior arrest record, Florida law mandated a twenty-five-year sentence.[30] In another case in April 2010, nineteen-year-old Hope Sykes was sentenced to fifteen years for selling twenty-five hydrocodone pills to an undercover officer.[31]

A number of states impose mandatory life imprisonment for possession of more than 600 grams of heroin or crack cocaine, even for those with no prior arrests or convictions. Michigan mandates life imprisonment for anyone arrested with over 650 grams of heroin or crack. The injustice and unreasonableness of these types of mandatory sentences is shown in a 1996 report by the National Criminal Justice Commission:

> In Mobile, Alabama, Nicole Richardson fell in love at age twenty with a small-time drug dealer who worked out of a local bar. One day, an undercover agent asked her where he could buy some drugs. She told him to talk to her boyfriend. For this degree of involvement, she was sentenced to ten years in prison with no possibility of parole. Her boyfriend had information on other drug dealers to trade. After cooperating with authorities, he received a prison sentence of five years.
>
> Michael Irish was a carpenter from Portland, Oregon, whose life savings had been wiped out to pay for the medical bills of his cancer-stricken wife. Irish, who had no criminal history, was caught and convicted of unloading boxes of hashish from a boat. Under the mandatory minimum law, he was sentenced to twelve years in prison with no possibility of parole—an incarceration that will cost (the state) at least $250,000.[32]

In the early 1990s, states began to establish life sentences for those convicted of a third felony, the "Three Strikes and You're Out" policy. Between 1993 and 1995, twenty-four states and the federal government established three-strikes laws. These laws were enacted to remove so-called superpredators from the streets, but they tended instead to give life sentences to the poor and the powerless.

In a study of three-strikes convictions, Willie Wisely found that 85 percent of those sentenced to life were nonviolent offenders. He concludes that, although the law was designed to permanently incarcerate violent predators, it ended up locking up characters like the Three Stooges. Wisely provides some examples of those who committed relatively minor three-strikes offenses:

> Larry Fisher, 35, was convicted of his third strike in Snohomish County superior court in Washington. He is in prison and will stay there for the rest of his life. Fisher was convicted of putting his finger in his pocket, pretending it was a gun, and robbing a sandwich shop of $151. An hour later police arrested him at a bar a block away while he was drinking a beer. Fisher's two prior strikes involved stealing $360 from his grandfather in 1986 and in 1986 robbing a pizza parlor of $100.
>
> In March 1995, Jerry Dewayne Williams of Los Angeles got 25 years to life for stealing a slice of pizza from a group of children on a pier. . . .
>
> In Monterey County, Joel Murillo faced a term of 35 years to life for stealing television sets. But, Judge Robert Moody exercised his discretion and disregarded a prior felony conviction, sentencing Murillo to an 18 year term.[33]

Ewing v. California

In the 2003 *Ewing v. California* decision, the Supreme Court upheld the Three Strikes and You're Out law. This California case involved Gary Albert Ewing who stole three golf clubs worth about $399 a piece from a sporting goods store. He put the clubs down his shirt and into his pants leg. Stiff-legged, he was caught limping and dragging one leg as he left the store. He was convicted and sentenced to life imprisonment. Ewing had about nine prior convictions, which included misdemeanors as well as felonies. Although he was never charged with an assault or violent crime, in one of his prior offenses he was convicted of breaking into a home and terrorizing the inhabitants.[34]

Ewing's attorney challenged the three-strikes law and the life sentence on the constitutional ground that they violated the Eighth Amendment: "Excessive bail shall not be required, nor excessive fines imposed, nor cruel and unusual punishment inflicted." The attorney argued that the Supreme Court had established a clear and strong precedent that the punishment of a crime should be proportional to the crime itself, and that the Eighth Amendment not only prohibits cruel and unusual punishment but forbids "excessive sanctions."[35] Only four Supreme Court justices agreed. In his dissenting opinion, Justice John Paul Stevens stated:

> The Eighth Amendment succinctly prohibits "excessive sanctions. . . ." Faithful to the Amendment's text, this Court has held that the Constitution directs judges to apply their best judgment in determining the proportionality of fines . . . and other forms of punishment, including the imposition of a death sentence. . . . Rather by broadly prohibiting excessive sanctions, the Eighth Amendment directs judges to exercise their wise judgment in assessing the proportionality of all forms of punishment.[36]

Writing for the majority, Justice Sandra Day O'Connor insisted that states had a compelling public purpose for imposing life sentences for repeat offenders and that these sentences did not violate the Eighth Amendment. O'Connor recited the history behind the enactment of this law. She discussed the Polly Klaas kidnapping, rape, and murder. She pointed out that the California State Legislature had tabled the law until Richard Allen Davis kidnapped Klaas from her home in Petaluma, California, repeatedly raped her, and then murdered her. O'Connor argued that "Davis had served only half of his most recent sentence (16 years for kidnapping, assault, and burglary). Had Davis served his entire sentence, he would still have been in prison on the day that Polly Klaas was kidnapped."[37] The Polly Klaas murder galvanized support for the three-strikes initiative. In response to this murder, California policymakers substantially increased prison sentences for repeat offenders. The state doubled the sentences for defendants with one prior serious or violent felony conviction. It mandated life sentences for those with two or more prior offenses.[38]

O'Connor insisted that states enact the three-strikes laws for the legitimate and compelling purpose of protecting the public safety. She agreed that the Eighth Amendment prohibits sentences that are grossly disproportionate to the crime. However, she disagreed that the three-strikes law and the life sentence imposed on Ewing violated the gross disproportionality rule. She cited the *Rummel v. Estelle* case:

> In Rummel, we held that it did not violate the Eight Amendment for a state to sentence a three-time offender to life in prison with the possibility of parole. Like Ewing, Rummel was sentenced to a lengthy prison term under a recidivism statute. Rummel's two prior offenses were a 1964 felony for fraudulent use of a credit card to obtain $80 worth of goods or services and a 1969 felony conviction for passing a forged check in the amount of $28.36. His triggering offense was a conviction for felony theft—obtaining $120.75 by false pretense.
>
> This court ruled that "[h]aving twice imprisoned him for felonies, Texas was entitled to place upon Rummel the onus of one who is simply unable to bring his conduct within the social norms prescribed by the criminal law of the state." The recidivism statute "is nothing more than a societal decision that when such a person commits yet another felony, he should be subjected to the admittedly serious penalty of incarceration for life, subject only to the state's judgment as to whether to grant him parole."[39]

O'Connor added: "Ewing's sentence is justified by the State's public-safety interest in incapacitating and deterring recidivist felons, and amply supported by his own long, serious criminal record. Ewing has been convicted of numerous misdemeanor and felony offenses, served nine separate terms of incarceration, and committed most of his crimes while on probation or parole."[40] O'Connor's logic helps explain the incarceration crisis. Life sentences are justified by the state's public safety interests, by society's need to protect itself from superpredators: from kidnappers, rapists, and murders who prey on the innocent and who kidnap, rape, and murder and then serve their time, only to get out to kidnap, rape, and murder again. To stop this cycle of rape, murder, incarceration, and more rape, murder, and incarceration—so the argument goes—it becomes necessary to incarcerate these violent superpredators for life. Life imprisonment for multiple violent offenders does not violate the gross proportionality rule. Arguably, such a sentence is proportionate to the multiple violent crimes. The problem with O'Connor's line of reasoning is that the law takes away the discretion of the judge to determine whether the sentence is indeed proportionate to the crime. The problem is that the life sentence is mandatory whether the crimes are rape and murder, stealing golf clubs, or forging bad checks.

The most serious problem is that these mandatory life sentences are driven by fear and hysteria. They seem rational in the face of a multiple rapists and murders like Davis. However, a life sentence for engaging in fraud to steal $80.00 and getting convicted, then stealing $29.36 and getting convicted, and then stealing $120.75 and getting a life sentence is grossly disproportionate to the crime. It is a penalty cost that is far removed from the cost of the crime. It violates most societies' sense of fairness and justice. Only the most repressive society in the world would sentence a person to life imprisonment for stealing less than $300.

Human Rights Violations in Juvenile Justice

In 2005, Human Rights Watch published a study that indicted the United States for its practice of sentencing children to life imprisonment without any chance of parole in violation of international agreements and standards.[41] Out of all the countries in the world, only a handful sentence children to life without parole. The report notes that "all countries except the United States and Somalia have ratified the Convention on the Rights of the Child, which explicitly forbids life imprisonment without possibility of release for offenses committed by persons below eighteen years of age."[42] The United States stands alone in terms of the number of youth offenders sentenced each year and the total number serving life sentences. The report adds, "Of the 154 countries for which Human Rights Watch was able to obtain data, only three currently have people serving life without parole for crimes they committed as children, and it appears that those three countries combined have only about a dozen such cases."[43] Today, the United States has over 2,700 youth offenders serving life sentences without parole. But this practice is new; it was rare in the United States prior to 1990. It arose out of a national hysteria over juvenile violence.[44]

Public fear over rising youth crime rates enabled policymakers to enact even more severe penalties. Governors and state legislatures made several changes in state law that made it easier to sentence youth offenders to life without parole. Some state policymakers simply lowered the age at which juveniles may be tried as adults. Twenty states eliminated the age limit, allowing courts to try children of any age as adults. Today, thirty-four states allow juveniles thirteen years old and younger to be tried as adults. Some states mandated that all juveniles charged with first degree murder be automatically tried as adults. Some have given prosecutors the discretion to decide whether to try juveniles as adults.

Despite the pervasive public fear of superpredators, few of the juveniles serving life sentences fit the description of the superpredator. The majority of those sentenced, about 60 percent, are first-time offenders:

The specter of "super predators" created much of the national furor over youth violence. Politicians and the public thought their communities were (or would be) besieged by vicious teenagers with long records of crime. Yet few of the child offenders sentenced to life without parole fit this super predator profile. Our research suggests that 59 percent of youth offenders received a life without parole sentence for their first-ever criminal conviction of any sort. These youths had neither an adult criminal record nor a juvenile adjudication. The other 39 percent had prior criminal records that ranged from convictions as adults for serious crimes such as robbery, to juvenile offenses such as getting into fights with other teenagers.[45]

Human Rights Watch provides some examples of cases in which juveniles were sentenced to life without parole. Stacey T. was fourteen years old when he committed the crime for which he was sentenced to life without parole. He was an excellent student, on his way from ninth to tenth grade. He had no prior record or encounters with the police. But he agreed to participate in the robbery of a drug dealer by letting two adults tie him up and pretend to murder him in order to convince the drug dealer that they were serious. The two adults tied up Stacey, took him outside, and pretended to murder him. Instead, they released him. They then tied up the drug dealer, put him in the trunk of the dealer's car, took him out to a park, and shot him to death. Stacey had agreed to assist with a robbery, not a murder, and he was not present at the murder. Nevertheless, he was convicted and sentenced to life without parole.[46]

Another example involved Samantha L., who was fourteen years old when she committed the crime for which she was sentenced to life. She took her boyfriend to her best friend's grandfather's house to ask to borrow money. When the grandfather said no to loaning her the money, she wanted to leave. Her boyfriend wanted to stay and talk. She went outside and waited in her boyfriend's truck. Later her boyfriend came out and told her that he killed the grandfather. She thought he was lying because he had no blood on himself. They drove away. She and her boyfriend were both arrested that night. Samantha was sentenced to life without parole for aiding and abetting a murder. She did have a prior record for assault, burglaries, and auto theft.[47] As these examples indicate, many of the youths sentenced to life were participants and followers, but few had committed murders themselves.

Double Human Rights Violations

Human Rights Watch contends that trying youths as adults and sentencing them to life without parole constitutes multiple human rights violations.[48] Youths incarcerated for life are presumed unredeemable and unsalvageable. They are often denied educational and vocational opportunities on the grounds that they will not need them because they will never be released back into the public. Some are placed in adult facilities and subjected to assaults and rapes by adult inmates.

The Race Issue

The most troubling aspect of the Human Rights Watch report is the high percentage of blacks youth offenders incarcerated:

> Our data reveal that blacks constitute 60 percent of the youth offenders serving life without parole nationwide and whites constitute 29 percent. In addition, the data show that black youth nationwide are serving life without parole sentences at a rate that is ten times higher than white youth (the rate for black youth is 6.6 as compared to .6 for white youth).
> Again, while the differences are dramatic, we do not know the crime rates, criminal histories, or other race-neutral factors that would allow us to draw conclusions about racial disparities in the sentencing policies of states. However, research studies have found that minority youths receive harsher treatment than similarly situated white youths at every stage of the criminal justice system from the point of arrest to sentencing. For example, Amnesty International's research indicates that one reason for the over-representation of black and other minority children in the criminal justice system is racial discrimination by law enforcement and justice authorities.[49]

The Supreme Court's Response

The Supreme Court's response to this human rights violation of sentencing children to die in prison has been slow and narrow. A few cases have come before the Court, but they have not put an end to the practice. Noteworthy are *Miller v. Alabama,* and *Hill v. Snyder* (a federal district court decision out of the state of Michigan).

Miller v. Alabama

In the *Miller v. Alabama* decision, the court struck down state laws that mandated a minimum of life imprisonment without any chance of parole for juvenile offenders. This decision involved two separate cases, each was a fourteen-year-old offender. The first case took place in Arkansas. It involved Kuntrell Jackson and two other youths. In November 1999, Jackson and the other youths decided to rob a video store. On the way to the store, Jackson learned that one of the youths, Derrick Shields, had a sawed-off shotgun hidden in his coat. Jackson decided to stay outside the store while the other two youths went inside:

Inside, Shields pointed the gun at the store clerk, Laurie Troup, and demanded that she "give up the money." Troup refused. A few moments later, Jackson went into the store to find Shields continuing to demand money. At trial, the parties disputed whether Jackson warned Troup that "[w]e ain't playin'" or instead told his friends, "I thought you all was playin'." When Troup threatened to call the police, Shields shot and killed her. The three boys fled empty-handed.

Arkansas law gives prosecutors discretion to charge 14-year-olds as adults when they are alleged to have committed certain serious offenses. The prosecutor here exercised that authority by charging Jackson with capital felony murder and aggravated robbery. Jackson moved to transfer the case to juvenile court, but after considering the alleged facts of the crime, a psychiatrist's examination, and Jackson's juvenile arrest history (shoplifting and several incidents of car theft), the trial court denied the motion. A jury later convicted Jackson of both crimes. Noting that "in view of [the] verdict, there's only one possible punishment," the judge sentenced Jackson to life without parole.[50]

Arkansas law allowed the prosecutor to try a fourteen year old as an adult. The law also mandated a sentence of death or no less than life imprisonment without any chance of parole for anyone convicted of a capital murder. In *Roper v. Simmons*, the Supreme Court had struck down the practice of executing juveniles who were younger than eighteen years old when they committed their crime.[51] In *Graham v. Florida,* the Court struck down mandatory life sentences without any chance of parole for juveniles involved in nonviolent crimes.

The second case involved another fourteen year old, Evan Miller. Miller had been in and out of foster care because his mother suffered from alcoholism and drug addiction and his stepfather physically abused him. Miller had his own problems, having attempted suicide four times, the first time when he was only six years old. When the crime he was convicted of occurred, he was living with his mother:

One night in 2003, Miller was at home with a friend, Colby Smith, when a neighbor, Cole Cannon, came to make a drug deal with Miller's mother. The two boys followed Cannon back to his trailer, where all three smoked marijuana and played drinking games. When Cannon passed out, Miller stole his wallet, splitting the $300 with Smith. Miller then tried to put the wallet back in Cannon's pocket, but Cannon awoke and grabbed Miller by the throat. Smith hit Cannon with a nearby baseball bat, and once released, Miller grabbed the bat and repeatedly struck Cannon with it. Miller placed a sheet over Cannon's head, told him "I am God, I've come to take your life," and delivered one more blow. The boys then retreated to Miller's trailer, but soon decided to return to Cannon's to cover up evidence of their crime. Once there, they lit two fires. Cannon eventually died from his injuries and smoke inhalation.[52]

As with the Arkansas case, Alabama law allowed the prosecutor to charge Miller as an adult. Also, Alabama law mandates a minimum sentence of life without parole for murder in the commission of arson. Miller was convicted and sentenced to life without any chance of parole. In both cases, neither the judge nor the jury had any discretion to consider mitigating circumstances. The judge could not consider the fact that Jackson was not the shooter and that there was no evidence that he had intended to hurt anyone. The judge could not consider Miller's and Jackson's age or any other mitigating circumstances. State law mandated that children convicted of murder be sentenced to life imprisonment without any chance of parole. The Supreme Court decision was narrow. It did not strike down excessively long prison sentences. It did not strike down the practice of sentencing children to life. It struck down state laws that mandated life sentences without parole for children convicted of murder, despite mitigating circumstances and over the objection of judges and juries: "By requiring that all children convicted of homicide receive lifetime incarceration without possibility of parole, regardless of their age and age-related characteristics and the nature of their crimes, the mandatory sentencing schemes before us violate this principle of proportionality, and so the Eighth Amendment's ban on cruel and unusual punishment."[53]

Michigan and Iowa Undermine Miller

This decision did not require the release of the thousands of prisoners who were children when they committed their crimes. The case of state of Michigan illustrates the narrowness of this ruling. Just after the *Miller v. Alabama* decision, thirteen inmates incarcerated in the state of Michigan sued for a probationary hearing. In *Hill v. Snyder,* a federal district court ruled that they were indeed entitled to probation hearings.[54] In response to this ruling Michigan attorney general Bill Schuette sent a letter to eighty-three county prosecutors stating that the Hill ruling applied only to those thirteen inmates. He added that neither the Miller nor the Hill ruling entitled inmates to retroactive parole hearings.[55] He subsequently appealed the case.

Michigan was not the only state to undermine the Miller decision. In another case cited by Amnesty International, Iowa governor Terry Brastad responded to the Miller decision by commuting the sentences of thirty-eight people sentenced to life without parole for committing a crime when they were younger than eighteen years old. He reduced the life sentence to sixty years without any chance of parole and without any consideration for mediating circumstances.[56] In other words, he undermined the Miller decision but guaranteed that they would die in prison by changing the sentences from life to sixty years.

Capital Punishment

The death penalty has been another area that has involved both human rights violations and racial repression. There are several problems with the death penalty: it is racially biased, it kills some innocent people, it is cruel punishment, and it does not deter crime. The *McCleskey v. Kemp* decision challenged the death penalty on grounds of racial bias. Warren McCleskey and four other men, all armed, had entered a furniture store to rob it. They tied up the store employees, but not before a silent alarm was activated. When a police officer answering the silent alarm came into the front of the store, four shots were fired and the officer was killed. McCleskey confessed to the robbery, but not to the murder. Although it was not a perfect match with his gun, the bullet that killed the officer came from a .38 revolver, the same type of gun McCleskey had used in the robbery. McCleskey was charged and convicted of the murder of a police officer.[57]

The major issue in this case was whether the death penalty was applied in a racially discriminatory manner and, if so, whether this application violated the equal protection clause of the Fourteenth Amendment. The case turned on a study conducted by David C. Baldus, Charles Pulaski, and George Woodworth (known as the Baldus study).[58]

The Baldus study indicated that there was substantial evidence of racial discrimination in the administration of the death penalty. Despite this evidence, the Supreme Court upheld the constitutionality of capital punishment. Justice Lewis F. Powell Jr. writing for the majority decided that the statistical evidence alone was insufficient to find any violation of the equal protection clause of the Fourteenth Amendment. Powell summarized the Baldus study:

> The Baldus study is actually two sophisticated statistical studies that examine over 2,000 murder cases that occurred in Georgia during the 1970s. The raw numbers collected by Professor Baldus indicated that defendants charged with killing white persons received the death penalty in 11% of the cases, but defendants charged with killing blacks received the death penalty in only 1% of the cases. . . .
>
> Baldus also divided the cases according to the combination of the race of the defendant and the race of the victim. He found that the death penalty was assessed in 22% of the cases involving black defendants and white victims . . . 1% of the cases involving black defendants and black victims. . . . Similarly, Baldus found that prosecutors sought the death penalty in 70% of the cases involving black defendants and white victims . . . 15% of the cases involving black defendants and black victims. . . .
>
> Baldus subjected his data to an extensive analysis, taking account of 230 variables that could have explained the disparities on nonracial grounds. One of the models concludes that, even after taking account of 39 nonracial variables, defendants charged with killing white victims were 4.3 times as likely to receive a death sentence as defendants charged with killing blacks.[59]

Justice Powell argued that, even if the Baldus study is assumed valid, statistical evidence of racial discrimination alone is insufficient to prove unconstitutional racial discrimination. Citing the appeals court's decision, Powell argued that, assuming the Baldus study was valid, the appeals court found the statistics "insufficient to demonstrate discriminatory intent or unconstitutional discrimination in the Fourteenth Amendment context, [and] insufficient to show irrationality, arbitrariness and capriciousness under any kind of Eighth Amendment analysis."[60] In other words, Powell found evidence of systemic discrimination insufficient to support a constitutional violation. He required proof that police, prosecutors, and judges were prejudiced and had engaged in purposeful or intentional discrimination:

> Our analysis begins with the basic principle that a defendant who alleges an equal protection violation has the burden of proving "the existence of purposeful discrimination." . . . Thus, to prevail under the Equal Protection Clause, McCleskey must prove that the decision makers in his case acted with discriminatory purpose. He offers no evidence specific to his own case that would support an inference that racial considerations played a part in his sentence. Instead, he relies solely on the Baldus study.[61]

Powell maintained that the standards of proof of discrimination for criminal justice cases are more stringent than those for Title 7 employment discrimination cases. In Title 7 employment discrimination cases, statistical evidence is sufficient to demonstrate a prima facie case of discrimination. Once this is established, the burden of proof shifts to the employer, who must demonstrate that the hiring standards are not arbitrary but are necessary for the job. In criminal justice cases, it is insufficient to show statistical evidence of discrimination alone. Defendants must present evidence of purposeful discrimination. Powell established an impossible standard for demonstrating illegal racial discrimination in death penalty cases. He required evidence of motive and then more evidence. That is, he required evidence that prosecutors, judges, and jurors intended to produce an adverse racial impact. Getting this type of evidence is extremely difficult in employment discrimination cases, as most employers are aware of antidiscrimination laws and are careful to conceal their motives. However, in setting up this difficult standard, Powell made it impossible to obtain the needed evidence. Powell insisted that prosecutors, judges, and jurors "cannot be called to testify to the motives and influences that lead to their verdict."[62] In other words, Powell required evidence of motive, but then prohibited the questioning of jurors, prosecutors, and judges to obtain that evidence.

Michelle Alexander makes this point more forcefully:

> On its face, the case appeared to be a straightforward challenge to Georgia's death penalty scheme. Once the Court's opinion was released, however, it be-

came clear the case was about much more that the death penalty. The real issue at hand was whether—and to what extent—the Supreme Court would tolerate racial bias in the criminal justice system as a whole. The Court's answer was that racial bias would be tolerated—virtually to any degree—so long as no one admitted it.[63]

Metaracism and Racial and Class Repression

Metaracism plays a role in enabling the United States to maintain one of the cruelest, most racially repressive criminal justice systems among developed nations. Undergirding this system are memories of the urban underclass literature and fearful images of superpredators, black street criminals, drug-crazed assailants, and black street gangs. Like earlier forms of racism, metaracism effectively desensitizes the nation to the suffering of people trapped for life in this penal system. With this racism, fear trumps mercy. Because of the way people on death row look, it is difficult to believe that anyone could be innocent or that the government, police, prosecutors, juries, or judges could make a mistake and send innocent people to prison. Nevertheless, innocent people end up there.

Michael Radelet, Hugo Bedau, and Constance Putnam document how overzealous prosecutions, perjured witnesses, erroneous testimony, mistaken identity, police negligence, incompetent defense counsels, and errors in judgment can result in innocent people ending up on death row. They demonstrate that, by conservative estimates, more than 400 people have been erroneously convicted of capital crimes between 1900 and 1991.[64] Bedau and Radelet estimate that more than thirty-five people known to be innocent were executed between 1900 and 1987.[65] Even with elaborate appeals processes and safeguards in place, human error is possible. Moreover, the likelihood of executing more innocent people increases as the number of inmates on death row increases, as appeals and other safeguards are abridged or eliminated, as public enthusiasm for executions rises, as the burden of proof shifts to the defendant on appeals, and as the federal courts establish stricter standards for proof of innocence in appeals cases, such as they did in the 1994 *Jacobs v. Scott* case—the case in which the court decided that proof that someone else committed the murder is insufficient to establish one's innocence.

Like earlier forms of racism, metaracism masks the pronounced class and racial biases. About 90 percent of prisoners on death row could not afford their own attorneys at the time of their trials. Although all low-income defendants in capital cases are entitled to a court-appointed attorney, and most courts provide additional resources for public defenders to conduct independent investigations, the court system remains biased in favor of the rich and against the poor. Wealthy defendants are able to afford a team of the best attorneys in the nation, independent DNA specialists, forensic scientists, and special investigators, while poor defendants have few resources even for independent laboratory tests. In this system, wealthy defendants who appear guilty are more likely to be acquitted and poor defendants who are innocent are more likely to end up on death row.

Although prosecutors take every precaution to avoid the possibility of racial bias, and the murder arrest rate for African American men tends to reflect their rate of committing murder, one particular bias stands out in the studies of race and capital punishment: "the average odds of receiving a death sentence among all indicted cases were 4.3 times higher in cases with white victims."[66] A 1990 General Accounting Office report on studies of race and the death sentence reached a similar conclusion: "Our synthesis of the 28 studies shows a pattern of evidence indicating racial disparities in the charging, sentencing and imposition of the death penalty after the Furman decision."[67] The *Furman v. Georgia* decision suspended the argued death penalties because the death penalty was administered in an arbitrary, freakish, and racially discriminatory manner. In his concurring opinion, Justice Thurgood Marshall presented these statistics:

> Regarding discrimination, it has been said that "it is usually the poor, the illiterate, the underprivileged, the member of the minority group—the man who, because he is without means, and is defended by a court-appointed attorney—who becomes society's sacrificial lamb. . . . Indeed, a look at the bare statistics regarding executions is enough to betray much of the discrimination. A total of 3,859 persons have been executed since 1930, of whom 1,751 were white and 2,066 were Negro. Of the executions, 3,334 were for murder; 1,664 of the executed murderers were white and 1,630 were Negro; 455 persons, including 48 whites and 405 Negros, were executed for rape.[68]

Given the depth of class and racial bias in the justice system, Marshall did not believe that capital punishment could ever be administered in a fair and unbiased manner. Indeed, as his statistics bear out, 89.1 percent of those executed for rape were black, and blacks comprised 53.5 percent of all those executed between 1930 and 1968.[69] Capital punishment is symptomatic of a repressive state. Most nations, except for the most repressive ones, have abolished capital punishment. Moreover, when repressive regimes are replaced by democratic ones, capital punishment is generally eliminated. When the apartheid regime in South Africa ended, so did capital punishment. The persistence of capital punishment in the United States is symptomatic of the persistence of both racism and classism. Capital punishment, life imprisonment without any chance of parole for nonviolent offenders, and systematic racial and class biases are signs of a society rendered callous and insensitive by undercurrents of racism.

Targeting Minority Communities

Amnesty International cited the United States for community-targeted police enforcement and racial profiling. A federal district court decision involving the city of New York illustrates this issue. On August 12, 2013, federal district judge Shira A. Scheindlin ruled that the city's style of police administration violated both the Fourth and the Fourteenth Amendments. The judge provided the following summary of the facts of this case: "Between 2004 and June 2012, the New York City Police Department conducted over 4.4 million Terry stops. The number of stops per year rose sharply from 314,000 in 2004 to a high of 686,000 in 2011. . . . Between 2004 and 2009, the percentage of stops where the officer failed to state a specific suspected crime rose from 1% to 36%."[70] In 2010, the city's population was about 23 percent black, 29 percent Hispanic, and 33 percent white. Nevertheless, of the 4.4 million people stopped, 52 percent were black and 31 percent were Hispanic; that is, 83 percent of those stopped were people of color. Only 10 percent were white. Among the blacks stopped, 1.0 percent of them had weapons and 1.8 percent of them had contraband other than weapons. Among the whites stopped, 1.4 percent had weapons and 2.3 percent had contraband other than weapons. Also, the police were more likely to use force among blacks than whites.[71]

Judge Scheindlin agreed that the racial composition of people stopped by the police should reflect the racial composition of residents of the neighborhoods and the racial composition of those arrested for crimes. However, she noted that the statistics indicated that blacks and Hispanics were more likely than whites to be stopped, even after controlling for these factors. She added, "This is so even in areas with low crime rates, racially heterogeneous populations, or predominately white populations."[72] The judge concluded that, when police officers searched those stopped without reasonable suspicion, they violated the Fourth Amendment's prohibition from unreasonable search and seizure. When the police targeted blacks and Hispanics for stops, they violated the equal protection clause of the Fourteenth Amendment.[73]

New York mayor Michael Bloomberg responded to the ruling with visible anger. He attacked the judge: "This is a very dangerous decision made by a judge who I think does not understand how policing works. . . . Nowhere in her 195-page decision does she mention the historic cuts in crime or the number of lives that have been saved. . . . You're not going to see any change in tactics overnight. . . . I wouldn't want to be responsible for a lot of people dying."[74] He argued that the New York City Police Department's policy of targeted enforcement had saved lives. He claimed that the judge had no background in police administration, that she did not understand the city's policy, and that she was prejudiced against the police from the beginning. He insisted that the aggressive targeted police enforcement policy was effective policing, and that it made the streets of New York safer. He added that the judge's decision was irresponsible, and announced that the city would be appealing the decision.[75]

The nation is already polarized over this issue because liberals ignored the violence and, thus, allowed conservatives to define the problem. Conservatives defined the problem in terms of out-of-control street violence brought under control by aggressive targeted police enforcement. They claimed that this is not racism because a high percentage of New York City murders had been committed by black and Hispanic men.

The problem is not that poverty is associated with violence. Social scientists have long documented this association between violence and poverty, a point that I note in Chapter 1 and one that is also presented by W. E. B. Du Bois.[76] William J. Wilson also refers to this when he demonstrates that most homicides in Chicago occurred in the areas of the city with the greatest concentration of poverty.[77] In a follow-up study with Robert Sampson, Wilson demonstrates this point further: crime and violence are strongly associated with concentrated poverty.[78] Indeed, cities with high rates of concentrated poverty like Baltimore, Washington, DC, Detroit, New Orleans, and Saint Louis have high homicide rates. Wilson explains the violence in terms of extreme inequality, concentrated poverty, social isolation, absence of positive role models, lack of supportive social networks, and social pathology.[79] On an international level, Amy Chuo demonstrates the strong association between extreme inequality and violence. Violence has been strongly associated with poverty most evident in areas with the most extreme inequality, such as Brazil.[80]

Although violence has been associated with poverty and inequality, the responses of the neoconservative and urban underclass literature, the mass media, and racial politics have done more to exacerbate rather than explain or solve the violence problem. As with welfare policy, neoconservatives define the problem in terms of liberal governments and the bad values and behavior of the poor. For example, Charles Murray claims that crime increased with the liberalization of the criminal justice system. He dehumanizes the urban poor in ways that encourage repression as the solution. Murray argues that the liberal policies of the 1960s changed the cost-benefit ratio, created incentives for committing crimes, and made crime less risky and less costly for poor people.[81] He adds that the liberal changes of the 1960s restricted police behavior, required police to have probable cause to stop a poor person on the street, required warrants issued by courts to search houses, and guaranteed poor felony defendants an attorney. According to Murray,

> Accompanying these changes in the numbers were changes in the rules of the game that once again disproportionately affected the poor. The affluent per-

son caught by the police faced effectively the same situation in 1960 and in 1970. The poor person did not. In 1960, he could be picked up more or less on the police officer's intuition. He was likely to be taken into an interrogation room and questioned without benefit of counsel. He was likely to confess in instances when, if a lawyer had been sitting at his side, he would not have confessed. He was likely to be held in jail until his court date or to have to post bail, considerable economic punishment in itself. If convicted he was likely to be given a prison term. By 1970, the poor person had acquired an array of protections and stratagems that were formerly denied him.[82]

Murray blames the rise of crime during the 1970s on the extension of rights to poor people. He insists that the extension of these rights "made crime less risky for poor people who were inclined to commit crimes if they thought they could get away with them."[83] The solution to the crime problem was to take away constitutional protections for inner-city suspects and to substantially increase the penalties for committing crimes. This is precisely the solution that contributes to the human rights violations that we see today.

The conservative academic literature also suggests that there were superpredators and career criminals in the streets, and that the best way of addressing this problem was to incarcerate more people for longer periods of time. Scholars like John DiIulio claim that most crimes were committed by a few superpredators.[84] In a study of convicted felons in their twenties in Philadelphia, Marvin Wolfang, Robert Figlio, and Thorsten Selling conclude that 6 percent of them committed more than half of all the crimes.[85] The policy solution was to target these criminals and lock them up. The expected results would be a dramatic drop in crime. Other studies conclude that rehabilitation did not work and that incarceration was more effective in protecting the public.

The mass media has played a major role in promoting hysteria over violent crime and public perception of the need for harsher criminal penalties. Television programming has focused more on violent crimes: crime scene investigations, gang violence, and terrorism. The media and the academic literature have promoted images of predatory street criminals concentrated in inner cities.

Political leaders have played a role in making the criminal justice system more repressive. This role goes back to the early 1970s, with the political campaigns of George Wallace, Richard Nixon, and Reagan, but it continued with Bill Clinton. At the state level, both Democratic and Republican politicians vied with each other to demonstrate to the public who was the toughest on crime. These leaders, the media, and the literature did much to promote hysteria over crime and to dehumanize inner-city residents and young black men in ways that have made it difficult to address the problem of violence in high-poverty urban areas in constructive ways.

David Kennedy suggests that both liberals and conservatives get it wrong. He insists that liberals get it wrong by ignoring or underestimating the extent of the violence problem and by overestimating the racism. According to Kennedy, the problem with the conservatives is not that they see the violence problems or that they see its association with poor black neighborhoods. The problem is that conservatives define issues in ways that dehumanize young black and Hispanic men and encourage police repression.[86] Entire black communities are denigrated as people talk about issues exclusively in terms of bad values, pathological behavior, female-headed households, and dangerous youth gangs.

Kennedy maintains that violence, particularly violence associated with youth gangs and drug dealers, is a serious problem in large urban areas, particularly in cities like Baltimore, Buffalo, Chicago, Detroit, Los Angeles, and Oakland. After extensive interviews with police officers, drug dealers, gang members, residents, and others, Kennedy sums up his view of the problem:

> Spend time, real time, with cops. Spend time, real time with angry communities. Spend time, real time with gang members and drug dealers. They are, none of them, their stereotypes. They are, all of them, in their own ways, strong and aspirational and resilient. They are, all of them, dealing as best they can with a world they did not make. They are all doing profoundly destructive things without fully understanding what they do. There is, on all sides, malice, craziness, and evil. But not much, it turns out, not much at all. There is on all sides, a deep reservoir of core human decency. (Yes, for those of you shaking your heads and about to put this book down, because you cannot believe this is true of cops, or the neighborhoods, or the gangbangers; truly. Bear with me. You'll see.)
>
> This is what is at the heart of America's shame of violent death and mass incarceration and unspeakable community fear and chaos. Those understanding and misunderstandings and the awful stereotypes they foster and reinforce, and the awful places into which they push ourselves and each other. The awful truth is that they are understandable, each and every one; they make perfect sense, each from their own perspective.[87]

Kennedy demonstrates that these residents are no different than residents anywhere else. They are good, decent, rational, and caring people who help each other and give each other emotional support. They value education and hard work. They aspire to move out of poverty and move up the ladder of social mobility. Although concentrated poverty areas have high rates of single mothers, they often receive support in raising their children from their mothers, sisters, neighbors, boyfriends, and former boyfriends. However, these areas do have high needs, yet they suffer from inadequate resources and institutional supports.[88]

Kennedy urges policymakers to change the style of police administration into one that empowers and humanizes residents, maximizes police-resident interaction and communication, and involves the entire community in efforts to reduce the violence. The current approach dehumanizes young black men and focuses on the control of minority communities. Kennedy's approach addresses the issue of police administration, improving the relationship between police officers and the community they are responsible for protecting. This approach ignores the social economic and environmental conditions that tend to produce crime.

In the final analysis, the US criminal justice system has become one of the most racially repressive systems in the world; yet because of the form of racism, the United States cannot begin to have a healthy and open dialogue of these problems. The problem is that the system is not based on the old style of racism with open and hateful bigots. There are no leaders calling for the racial repression of blacks. Because of this absence of the bigots, conservative leaders insist with passion that there is no racism, that racism is a thing of the past, and that it is a figment of the liberal imagination.

The problem is that racial repression is deeply embedded in US society. It is associated with concentrated urban poverty and extreme inequality, with a dominant culture that dehumanizes the urban poor and depicts young inner-city black men as potential thugs, drug dealers, and street criminals who threaten middle-class society. This culture enables the emergence of a cruel, sadistic, violent, and unmerciful justice system. It is related to a form of politics that exploits the fears and anxieties triggered by this dominant culture.

This repressive system did not spring up magically out of metaracism. The corporate-centered coalition played a role. The conservative think tanks produced the neoconservative and urban underclass literature that dehumanizes the poor and that calls for the repressive policies. Also, corporate policymaking organizations, such as the American Legislative Exchange Commission, played a major role in producing and promoting model repressive legislation. Marvin Meadors provides a revealing expose of the role of ALEC:

> How is model legislation drafted by the American Legislative Exchange Council (ALEC) undermining democracy? . . .
>
> ALEC is funded by the usual suspects: the Koch brothers, Exxon Mobil, and the NRA to name a few. . . .
>
> In addition to the Florida bill that ALEC and the NRA call the "Castle Doctrine Act," also known as the "Stand Your Ground," law which will likely be used as a defense in the Trayvon Martin killing, ALEC model bills have served as the template for "voter ID" laws that swept the country in 2011 for the "voucher" programs that privatize public education for anti-environmental bills. . . .
>
> ALEC's model legislation has been instrumental in the explosive growth of the prison population. It helped pioneer "three strikes" laws, mandatory minimum sentencing laws, and truth in sentencing laws which served to abolish or curb parole so convicts are made to serve the entire length of their sentence. "Because of truth-in-sentencing and other tough sentencing measures, state prison populations grew by half a million inmates in the 1990s

even while crime rates fell dramatically." In fact, one of ALEC's benefactors, the Corrections Corporation of America (CCA) made an offer to cash-strapped states to buy up their prison populations at a cost savings as long as the state kept their prisons 90 percent filled to capacity.[89]

Conclusion

In this chapter, I suggested that metaracism and the conservative coalition contributed to the emergence of one of the most racially repressive criminal justice systems in the developed world. As argued in earlier chapters, metaracism has functioned to normalize and legitimize this repression and to desensitize society to the suffering of the oppressed. I argue in this chapter that metaracism not only enabled society to tolerate this level of repression, but it undergirds the sense of righteousness and indignation of key political officials—mayors, prosecutors, state attorney generals, etc.—in defending draconian sentences, racial profiling, capital punishment, lifetime incarceration of nonviolent criminals, and sentences of offenders as young as 14 years old. In this chapter I also drew from David Kennedy's research to suggest alternative solutions to the high level of violence in high poverty areas. Any alternative requires the reverse of racializing—it requires humanizing, empathizing, and communicating among all parties involved.

In Chapter 8, I turn my attention to the issue of voting. I argue that contemporary racism, much like old-fashioned racism, is based not on democratic principles, but on efforts to undermine democracy by suppressing the votes of minorities.

Notes

1. Human Rights Watch, *The Rest of Their Lives: Life Without Parole for Child Offenders in the United States* (New York: Human Rights Watch and Amnesty International, October 12, 2005); Human Rights Watch, "Nation Behind Bars: Human Rights Solution," May 2014. http://www.hrw.org/sites/default/files/related_material/2014_US_Nation_behind_bars_0.pdf; Amnesty International, "Entombed: Isolation in the U.S. Federal Prison System," http://amnestyusa.org/research/reports/entombed-isolation-in-the-us-federal-prison-system; Human Rights Watch, "United States," *World Report: Events of 2013* (2013).

2. Lauren Glaze and Erika Parks, "Correctional Populations in the United States, 2011," US Department of Justice, Office of Justice Programs, Bureau of Justice Statistics, 2012.

3. Alexander Lichtenstein and Michael Kroll, "The Fortress Economy: The Economic Role of the U.S. Prison System," in Elihu Rosenblatt, ed., *Criminal Injustice: Confronting the Prison Crisis* (Boston: South End Press, 1996), p. 22.

4. Incarceration data are from William Sabol, Todd Minton, and Paige Harrison, "Prison and Jail Inmates at Midyear 2006," *Bureau of Justice Statistics Bul-*

letin, NCJ217675 (June 2007), pp. 8–9. Population data are from US Department of Commerce, "Resident Population by Sex, Race, and Hispanic Origin Status: 2000–2006, Table 6," *Statistical Abstracts,* http://www.census.gov/compendial/stab /2008/tables/08s0006.pdf.

5. The Sentencing Project, "Racial Disparities," 2013. http://www.sentencing project.org/template/page.cjm?id=123.

6. Michelle Alexander, *The New Jim Crow: Mass Incarceration in the Age of Colorblindness* (New York: New Press, 2010).

7. Marc Mauer, *Race to Incarcerate* (New York: New Press, 1999), p. 147.

8. Ibid.

9. Ibid.

10. The Sentencing Project, "The Federal Prison Population: A Statistical Analysis," 2004. http://www.sentencingproject.org/doc/publications/inc-federalprisonpop.pdf.

11. Alexander, *The New Jim Crow.*

12. Ibid.

13. American Civil Liberties Union, "The War on Marijuana in Black and White: Billions of Dollars Wasted on Racially Biased Arrests" (New York: ACLU, June 2013), p. 15.

14. Ibid, p. 20.

15. Ibid, p. 43.

16. Ibid.

17. American Civil Liberties Union (ACLU), "New ACLU Report Finds Overwhelming Racial Bias in Marijuana Arrests," press release (New York: ACLU, June 4, 2013). http://www/criminal/law/reform/new-aclu-report-finds-overwhelming -racial-bias-in-majuana-arrests.

18. American Civil Liberties Union, "The War on Marijuana in Black and White," p. 10.

19. Ibid.

20. "The Fair Sentecing Act Corrects a Long-time Wrong in Cocaine Cases," *Washington Post,* April 3, 2010. http://www.washingtonpost.com/wp-dyn/content /article/2010/08/02/AR2010080204360.html.

21. *United States v. Blewett,* 12-5226/12-5582 (May 17, 2013).

22. Ibid. See also, US Sentencing Commission, Annual Report 2011. http://www .ussc.gov/research-and-publications/annual-reports-sourcebooks/2011/annual-report -2011.

23. Ibid.

24. Ibid. See also, Dan Weikel, "War on Crack Targets Minorities over Whites," *Los Angeles Times,* May 21, 1995. http://articles.latimes.com/1995-05-21/news/mn -4468_1_crack-cocaine. These alarming numbers are not unlike the Supreme Court's early cases of facially neutral laws creating an overwhelmingly disparate result.

25. Ibid.

26. Ibid.

27. *Dorsey v. United States,* 567 U.S. 132 S. Ct. 2321 (2012).

28. Ryan Reilly, "Eric Holder Outlining New Justice Department Drug Sentencing Reforms," *Huffington Post,* August 12, 2013. http://www.huffingtonpost.com /2013/08/12/eric-holder-drug-sentencing_n_3741524.html.

29. Human Rights Watch, "United States," *World Report: Events of 2012* (New York: Human Rights Watch, 2013). This reports applauds the state of Connecticut for abolishing the death penalty, but cites the United States for executing forty-two people. http://www.hrw.org/world-report/2013/country-chapters/united-states; Amnesty International, "Death Penalty: Countries Continue to Execute People with

Mental and Intellectual Disabilities," October 10, 2014. http://www.amnesty.org/en /news/death-penalty-countries-continue-to-execute-people-with-mental-and -intellectual-disabilities-2014.

30. Conor Friedersdorf, "Father of Three Gets 25 Years for Selling $1,800 Worth of Painkillers," Business Insider (Australia), April 4, 2013. http://www .businesinsider.com.au/unjust-prison- sentence-war-on-drugs-2013-4.

31. Cindy Swirko, "Cummings Cousin Gets 15-Year Sentence: Hope Sykes Pleaded No Contest to One Count of Trafficking Prescription Narcotics," *Gainesville Sun,* April 27, 2010, http://www.gainesville.com/article/20100428 /ARTICLES/4281005/1002.

32. Steven Donziger, ed., *The Real War on Crime: The Report of the National Criminal Justice Commission* (New York: HarperCollins, 1996), pp. 25–27.

33. Willie Wisely, "Who Goes to Prison," in Daniel Burton-Rose and Paul Wright, eds., *The Celling of America: An Inside Look at the U.S. Prison Industry* (Washington, DC: Common Cause Press, 1998), pp. 16, 21–22.

34. *Ewing v. California,* 538 U.S. 11 (2003).

35. Ibid.

36. Ibid.

37. Ibid.

38. Ibid.

39. *Rummel v. Estelle* 445 U.S. 263 (1980).

40. *Ewing v. California.*

41. Human Rights Watch, *The Rest of Their Lives: Life Without Parole for Child Offenders in the United States* (New York: Human Rights Watch and Amnesty International, October 12, 2005).

42. Ibid, p. 5

43. Ibid.

44. Ibid, p. 2.

45. Ibid, p. 28.

46. Ibid, pp. 29–30.

47. Ibid, pp. 23–24.

48. Ibid, p. 2.

49. Ibid, p. 39.

50. *Miller v. Alabama,* 567 U.S. (2012).

51. *Roper v. Simmons,* 543 U.S. 551 (2005).

52. *Miller v. Alabama.*

53. Ibid.

54. *Hill v. Snyder,* case no. 10-14568, U.S. District Court of Michigan, Southern District (2013).

55. *MiLW Blog,* Michigan Lawyers Weekly, February 15, 2013, http://www .milawyersweekly.com/milwblog/2013/02/15/the-law-as-applied.

56. Amnesty International, *Annual Report 2013: The State of the World's Human Rights,* 2013. http://www.amnesty.org/region/usa/report-2013-#section-157-6.

57. *McCleskey v. Kemp,* 481 U.S. 279 (1987).

58. David Baldus, Charles Pulaski, and George Woodworth, *Equal Justice and the Death Penalty: A Legal and Empirical Analysis* (Boston: Northeastern University Press, 1990).

59. *McCleskey v. Kemp*; Baldus, Pulaski, and Woodworth, *Equal Justice and the Death Penalty.*

60. *McCleskey v. Kemp.*

61. Ibid.

62. Ibid.

63. Alexander, *The New Jim Crow,* p. 107.

64. Michael Radelet, Hugo Bedau, and Constance Putnam, *In Spite of Innocence: Erroneous Convictions in Capital Cases* (Boston: Northeastern University Press, 1992).

65. Hugo Bedau and Michael Radelet, "Miscarriages of Justice in Potentially Capital Cases," *Stanford Law Review* 40, no. 1 (1987): 21–179.

66. *McCleskey v. Kemp.*

67. US General Accounting Office, "Death Penalty Sentencing" (Washington, DC: Government Printing Office, 1990), pp. 5–6.

68. Thurgood Marshall, Concurring Opinion, in *Furman v. Georgia,* 408 U.S. 238.

69. Ibid.

70. *Floyd, et al. v. City of New York, et al.,* 813 F. Supp. 2d 457 (2013).

71. Ibid.

72. Ibid.

73. Ibid.

74. Danielle Tcholakian, "Bloomberg Lashes Out at Stop-and-Frisk Judge in Response to Ruling," *Metro.US,* August 12, 2013.

75. Ibid.

76. William E. B. DuBois, *The Philadelphia Negro* (Philadelphia: University of Pennsylvania Press, 1996).

77. William J. Wilson, *The Truly Disadvantaged: The Inner City, the Underclass, and Public Policy* (Chicago: University of Chicago Press, 1987), p. 25.

78. William Julius Wilson and Robert Sampson, "Toward a Theory of Race, Crime and Urban Inequality," in John Hagan and Ruth Peterson, eds., *Crime and Inequality* (Stanford: Stanford University Press, 1995).

79. Ibid.; Wilson, *The Truly Disadvantaged.*

80. Amy Chua, *World on Fire: How Exporting Free Market Democracy Breeds Ethnic Hatred and Global Instability* (New York: Doubleday, 2003), p. 6.

81. Charles Murray, *Losing Ground: American Social Policy, 1950–1980* (New York: Basic Books, 2003 [1984]), pp. 169–170.

82. Ibid., p. 170.

83. Ibid.

84. John DiIulio, "The Coming of the Super-Predators," *Weekly Standard,* 1, no. 11 (November 27, 1995). http://www.weeklystandard.com/Content/Protectvsbrv.asp.ed/Articles/000/000/007/011.

85. Marvin Wolfang, Robert Figlio, and Thorsten Selling, *Delinquency in Birth Cohort* (Chicago: University of Chicago Press, 1987 [1972]).

86. David Kennedy, *Don't Shoot* (New York: Bloomsbury, 2011).

87. Ibid., p. 21.

88. Ibid.

89. Marvin Meadors, "How Are ALEC Laws Undermining Our Democracy?" *Huffington Post,* April 4, 2012.

8

Minority Voter Suppression

I begin this chapter with a discussion of the importance of the right to vote in a democratic society. I then focus on the present massive and coordinated movement to suppress the minority vote in the United States.

The extent to which a state guarantees the right to vote for all of its voting age citizens is the measure of a democratic society. The Philadelphia Constitutional Convention of 1787 did not produce a democratic society. It produced a republic in which power was concentrated in the hands of the privileged economic elites and the masses. The constitution that came out of that convention gave the power to determine the qualifications for voting to the state governments. Dominated by upper-class property owners, these governments restricted the right to vote to male members of that class. But all white men attained the right to vote during the 1830s, as state governments eliminated property-owning requirements.

Black men acquired the right to vote in 1870, with the ratification of the Fifteenth Amendment. This amendment superseded the Tenth Amendment by giving the federal government direct power over the states in order to protect black voter rights. However, by the beginning of the twentieth century, blacks in the South had lost the right to vote because Southern states were using the old familiar devices to suppress the black vote: poll taxes, literacy tests, character tests, felony conviction disenfranchisement, and racial gerrymandering. The US Congress failed to exercise its powers under the Fifteenth Amendment to protect black voting rights. And the Supreme Court allowed Southern states to deny blacks the right to vote, as long as the denial appeared race neutral.

However, blacks did not lose the right to vote in the way that conventional wisdom portrays it. Conventional wisdom suggests that the white masses disenfranchised blacks through a democratic process. But in fact a prominent historian of the rise of Jim Crow, C. Vann Woodward argues, "It is one of the paradoxes of Southern history that political democracy for the white man and racial discrimination for the black were often products of the same dynamics."[1] He explains, "As the Negroes invaded the new mining and industrial towns . . . , and as the two races were brought into rivalry for subsistence wages in the cotton fields, mines, and wharves, the lower-class white man's demand for Jim Crow laws became more insistent."[2]

Contrary to conventional wisdom, the United States was not an exceptional democracy. Democracy failed in the United States. Blacks were never disenfranchised through white democracy. Black voter suppression over 100 years ago, as it is today, was driven by the dominant class. The black disenfranchisement movement of the late nineteenth century was led by powerful white Southern landowners who were enraged by state governments under an integrated Republican Party that taxed the rich to provide benefits and protections for the poor, vulnerable, and underprivileged citizens of the state.

Pursuing this class conflict thesis, J. Morgan Kousser investigated both the leaders in the Southern state legislatures and the voters involved in the movement to disenfranchise blacks. He discovered that the movement was not led by white workers or white sharecroppers, but by members of the Southern white aristocracy who formed the class of wealthy white landowners. Kousser describes the leaders of the movement to disenfranchise blacks: "Not only did the vast majority of the leaders reside in the black belt, almost all of them were affluent and well educated, and they often bore striking resemblance to antebellum 'patricians.' Indeed, almost every one was the son or grandson of a large planter, and several of the older chiefs had been slaveholders before the war."[3] Kousser notes a positive correlation between wealth and the vote in favor of disenfranchisement. The more wealthy that a voting district was, the greater was the proportion of voters voting in favor of disenfranchisement.[4]

The movement was not a paradox of democracy for whites and disenfranchisement for blacks. It was antidemocratic and racist movement that was influenced by stereotypical images of blacks as illiterate, incompetent, inferior beings who were incapable of making rational political decisions. It was driven by the greed of members of the dominant class, their sense of privilege, and their belief that they were entitled to rule the South and the nation.

This movement not only took away the vote from blacks, but also from poor whites. Rich white Southerners used bribery, threats, and violence to destroy the Republican Party. This dominant class seized control of state governments and passed laws that disenfranchised both blacks and whites. Jack Bloom illustrates this point well with data that indicate that overall voter participation in Louisiana declined between 1896 and 1900 by 90 percent among black voters and 60 percent among white voters. Almost all blacks lost the right to vote as did most poor whites and white workers.[5]

Advances in Voter Rights

Voting rights began to expand, but not without a fight. The nonviolent civil rights movement of the 1950s and 1960s met stubborn and violent resistance from established political powers and from organized white supremacists. The months before the passage of the Voting Rights Act of 1965 were rift with violence. Several white and black civil rights activists were murdered between June 1964 and May 1965. James Chaney, Andrew Goodman, and Michael Schwerner were murdered in June of 1964. Viola Liuzzo was murdered in March of 1965. During the voting rights demonstrations in Selma, Alabama, in March 1965, nonviolent civil rights demonstrators were attacked by state troopers and local police— they were beaten, trampled by horses, and shot. With the strong support of President Lyndon Johnson, Congress passed the Voting Rights Act in 1965.

The period from 1965 to 2000 was one of unprecedented expansion in voter rights. The Voting Rights Act of 1965, amended in 1970, 1975, 1982, and 2006, was one of the most expansive pieces of civil rights legislation ever passed. Several of its sections stand out. Section 2 prohibits voting practices and procedures that have a racially discriminatory intent and effect. Section 4 contains a trigger clause, which prompts a federal reaction if a state or county has registered less than 50 percent of its voting age population. This provision allows the Justice Department to assign federal registrars to register people to vote and federal examiners to monitor elections. Section 5 contains a preclearance provision; that is, those states or counties that trigger the federal reaction from Section 4 are required to clear any major changes in their voting laws with either the Justice Department or the federal district court of Washington, DC.

Voting rights were expanded with the amendments to the Voting Rights Act. The Voting Rights Act of 1975 added protections for language minorities. The Voting Rights Act of 1982 provided guidelines for challenging at-large elections. These guidelines do not guarantee the election of blacks, but they allow courts to consider the totality of the circumstances in cities where blacks are not represented on city councils. These circumstances include evidence of racial discrimination in local political parties, racial polarizations in voting patterns, and biased impacts of at-large elections. The 1982 law encouraged states to draw election districts in ways open to the public and fair to racial minorities.

The 1990s saw both advancement and regression. Advancement came with the passage of the National Voter Registration Act of 1993 that required states to allow individuals to register to vote at state departments of motor vehicles and public assistance and disability offices. It also allowed mail-in registration and encouraged organizations to engage in voter registration drives.

The regression in voting rights occurred in the *Shaw v. Reno* decision.[6] In this decision, the Supreme Court struck down a North Carolina congressional redistricting plan deliberately designed to create two majority black districts in order to allow for the election of black representatives. The plan was a response to the fact that, although blacks constituted 22 percent of the population of North Carolina, from 1900 to 1992 not one black congressperson had been elected to represent the state. The redistricting led to the election of two black representatives. Critics claim that the state violated the Constitution by using race as a basis to create black congressional districts, that these black districts constituted a form of apartheid similar to the South African apartheid regime, and that the creation of two majority black districts discriminated against whites.[7]

Defenders of the redistricting plan claim that taking race into consideration was necessary to prevent racial discrimination, that reducing discrimination against blacks does not constitute discrimination against whites, and that the election of two blacks still left blacks underrepresented in North Carolina. Moreover, the South African apartheid regime created districts that were 100 percent black whereas North Carolina created a district that was 57 percent black.[8]

The Supreme Court ruled against the state and struck down the congressional districts as a form of racial gerrymandering. Justice Sandra Day O'Connor wrote the majority opinion. She noted that the congressional district was drawn in such a bizarre way that it was "unexplainable on grounds other than race." She added that it had an unsettling resemblance to "the most egregious racial gerrymandering of the past" and an "uncomfortable resemblance to political apartheid."[9] The Court ruled that race cannot be taken in consideration when drawing congressional districts lines.

Kousser notes that, up until the Shaw decision, the court had required evidence of a discriminatory effect and purpose to demonstrate a case of illegal racial gerrymandering. He adds that, in the Shaw decision, there was no evidence of a discriminatory effect or purpose, and concludes that the Supreme Court created a new and double standard. In states with black populations of over 20 percent, if the construction of congressional districts produced no black representatives, then the standard for demonstrating a constitutional violation would be evidence of a discriminatory effect and purpose. However, if the state redrew district lines to allow for the election of black representatives, then the use of race alone would become the new standard. In other words, all that would be required to demonstrate a constitutional violation is the fact that the state used race to draw the districts.

Kousser considers this new standard a setback in the movement to expand voting rights for minorities.[10]

Minority Vote Dilution and Racial Gerrymandering

The literature on gerrymandering identifies two major tactics: packing and cracking. Packing refers to drawing district lines in such a way as to concentrate opponents or minorities in a single district in order to reduce their political influence or voting strength. Cracking refers to spreading opponents or minorities into several districts so as to substantially reduce their political influence. The courts allow partisan gerrymandering, the practice of one political party drawing election districts in ways to dilute the political strength of the other political party, but prohibits racial gerrymandering. But these two forms of gerrymandering often overlap. Indeed, this has been the case in the most recent incidents of racial gerrymandering.

A number of studies attribute the Republican majority in the US House of Representatives to partisan gerrymandering. Whereas the majority of votes casted for members of Congress went to Democrats by a margin of over a million votes, Republicans won a majority of House seats.

In the *League of Latino American Citizens v. Perry* decision the Supreme Court struck down a racially gerrymandered congressional district in Texas.[11] At the same time, the Court upheld partisan gerrymandering. The problem was that party lines and racial lines were often the same line; partisan gerrymandering often resulted in racial gerrymandering. As the Republican Party has become emboldened by the voter suppression movement, evidence of racial gerrymandering has increased. For example, between 2000 and 2010, the Hispanic population of Texas increased by 41.85 percent while the black population increased by 19.21 percent and the white population by only 2.91 percent.[12] The white population of Texas has declined. Nevertheless, after redrawing congressional election districts, the number of minority representatives has declined while the number of white representatives has increased.[13]

Ari Berman describes gerrymandering in Texas:

> Texas gained 4.3 million new residents from 2000–2010. Nearly 90 percent of that growth came from minority citizens (65 percent Hispanic, 13 percent African American, 10 percent Asian). As a result, Texas gained four new Congressional seats, from thirty-two to thirty-six. Yet, under the Congressional redistricting map passed by Texas Republicans following the 2010 election, white Republicans were awarded three of the four new seats that resulted from Democratic-leaning minority population growth. The League of Women Voters called the plan "the most extreme example of racial gerrymandering among all the redistricting proposals passed by lawmakers so far this year."[14]

The Current Voter Suppression Movement

The twenty-first century has been shaken by another voter suppression movement, which has been going on for more than a decade. The first voter suppression movement emerged near the end of the nineteenth century specifically to destroy the Reconstruction regime. Driven by several factors, it has recently intensified: the success of early voter suppression efforts, the weak opposition, the dramatic increase in the minority population and voter turnout, and the election of a black president. As with previous voter suppression movements, this one has been led by the dominant economic class. It has been undergirded by the rise of a powerful conservative coalition.

Below I discuss the voter suppression movement and document the extent of the movement and the efforts of this movement to pass laws restricting voting and voter registration. I identify the key leaders of this movement. Early signs of voter suppression appeared in a US Civil Rights Commission report in 2001.[15] The Help America Vote Act (HAVA) of 2002 encouraged further suppression. The 2004 election exhibited increased signs, but resistance to suppression emerged in the 2008 election. The suppression movement launched a frontal assault in 2011.

Voter Fraud

The main argument used to justify voter suppression laws is that they are designed to prevent voter fraud and ensure integrity in elections. Proponents of the new laws to suppress the vote—such as new identification requirements to vote and the birth certificate requirement to register—argue that voter fraud is a problem.

A number of scholars see the charge of voter fraud as a partisan pretext for suppressing the vote: for passing voter suppression laws, intimidating voters, and assaulting organizations that engage in voter registration drives. Andrew Gumbel examines the history of voting, voter fraud, and voter suppression in the United States.[16] Greg Palast focuses on contemporary efforts to take away people's right to vote.[17] Francis Piven, Lorraine C. Minnite, and Margaret Groarke suggest that charges of voter fraud were wildly exaggerated to generate fear and dissuade some people from voting. They claim that the Republican Party used false charges of voter fraud to intimidate voters and voter registration organizations:

> The exaggerated charges of registration fraud have been used by Republican Party operatives and their conservative and business allies to justify a crackdown on groups like ACORN, America Coming together, and the NAACP, which have registered millions of low-income Americans in recent years. For example, in one preposterous lawsuit filed by two Ohio voters, one of

whom it was later revealed, had been "indemnified" by a now defunct Republican Party front group, plaintiffs charged America Coming Together, ACORN, the Ohio AFL-CIO, and the NAACP Voter Fraud with engaging in a criminal conspiracy to traffic drugs in order to raise funds for their fraudulent voter registration activities. The case had to be withdrawn after the plaintiffs were deposed and found to grasp few of the details of the case or even why they had brought the litigation. But this was not before the Republican-controlled state legislature passed a four hundred page election "reform" bill that the League of Women Voters of Ohio warned would result in voter "confusion, uncertainty, disenfranchisement, distrust, and an overburdened election system."[18]

Voter Irregularities in Florida in the 2000 Presidential Election

The first evidence of a deliberate and systematic effort to suppress the vote appeared in Florida in the aftermath of the 2000 presidential election. This effort was successful. There were no repercussions, no vast counterdemonstrations, and no one was held accountable. The US media exposed a couple of irregularities, such as confusing ballots, in which people voted for the wrong candidate, and dimpled chads, the failure to punch a hole all the way through a punch card ballot. The media blamed the voters for making the wrong choice, for being misinformed, and for misreading ballot instructions.

The US Civil Rights Commission conducted a thorough investigation, complete with extensive voting data, hearings, eyewitness testimony, and countless interviews with the state officials and private contractors involved. The commission documents substantial irregularities in the administration of the election, and concludes that these irregularities produced blatant racial and class biases in voter suppression. It identifies several ways in which the right to vote was denied to legally registered US citizens, most of whom happened to be the most vulnerable and the least privileged—low-income white, black, and disabled citizens. These ways identified by the commission include: spoiled ballots, police checkpoints, felony disenfranchisement, false positive purges without notice or appeal, unequal allocation of resources, and early closing of polling venues.[19]

Spoiled ballots are those that are not counted, but disposed of because of some irregularity or error. Whereas the US media blamed the irregularities and errors on the voters themselves, the US Civil Rights Commission concludes that only about 1 percent of the spoilage was attributable to voter error. The commission attributes the spoilage to punch card ballots, in which voters punch the card to indicate their choice for president. Although the voter's choice was clear as indicated by the punched indentation, the vote was thrown out in cases where there was paper residue in the hole made by the indentation (i.e., a dimpled chad). The Florida Supreme Court required the counting of all votes in which the voter choice was clear, but the US Supreme Court overturned the state court's decision. The votes were thrown out and never counted. Moreover, the commission notes that punch card voting machines were concentrated in poor and predominated black districts. Consequently, the majority of spoiled ballots were cast by black voters. Moreover, "black voters were nearly 10 times more likely than non-black voters to have their ballots rejected."[20] The commission concludes:

> approximately 11 percent of Florida voters were African Americans; however, African Americans cast about 54 percent of the 180,000 spoiled ballots in Florida during the November 2000 election based on estimates derived from county-level data. These statewide estimates were corroborated by the results in several counties based on actual precinct data. Poor counties, particularly those with large minority populations, were more likely to possess voting systems with higher spoilage rates than the more affluent counties with significant White populations. There is a high correlation between counties and precincts with a high percentage of African American voters and the percentage of spoiled ballots
>
> Where precinct data were available, the data show that 83 of the 100 precincts with the highest number of spoiled ballots are black majority precincts.[21]

The US Civil Rights Commission had initially expressed disbelief over testimony from witnesses who claimed that they faced police checkpoints or roadblocks on streets leading to voting venues. The police checkpoints were verified by the director of the Florida Highway Patrol. The commission notes that the Voting Rights Act prohibited local or state police from intimidating voters en route to the polling venues.[22]

Several voting venues were closed early, denying voters who arrived before the scheduled closing time the right to vote, according to the US Civil Rights Commission report. Some polling places closed at the designated time of 7 P.M., but those who were already in the building waiting for their turn to vote were denied the right to vote, which is a violation of state voting rules that require those present before the closing an opportunity to vote. Most early closings occurred in low-income minority precincts.

The US Civil Rights Commission report also describes an investigation on the scrubbing of voter registration rolls. It points out that there was nothing unusual about scrubbing the rolls. States periodically review voting rolls to eliminate voters who have died or moved out of the state. The state of Florida as well as several other Southern states permanently ban citizens with felony convictions from voting, even after they served their time and completed all of the requirements of their sentence. This type of ban emerged with poll taxes, literacy tests, character tests, and other mechanisms designed to disenfranchise blacks in ways that circumvent the Fifteenth Amendment. The commission notes that this provision denies the right to vote to close to 4 million voting age citizens and 13 percent of the voting age black male population nationally and disenfranchises about 31 percent of the voting age black male population in Florida.[23] The report suggests that the purge of those with felony convictions contained several false positives; that is, a large number of law-abiding citizens with no record of a felony were purged from the voting rolls and denied the right to vote. When denying the right to vote to those voters who were illegally purged from the voter rolls, Florida offered no alternative, no opportunity to challenge the purge, and no provisional ballot. Moreover, legitimately registered voters with no felony record who were purged from the rolls were never notified that they were deregistered. Also, a large percentage of those purged were black. The report adds, "For instance, in the state's largest county, Miami-Dade, more than 65 percent of the names on the purge list were African American, who represented only 20.4 percent of the population."[24]

The US Civil Rights Commission paints a picture of a complex, unco-ordinated, and vague process involving many actors—including Florida secretary of state Katherine Harris and governor Jeb Bush, the Florida Elec-tion Board, the local election boards, and a private contractor, Database Technologies—with no one assuming major responsibility for the outcome. However, the impact of the process was unambiguous: the irregularities in Florida produced an electoral process that was extremely and egregiously biased against blacks and poor whites.[25]

The foreign media investigated other aspects of the election. For exam-ple, Palast of the BBC discovered that voter registration forms from an aggressive registration drive among black students were officially turned in but never processed. Palast discovered evidence that large numbers of bal-lots from low-income and minority districts were destroyed. Palast con-cludes that, although there was no evidence of a conspiracy, the evidence indicates that there was a systematic effort to suppress the votes from pre-dominantly black and low-income precincts.[26]

Palast titled an article "The Silence of the Media Lambs," a play on the movie *The Silence of the Lambs,* in which he expressed astonishment about the relative silence of the US media over the extent of the civil rights viola-tions in what appeared to be a deliberate effort to steal votes and steal the 2000 election. He was surprised over the lack of outrage and protests from civil rights groups, which may have encouraged further voter suppression efforts.[27]

The Help America Vote Act of 2002

In response to the irregularities in Florida during the 2000 election and somewhat in response to the US Civil Rights Commission report, Congress passed the Help America Vote Act (HAVA) in 2002. The act mandated that precincts provide provisional ballots for voters who attempt to vote but are stopped because of disputes over their eligibility to vote because their names no longer appear on the voter registration rolls, because of unacceptable identification cards (IDs), because of errors on the registration names or addresses, or because of any other reason. The act created the federal Election Assistance Commission, requires states to improve their election administrative procedures, and provides federal money to assist states in replacing older voting machines (particularly the punch card machines) with more up-to-date machines.[28]

Palast insists that HAVA was crafted by President George W. Bush's senior counselor Karl Rove in order to enable further voter suppression. Palast argues that three provisions of the act set the stage for more suppression. First, the law established a federal voter identification requirement. That is, it requires any voter who registers to vote by mail and who has not previously voted to show a valid photo ID or a current utility bill before voting. This provision set the stage for a surge in state voter identification laws. Second, the law requires states to centralize their voter registration rolls and to maintain these rolls. Palast contends that this provision encourages other states to engage in the type of purge of the voter registration rolls that Florida had engaged in immediately prior to the 2000 presidential election: "In Colorado, another electoral swing state, the Republican secretary of state used new HAVA powers to wipe away one in five voters (19.4 percent) off the state's voter rolls, double Barack Obama's 2008 victory margin. Why? Don't know. Notably, the names were overwhelmingly Hispanic."[29] He argues further,

> Weirdly, Wisconsin voter registrations show a drop of 107,000 in the first six months of 2011, even before a mass attack on the list by the GOP-controlled legislature. Despite the fact that Wisconsin has no known history of fictional or dead people actually voting, the cost to real, live voters is devastating the "matching" rules that knocked out 42 percent of registrants in California are far more severe in Wisconsin; and in Wisconsin, first-time registrants must mail in ID (as must first-time voters). The result is that only a third of Hispanic citizens in Wisconsin are registered to vote. And students? Forget it: using a formula from the Brennan Center for Justice at New York University Law School, we can calculate that about 97,850 Wisconsin voters under the age of twenty-nine lost their rights due to the new ID law.[30]

Third, the law allows for a shift to the new high-tech voter machines. Palast suggests that this provision allowed for the use of high-tech voting machings to better rig or suppress votes. In researching the problems with voting machines, Palast looked into allegations of a connection between key Republican strategists and a company that produced high-tech voter machines. Palast suspects that Rove had worked with Jack Abramoff, a lobbyist who ended up being charged and convicted of illegal influence ped-dling. Palast claims that Abramoff worked for Diebold (now Premier Elec-tions Solutions), a company that manufactured voting machines, and that Rove saw the opportunity for using the high-tech voting machines to influ-ence the outcome of elections. Following leads in his investigation, Palast interviewed members of a task force investigating this same issue. He met with Paul Hultin, Colorado's voting task-force attorney and asked him about this connection:

> Hultin suggested one answer to me. "It's very disturbing," he said. "This law was corruptly influenced. Jack Abramoff who was a lobbyist for Diebold, the largest manufacturer of electronic vote machines. He's in prison—and [Con-gressman] Bob Ney, who was the Chairman of the Government Operations committee, is in prison for selling favors to Jack Abramoff in connection with [the Help America Vote] Act. So a subsidy went out: $1.5 billion to subsidize purchases of Diebold machines."
> So?
> "Their software loses votes." Hultin paused. "Systematically."
> So?
> "So," said the conservative official, "connect the dots."[31]

Palast discovered that when the memory card is removed from a Diebold voting machine, votes are lost. Palasts explains: "It simply looks like 'undervote,' or spoilage, to the counters. Again, this is not about switching votes from one candidate to another, but the subtle, nastier method, the untraceable 'glitch.' But glitches that seem to occur overwhelmingly in Black, Brown, and Bluish precincts."[32] Palast goes further to suggest that Diebold machines have been used to suppress minority votes and influence the outcome of elections, particularly the 2006 election over a House of Representatives seat that Cynthia McKinney lost:

> In a tight contest in Georgia, Diebold machines simply refused to operate and record votes in several black precincts. According to the company, the machines don't work well in very humid, hot conditions. "Well, what do you think we get in Georgia in July!" the losing candidate, Congresswoman Cynthia McKinney, told me. In the white precincts, voting was held in air-conditioned suburban school gyms.[33]

Palast insists that HAVA, far from helping people vote, helps to suppress the black vote. It also set the stage for an all-out assault on voter rights.

Voter Suppression in Ohio in 2004

Despite the passage of HAVA, voting problems persisted in the 2004 presi-dential election. A number of states experienced many of the same types of irregularities that occurred in Florida during the 2000 election. Insofar as these irregularities were related to actions that had the effect of reducing or diluting the minority vote, they constituted forms of voter suppression. Indeed, as in the Florida case, the actions of state officials and in some cases party activists blocked voter registrations; prevented legitimately registered voters from voting; discouraged or intimidated voters; and squashed, eliminated, or did not count actual votes. These actions constituted voter suppression. Voter suppression involved problems with voter registrations, erroneous purges of voter registration rolls, spoiled ballots, unequal allocation of voting resources, faulty voter machines, and illegal tactics. As in the Florida case, these problems were most pronounced in low-income, predominantly black, urban communities.[34]

Robert Kennedy summarizes the data and evidence from congressional reports, news stories, and eyewitness accounts, and concludes that the 2004 election was stolen: "Nationwide, according to the federal commission charged with implementing election reforms, as many as 1 million ballots were spoiled by faulty voting equipment—roughly one for every 100 cast."[35] Kennedy focuses on the state of Ohio:

> The reports were especially disturbing in Ohio, the critical battleground state that clinched Bush's victory in the Electoral College. Officials there purged tens of thousands of eligible voters from the rolls, neglected to process registration cards generated by Democratic voter drives, shortchanged Democratic precincts when they allocated voting machines and illegally derailed a recount that could have given Kerry the presidency. A precinct in an evangelical church in Miami County recorded an impossibly high turnout of ninety-eight percent, while a polling place in inner-city Cleveland recorded an equally impossible turnout of only seven percent.[36]

What happened in Ohio was classic voter suppression. State actions had a disproportionate and substantial impact on voters in predominantly low-income, black, and urban areas.

Blocked Registrations

According to a report by the House Judiciary Committee Democratic Staff, voting problems emerged in Ohio months before the election began. There were several problems with the registration process. The first problem involved registration forms. Ohio secretary of state Kenneth Blackwell issued an order for local election boards not to accept voter registration forms unless they were written on the appropriate paper in terms of exact weight and thickness. When forms were turned in on the wrong size or thickness of paper, election boards were instructed to use the form as an application for the proper form. That is, the improper form was rejected and a proper form was mailed out to the applicant. Blackwell rejected and discarded forms that were supplied by local newspapers, forms that were used by local election boards, and surprisingly forms that originated from his office. After being threatened with a lawsuit, he rescinded his order and began accepting registration forms about six days before deadline for registering to vote in Ohio. The report adds, "Mr. Blackwell's widely reviled decision to reject voter registration applications based on paper weight may have resulted in thousands of new voters not being registered in time for the 2004 election."[37]

The second problem involved the processing of the forms. Because of the large number of registration forms, all the forms were not processed in time for the election. Thousands of people who had registered to vote could not vote, even though they had filed their application form before the deadline. Voter registrations were also rejected because of data entry errors or errors of omission. The House Judiciary Committee Democratic Staff report observes, "The Greater Cleveland Voter Registration Coalition projects that in Cuyahoga County alone over 10,000 Ohio citizens lost their right to vote as a result of official registration errors."[38]

Purges of Voter Registration Rolls

Ohio secretary of state Blackwell, who was cochair of the Ohio Committee to Re-elect George W. Bush, engaged in a number of activities that had the effect of suppressing the vote, particularly the minority and Democratic vote. Blackwell claimed that the cochair status was a nominal position and that he believed that he was acting in a fair and unbiased manner. Nevertheless, he had local election boards scrub the voter registration rolls to eliminate those who were no longer legitimately registered and those who had died or had long since moved to another state. Unlike Florida, Ohio does not prevent convicted felons who have completed their sentences from voting. Ohio did not hire a private firm to scrub its rolls. Nevertheless, the guidelines for scrubbing the rolls were calculated to eliminate large numbers of legitimately registered voters. Blackwell asked election workers to eliminate from the rolls the voters who had not voted in the past two national elections. As in the Florida case, those voters who were erroneously eliminated from the rolls were not notified. Kennedy claims,

> Instead of welcoming the avalanche of citizen involvement sparked by the campaign, Blackwell permitted election officials in Cleveland, Cincinnati and Toledo to conduct a massive purge of their voter rolls, summarily expunging the names of more than 300,000 voters who had failed to cast ballots in the previous two national elections. In Cleveland, which went five-to-one for Kerry, nearly one in four voters were wiped from the rolls between 2000 and 2004.[39]

The purges were particularly severe in inner-city precincts. In Cleveland, about 25 percent of the names on the voter registration rolls were purged. These purges substantially suppressed voter turnout in these areas. In one Cleveland inner-city precinct, voter turnout was 7.1 percent, the lowest in the state. This low turnout was no doubt the result of the purges.[40]

According to HAVA and Ohio law, people who come to vote and discover that their names are not on the voter registration rolls are entitled to provisional ballots. However, Blackwell developed a narrow administrative interpretation of HAVA and Ohio law. His interpretation restricted both the granting of provisional ballots and the counting of them. Whereas Ohio law had allowed for provisional ballots in the past when a voter turned up at the wrong precinct, Blackwell required that voters whose names were not on the rolls to prove that they resided in the precinct in which they were attempting to vote. In some cases, voters were not informed that they were entitled to provisional ballots and were not given them. In other cases, they were given provisional ballots, but these ballots were discarded if the voters could not prove that they lived in the precinct. The House Judiciary Committee Democratic Staff report explains:

> While the Help America Vote Act provided that voters whose names do not appear on poll books are to sign affidavits certifying that they are in the correct "jurisdiction" to mean "precinct." Alleging that allowing voters to use provisional ballots outside their own precincts would be "a recipe for Election Day chaos," Secretary Blackwell required such ballots to be cast in the actual precincts of voters otherwise they would be discarded entirely.[41]

Spoiled Ballots

As explained above, spoiled ballots are votes that are not counted. In fact, next to the large number of people purged from the voter registration rolls, the most serious problem in the 2004 election was the extraordinary large number of spoiled—uncounted or discarded—votes. There are three sources of spoiled ballots: old punch card machines, discarded provisional votes, and malfunctioning machines. The large number of discarded provisional votes was discussed earlier. The House Judiciary Committee Democratic Staff report notes the following on punch card ballots: "According to a *New York Times* investigation, the problem [with spoiled ballots] was pronounced in minority areas, typically Kerry strongholds. In Cleveland ZIP codes where at least 85% of the population is black, precinct results show that one in 31 ballots registered no vote for president, more than twice the rate of largely white ZIP codes where one in 75 registered no vote for president. Election officials say that nearly 77,000 of the 96,000 [spoiled] ballots were punch cards."[42] The report also notes cases in which state-of-the-art voting machines flipped the vote from John Kerry to George W. Bush.

In other words, the voting machines were rigged; when a voter pushed the button for Kerry, the machine registered a vote for Bush.

Palast insists that there was a large number of spoiled or uncounted ballots in the 2004 election and that the chance of a spoiled vote was not random.[43] The uncounted votes came disproportionately from minority communities:

> The "uncount" and racial disparity is at its worst in swing states where the motive to steal is highest. In New Mexico in 2004, no fewer than 16,469 missing ballots, almost exclusively found in pueblo and Hispanic precincts, swamped Bush's "victory margin" of 5,988.
>
> As in every state (no exceptions), the un-count in New Mexico had a dark racial hue. Just one in a hundred (1.11 percent) of Anglo presidential ballots failed to record a choice. But four times as many Hispanic ballots were blank (4.43 percent), and seven times as many native American ballots were blank (7.05). But note carefully: when ballots are read optically, the racial difference disappears.
>
> In all, Hispanic, Native American, or black voters cast 89 percent (nearly nine out of ten) of ballots that bit the desert dust.[44]

Palast also notes that the Election Assistance Commission (EAC) reported that 133,289 ballots were not counted for trivial reasons such as extra marks on the ballot. He says that the highest percentage of spoiled ballots came from predominantly Hispanic and low-income precincts.[45]

Unequal Allocation of Resources

Another serious problem of the 2004 election was long voting lines, resulting from an inadequate number of voting machines, particularly in low-income predominantly black precincts. Evidence suggests that this impact was not an accident. Although voter registration drives were up in predominantly black districts and election officials were expecting a higher than usual turnout, in some inner-city precincts there were not more but fewer voting machines. The state of Ohio had money from the federal government to purchase additional voting machines, but the state made a decision not to allocate more money to high-poverty districts. The unequal allocation of machines was done deliberately. The consequence was long lines that discouraged voters. The city of Cleveland was hit especially hard; the average wait in line to vote in Cleveland during the 2004 election was four hours and some people waited for longer than six or seven hours.[46]

Intimidation and Illegal Activities

Just as there was evidence of police intimidation and illegal tampering with the 2000 presidential election in Florida, similar evidence emerged during the 2004 election in Ohio and the nation. There was an incident in which the Sandusky County Republican Party contacted the county sheriff's office to investigate registered voters for possible voter fraud involving incorrect or nonexisting addresses. The House Judiciary Committee Democratic Staff report notes, "Among other things, the Republican Party arranged for the Sandusky County sheriff to visit the residence of 67 voters with wrong or non-existing addresses."[47]

Two other forms of intimidation emerged during the 2004 presidential election: caging and challengers. Caging has generally involved officials mailing a letter to registered voters to verify registration status and address. The letter is marked "do not forward, return to sender." If the letter is returned, the officials use the returned letter to remove the name from the registration rolls. The House Judiciary Committee Democratic Staff report explains,

> The caging tactics were so problematic that a federal district court in New Jersey and a panel of the Third Circuit found that the Republican Party was egregiously in violation of the 1982 and 1987 decrees that barred the party form targeting minority voters for challenges at the polls. They found sufficient evidence that the Ohio Republican Party and the RNC conspired to be "disruptive" in minority-majority districts and enjoined the party from using the list.[48]

During the 2004 election, Republican officials targeted for caging neighborhoods that had high numbers of Democratic, low-income, and minority voters.[49]

Republicans also sent challengers to the polls. These challengers were throwbacks to the pre–Voting Rights Act age. Challengers attempt to stop a voter by finding something wrong with the registration or an inconsistency between an ID, signature, address, or something else to call the validity of the registration into question. Republicans targeted low-income minority precincts. Although challengers were not that successful in finding errors, they were successful in intimidating legitimate voters.[50]

The 2008 and 2012 Elections

The 2008 presidential election was a drama that involved three competing tales: a tale of persisting voter suppression, a tale of increasing resistance, and a tale of record-breaking voter turnout. The same practices that were used to suppress the vote in 2004 reappeared in 2008: purges, blocked registrations, and caging. The 2008 election added some practices that magnified the suppression. In their article on the 2008 voter roll purges, Wendy Weiser and Margaret Chen note what they call the "No Match, No Vote" policy whereby some states matched names and addresses from their voter registration computer data base with names and addresses from other state computer data bases. If the addresses of the names did not match, they were purged from the voter registration rolls:

> The problem is the computer match processes states use are inherently unreliable. Between 15% and 30% of all match attempts fail because of typos, other administrative errors, and minor discrepancies between database records, such as a maiden name in one record and a married name in another or a hyphen in one record and not another. No match, no vote policies can block hundreds of thousands of voters through no fault of their own.[51]

Weiser and Chen estimate that states using various strategies to reject registration forms and to purge registered voters from the rolls will prevent millions of citizens from voting. Besides the No Match, No Vote rule, these strategies include strict rules that would reject voter registration forms for having missing information, extra marks, or trivial errors. The 2008 election marked the rapid rise of state laws mandating state issued IDs before voting, while at the same time making it more difficult to obtain these IDs. For example, whereas states would issue a driver's license to a new resident who had a driver's license from a previous state residence, states began to require a birth certificate, a social security card, and a utility bill before issuing a driver's license or state ID. These laws impacted the most vulnerable voters, particularly older people, students, and low-income voters.

The impact of voter suppression in the 2008 election is summarized by Palast: "In the 2008 election, no fewer than 767,023 provisional ballots were cast and not counted; 1,451,116 ballots were "spoiled," not counted; [and] 488,136 absentee ballots were mailed in, but not counted."[52]

The second story is one of resistance. The state of Ohio provides a prime example. As mentioned above, to check the validity of registrations Ohio election officials sent out millions of letters marked to not forward, but return to sender. Over 600,000 of these letters were returned. Election officials considered automatically purging these names from the rolls. However, by 2008, Ohio was under a Democratic administration. The Democratic secretary of state issued a directive indicating that the returned mail was not sufficient to purge names from the roll.

In other states, civil rights groups sued state officials attempting to suppress the vote. A number of suits were filed by the Mexican American Legal Defense and Education Fund and the Lawyers' Committee for Civil Rights Under Law against the state of Georgia for purging several thousand Mexican Americans from the voter registration rolls because their names did not match state computers on naturalized citizens.[53] The NAACP Legal Defense and Educational Fund filed several lawsuits to stop voter suppression. Most of the lawsuits targeted states for voter identification laws and for permanently barring convicted felons from voting even after they completed their sentence.[54]

The third story is one of triumph. Just before the 2008 election, there was a strong effort to increase opportunities for voting. In response to the voter suppression measures of the 2004 election, a number of states passed laws and established rules to expand the vote. Many states substantially expanded the number of days for early voting. Voter turnout among African Americans reached record-breaking highs during the 2008 election and the black/white gap in turnout practically disappeared. For example, black voter turnout in 1988 was about 55.1 percent. It dropped to just above 50 percent in 1996, but increased to 53.5 percent in 2000, and further to 60.3 percent in 2004. It reached a record-breaking high of 65.2 percent in 2008, which was only slightly under the white turnout rate of 66.1 percent. However, among young voters between the ages of eighteen and twenty-nine years old, the black voter turnout rate of 58.2 percent exceeded the white voter turnout rate of 52.1 percent. The 2008 election was exceptional, but the 2012 election was better. The black voter turnout reached 66.2 percent, compared to 64.4 percent for whites and 48.0 percent for Hispanic voters.[55] Although voter suppression persisted, voter turnout among blacks increased.

An All-Out Frontal Assault on the Rights of Voters

The struggle over voter suppression did not end after the 2008 election. On the contrary, it intensified. Just after the 2010 election, there was an all-out assault on voter rights: a multipronged attack to block registrations, to reduce the number of voters, to restrict actual voting, and to cut back on the number of days of early voting for president. Indeed, in 2011 alone, fourteen states enacted about twenty-five laws designed to restrict the right to vote and suppress the votes of the most vulnerable and disadvantaged citizens.

As noted, a number of states expanded the number of days for early voting for the 2008 presidential election because of the long lines at the polls during the 2004 election. By the beginning of 2012, many of those states rescinded or reduced the number of days for early voting. Since a large percentage of black and low-income voters had taken advantage of the early voting in 2008, cutting the days of early voting would have had the obvious impact of suppressing the black vote. In most cases, the NAACP and the Obama administration challenged the cuts in early voting days, including in Florida, Georgia, Maine, Maryland, North Carolina, Ohio, Tennessee, and West Virginia. These cuts in early voting were challenged in court on grounds that they suppressed the minority vote, as a large percentage of minorities participated in early voting.

Voter Identification

Another controversial method of suppressing the vote includes strict voter identification laws. State voter identification laws multiplied after the passage of HAVA in 2002. This law required first-time voters registering through the mail to show a valid photo ID such as a driver's license or military identification, or a utility bill, bank statement, government check, or other government document showing the person's name or address. States responded to HAVA by passing state voter identification laws. These state laws range from lenient to moderate to strict. Lenient laws allow a large number of acceptable identification documents: photo identification (e.g., state driver's licenses, state IDs, nursing home identification, college identification, military identification) or nonphoto identification (e.g., utility bills, bank statement, payroll check). Strict laws limit the types of acceptable IDs. Texas provides a good example of strict laws. Texas law limited the kinds of acceptable IDs to a driver's license or a concealed weapon permit, and would not accept college photo IDs. Critics claim that this restriction was deliberately designed to advantage Republicans (as they were more likely to have concealed weapon permits) and disadvantage Democrats (as college students were more likely to vote Democrat). The courts recently struck down the Texas voter ID law. Moderate laws are between the two extremes.[56]

Indiana enacted a moderate voter identification law. The law requires a voter to present a state-issued photo ID before being allowed to vote. The Indiana Democratic Party and several civil rights organizations immediately challenged the law on grounds that it placed an undue burden on elderly, disabled, indigent, and minority voters; that it was neither necessary nor appropriate to achieve its stated goal of preventing voter fraud; that it arbitrarily disfranchised qualified voters; and that it constituted a de facto poll tax. The state insisted that the law was needed to prevent voter fraud, to enhance the integrity of elections, and to maintain public confidence in the democratic system. In the 2008 *Crawford v. Marion County Election Board* decision, the Supreme Court upheld the law. It noted that neither side had any evidence to support its arguments. The state of Indiana could not find a single case of voter fraud that would have been prevented by this law. However, civil rights groups could not find a single person that was denied the right to vote because of this law. The court claimed that the number of people without state identification was exaggerated and that the state offered to provide state IDs for free to those who could not afford them and provisional ballots to those who did not have identification when they voted. Moreover, the state gave voters without identification a grace period of ten days to provide it in order to have their provisional ballot counted. The court allowed state ID laws as long as they had provisions for poor people and offered provisional ballots for those without IDs. This decision validated the constitutionality of these moderate and lenient laws and encouraged other states to enact similar laws.[57]

Recently, several states passed more restrictive ID laws, impacting both the voter registration process and the voting process. Five states—Alabama, Arizona, Georgia, Kansas, and Tennessee—passed laws to require proof of citizenship in order to register to vote. The Arizona law is being challenged within the Supreme Court. Most of these five states would accept a passport, birth certificate, or naturalization papers for proof of citizenship. Since passports cost over $100 and naturalization papers can cost over $300, these requirements may be cost prohibitive for the very poor. Birth certificates can also be costly to the poor because they often cost more than $20. Getting a birth certificate may be impossible for some older black people born during the Jim Crow era in the South. Prior to the passage of the Civil Rights Act of 1964, white Southern hospitals excluded blacks. Consequently, many older blacks were born at home and never had the luxury of having a birth certificate. Since birth certificates are required to get most state IDs, this requirement has already disenfranchised a significant percentage of older blacks.

Many states require the address on a photo ID card to match the address on the voter registration roll. Poor voters are more likely to change residences between presidential elections. If they update their driver's license as prescribed by law, they are likely to be stopped at the polls unless they also update their voter registration information. This requirement puts additional burdens on poor voters.

In a report for the Center for American Progress, Scott Keyes and colleagues compiled several anecdotal cases documenting how these ID laws impede individual voting rights:

> *Ruthelle Frank.* Ruthelle is an 84-year-old former elected official who voted in every election for the last 63 years, yet she will be unable to obtain a voter ID unless she pays a fee to obtain a birth certificate from the Wisconsin government—despite the fact that the Constitution explicitly forbids any voter from being charged a fee in order to vote. Worse, because the attending physician at her birth misspelled her name on her original birth certificate, she may need to pay hundreds of dollars in court fees to petition the state judiciary to correct her certificate before she can obtain a voter ID.
>
> *Paul Carroll.* Paul is an 86-year-old World War II veteran who has lived in the same Ohio town for four decades. Yet when he attempted to vote in the recent Ohio primary, he was told his photo ID from the Department of Veterans Affairs was not good enough because it did not include his address.
>
> *Dorothy Cooper.* Dorothy is a 96-year-old African-American woman who says she has voted in every election but one since she became eligible to vote. Yet when she attempted to obtain a voter ID she was turned away because she did not have a copy of her marriage license. In a subsequent interview Dorothy said that she didn't even have problems voting in Tennessee "during Jim Crow days—only now under voter ID."

Thelma Mitchell. Thelma is a 93-year-old woman who cleaned the Tennessee Capitol for 30 years. She never received a birth certificate, however, because she was delivered by a midwife in Alabama in 1918 and there was no record of her birth. When she attempted to obtain a voter ID, she was turned away for lack of a birth certificate by a clerk who suggested she could be an illegal immigrant.[58]

In addition to imposing a disproportionate burden on older minority voters, some state voter ID laws have been administered in a racially discriminatory manner. Ryan Haygood describes this practice:

Moreover, due to discriminatory enforcement, these laws place disproportionate burdens on all minority voters, not just those who lack a photo ID. Nationally, 70% of all African American voters and 65% of all Latino voters were asked to show photo identification at the polls during the 2008 election, as oppose to only 51% of white voters. As a result, eligible African American voters were forced to cast provisional ballots at a rate four times higher than were white voters. As noted above, provisional ballots are often not counted as frequently as regular ballots. The racially discriminatory effects of photo ID laws have not been lost on some of the proponents of such laws. In October 2011, political strategists in South Carolina publicly boasted that suppression of the African American vote was "why we need [v]oter ID [laws] in [South Carolina]."[59]

Supporters of voter ID laws insist that they are needed to prevent fraud; that they ensure the integrity of elections; that presenting an ID card is normal, as they are required for airplane travel; and that the laws have no impact on elections. These supporters grossly overestimate the extent of voter fraud and the impact of these laws.

Foreclosures and Voters

Palast reports on a disturbing story involving the city of Detroit that occurred just before the November 2008 presidential election. Palast suggests that he was informed that a law firm that handled mass foreclosures gave the foreclosure address list to the Michigan Republican Party, and the party used the list to challenge voter rolls. He came to Detroit to investigate and was directed to the Trott Brothers Law Firm. He questioned officials about the reports:

We pretended to film some executives, following them through the security doors, into the main lobby, and up to Mr. Trott's office. Did the Trott Brothers give their lists of properties they slated for foreclosure to the GOP?

Their answer was to call security. On the ground floor, as we stalled while getting hustled out, we saw to our left what looked like just another division of the Trott & Trott foreclosure factory. Except for a small sign that said, John McCain for President, Michigan State headquarters.

> Mystery solved. That was quick investigation. Still, we slipped back in to ask if the Republican campaign was using Trott & Trott foreclosure lists to eliminate citizens' voting rights.

Palast says that the answer he got was what he expected. An official from the law firm said, "You wouldn't want illegal voters to cast ballots, would you?" Palast ended the story by saying, "Today, Trott & Trott is legal counsel to the Mitt Romney for President campaign."[60]

The Court Weakens the Voting Rights Act

The Supreme Court played a role in weakening voter rights in the *Shelby County, Alabama v. Holder* decision. In this decision, the court struck down Section 4 of the Voting Rights Act of 1965, which provided the formula for identifying states that fall in the Section 5 preclearance provision. The preclearance provision requires states to obtain permission from either the Justice Department or a three-panel federal court before changing their voting laws. The Court ruled that the practice of requiring state governments to obtain permission from the federal government before enacting new laws violates the sovereignty of the states and drastically departs from the principles of federalism established by the Constitution. The Court argued that, in the past, it had allowed the federal government to subject a few states to this preclearance practice because these states had engaged in the flagrant, pervasive, and rampant practice of racial discrimination in voting and this practice had substantially suppressed the black vote. However, the criteria for identifying states for preclearance was established fifty years ago. Since that time, these states have ceased the direct and blatant practice of racial discrimination in voting.[61]

The Court concluded that the conditions that necessitated this drastic departure from the principles of federalism and federal violation of state sovereignty no longer existed by 2004. According to the Court, continuing to single out these states violates the principle that all states enjoy equal sovereignty.[62]

Justice Ruth Bader Ginsburg, writing the dissenting opinion disagreed on factual grounds. She argued that contrary to the majority opinion, Congress did not rely on 1965 facts to reenact the Voting Rights Act of 2006. Congress relied on current facts in deciding to renew Sections 4 and 5 of the Voting Rights Act. She further argued that the facts indicate that although there has been substantial progress, there was substantial evidence of second-generation discrimination. This discrimination involved vote dilution as Justice John Roberts Jr. argued in the majority decision. It also involved, not isolated or incidental cases, but thousands of cases of blatant, purposeful, and persistent discrimination occurring from 1982 up to the passage of the act in 2006. These cases were documented in congressional testimony, court decisions, and independent studies. They included both Section 5 preclearance and Section 2 lawsuits, as well as FBI reports and recordings. The vote dilution cases involved many incidents of the deliberate elimination of majority black districts with the impact of eliminating black elected officials. Ginsburg demonstrated that, although a higher percentage of blacks than whites are registered to vote in states like Alabama, studies "indicated that racial discrimination in voting remains concentrated in the jurisdictions singled out for preclearance." She added, "Although covered jurisdictions accounted for less than 25 percent of the country's population, the Katz study revealed that they accounted for 56 percent of successful Section 2 litigation since 1982." The covered jurisdictions were more likely to be found guilty of violating Section 2.[63] Ginsburg cited the FBI investigation of Alabama state legislators talking openly about engaging in efforts to reduce black voter turnout:

> A recent FBI investigation provides a further window into the persistence of racial discrimination in state politics. Recording devices worn by state legislators cooperating with the FBI's investigation captured conversations between members of the state legislature and their political allies. The recorded conversations are shocking. Members of the state Senate derisively refer to African-Americans as "Aborigines" and talk openly of their aim to quash a particular gambling-related referendum because the referendum, if placed on the ballot, might increase African-American voter turnout. . . . (Legislators and their allies expressed concern that if the referendum were placed on the ballot, "'[e]very black, every illiterate' would be 'bused [to the polls] on HUD [Department of Housing and Urban Development] financed buses.'")
>
> Ginsburg pointed out that these conversations did not occur during the 1870s or the 1960s. They occurred in 2010. She quoted the district judge presiding over the case as saying that the recorded conversations provided "compelling evidence that political exclusion through racism remains a real and enduring problem in Alabama." The evidence demonstrates that racist sentiments "remain regrettably entrenched in the high echelons of state governments."[64]

Ginsburg provided several other examples of cases of racial discrimination in voting practices in Alabama. One case involved a redistricting plan from the City of Calera, located in Shelby County.[65] In 2008, this city developed a redistricting plan that would eliminate its only black district and black councilman. The city developed and implemented the plan, ignoring the preclearance requirement. With the loss of the black district, the only black councilman was voted out of office. The Justice Department took the city to court to force it to restore the majority black district. In another case, in the late 1980s, the city of Pleasant Grove annexed white areas, but deliberately refused to annex black areas.[66] The

Supreme Court stepped in to stop the practice. In 1985, the Supreme Court struck down a provision of the Alabama Constitution that prohibited individuals convicted of misdemeanor offenses involving moral turpitude from voting. These practices in Alabama were reminiscent of racial practices prevalent in the state over 100 years ago: character tests, blatant racial discrimination, racially discriminatory redistricting. By presenting these cases, Ginsburg demonstrated that the five justices that struck down Section 4 of the Voting Rights Act because they believed that racial discrimination in voting had ended in the South were just as blind to racial discrimination in voting in the South as the members of the court over 100 years ago.

Explaining Voter Suppression

The voter suppression movement of the twenty-first century bears a striking and disturbing resemblance to the voter suppression movement that overthrew the Reconstruction regime. Both movements emerged in reaction to progressive regimes. Both involved broad-based mass movements that were led and supported by leaders from the dominant class.

Palast sums up the origins of this voter suppression movement in the title of his book, *Billionaires and Ballot Bandits*. He sees this movement driven by greed and a lust for power. He suggests that it is associated with the drive of multibillionaires to dominate the political arena and to influence the outcome of elections. It is not enough to offer hundreds of millions of dollars to get their candidates elected, to lobby elected officials, and to influence public opinion. They also feel the need to suppress the votes of the masses, the middle and low-income voters, and minority voters, that is, those voters likely to support the equal opportunity regime. He identifies key players. For example, Paul Weyrich, a cofounder of the Heritage Foundation and a major player in the founding of the Christian Coalition, was an early advocate of voter suppression. To illustrate his point, he provides the following quote from Weyrich at a dinner with President Reagan:

> Now many of our Christians have what I call the goo-goo syndrome—good government. They want everybody to vote. I don't want everybody to vote. Elections are not won by a majority of people, they never have been from the beginning of our country and they are not now. As a matter of fact, our leverage in the elections quite candidly goes up as the voting populace goes down.[67]

Palast identifies the Koch brothers as players in promoting the idea of voter suppression. He quotes multibillionaire Charles Koch saying, "I want my fair share—and that's all of it."[68] Suppressing the minority vote becomes part of the strategy in controlling the outcome of elections. Palast provides this example with Republican strategist Karl Rove:

> In Florida and Iowa, Democratic registrations are down from their 2010 levels while Republican numbers are up. For example, nearly 29,000 Democrats have disappeared from the Iowa registration rolls since January 2011. . . . In Arizona, Democrats are down 58,000 . . . and there are now 176,000 fewer Democrats registered in Pennsylvania in November 2010.[69]

Palast makes it clear that Rove is not just predicting the outcome of elections. He is planning the outcomes. Palast quotes from a *Wall Street Journal* article written by Rove to illustrate the deliberateness of minority voter suppression: "Even a small drop in the share of black voters would wipe out [Obama's] margin in North Carolina."[70] Haygood's perspective overlaps with that of Palast's. Both see the voter suppression movement supported by right wing billionaires like the Koch brothers and organizations like ALEC. Haywood puts it mildly when he says,

> ALEC founder Paul Weyrich made the point of voter suppression tactics clear when he stated that "our leverage in the elections quite candidly goes up as the voting populace goes down." The attack on voting rights is not about protecting our democratic process; it is about control and manipulation of the electorate by any means, no matter how discriminatory.[71]

ALEC, founded by the Koch brothers, is key to understanding the voter suppression movement.

Journalist Ari Berman sees the same parallel between the old voter suppression movement and the current movement:

> As the nation gears up for the 2012 Presidential election, Republican officials have launched an unprecedented, centrally coordinated campaign to suppress the elements of the Democratic vote that elected Barack Obama in 2008. Just as Dixiecrats once used poll taxes and literacy tests to bar black Southerners from voting, a new crop of GOP governors and state legislators has passed a series of seemingly disconnected measures that could prevent millions of students, minorities, immigrants, ex-convicts and the elderly from casting ballots.[72]

Berman goes beyond Palast and Haygood and identifies ALEC as the main organization coordinating the voter suppression movement:

> But since the 2010 election, thanks to a conservative advocacy group founded by Weyrich, the GOP's effort to disrupt voting rights has been more widespread and effective than ever. In a systematic campaign, orchestrated by the American Legislative Exchange Council—and funded in part by David and Charles Koch, the billionaire brothers who bankrolled the Tea party—38 states introduced legislation this year designed to impede voters at every step of the electoral process.[73]

Conclusion

In this chapter, I identified the voter suppression movement and described the many ways in which voters are prevented from voting. I drew similarities between this movement and the reactionary movement associated with the overthrow of the Reconstruction regime. I concluded by asserting that this voter suppression movement is part of a larger reactionary movement to undermine the equal opportunity regime. In the next chapter, I examine this larger reactionary movement in more detail and look at alternative research that challenges this thesis.

Notes

1. C. Vann Woodward, *Origins of the New South, 1877–1913* (Baton Rouge: Louisiana State University Press, 1966 [1951]), p. 211.

2. Ibid.

3. J. Morgan Kousser, *The Shaping of Southern Politics: Suffrage Restrictions and the Establishment of the One-Party South, 1880–1910* (New Haven: Yale University Press, 1974), p. 247.

4. Ibid.

5. Jack Bloom, *Class, Race, and the Civil Rights Movement: The Changing Political Economy of Racism* (Bloomington: Indiana University Press, 1987).

6. *Shaw v. Reno,* 509 U.S. 630 (1993).

7. Morgan Kousser, *Colorblind Injustice: Minority Voting Rights and the Undoing of the Second Reconstruction* (Chapel Hill: University of North Carolina Press, 1999).

8. Ibid.

9. *Shaw v. Reno.*

10. Kousser, *Colorblind Injustice.*

11. *League of Latino American Citizens v. Perry,* 548 U.S. 399 (2006).

12. Maya Halebic, "Texas Population Growth, Projections, and Implications," Saber Research Institute, San Antonio, March 2012, p. 9.

13. Ari Berman, "Texas Redistricting Fight Shows Why Voting Rights Act Still Needed," *The Nation,* June 5, 2013. http://www.thenation.com.blog/174652/texas-redistricting-fight-shows-why-voting-rights-act-still-needed.

14. Ari Berman, "Most Extreme Example of Racial Gerrymandering: Federal Court Blocks Discriminatory Texas Redistricting Plan," *The Nation,* August 28, 2012. http://www.mykeystrokes.com2012/08/29/most-extreme-example-of-racial-gerrymandering-federal-court-blocks-discriminatory-texas-redistricting-plan-3/.

15. US Civil Rights Commission, *Voter Irregularities in Florida* (Washington, DC: Government Printing Office, 2001).

16. Andrew Gumbel, *Steal This Vote: Dirty Elections and the Rotten History of Democracy in America* (New York: Nation Books, 2005).

17. Greg Palast, *Billionaires and Ballot Bandits: How to Steal an Election in 9 Easy Steps* (New York: Seven Stories Press, 2012).

18. Francis Piven, Lorraine C. Minnite, and Margaret Groarke, *Keeping Down the Black Vote: Race and the Demobilization of American Voters* (New York: New Press, 2009), p. 199.

19. US Civil Rights Commission, *Voting Irregularities in Florida During the 2000 Presidential Election* (Washington DC: Government Printing Office, 2001). http://www.permanent.access.gop.gov/lps13588/lps13588/main.htm.

20. Ibid.

21. Ibid.

22. Ibid.

23. Ibid.

24. Ibid.

25. Ibid.

26. Gregg Palast, "The Silence of the Media Lambs: The Election Story Never Told," *Third World Traveler,* May 24, 2001. http://www.alternet.org/story/1654 /silence_of_the_media_lambs/.

27. Ibid.

28. Summary of HAVA from US Election Assistance Commission's website, http://www.eac.gov/about_the_eac/help_america_vote_act.aspx.

29. Palast, *Billionaires and Ballot Bandits,* p. 27.

30. Ibid., pp. 32–33.

31. Ibid, p. 218.

32. Ibid.

33. Ibid., p. 214.

34. Ibid.

35. Robert Kennedy, "Was the 2004 Election Stolen?" *Rolling Stone,* June 15, 2006. See also International Endowment for Democracy website, http://www.iefd .org/articles/was_2004_election_stolen.php.

36. Ibid.

37. House Judiciary Committee Democratic Staff, *Preserving Democracy: What Went Wrong in Ohio,* Status Report (Washington, DC: Government Printing Office, January 5, 2005), p. 5. http://www.openvotingconsortium.or/files/conyersreport.pdf.

38. Ibid., p. 6.

39. Kennedy, "Was the 2004 Election Stolen?"

40. Ibid.

41. House Judiciary Committee Democratic Staff, *Preserving Democracy,* p. 31.

42. Ibid.; James Dao et al., "Voting Problems in Ohio Spur Call for Overhaul," *New York Times,* December 24, 2004, p. A1.

43. Palast, *Billionaires and Ballot Bandits,* p. 207.

44. Ibid, pp. 205–206.

45. Ibid, p. 206.

46. Kennedy, "Was the 2004 Election Stolen?"

47. House Judiciary Committee Democratic Staff, *Preserving Democracy.*

48. Ibid., pp. 41–42.

49. Kennedy, "Was the 2004 Election Stolen?"

50. Ibid.

51. Wendy Weiser and Margaret Chen, *Recent Voter Suppression Incidents* (New York: Brennan Center for Justice at New York School of Law, November 3, 2008), p. 1. www.brennancenter.org/sites/default/files/legacy/Democracy/VoterSuppression Incidents.pdf.

52. Palast, *Billionaires and Ballot Bandits,* p. 17.

53. See Mexican American Legal Defense and Education Fund website, http:// www.maldef.org/voting_rights/litigation/morales_v_handel/ for information on *Morales v. Georgia Secretary of State Karen Handel.*

54. See the NAACP Legal Defense and Educational Fund website, www .naacpldf.org.

55. US Department of Commerce, US Census Bureau, *The Diversifying Electorate—Voting Rates by Race and Hispanic Origin in 2012 (and Other Recent Elections)* (Washington, DC: US Department of Commerce, US Census Bureau, May 2013).

56. Sari Horwitz, "Texas Voter-ID Law is Blocked," *Washington Post,* August 30, 2012. http://www.washingtonpost.com/world/national-security/texas-voter-id -law-struck-down/2012/08/30/4a07e270-f2ad-11e-adc6-87dfa83ff430_story.html.

57. *Crawford v. Marion County Election Board,* 553 U.S. 181 (2008).

58. Scott Keyes, Ian Millhiser, Tobin Van Ostern, and Abraham White, *Voter Suppression 101: How Conservatives Are Conspiring to Disenfranchise Millions of Americans* (Washington, DC: Center for American Progress, April 4, 2012). http://cdn.americanprogress.org/wp-contnet/uploads/issues/2012/04/pdf/voter _suppression.pdf.

59. Ryan Haygood, "The Past as Prologue: Defending Democracy Against Voter Suppression Tactics on the Eve of the 2012 Elections," *Rutgers Law Review* 64, no. 4 (2012): 1055–1056.

60. Palast, *Billionaires and Ballot Bandits,* p. 270.

61. *Shelby County, Alabama v. Holder,* 570 U.S. 193 (2013).

62. Ibid.

63. Ibid.

64. Ibid.

65. Ibid.

66. Ibid

67. Palast, *Billionaires and Ballot Bandits,* p. 114.

68. Ibid, p. 43.

69. Ibid, p. 33.

70. Ibid, p. 21.

71. Haygood, "The Past as Prologue," p. 1057.

72. Ari Berman, "The GOP War on Voting," *Rolling Stone,* August 30, 2011. http://www/rollingstone.com/politics/news/the-gop-war-on-voting-20110830.

73. Ibid.

9

Metaracism at a Crossroads

Today this nation is engaged in an epic political conflict, the outcome of which will determine its future. On one side of the battle line is a corporate-centered conservative coalition. At the core of this coalition are powerful business and corporate interests, Christian fundamentalists, and Tea Party organizations. The coalition includes hundreds of business organizations, corporate think tanks, corporate political action committees and thousands of trade organizations, and corporate policymaking organizations.

On the other side of the battle line is an egalitarian coalition. This coalition has consisted of the New Deal, civil rights, antipoverty, and civil liberties coalitions. This coalition has supported the New Deal and Great Society programs. These programs formed part of the equal opportunity regime that enabled upward social mobility, reduced inequality, and ameliorated racial oppression.

These two coalitions are engaged in a battle that is reminiscent of past struggles (e.g., the Civil War and the Redeemer movement) that determined the fate of this nation—whether it would rise out of the conflict as a more just nation or whether it would sink into the quicksand of a more racially oppressive society. The Civil War ended slavery and produced the Reconstruction regime that moved this nation in a progressive direction. The Redeemer movement exterminated the Reconstruction regime. Led by the dominant Southern class, in alliance with the Northern industrial and financial sectors, this movement was energized by racism. It established the system of Jim Crow segregation and aversive dominative racism.

Today, the conservative coalition is engaged in a reactionary assault on the equal opportunity regime. Because the equal opportunity regime is defended by the egalitarian coalition, this assault brings the conservative coalition in direct conflict with the egalitarian coalition.

257

Metaracism has energized the conservative coalition in its assault. Although metaracism eschewed hard-core racism, it has functioned much like the older forms of racism. It contains racial images, narratives, and ideas that have dehumanized the poor, desensitized society to poverty, detracted attention from extreme inequality, supported a punitive and exploitive social welfare system, encouraged the formation of a racially repressive criminal justice system, and enabled the superexploitation of the working poor.

This current reactionary movement has already inflicted enormous damage on the equal opportunity regime in several policy areas that I have discussed in this book: criminal justice, social welfare, education, employment discrimination, finance, rules of the market, and democratic governance. It has created one of the most racially repressive criminal justice systems in the world and has incurred the condemnation of international human rights organization. It has taken a minimalist social welfare system, weakened the social safety net, and enhanced the exploitation of the working poor. It has allowed the expansion of a form of predatory lending that contributed to the collapse of black wealth and the increase in black/white disparities in wealth. It has practically ended affirmative action. It has weakened anti–employment discrimination programs and increased tolerance for employment discrimination. It has contributed to the highest levels of inequality since the Gilded Age.

The reactionary movement has undermined this nation's democratic system. It has endeavored to suppress the minority vote. It has drowned out the voices of the poor. It has created a system of money-driven elections and corporate-sponsored politicians.

In association with metaracism, this reactionary movement has engaged in a form of racial politics involving scapegoating, racializing, victim blaming, and diversionary politics. Scapegoating has involved right-wing organizations' efforts to convince whites who had lost their jobs or farms to blame minorities: the immigrants, the blacks, and the Hispanics. Scapegoating has long been a racist practice of redirecting rage from the dominant class to vulnerable minorities. Racializing has emerged as the secret weapon of neoliberals who could not convince the US public to oppose social programs. Racializing allows them to build this opposition by redefining social programs as being race targeted, that is, as programs designed to assist blacks and other minorities. Racializing is accompanied by racial stereotypes that provoke opposition and anger against both the programs and the minorities.

Diversionary politics has emerged as the new way to exonerate neoliberal policies for the near collapse of the financial market. Political leaders simply blamed the near collapse on overgenerous liberal housing programs that granted mortgages to unqualified minorities who could not afford to repay their loans. In this way, political leaders could continue to promote the myth of markets that cannot fail and to continue to turn blacks into scapegoats.

This practice not only absolved the deregulation movement and the predatory lending frenzy of any responsibility for the financial collapse. It put the blame on nonexisting liberal policies and on blacks themselves. This practice provided cover for neoliberalism. It generated contempt and hostility toward the millions of homeowners who lost their homes. As subtle as this practice was, it was racism pure and simple.

Blaming the victim is a major feature of metaracism. This practice reinforces neoconservatism and neoliberalism, which exonerates the free market of any blame for poverty. Instead, it blames poverty on the bad values and behavior of the poor. This practice makes it easier to cut social programs for the poor.

Like past reactionary movements, the current movement exploits the new form of tyranny that defines *tyranny* as the use of governmental powers to ameliorate oppression. Tyranny has become welfare spending, the Affordable Care Act, the stimulus package, and other social programs.

The election of the first black president was not the signal of a post–civil rights society or a new age of progressivism. It was simply an indication that the egalitarian coalition still exists. It masks the emergence of a powerful conservative coalition that challenges the egalitarian coalition and threatens the equal opportunity regime.

As the conservative coalition assaults the equal opportunity regime, it engages the egalitarian coalition that defends this regime, producing the current epic conflict. The outcome of this conflict will determine whether this nation would move forward in efforts to ameliorate racial oppression or move backward as it continues to promote racial oppression.

The Color-Blind vs. the Color-Conscious Alliance Thesis

This view of a conflict between a progressive coalition and a reactionary one contrasts sharply with the view provided by political scientists Desmond King and Rogers M. Smith. Because of the importance of their insightful and brilliant contributions to contemporary racial politics and because their analysis contradicts the one that I present in this book, I devote considerable space in this chapter to reviewing and critiquing their position.

In their work King and Smith identify color-blind alliances (political groups that oppose affirmative action and other so-called race conscious policies and are likely to see the shootings of Michael Brown and Trayvon Martin as unrelated to race) and color-conscious alliances (political groups that are likely to support affirmative action policies and are likely to see the shootings of Brown and Martin as race related). King and Smith point out that these alliances are fluid.[1] That is, although there is a stable core of organizations making up each alliance, different organizations operate in different issue areas. For example, the housing organizations that operate in the housing issue area do not operate in the criminal justice, affirmative action, or other issue areas. This perspective on shifting political interests from one issue area to the next is well grounded in the public policy literature.[2]

King and Smith insist that the racial conflicts carried out in these issue areas today bear little resemblance to the conflicts of the past such as the clashes over slavery and the Jim Crow system, where there was a clear right side promoting justice and freedom and a clear wrong side protecting slavery and a racial caste. Instead, they argue that there are no clear right or wrong sides in these current racial conflicts. They contend that there are valid points and strengths and weaknesses on both sides. They maintain that in every relevant issue area—affirmative action, criminal justice, education, immigration, etc.—the color-blind alliance is supported by genuine non-racist ideas. That is, proponents of the color-blind alliance sincerely identify with the proposition of Martin Luther King Jr. that people need to be judged by the content of their character and not by the color of their skin. Color-blind advocates believe in personal responsibility. They have a strong sense of morality. They are disturbed by liberals attempting to change laws because too many blacks are getting arrested and going to prison, even though there is a high rate of violence and criminal activity among blacks. They see giving people jobs on the basis of color as morally wrong, whether the jobs are given to blacks or to whites. They believe in rewarding good character and punishing bad behavior. They are fundamentally opposed to racially targeted public programs. They believe that instead of helping people, these programs promote dependency:

> Color-blind proponents argue that it is a moral and policy error to focus on social "root causes" of crime to be addressed, in part, by race-targeted programs. They condemn any criticism of the racially disparate consequences of punitive laws as fostering permissive attitudes that disastrously deny personal responsibility of misconduct, and as failing to recognize the benefits minority communities receive from the incarceration of the criminals in their midst.[3]

They contend further, "Color-blind proponents have long believed that promises of race-conscious assistance tempt blacks and Latinos away from doing what they need to do for themselves if they are to succeed in America."[4] King and Smith claim that the two competing alliances need to work together and find common ground. However, unfortunately, the two sides are polarized because they draw the wrong lessons from history; that is, because compromise with slavery and Jim Crow was wrong in the past, compromise is wrong today:

When American political parties and political leaders sought to compromise and evade issues of slavery and Jim Crow racial segregation, they were seeking to avoid confronting injustices with which there should have been no compromise. Today, those past American leaders who supported concessions to proponents of racial inequality, like Senators Henry Clay and Stephen Douglas in the antebellum years, and Justice Joseph Bradley and President Woodrow Wilson in the late nineteenth and early twentieth century, are widely seen as having acted shamefully. It is the Americans who stood fast against slavery's spread like Abraham Lincoln and against segregation like Martin Luther King Jr. who are now iconic symbols of the politics of moral principle.

Yet partly as a result, today, proponents of both color-blind and race-conscious policies have drawn the wrong lesson from this history. They see themselves as just such champions of principle, and they often imply that today, as in the past, compromise with their opponents would be immoral. Some on each side charge that despite the members of the rival alliance's professed allegiance to the modern civil rights movement, their positions are racist.[5]

A Critique of King and Smith

In comparing King and Smith's perspective with the view that I present in this book, two issues emerge: one is small, the other colossal.

The small issue has to do with the way the two perspectives present power arrangements. King and Smith are absolutely correct in their presentation of fluid power arrangements. Indeed, the political science and public policy literature describes power arrangements in the process of making public policies as fluid.[6] However, even though there are indeed different organized interests active in different issue areas, the entire political system tends to be biased in favor of business and corporate interests. Moreover, in recent times these business and corporate interests have become more active and more powerful.[7] King and Smith concede that there are a number of core interests that cross most policy issue lines. Moreover, conservative think tanks and the American Legislative Exchange Council have been involved in almost every policy area that impacts racial issues. Progressive and reactionary policy cultures have operated to shape policies in almost every issue area that impacts race.

The colossal issue has to do with the question of whether the conflict between competing alliances or coalitions is similar to the conflicts of the past; that is, conflicts where one side opposed racial oppression and the other side supported it and conflicts where the outcome determined the future of the nation. Here, I find a number of serious problems with King and Smith's view.

First, I take issue with King and Smith's assessment of historical figures such as Lincoln, Bradley, and Wilson.[8] Contrary to their assessment, Lincoln was not uncompromising over the issue of slavery. His position on slavery was influenced by his practical views about the unity of the nation. In a letter dated August 22, 1862, Lincoln said:

> My paramount object in this struggle is to save the Union, and is not either to save or to destroy slavery. If I could save the Union without freeing any slave I would do it, and if I could save it by freeing all the slaves I would do it; and if I could save it by freeing some and leaving others alone I would also do that. What I do about slavery, and the colored race, I do because I believe it helps to save the Union; and what I forbear, I forbear because I do not believe it would help to save the Union.[9]

Contrary to King and Smith, President Lincoln was willing to compromise over the issue of slavery. The Confederacy was uncompromising in its defense of slavery. It was adamant about its right to expand slavery and extend it into the territory gained from Mexico in the Mexican-American War.

Whereas Lincoln was a compromiser over slavery, Justice Bradley and President Wilson were uncompromising in their support of racial segregation. Bradley was fundamentally opposed to civil rights laws. Like Justice Antonin Scalia (see Chapter 2), Bradley referred to these laws as granting special favors to blacks. He authored the majority opinion in the *Civil Rights Cases* of 1883, which struck down the Civil Rights Act of 1875.[10] This act prohibited racial discrimination in public places such as theaters, railroads, and steamboats. Bradley argued that the federal government had exceeded its powers under the constitution by passing this Civil Rights Act. Although the Fourteenth Amendment explicitly expanded federal powers in the area of civil rights, Bradley in the nineteenth century and reactionary conservatives in the twenty-first century deny this expansion. This *Civil Rights Cases* of 1883 decision set the stage for the rise of Jim Crow laws.

President Wilson was also a promoter of racial segregation. He sympathized with the Ku Klux Klan and imposed racial segregation on workstations, cafeterias, restrooms, and other places inside federal agencies. In order to be able to exclude qualified blacks from federal employment, his administration introduced the practice of attaching the pictures of job applicants who had passed the test to qualify for employment to their file folders.[11]

Second, I take issue with King and Smith's list of groups on both sides of the criminal justice issue area is inaccurate and incomplete. For one example, this list is included on the color-blind alliance women's groups concerned with the issues of rape and domestic violence. These groups were not involved in pushing for the types of draconian laws that define the current racially repressive criminal justice system. Battered women's groups pushed hard for the Violence Against Women Act of 1994. Contrary to King and Smith, opponents of this act were well represented on the color-blind alliance and supporters of this act were part of the color-conscious alliance. For example, in *United States v. Morrison,* the color-blind side of the Supreme Court struck down parts of this act.[12] The color-conscious side of the Court defended the entire act. In 2013, when Congress reauthorized this act, the color-conscious alliance supported it. The color-blind alliance opposed it.

There are some critically important organizations missing from King and Smith's alliances. The organization that is most noticeably missing from the color-blind alliance in the criminal justice issue area is ALEC. More than any political organization in this country, the corporate-controlled ALEC played the dominant role in establishing a racially repressive criminal justice system. Mike Elk and Bob Sloan set the record straight on ALEC:

> Somewhat more familiar is ALEC's instrumental role in the explosion of the U.S. prison population in the past few decades. ALEC helped pioneer some of the toughest sentencing laws on the books today, like mandatory minimums for non-violent drug offenders, "three-strikes" laws, and "truth in sentencing" laws. In 1995 alone, ALEC's Truth in Sentencing Act was signed into law in twenty-five states. More recently, ALEC had proposed innovative "solutions" to the overcrowding it helped create, such as privatizing the parole process through "the proven success of the private bail bond industry," as it recommended in 2007 . . . ALEC has also worked to pass state laws to create private for-profit prisons, a boon to two of its major corporate sponsors: Corrections Corporation of America and GEO Group (formerly Wackenhut Corrections), the largest private prison firms in the country.[13]

ALEC not only played a key role in the passage of mandatory sentencing, truth in sentencing, and three-strikes laws, it played a major role in promoting the rise of the prison industry complex and in the passage of the infamous stand your ground laws. ALEC has been a leader in the reactionary movement that produced racial repression. The failure to acknowledge ALEC is significant because the involvement of this organization is consistent with the theme of this book that corporate organizations played a crucial role in the reactionary coalition.

King and Smith also missed a couple of important organizations in their color-conscious alliance: Amnesty International and Human Rights Watch. Amnesty International had been campaigning for decades to get the United States to end capital punishment, as it has considered the death penalty to be the ultimate human rights violation and one that is tainted with racial bias. In 2012, Amnesty International called on the United States to end the death penalty.[14] Several years earlier, Human Rights Watch had cited the United States for a number of human rights violations, most notably for sentencing children to life imprisonment without any chance of parole and for racial biases in the sentencing since the overwhelming majority of those sentenced to life without parole were children of color.[15] (See Chapter 7.)

In a 2008, Human Rights Watch cited the United States for racial targeting in its drug enforcement policy:

> Ostensibly color-blind, the U.S. drug war has been and continues to be waged overwhelmingly against black Americans. Although white Americans constitute the large majority of drug offenders, African American communities continue as the principal "fronts" in this unjust effort. Defenders of the current anti-drug efforts claim they want to protect poor minority communities from addiction as well as the disorder, nuisance, and violence that can accompany drug dealing. But the choice of imprisonment as the primary anti-drug strategy, and the effect of this policy on neighborhoods, evokes the infamous phrase from the Vietnam War, "it became necessary to destroy the town in order to save it."[16]

When these human rights organizations raised concerns about racial biases within the US justice system, they became part of the color-conscious coalition. As Amnesty International and Human Rights Watch turned the spotlight on these human rights violations, the claim that these laws are fair and just lost all validity.

Third, I propose that King and Smith accepted uncritically some of the biased assumptions and terminology used by proponents of the color-blind alliance. A prime example is their use of the term "race-conscious assistance." They note, "Color-blind proponents have long believed that promises of race-conscious assistance tempt blacks and Latinos away from doing what they need to do for themselves if they are to succeed in America."[17] This expression is not a reflection of the objective reality of public policies. It is a function of the racializing of federal assistance programs; that is, it erroneously characterizes race-neutral programs as racially targeted programs. Programs such as Temporary Assistance for Needy Families, the Supplemental Nutrition Assistance Program, job training, and offender reentry are race neutral, but they are often presented as race-conscious assistance programs by the color-blind alliance. This characterization has generally been followed by racial stereotypes of program recipients. This whole process of racializing federal programs is a function of metaracism.

As noted above, King and Smith give credence to the color-blind alliance's assumption that extremely high incarceration rates benefit black communities. The tragedy and fallacy of this color-blind assumption is shown in Matt Lauer's interview of former New York City police commissioner Bernard Kerik on the November 1, 2013, *Today* show. Kerik had served a three-year sentence for federal tax evasion. During the course of the interview, Kerik placed a nickel in Lauer's hand. Kerik said that while in prison he met good, decent, hardworking fathers and husbands who he had put there for possessing crack cocaine of the same weight as that nickel. He confessed that he had believed in that policy. He believed that he was doing something good. Instead, he needlessly destroyed people's lives, wrecked families, and disrupted communities.[18]

Fourth, I contend that it seems that in an effort to remain fair, balanced, and objective, King and Smith have unknowingly and unwittingly white-washed the color-blind alliance and colored the color-conscious alliance. The October 23, 2013, episode of *The Daily Show with Jon Stewart* provides a good example of this whitewashing and coloring. In the episode with guest Aasif Mandvi, a *Daily Show* regular, Mandvi interviews Representative John Lewis (D–GA) and Don Yelton, a precinct captain and Republican Executive Committee member in North Carolina.[19]

During the course of the interview, Yelton used the N-word several times. He claimed that he was not racist, although he said that he had been called a bigot. He insisted that he had black friends. He stated that the new voter registration laws were enacted to enhance the integrity of elections and to prevent fraud. However, he admitted that the new laws were indeed designed to reduce the number of Democrats voting. He argued that "you don't want people who are too lazy and too stupid to get a state identification card to vote and elect the president anyway."[20]

In the interview, Lewis raised many of the same concerns about the color-blind and color-conscious perspectives discussed by King and Smith: that the color-conscious and color-blind alliances accuse each other of racism and that both sides evoke the name and legacy of Martin Luther King Jr. Lewis claimed that he supported all people, regardless of color, and that the voter suppression movement today is motivated by the same racism as it was back in the 1960s. Mandvi showed Lewis a picture of the leaders of the 1963 March on Washington and said that these leaders would not make the same claims that Lewis was making today. However, Lewis pointed out that he was in the picture, next to Martin Luther King Jr.[21]

Indeed, the belief that the color-blind alliance has the same legitimate claim to the legacy of Martin Luther King Jr. as civil rights leaders today is belied by the fact that many of these leaders had worked with him fifty years ago. Some like Lewis had shared the podium with him. Some like Jesse Jackson were with him when he was assassinated. Lewis explained that civil rights leaders were color conscious because the only possible way to see the reality of racial injustice was to be able to see color.[22]

The claim of color-blind alliance members to the legacy of Martin Luther King Jr. is also belied by the fact that many of its members had fought against civil rights policies in the past. Fifty or sixty years ago, some of these members were part of the racist right. For example, King and Smith include the late Senator Robert Byrd on the color-blind list. Byrd filibustered against the Civil Rights Act of 1964, and in his younger years he had been an active leader in his local Ku Klux Klan.

Yelton's views place him in the color-blind alliance. His views bear strong similarities to the position of the Southern Redeemers who overthrew the Reconstruction regime. Over a hundred years ago, while they claimed to be restoring the glory of the South and integrity and common sense to elections, Southern leaders passed a series of color-blind laws such as the character test, the literacy test, and poll taxes. They made the same claims that Yelton made when he was interviewed by Mandvi: they didn't want dumb, illiterate, lazy bums of bad character voting. Like those of a century ago, today's color-blind laws are used in racially biased ways.

Contrary to King and Smith's analysis, the conflict between the color-blind and the color-conscious alliances is not one in which there are good and bad points on each side. It is not one in which each side could benefit from the wisdom and insight of the other.

The Old Redeemer and New Reactionary Movements

Contrary to King and Smith's view, the new reactionary movement has a number of striking similarities with the old Redeemer movement. Both movements have grossly exaggerated the problems of the progressive regimes; demonized progressives; and engaged in a ruthless, relentless, and uncompromising assault on the progressive regimes—Reconstruction and equal opportunity. Both movements have used race and racism strategically to normalize extreme inequality, to legitimize the redistribution of wealth, and to support racial oppression. Both have used racism to support an assault on equal opportunity regimes and to encourage extreme racial repression.

The reactionary movement is engaged in an all-out assault on the equal opportunity regime. It has pushed to ban any form of race-conscious affirmative action policies, to weaken employment discrimination laws, to roll back regulations that protect the most vulnerable from consumer fraud and predatory lending, to suppress minority voting rights, to outlaw labor unions, to further erode or eliminate the minimum wage, and to cut back social security and public assistance programs.

There are some differences. The racism of the Redeemer movement was hard core and blatant. It entailed biological and genetic determinism that was applied to entire racial groups. The racism of the reactionary movement is soft core and subtle; it involves coded language and cultural determinism applied primarily to low-income blacks. The Redeemer movement squashed the Reconstruction regime in less than two decades. The reactionary movement is meeting with resistance as the egalitarian coalition has pushed back. This is not the first time that the egalitarian coalition and equal opportunity regime has been challenged by a counter movement led by corporate interests. In the 1980s, Frances Piven and Richard A. Cloward had this to say about the emergence of the welfare state and the corporate assault on it:

> The emergence of the welfare state was a momentous development in American history. It meant that people could turn to government to shield them from the insecurities and hardships of an unrestrained market economy. One purpose of this essay is to explain why the business oriented leaders who came to power with the election of Reagan in 1980 are trying to dismantle these protections.
>
> Our other purpose is to say why we think they are likely to fail. This is not the first time men of property have combined to strip away the state programs on which the unemployed, the unemployable, and the working poor depend for their subsistence. However, if our conclusion turns out to be correct, it will be the first time the propertied met defeat. Despite temporary setbacks, they have always managed in the past to eliminate whatever sources of subsistence were, from time to time, provided by the state. If the present-day corporate mobilization fails, that will be as significant as the emergence of the welfare state itself. It will mean that the developments in American society which brought the welfare state into being are also sufficient to ensure its persistence.[23]

Piven and Cloward conclude that "although the corporate mobilization in our time is formidable, its success depends finally on the inability of the American people in the twentieth century to see through the mystifications of propaganda drawn from the nineteenth century. Its success also depends ultimately on the acquiescence of Americans before the combined power of state and capital. Both premises have proved wrong before."[24] As they predicted, the corporate assault on the welfare state failed during the 1980s. It failed because most people did not believe in the reactionary political culture—neoconservatism or neoliberalism. It failed because of the power of democracy, the vote, and organized labor. And it failed because racism had receded, although Ronald Reagan used racist images to attack these programs.

However, since the 1980s some things have changed to the disadvantage of the egalitarian coalition. Political power has shifted to the right. The corporate-centered conservative coalition has grown much stronger, much larger, and more pervasive—supporting the Republican Party and pushing the Democratic Party to the right. This conservative coalition has become more effective in racializing social programs and using racial code words.

After the 2008 election, the far right and the Tea Party movement emerged to become a major wing of the Republican Party and to occupy key congressional offices. As the political right ascended, the political left declined. Today, the left is disorganized and weak. Nevertheless, a few scholars have fought back from the left, criticizing both the egalitarian and reactionary coalitions. This criticism provides support for the dismissal view of class and racial politics that I have presented in this book.

A Leftist Critique of the Egalitarian Coalition and the Barack Obama Administration

Marxist scholar David Harvey insists that the egalitarian coalition has been too particularistic and has failed to use the issue of class to build a united working-class movement. That is, it has emphasized the rights of identity groups, but neglected working-class issues that cut across racial, gender, and sexual orientation lines. To make his point, he uses the example of a tragic fire that occurred in 1991 at a chicken processing plant in Hamlet, North Carolina, in which twenty-five people died, including twelve African Americans and eighteen women:

> I think it is instructive here to note that as far as I know, none of the institutions associated with such new social movements saw fit to engage politically with what happened in Hamlet, North Carolina. Women's organizations, for example, were heavily preoccupied with the question of sexual harassment and mobilizing against the Clarence Thomas appointment, even though it was mainly women who died in the North Carolina fire and women who continue to bear an enormous burden of exploitation in the "Broiler Belt." And apart from the Rainbow Coalition and Jesse Jackson, African-American (and Hispanic organizations) also remained strangely silent on the matter, while some ecologists (particularly the animal rights wing) exhibited more sympathy for the chickens than for the workers.[25]

Harvey argues that the question of whether the fire was inevitable or not is debatable. However, there is no question that the deaths of the twenty-five workers was avoidable: they were the result of the fact that there were no safety inspections of the plant for over eleven years. The sprinkler system did not work. The exit doors were locked. This fire occurred in an area hit hard by the farm crisis of the 1980s. Poverty was high and wages were low. Labor unions were nonexistent so the workers had no power and no voice within the state legislature. Neither political party responded to this tragedy. There were no demands for stricter safety regulations or calls for increased support for workers, for unions, for higher wages, or for better working conditions for all workers—black or white, men or women. Aside from Jesse Jackson's Rainbow Coalition, civil rights and women rights groups were silent. They failed to respond to the issues that impacted the working-class poor.[26]

Cornel West offers considerable insight into the current reactionary movement. Chris Hedges explains West's insights and concerns about the Obama administration:

> This was maybe America's last chance to fight back against the greed of the Wall Street oligarchs and corporate plutocrats, to generate some serious discussion about public interest and common good that sustains any democratic experiment. . . . We are squeezing out all of the democratic juices we have. The escalation of the class war against the poor and the working class is intense. More and more working people are beaten down. They are world-weary. They are into self-medication. They are turning on each other. They are scapegoating the most vulnerable rather than confronting the most powerful. It is a profoundly human response to panic and catastrophe. I thought Barack Obama could have provided some way out. But he lacks backbone.[27]

According to Hedges, West argues that there is a reactionary movement engaged in an assault on the working class and that the Democrats and the Obama administration are doing little about it. West insists that the white working class has turned to scapegoating the most vulnerable rather than confronting the conservative coalition and corporate sector, and that President Obama has lacked the courage to stand up to this coalition, to advocate for the poor and the working class, and to lead the nation in a more progressive direction.[28]

In his book *Democracy Matters,* West develops a much broader critique of the reactionary movement. He acknowledges that this nation is at a crossroads and engaged in an epic battle that will determine its future. He sees an epic battle between democratic-led globalization versus corporate-led globalization. He sees corporate-led globalization promoting free-market fundamentalism, authoritarianism, and aggressive militarism.[29] He insists that free-market fundamentalism is just as dangerous as religious fundamentalism, for both trivialize concern for public interest and public welfare. The culture of denial remains a problem. West suggests that, although people in the United States see themselves as exceptional because of their commitment to democracy and freedom, they are instead exceptional because of their refusal to acknowledge their deeply racist roots and the contradiction in their history of a commitment to freedom marred by the promotion of slavery and racial oppression.[30]

West also recognizes media bias as a problem for democracy. The problem is that the media provides an outlet for the corporate sector and the well-endowed and organized groups, but blocks access for and silences the voices of the poor and oppressed. Of the media, West notes, "Meanwhile the market-driven media—fueled by our vast ideological polarization and abetted by profit-hungry monopolies—have severely narrowed our political 'dialogue.' The major problem is not the vociferous shouting from one camp to the other; rather it is that many have given up even being heard."[31]

West argues that Christian fundamentalists are a major part of the reactionary movement. These fundamentalists have joined with the plutocrats in an assault on both the equal opportunity state and progressive Christians. West insists that the Christian fundamentalist movement emerged as a backlash of the success of Martin Luther King Jr. and the Christian-led civil rights movement: "The politicization of Christian fundamentalism was a direct response to King's prophetic Christian legacy. It began as a white backlash against King's heritage in American public life, and it has always had a racist undercurrent—as with Bob Jones University, which until recently barred interracial dating."[32] He identifies the Christian fundamentalist movement as part of "the Republican Party's realignment of American politics—with their use of racially coded issues (busing, crime, affirmative action, welfare) to appeal to southern conservatives and urban white centrists."[33]

West maintains that Christian fundamentalists began their ascent to power with an attack on progressive Christians: With the backing of the Plutocrats, Christian fundamentalists have attacked organizations such as the World Council of Churches, the National Council of Churches, and liberal mainline denominations (Episcopalians, Presbyterians, Lutherans, and Congregationalists) because these progressive religious organizations have spoken out in defense of the rights of people of color, workers, women, gays, and lesbians.[34]

West makes it clear that Christian fundamentalists, allied with free-market fundamentalists and plutocrats, have drowned out the voices of progressive Christians and promoted a form of market-driven nihilism devoted to the rich, devoid of compassion for the poor, and hostile to any sense of social justice. West's insightful analysis shows a reactionary movement that is driven by greed, engagement in a war against the poor, and promotion of racial stereotypes; that is led by the dominant corporate class, with the support of Christian fundamentalists; and that is bringing this nation down a dangerous and self-destructive path.

West ignores the context within which the Obama administration has been operating: as an administration constrained and under siege. With few exceptions (perhaps Andrew Johnson), the Obama administration has been subjected to the most severe and relentless assault from the opposition party than any other administration. Few, if any, presidents of the United States faced a Congress in which leaders of the opposite party publicly stated that they were committed to making the president a one-term president and in which opposition party leaders devoted a large part of their time, energy, and efforts to blocking the president's proposals and targeting a single signature program, the Affordable Care Act. Few, if any, presidents had their

State of the Union address interrupted by an opposition party member shouting out, "You lie." The level of opposition to President Obama's administration has been unprecedented.

Nevertheless, even under these extraordinary circumstances, the Obama administration has made significant progress in select areas. This administration can point to a number of landmark achievements: the Lilly Ledbetter Fair Pay Act, the stimulus bill, the Affordable Care Act, cash for clunkers, and the end of discrimination against gay men and lesbians in the military.

There have been both progress and setbacks. Although President Obama's Justice Department has fought tirelessly against the minority voter suppression movement, the Supreme Court found state voter identification laws valid and struck down Section 4 of the Voting Rights Act. Although the Obama administration achieved some modest reform of racially biased drug laws, reform measures have been too small to make a substantial difference. Although the president has had some conversations on racial issues, his entire administration had been dogged by racist attacks.

At least, President Obama has advocated progressive change in select areas. He spoke out in favor of raising the minimum wage, in support of the rights of workers to organize and engage in collective bargaining, and for the need to reform an exceedingly punitive and racially biased criminal justice system. He advocated an increase in spending to rebuild this nation's infrastructure and to maintain spending for SNAP, unemployment, social security, Medicare and Medicaid, and other programs. The president pushed back against the conservative coalition and the Republican Party, although he could not prevent cuts in a few select equal opportunity programs.

One criticism of the Obama administration stands out. The president never acknowledged the inadequacy of the support for poor women with children. Moreover, he supported the so-called welfare reforms that trashed the Aid to Families with Dependent Children program.[35] However, given the extent of metaracism, had the president supported welfare, he would have been buried politically. This is the racially charged context within which he has operated.

Where Do We Go from Here?

If any major point emerges from this book, it must be this one: the struggle for racial equality and justice has never been a zero-sum game and it is ongoing. Contrary to metaracism and reactionary ideology, progressive programs that have reduced racial inequalities and produced equal opportunity have contributed to expanded opportunities, income, and wealth for all people in this country.

Nevertheless, the conservative coalition is likely to continue to hack away at equal opportunity programs and promote a neoliberal agenda that is bound to aggravate racial oppression. As Republicans propose substantial cuts to social programs, Democrats are likely to reduce the cuts. Over time, this process will probably contribute to a slow erosion of equal opportunity programs, a continual growth in inequality, and a widening of the black/ white gaps in income, wealth, and education.

As the egalitarian coalition weakens and the reactionary coalition gains momentum, Congress will remain fixated on the budget deficit and the national debt, continuing in its current budget-cutting mode. Republicans will propose substantial cuts, mediated by Democrats. However, in time, the downward spiral will cease. It will cease as this nation becomes more diverse with changing demographics. It will cease when people realize that this paradox of racial progress and regression is a result of the epic battle between progressive and reactionary forces. It will cease when people realize that racism is not an isolated incidental problem that will correct itself when exposed to Christianity and the American creed, but it is now and always has been part of and symptomatic of larger problems deeply rooted in the US economy, culture, institutions, and politics. It will cease when people understand the extent of the problems of inequality; the extent to which democracy has already been undermined by voter suppression and money-driven and corporate-sponsored elections; and the extent to which racism desensitizes them to these larger problems of democracy, inequality, poverty, and police repression and the dangers posed by the looming reactionary movement. People must realize that what happens to those most oppressed happens to all of us; that is, the advancement of the oppressed has historically contributed to the advancement of all. This realization will eventually precipitate a resurgence in the egalitarian coalition.

This same principle applies to immigration policy, another policy area infected by racism that would require another entire book to discuss. The point here that the current anti-immigration hysteria is part of the same metaracism. Latino immigrants are used as scapegoats just like African Americans. Moreover, the oppressive treatment of Latino immigrants from Central and South America diminishes everyone in this country. The struggle for immigration reform must emerge as part of the egalitarian coalition.

Indeed, Thomas Paine's progressive vision was not that of the neoliberals or neoconservatives who strive for limited government and open markets. It was not a vision coming from anti-immigration hysteria. It was not a vision of an exclusionary repressive United States. Paine's vision was of a nation truly committed to justice, equal opportunity, and prosperity for all. A realization of these principles should energize the egalitarian coalition and push this nation back on the road toward justice. To paraphrase Martin Luther King Jr., the arc of history is long, but it bends toward justice.

Notes

1 Desmond King and Rogers M. Smith, *Still a House Divided: Race and Politics in Obama's America* (Princeton: Princeton University Press, 2011), pp. 15–16.

2. See Carter A. Wilson, *Public Policy: Continuity and Change* (Long Grove, IL: Waveland Press, 2013).

3. King and Smith, *Still a House Divided*, pp. 218–219.

4. Ibid., p. 269.

5. Ibid., p. 11.

6. Robert Dahl, *Who Governs? Democracy and Power in an American City* (New Haven: Yale University Press, 2005); Hugh Heclo, *Issue Networks and the Executive Establishment* (Englewood Cliffs, NJ: Prentice Hall, 1995); Nelson Polsby, *Community Power and Political Theory* (New haven: Yale University Press, 1963).

7. Charles Lindblom, *Politics and Markets: The World's Political Economic Systems* (New York: Basic Books, 1977); Elmer Schattschneider, *The Semisovereign People: A Realist's View of Democracy in America* (Fort Worth, TX: Harcourt Brace, Jovanovich College Publishers, 1975).

8. King and Smith, *Still a House Divided*, p. 11. I take issue with this statement: "It is the Americans who stood fast against slavery's spread like Abraham Lincoln."

9. Abraham Lincoln, "Letter to Horace Greeley," in Roy Basler, ed., *The Collected Works of Abraham Lincoln,* Vol. 5, August 22, 1865 (New Brunswick, NJ: Rutgers University Press, 1953), p. 388.

10. Justice Joseph Bradley made this point clear in his majority opinion in the *Civil Rights Cases,* 109 U.S. 3 (1883).

11. Desmond King and Rogers M. Smith, "Racial Orders in American Political Development," *American Political Science Review* 99 (2005): 75–99.

12. *United States v. Morrison,* 529 U.S. 598 (2000).

13. Mike Elk and Bob Sloan, "The Hidden History of ALEC and Prison Labor," *The Nation,* August 1, 2011.

14. Amnesty International, "USA Senseless Killing After Senseless Killing: Texas Inmate with Mental Disability Claim Facing Execution for Murder Committed as Teenager" (London: Amnesty International, 2012).

15. Human Rights Watch, *The Rest of Their Lives: Life Without Parole for Child Offenders in the U.S.* (London/New York: Human Rights Watch and Amnesty International, October 12, 2005).

16. Human Rights Watch, "Targeting Blacks: Drug Law Enforcement and Race in the United States" (New York: Human Rights Watch, 2008). http://hrw.org./sites/default/files/reports/us0508_1.pdf.

17. King and Smith, *Still a House Divided,* p. 269.

18. Bernard Kerick, former New York City police commissioner interviewed by Matt Lauer, *Today,* NBC, November 1, 2013. http://www.today.com/.../nypd-chief-turned-inmate-kerick-prison-system-broken-8c11509923.

19. Representative John Lewis (D-GA) and Don Yelton, a precinct captain and Republican executive committee member, in North Carolina, interviewed by Aasif Mandvi, "Suppressing the Vote," *The Daily Show with Jon Stewart,* Comedy Central, October 23, 2013. http://www.thedailyshow.com/...October-23-2013/suppressing-the-vote.

20. Ibid.

21. Ibid.

22. Ibid.

23. Frances Piven and Richard A. Cloward, *The New Class War: Reagan's Attack on the Welfare State and Its Consequences* (New York: Pantheon Books, 1982), pp. ix–x.

24. Ibid.

25. David Harvey, *Justice, Nature and the Geography of Difference* (Cambridge, MA: Blackwell, 1996), p. 341, quoted in Carolyn Gallaher, *On the Fault Line: Race, Class and the America Patriot Movement* (Lanham, MD: Rowman and Littlefield, 2002), p. 37.

26. Ibid.

27. Chris Hedges, "The Obama Deception: Why Cornel West Went Ballistic," *Truthdig*, May 16, 2011. http://www.truthdig.com/report/item/the_obama_deception _why_cornel_west_went_ballistic_20110516/.

28. Ibid.

29. Ibid., p. 22.

30. Ibid., p. 41.

31. Ibid., p. 7.

32. Ibid., p. 164.

33. Ibid.

34. Ibid., pp. 165–166.

35. Barack Obama, *The Audacity of Hope: Thoughts on Reclaiming the American Dream* (New York: Crown, 2006).

Bibliography

Adorno, Theodor, Else Frenkel-Brunswik, Daniel Levison, and R. Levitt. *The Authoritarian Personality.* New York: Harper, 1950.

Alexander, Michelle. *The New Jim Crow: Mass Incarcerations in the Age of Colorblindness.* New York: New Press, 2010.

Allport, Gordon. *The Nature of Prejudice.* Garden City, NY: Doubleday, 1958.

Altemeyer, Bob. *The Authoritarian Specter.* Cambridge: Harvard University Press, 1996.

American Civil Liberties Union (ALCU). "New ACLU Report Finds Overwhelming Racial Bias in Marijuana Arrests." ACLU press release, June 4, 2013.

Amnesty International. *Annual Report 2013: The State of the World's Human Rights.* 2013. http://amnesty.org/region/usa/report-2013-#section-157-6.

Auletta, Ken. *The Underclass.* New York: Random House, 1982.

Baldus, David, Charles Pulaski, and George Woodworth. *Equal Justice and the Death Penalty: A Legal and Empirical Analysis.* Boston: Northeastern University Press, 1990.

Bartel, Larry. *Unequal Democracy: The Political Economy of the New Gilded Age.* Princeton: Princeton University Press, 2008.

Baumgartner, Frank, and Bryan Jones. *Agendas and Instability in American Politics.* Chicago: University of Chicago Press, 2009.

Bedau, Hugo, and Michael Radelet. "Miscarriages of Justice in Potentially Capital Cases." *Stanford Law Review* 40, no. 1 (1987): 21–179.

Bellah, Robert, Richard Madsen, William Sullivan, Ann Swidler, and Steven Tipon. *Habits of the Heart: Individualism and Commitment in American Life.* Berkeley: University of California Press, 2008.

Bergin, David, and Helen Cooks, "High School Students of Color Talk About Accusations of 'Acting White.'" *Urban Review* 34, no. 2 (2002): 113–135.

Berman, Ari. "Texas Redistricting Fight Shows Why Voting Rights Act Is Still Needed." *The Nation,* June 5, 2013.

Biddle, Bruce, and David Berliner. *Manufactured Crisis: Myths, Fraud, and the Attack on America's Public Schools.* Reading, MA: Addison-Wesley, 1996.

———. "A Research Synthesis/Unequal School Funding in the United States." *Educational Leadership* 59, no. 8 (2002): 48–59.

Billingsley, Andrew. *Climbing Jacob's Ladder: The Enduring Legacy of African-American Families* (New York: Simon & Schuster, 1993).

Billingsley, Andrew, and Cleopatra H. Caldwell. "The Church, the Family, and the School in the African American Community," *Journal of Negro Education* 60, no. 3 (1991): 427–440.

Bishaw, Alemaye. "Areas with Concentrated Poverty: 2006–2010," *American Community Survey Briefs.* Washington, DC: US Department of Commerce, Economics, and Statistics Administration, US Census Bureau, 2011.

Bloom, Jack. *Class, Race, and the Civil Rights Movement: The Changing Political Economy of Racism.* Bloomington: Indiana University Press, 1987.

Bluestone, Barry, and Bennett Harrison. *The Deindustrialization of America.* New York: Basic Books, 1982.

Bolen, Ed, Dottie Rosenbaum, and Robert Greenstein. "GOP's Additional SNAP Cuts Would Increase Hardship in Areas with High Unemployment." Washington DC: Center for Budget Priorities, August 18, 2013

Bottari, Mary. "A Field Guide to the Koch O'Nut's Behind the Near Government Default." *PR Watch,* October 21, 2013. http://www.Truth-out.org/news/item/1954-a-field-guide-to-the-koch-o-nuts-behind-the-near-government-default.

Bower, William, and Glenn Pierce. "Deterrence or Brutalization: What Is the Effect of Executions?" *Crime and Delinquency* 26, (1980): 453–484.

Brock, David. *The Republican Noise Machine: Right-Wing Media and How It Corrupts Democracy.* New York: Three River Press, 2004.

Burton-Rose, Daniel. *The Celling of America: An Inside Look at the U.S. Prison Industry.* With Dan Pens and Paul Wright. Monroe, ME: Common Courage Press, 1998.

Cazenave, Noel. *The Urban Racial State: Managing Race Relations in American Cities.* Lanham, MD: Rowman and Littlefield, 2011.

Ciotti, Paul. "America's Most Costly Educational Failure." Commentary. Washington, DC: Cato Institute, 2012. http://cato.org/publication/commentary/americas-most-costly-educational-failure.

———. *Money and School Performance: Lessons from the Kansas City Desegregation Experiment.* Stanford, CA: Hoover Institution Press; San Francisco: Pacific Research Institute, 2001.

Chua, Amy. *World on Fire: How Exporting Free Market Democracy Breeds Ethnic Hatred and Global Instability.* New York: Doubleday, 2003.

Chubb, John, and Terry Moe. *Politics, Markets and America's Schools.* Washington, DC: Brookings Institution, 1990.

Cobb, Roger, and Charles Elder. *Participation in American Politics: The Dynamics of Agenda Building.* Baltimore: Johns Hopkins University Press, 1983.

Coleman, James. *Equality of Educational Opportunity.* Washington, DC: Government Printing Office, 1966.

Collins, Jane L., and Victoria Mayer. *Both Hands Tied: Welfare Reform and the Race to the Bottom of the Low-Wage Labor Market.* Chicago: University of Chicago Press, 2010.

Collins, Patricia. *Black Feminist Thought: Knowledge, Consciousness and the Politics of Empowerment.* New York: Routledge Press, 2000.

Cook, Philip, and Jens Ludwig. "Weighing the Burden of Acting White: Are There Race Differences in Attitudes Toward Education?" *Journal of Policy Analysis and Management* 16, no. 2 (1997): 256–278.

Caper, Laura. "The Negro Family and the Moynihan Report." In Lee Rainwater and William Yancey (eds.), *The Moynihan Report and the Politics of Controversy.* Cambridge: MIT Press, 1996 [1967].

Coulter, Ann. *Guilty: Liberal "Victims" and Their Assault on America.* New York: Crown Forum, 2008.

Currie, Elliot. *Confronting Crime: An American Challenge.* New York: Pantheon Books, 1985.

Dahl, Robert. *Who Governs? Democracy and Power in an American City.* New Haven: Yale University Press, 2005.

Derber, Charles. *The Wilding of America: How Greed and Violence Are Eroding Our Nation's Character.* New York: St. Martin's Press, 1996.

Diamond, Sara. *The Roads to Dominion: Right-Wing Movements and Political Power in the United States.* New York: Guilford Press, 1995.

DiIulio, John. "The Coming of the Super-Predators." *Weekly Standard,* November 27, 1995.

DiTomaso, Nancy. *The American Non-Dilemma: Racial Inequality Without Racism.* New York: Russell Sage Foundation, 2013.

Donziger, Steven (ed.). *The Real War on Crime: The Report of the National Criminal Justice Commission.* New York: HarperCollins, 1996.

DuBois, W. E. B. *Black Reconstruction in America, 1860–1880.* New York: Atheneum, 1969.

———. *The Philadelphia Negro.* Philadelphia: University of Pennsylvania Press, 1996.

———. *The World and Africa.* Millwood, NY: Kraus Thomson Organization, 1976.

Dyer, Joel. *Harvest of Rage: Why Oklahoma City Is Only the Beginning.* Boulder, CO: Westview Press, 1998.

Dyson, Eric Michael. *Is Bill Cosby Right or Has the Black Middle Class Lost Its Mind?* New York: Basic Civitas Books, 2008.

Eben, Harrell. "Study: Racist Attitudes Are Still Ingrained." *Time,* January 8, 2009.

Eberhardt, Jennifer, Paul Davies, Valerie Purdie-Vaughns, and Sheri Johnson. "Looking Deathworthy: Perceived Stereotypicality of Black Defendants Predicts Capital-Sentencing Outcomes." *Psychological Science* 17, no. 5 (2006): 383–386.

Eberhardt, Jennifer, Valerie Purdie, Phillip Goff, and Paul Davies. "Seeing Black: Race, Crime, and Visual Processing." *Journal of Personality and Social Psychology* 87, no. 6 (2004): 876–893.

Edsall, Thomas. *The Age of Austerity: How Scarcity Will Remake American Politics.* New York: Anchor Books, 2012.

———. *The New Politics of Inequality.* New York: W. W. Norton, 1984.

———. "The Persistence of Racial Resentment." *New York Times,* February 6, 2013.

Edsall, Thomas, and Mary Edsall. *Chain Reaction: The Impact of Race, Rights, and Taxes on American Politics.* New York: W. W. Norton, 1992.

Ehrenreich, Barbara. *Nickel and Dimed: On (Not) Getting By in America.* New York: Metropolitan Books, Henry Holt, 2001.

Elk, Mike, and Bob Sloan. "The Hidden History of ALEC and Prison Labor," *The Nation.* August 1, 2011. http://www.thenation.com.

Erickson, David, Carolina Reid, Lisa Nelson, Anne O'Shaughnessy, and Alan Berube (eds.). *The Enduring Challenge of Concentrated Poverty in America: Case Studies from Communities Across the U.S.* A Joint Project of the Community Affairs Office of the Federal Reserve System and the Metropolitan Policy Program at the Brookings Institution. Richmond, VA: Federal Reserve Bank of Richmond, 2008.

Evers, Williamson. *Victims Rights, Restitution and Retribution.* Oakland, CA: Independent Institute, 1996.

Fainstein, Norman. "The Underclass/Mismatch Hypothesis as an Explanation for Black Economic Deprivation. *Politics and Society* 15, no. 4 (1987): 403–451.

Fanon, Frantz. *Black Skin/White Mask.* New York: Grove Press, 1967.

Farmer, James. "The Controversial Moynihan Report." In Lee Rainwater and William Yancey (eds.), *The Moynihan Report and the Politics of Controversy.* Cambridge: MIT Press, 1996 [1967].

Ferguson, Ronald. "A Diagnostic Analysis of Black-White GPA Disparities in Shaker Heights, Ohio." In *Brookings Papers on Education Policy.* Washington, DC: Brookings Institution, January 2001.

Financial Crisis Inquiry Commission. *The Financial Crisis Inquiry Report: Final Report of the National Commission on the Causes of the Financial and Economic Crisis in the United States.* Seattle: Pacific Publishing Studio, 2011.

Foner, Eric. *Reconstruction: America's Unfinished Revolution, 1863–1877.* New York: Harper and Row, 1988.

Foner, Philip. *Organized Labor and the Black Worker, 1619–1981.* New York: International, 1982.

Frank, Thomas. *What's the Matter with Kansas: How Conservatives Won the Heart of America.* New York: Henry Holt, 2005.

Fredrickson, George. *Racism: A Short History.* Princeton: Princeton University Press, 2002.

Freire, Paulo. *Pedagogy of the Oppressed.* Trans. Myra B. Ramos. New York: Continuum, 1993.

Friedersdorf, Conor. "Father of Three Gets 25 Years for Selling $1,800 Worth of Painkillers." *The Atlantic,* April 3, 2013.

Friedhoff, Alec, and Howard Wial. "Bearing the Brunt: Manufacturing Job Loss in the Great Lakes Region, 1995–2005." Washington, DC: Urban Institute, 2006.

Friedman, Milton. *Capitalism and Freedom.* Chicago: University of Chicago Press, 1962.

Friedman, Milton. *Free to Choose.* With Rose Friedman. New York: Harcourt, 1980.

Galbraith, James. *The Predatory State: How Conservatives Abandoned the Free Market and Why Liberals Should Too.* New York: Free Press, 2008.

Gallaher, Carolyn. *On the Fault Line: Race, Class and the America Patriot Movement.* Lanham, MD: Rowman and Littlefield, 2002.

General Accounting Office. *Death Penalty Sentencing.* Washington, DC: Government Printing Office, 1990.

Geoghegan, Thomas. *Were You Born On the Wrong Continent? How the European Model Can Help You Get A Life.* New York: New Press, 2010.

Gilder, George. *Wealth and Poverty.* New York: Basic Books, 1981.

Gilens, Martin. *Why Americans Hate Welfare: Race, Media, and the Politics of Antipoverty Policy.* Chicago: University of Chicago Press, 1999.

Goldberg, Theo David. *Racist Culture: Philosophy and the Politics of Meaning.* Cambridge: Blackwell Press, 1994.

Goldstein, Joseph. "Judge Rejects New York's Stop-and-Frisk Policy." *New York Times,* August 12, 2013.

Gordon, Linda. *Pitied but Not Entitled: Single Mothers and the History of Welfare, 1890–1935*. Cambridge: Harvard University Press, 1994.

Gossett, Thomas. *Race: The History of an Idea in America*. New York: Schocken, 1971.

Gould, Stephen Jay. *The Mismeasure of Man*. New York: W. W. Norton, 1996.

Government Accountability Office (GAO). *Consumer Protection: Federal and State Agencies Face Challenges in Combating Predatory Lending*. Washington, DC: Government Printing Office, 2004.

Gramsci, Antonio. *Selections from the Prison Notebooks of Antonio Gramsci*, edited and translated by Quintin Hoare and Geoffrey Smith. New York: International, 1980.

Green, Philip. *The Pursuit of Inequality*. New York: Pantheon Books, 1981.

Greenberg, Stanley. "Report on Democratic Defection." Washington, DC: The Analysis Group, April 15, 1985.

Greider, William. *Who Will Tell the People: The Betrayal of American Democracy*. New York: Touchstone, 1993.

Gumbel, Andrew. *Steal This Vote: Dirty Elections and the Rotten History of Democracy in America*. New York: Nation Books, 2005.

Hacker, Jacob, and Paul Pierson. *Winner-Take-All: How Washington Made the Rich Richer and Turned Its Back on the Middle Class*. New York: Simon and Schuster, 2011.

Hamilton, Alexander. "Report on Manufactures," December 5, 1791.

Hamilton, Alexander, James Madison, and John Jay. *The Federalist Papers*. With an introduction and commentary by Gary Wills. New York: Bantam Classics, 2003.

Hancock, Ange-Marie. *The Politics of Disgust: The Public Identity of the Welfare Queen*. New York: New York University Press, 2004.

Hanushek, Eric. "The Impact of Differential Expenditures on School Performance," *Educational Research* 18, no. 4 (1989).

Harrington, Michael. *The Other America: Poverty in the United States*. New York: Macmillan 1964 [1962].

Harrison, Bennett, and Barry Bluestone. *The Great U-Turn: Corporate Restructuring and the Polarizing of America*. New York: Basic Book, 1990.

Harvey, David. *A Brief History of Neoliberalism*. Oxford: Oxford University Press, 2007.

———. *The Conditions of Postmodernism: An Inquiry into the Origins of Cultural Change*. Cambridge: Blackwell Press, 1989.

———. *Justice, Nature and Geography of Difference*. Cambridge: Blackwell, 1996.

———. *The Limits of Capital*. New York: Verso, 1999 [1982].

Hauter, Wenonah. *Foodopoly: The Battle over the Future of Food and Farming in America*. New York: New Press, 2012.

Hayek, Frederick. *The Road to Serfdom*. Chicago: University of Chicago Press, 1956 [1944].

Haygood, Ryan. "The Past as Prologue: Defending Democracy Against Voter Suppression Tactics on the Eve of the 2012 Elections." *Rutgers Law Review* 64, no. 4 (2012): 1019–1064.

Heclo, Hugh. *Issue Networks and the Executive Establishment*. Englewood Cliffs, NJ: Prentice Hall, 1995.

Hedges, Chris. *American Fascists: The Christian Right and the War on America*. New York: Free Press. 2006.

————. "The Obama Deception: Why Cornel West Went Ballistic." *Truthdig,* May 16, 2011. http://www.truthdig.com/report/item/the_obama_deception_why_cornel _west_went_ballistic_20110516.

Henry, P. J., and David Sears. "The Symbolic Racism 2000 Scale." *Political Psychology* 23 (2002): 253–283.

Herrnstein, Richard, and Charles Murray. *The Bell Curve: Intelligence and Class Structure in American Life.* New York: Simon and Schuster, 1996.

Hill, Herbert. *The AFL-CIO and the Black Worker: Twenty-Five Years After the Merger.* Louisville, KY: National Association of Human Rights Workers, 1982.

————. *Black Labor and the American Legal System: Race, Work and the Law.* Madison: University of Wisconsin Press, 1985.

Hill-Collins, Patricia. *Black Feminist Thought: Knowledge Construction and the Politics of Empowerment.* New York: Routledge, 1990.

Hitchens, Christopher. *Thomas Paine's Rights of Man: A Biography.* New York: Grove Press, 2006.

Hochschild, Jennifer, "The Politics of the Estranged Poor," *Ethics* 101, no. 3 (1991): 560–578.

Hoffer, Eric. *The True Believer: Thoughts on the Nature of Mass Movements.* New York: Harper and Row, 1966 [1951].

Hofstadter, Richard. *The American Political Tradition.* New York: Vintage Books, 1948.

Holland, Joshua. *The Fifteen Biggest Lies About the Economy: And Everything Else the Right Doesn't What You to Know About Taxes.* Hoboken, NJ: John Wiley, 2010.

Holloway, Sparks, "Queens, Teens, and Model Mothers: Race, Gender and the Discourse of Welfare Reform." In Sanford Schram, Joe Soss, and Richard Fording (eds.), *Race and the Politics of Welfare Reform.* Ann Arbor: University of Michigan Press, 2003.

Holton, Woody. *Forced Founders: Indians, Debts, Slaves and the Making of the American Revolution in Virginia.* Chapel Hill: University of North Carolina Press, 1999.

Horwitz, Sari. "A Drug-Selling Machine That Was All Business." *Washington Post,* April 24, 1988.

House Judiciary Committee Democratic Staff. *Preserving Democracy: What Went Wrong in Ohio?* Status Report. Washington, DC: Government Printing Office, January 5, 2005.

Hudson, Michael. *The Monster: How a Gang of Predatory Lenders and Wall Street Bankers Fleeced America and Spawned a Global Crisis.* New York: Times Books, Henry Holt, 2010.

Hudson, William. *American Democracy in Peril: Seven Challenges to America's Future.* Chatham, NJ: Chatham House, 1995.

Hughes, Charles, and Michael Tanner. "The Work Versus Welfare Trade-Off, 2013: An Analysis of the Total Level of Welfare Benefits." Washington, DC: Cato Institute, 2010.

Human Rights Watch, *The Rest of Their Lives: Life without Parole for Child Offenders in the United States.* London/New York: Human Rights Watch/ Amnesty International, October 12, 2005.

Institute for Research and Education on Human Rights (IREHR). "Tea Party Nationalism: A Critical Examination of the Tea Party Movement and the Size and Scope and Focus of Its National Factions." Kansas City, MO: IREHR, 2010.

Jacobs, Lawrence, and Theda Skocpol. *Health-Care Reform and American Politics: What Everyone Needs to Know.* New York: Oxford University Press, 2012.

Jacoby, Susan. *Freethinkers: A History of American Secularism.* New York: Metropolitan Books, Henry Holt, 2004.

Jaspin, Elliot. *Buried in the Bitter Waters: The Hidden History of Racial Cleansing in America.* New York: Basic Books, 2008.

Johnson, Haynes. *Sleepwalking Through History: America in the Reagan Years.* New York: Anchor Books, 1992.

Johnston, David Cay. *Free Lunch: How the Wealthiest Americans Enrich Themselves at the Government's Expense (and Stick You with the Bill).* New York: Penguin Books, 2007.

A Joint Project of the Community Affairs Office of the Federal Reserve System and the Metropolitan Policy Program at the Brookings Institution. *The Enduring Challenge of Concentrated Poverty in America: Case Studies from Communities Across the United States of America.* Cleveland, OH: Federal Reserve Bank, 2008.

Juhasz, Antonia. *The Tyranny of Oil: The World's Most Powerful Industry—and What We Must Do to Stop It.* New York: HarperCollins, 2008.

Kaplan, Ester. *With God on Their Side: George W. Bush and the Christian Right.* New York: New Press, 2004.

Kasarda, John, "Urban Change and Minority Opportunities." In Paul Peterson (ed.), *The New Urban Reality.* Washington, DC: Brookings Institution, 1985.

Katz, Michael. *The Undeserving Poor: From the War on Poverty to the War on Welfare.* New York: Pantheon Books, 1989.

Katznelson, Ira. *When Affirmative Action Was White: An Untold History of Racial Inequality in Twentieth Century America.* New York: W. W. Norton, 2005.

Kawakami, Kerry, Elizabeth Dunn, Francine Karmali, and John Dovidio. "Mispredicting Affective and Behavioral Responses to Racism." *Science* 323 (2009): 276–278.

Kennedy, David. *Don't Shoot.* New York: Bloomsbury Press, 2011.

Kennedy, Robert. "Was the 2004 Election Stolen?" *Rolling Stone,* June 5, 2006.

Keyes, Scott, Ian Millhiser, Tobin Van Ostern, and Abraham White. *Voter Suppression 101: How Conservatives Are Conspiring to Disenfranchise Millions of Americans.* Washington, DC: Center for American Progress, April 2012.

Keynes, John Maynard. *General Theory of Employment, Interest and Money.* New York: Harcourt, Brace, 1962.

King, Desmond, and Rogers M. Smith. "Racial Orders in American Political Development." *American Political Science Review* 99 (2005): 75–92.

———. *Still a House Divided: Race and Politics in Obama's America.* Princeton, NJ: Princeton University Press, 2011.

Kirschenman, Joleen, and Kathryn Neckerman. "We'd Love to Hire Them, But . . . : The Meaning of Race for Employers." In Paul Peterson and Christopher Jencks (eds.), *The Urban Underclass.* Washington, DC: Brookings Institution, 1991.

Klein, Naomi. *The Shock Doctrine: The Rise of Disaster Capitalism.* New York: Metropolitan Books, Henry Holt, 2007.

Kousser, J. Morgan. *Colorblind Injustice: Minority Voting Rights and the Undoing of the Second Reconstruction.* Chapel Hill: University of North Carolina Press, 1999.

———. *The Shaping of Southern Politics: Suffrage Restrictions and the Establishment of the One-Party South, 1880–1910.* New Haven: Yale University Press, 1974.

Kovel, Joel. *White Racism: A Psychohistory.* New York: Columbia University Press, 1984.

Kozol, Jonathan. *Death at an Early Age: The Destruction of the Hearts and Minds of Negro Children in Boston.* Boston: Houghton Mifflin, 1967.

———. *Savage Inequality: Children in America's Schools.* New York: Harper Perennial, 1992.

———. *The Shame of the Nation: The Restoration of Apartheid Schooling in America.* New York: Crown Publishers, 2005.

Kroll, Andy. "You Need to See These 5 Shocking Facts About the Money in the 2012 Election." *Mother Jones,* January 2013. http://motherjones.com/mojo/2013/01/2012.

Krugman, Paul. *The Conscience of a Liberal.* New York: W. W. Norton, 2007.

———. "Why We're in the Gilded Age." *New York Review of Books,* May 8, 2014.

Kuhn, Thomas. *The Structure of Scientific Revolutions.* Chicago: University of Chicago Press, 1970.

Kushnick, Louis. "The Political Economy of White Racism in the United States." In Benjamin Bowser and Raymond Hunt (eds.), *Impacts of Racism on White Americans.* Thousand Oaks, CA: Sage, 1996.

Kuttner, Robert. *Economic Illusions: False Choices Between Prosperity and Social Justice.* Boston: Houghton-Mifflin, 1987.

———. *The Squandering of America: How the Failure of Our Politics Undermines Our Prosperity.* New York: Alfred A. Knopf, 2007.

Lakoff, George. *Moral Politics: How Liberals and Conservatives Think.* Chicago: University of Chicago Press, 2002.

Le Duox, Joseph. *The Emotional Brain: The Mysterious Underpinnings of Emotional Life.* New York: Touchstone, 1996.

Lekachman, Robert. *The Age of Keynes.* New York: Vintage Books, 1968.

Lewis, Oscar. "Culture and Poverty." In Daniel Moynihan (ed.), *On Understanding Poverty: Perspectives from Social Sciences.* New York: Basic Books, 1969.

Lichtenstein, Alexander, and Michael Kroll. "Fortress Economy: The Economic Role of the U.S. Prison System." In Elihu Rosenblatt (ed.), *Criminal Injustice: Confronting the Prison Crisis.* Boston: South End Press, 1996.

Lieberman, Matthew, Ahmad Hariri, Johanna Jarcho, Naomi Eisenberger, and Susan Bookeimer. "An fMRI Investigation of Race Related Amygdala Activity in African-Americans and Caucasian American Individuals." *Nature Neuroscience* 8, no. 6 (2005): 720–722.

Liebow, Elliot. *Tally's Corner: A Study of Negro Street Corner Men.* Boston: Little, Brown, 1967.

Lincoln, Abraham. "Letter to Horace Greeley." In Roy Basler (ed.), *The Collected Works of Abraham Lincoln,* Vol. 5, August 22, 1865. New Brunswick, NJ: Rutgers University Press, 1953.

Lindblom, Charles. *Politics and Markets: The World's Political Economic Systems.* New York: Basic Books, 1977.

Lioz, Adam, and Blair Bowie. "Billion-Dollar Democracy: The Unprecedented Role of Money in the 2012 Election." January 2013. www.demos.org/sites.

Locke, John. *Second Treatise on Government.* New York: New York University Press, 2002.

Lofgren, Mike. *The Party Is Over: How Republicans Went Crazy, Democrats Became Useless and the Middle Class Got Shafted.* New York: Viking, 2011.

Lopez, Ian. *Dog Whistle Politics: How Coded Racial Appeals Have Reinvented Racism and Wrecked the Middle Class.* Oxford: Oxford University Press, 2014.
———. *White by Law: The Legal Construction of Race.* Philadelphia: Temple University Press, 1995.
Mauer, Marc. *Race to Incarcerate.* New York: New Press, 1999.
Mead, Lawrence. *Beyond Entitlement: The Social Obligation of Citizenship.* New York: Free Press, 1986.
Meadors, Marvin. "How Are ALEC Laws Undermining Our Democracy?" *Huffington Post,* April 4, 2012.
Merida, Kevin. "Being a Black Man." *Washington Post,* January 8, 2007.
Mills, Linda G. *A Penchant for Prejudice: Unraveling Bias in Judicial Decision Making.* Ann Arbor: University of Michigan Press, 1999.
Monnat, Shannon. "Toward a Critical Understanding of Gendered Color-Blind Racism Within the U.S. Welfare Institution," *Journal of Black Studies* 404 (2010): 637–652.
Morrison, Toni. *Playing in the Dark: Whiteness and the Literary Imagination.* Cambridge, MA: Harvard University Press, 1992.
Mosteller, Frederick. "The Tennessee Study of Class Size in the Early School Grades," *The Future of Children* 5, no. 2 (1995).
Moynihan, Daniel. *The Negro Family: A Case for National Action.* Washington, DC: US Department of Labor, 1965.
Murray, Charles. *Losing Ground: American Social Policy, 1950–1980.* New York: New York University Press, 2003 [1984].
Myrdal, Gunnar. *An American Dilemma: The Negro Problem and Modern Democracy.* New York: Harper, 1944.
Neubeck, Kenneth, and Noel Cazenave. *Welfare Racism: Playing the Race Card Against America's Poor.* New York: Routledge, 2001.
Noah, Timothy. *The Great Divergence: America's Great Inequality Crisis and What We Can Do About It.* New York: Bloomsbury Press, 2012.
Nopper, Tamara. "Beyond the Bootstrap: How Korean Banks and U.S. Government Institutions Contributed to Korean Immigrant Entrepreneurship in the United States." PhD dissertation, Temple University, 2008.
Nozick, Robert. *The State, Private Property and Utopia.* New York: Basic Books, 1974.
Obama, Barack. *The Audacity of Hope: Thoughts on Reclaiming the American Dream.* New York: Crown, 2006.
Ogbu, John. *Black American Students in an Affluent Suburb: A Study of Academic Disengagement.* Mahwah, NJ: Lawrence Erlbaum, 2003.
Paine, Thomas. *Thomas Paine Reader.* Edited by Michael Foot and Isaac Kramnick. New York: Penguin Books, 1987.
———. "Agrarian Justice." In Jessica Kimpell (ed.), *Peter Linebaugh Presents Thomas Paine: Common Sense, Rights of Man and Agrarian Justice.* New York: Verso, 2009.
Palast, Greg. *The Best Democracy Money Can Buy: An Investigative Reporter Exposes the Truth About Globalization, Corporate Cons and High Finance Fraudsters.* London: Pluto Press, 2002.
———. *Billionaires and Ballot Bandits: How to Steal an Election in 9 Easy Steps.* New York: Seven Stories Press, 2012.
———. "The Silence of the Media Lambs: The Election Story Never Told." *Third World Traveler,* May 24, 2001,

Pareene, Alex. "Why Rush Limbaugh and the Right Turned on Trayvon Martin." *Salon,* April 2, 2012.

Parker, Christopher. "WISE Multi-state Survey of Race and Politics." University of Washington Institute for the Study of Ethnicity, Race and Sexuality, 2010. http://depts.washington.edu/uwise/racepolitics.html.

Parker, Christopher, and Matt Barreto. *Change They Can't Believe In: The Tea Party and Reactionary Politics.* Princeton: Prenceton University Press, 2013.

Parker, Richard. "Sam Houston, We Have a Problem," *New York Times,* January 31, 2011.

Payne, Ruby. *A Framework for Understanding Poverty.* Highlands, TX: Aha! Process, 2005.

Persons, Georgia (ed.). *Beyond the Boundaries: A New Structure of Ambition in African American Politics.* New Brunswick, NJ: Transaction, 2009.

Peterson, Peter. *Running on Empty: How the Democratic and Republican Parties Are Bankrupting Our Future and What Americans Can Do About It.* New York: Picador, 2005.

Piketty, Thomas. *Capital in the Twenty-first Century.* Cambridge: Harvard University Press, 2014.

Piven, Frances Fox. "Why Welfare Is Racist." In Sanford Schram, Joe Soss, and Richard Fording (eds.), *Race and the Politics of Welfare Reform.* Ann Arbor: University of Michigan Press, 2003.

Piven, Frances Fox, and Richard A. Cloward. *The New Class War: Reagan's Attack on the Welfare State and Its Consequences.* New York: Pantheon Books, 1982.

———. *Poor People's Movements: Why They Succeed, How They Fail.* New York: Vintage Books, 1979.

Piven, Frances, Lorraine C. Minnite, and Margaret Groarke. *Keeping Down the Black Vote: Race and the Demobilization of American Voters.* New York: New Press, W. W. Norton, 2009.

Prager, Devah. *Marked: Race, Crime, and Finding Work in an Era of Mass Incarceration.* Chicago: University of Chicago Press, 2007.

Prins, Nomi. *It Takes a Pillage: Behind the Bailouts, Bonuses and Backroom Deals from Washington to Wall Street.* Hoboken, NJ: John Wiley, 2009.

Quadagno, Jill. *The Color of Welfare: How Racism Undermined the War on Poverty.* New York: Oxford University Press, 1994.

Radelet, Michael, Hugo Bedau, and Constance Putnam. *In Spite of Innocence: Erroneous Convictions in Capital Cases.* Boston: Northeastern University Press, 1992.

Rainwater, Lee, and William Yancey (eds.). *The Moynihan Report and the Politics of Controversy.* Cambridge: MIT Press, 1996 [1967].

Rana, Aziz. *The Two Faces of American Freedom.* Cambridge: Harvard University Press, 2010.

Rand, Ayn. *Atlas Shrugged.* New York: New American Library, 1957.

———. *Capitalism, the Unknown Ideal.* With Nathaniel Branden, Alan Greenspan, and Robert Hessen. New York: Signet, 1985 [1967].

Randall, Ronald. "Presidential Powers Versus Bureaucratic Intransigence: The Influence of the Nixon Administration on Welfare Policy." *American Political Science Review* 73, no. 3 (1979): 795–810.

Ravitch, Diane. *Reign of Error: The Hoax of the Privatization Movement and the Danger to America's Public Schools.* New York: Alfred A. Knopf, 2013.

Reich, Robert. *Beyond Outrage: What Has Gone Wrong with Our Economy and Our Democracy and How to Fix It.* New York: Vintage Books, 2012.

———. *Supercapitalism: The Transformation of Business, Democracy and Everyday Life*. New York: Vintage Books, 2008.

Ricci, David. *The Transformation of American Politics: The New Washington and the Rise of Think Tank Politics*. New Haven: Yale University Press, 1993.

Ricketts, Erol. "The Origin of Black Female-Headed Families." Funded by the Equal Opportunity Division of the Rockefeller Foundation, University of Wisconsin, Madison, Institute for Research on Poverty. http://www.irp.wisc.edu /publications/focus/pdfs/foc121e.pdf.

Roberts, Dorothy. *Killing the Black Body: Race, Reproduction, and the Meaning of Liberty*. New York: Vintage Books, 1997.

———. "Welfare and the Problem of Black Citizenship." *Yale Law Journal* 105 (1996): 1563–1607.

Roediger, David. *The Wages of Whiteness: Race and the Making of the American Working Class*. New York: Verso, 1991.

Ronquillo, Jaclyn, Thomas Denson, Brian Lickel, Zhong-Lin Lu, Anirvan Nandy, and Keith Maddox. "The Effects of Skin Tone on Race-Related Amygdala Activity: An fMRI Investigation," *Social Cognitive and Affective Neuroscience* 2, no. 1 (2007): 39–44.

Rose, Nancy. *Workfare or Fair Work: Women, Welfare, and Government Work Programs*. New Brunswick, NJ: Rutgers University Press, 1995.

Ross, Heather, and Isabel Sawhill. *Time of Transition: Growth of Families Headed by Women*. Washington, DC: Urban Institute, 1975.

Sacks, Peter. *Tearing Down the Gates: Confronting the Class Divide in American Education*. Berkeley: University of California Press, 2007.

Salzberger, A. G. "Kansas City, MO School District Loses Its Accreditation." *New York Times*, September 20, 2011.

Saulny, Susan. "Board's Decision to Close 28 Kansas City Schools Follows Years of Inaction." *New York Times*, March 11, 2010.

Saxton, Alexander. *The Rise and Fall of the White Republic: Class Politics and Mass Culture in Nineteenth Century America*. New York: Verso, 1990.

Schama, Simon. *Rough Crossings: Britain, the Slaves and the American Revolution*. New York: HarperCollins, 2006.

Schattschneider, Elmer. *The Semi-sovereign People: A Realist's View of Democracy in America*. Fort Worth, TX: Hartcourt Brace Jovanovich College, 1975.

Schrag, Peter. *Final Test: The Battle for Adequacy in America's Schools*. New York: New Press, 2003.

Schram, Sanford, Joe Soss, and Richard Fording (eds.). *Race and the Politics of Welfare Reform*. Ann Arbor: University of Michigan Press, 2003.

The Sentencing Project. "The Federal Prison Population. A Statistical Analysis." 2004. http://www.sentencingproject.org/doc/publications/inc-federalprisonpop.pdf.

Serwer, Adam. "The Right Goes Nuts over Obama's Trayvon Comments." *Mother Jones*, March 23, 2012.

Shklar, Judith. *American Citizenship: The Quest for Inclusion*. Cambridge: Harvard University Press, 1991.

Sidel, Ruth. *Keeping Women and Children Last*. New York: Penguin, 1996.

Sitkoff, Harvard. *The Struggle for Black Equality, 1954–1992*. New York: HarperCollins, 1993 [1981].

Skocpol, Theda, and Vanessa Williamson. *The Tea Party and the Remaking of the Republican Conservatism*. New York: Oxford University Press, 2012.

Smedley, Audrey. *Race in North America: Origin and Evolution of a Worldview*. Boulder, CO: Westview Press, 1993.

Smith, Hedrick. *Who Stole the American Dream?* New York: Random House, 2012.

Smith, Robert, and Richard Seltzer. *Race, Class and Culture: A Study in Afro-American Mass Opinion.* New York: State University of New York Press, 1992.

Smith, Rogers. *Civic Ideas: Conflicting Visions of Citizenship in U.S. History.* New Haven: Yale University Press, 1997.

Snowden, Frank. *Blacks in Antiquity.* Cambridge: Harvard University Press, 1970.

Soss, Joe, Richard Fording, and Sanford Schram. *Disciplining the Poor: Neoliberal Paternalism and the Persistent Power of Race.* Chicago: University of Chicago Press, 2011.

Sowell, Thomas. "Largesse for Losers." *National Review Online,* April 10, 2012. http://www.nationalreviewdom/articles/295600?/largesse-for-losers-thomas -sowell.

———. *Migrations and Cultures: A World View.* New York: Basic Books, 1996.

———. *Race and Economics.* New York: Longman, 1975.

Steel, Claude. *Whistling Vivaldi and Other Clues to How Stereotypes Affect Us.* New York: W. W. Norton, 2010.

Steinberg, Stephen. *The Ethnic Myth: Race, Ethnicity and Class in America.* Boston: Beacon Press, 1989.

———. "Poor Reason: Culture Still Doesn't Explain Poverty. *Boston Review,* January 13, 2011.

———. *Turning Back: The Retreat from Racial Justice in American Thought and Policy.* Boston: Beacon Press, 1995.

Steinfield, Melvin. *Our Racist Presidents: From Washington to Nixon.* San Ramon, CA: Consensus Press, 1972.

Stiglitz, Joseph. *The Price of Inequality.* New York: W. W. Norton, 2012.

Swirko, Cindy. "Cummings Cousin Gets 15-Year Sentence: Hope Sykes Pleaded No Contest to One Count of Trafficking Prescription Narcotics." *Gainsville Sun,* April 27, 2010.

Takaki, Ronald. *Iron Cages: Race and Culture in Nineteenth Century America.* Oxford: Oxford University Press, 1990.

Tanner, Michael. *The End of Welfare.* Washington, DC: Cato Institute, 1996.

Tanner, Michael, and Charles Hughes. *The Work Versus Welfare Trade-Off 2013: An Analysis of the Total Level of Welfare Benefits.* Washington, DC: Cato Institute, 2013.

Tcholakian, Danielle. "Bloomberg Lashes Out at Stop-and-Frisk Judge in Response to Ruling." *Metro.US,* August 12, 2013. www.metro.us/.../bloomberg-lashes -out-at-stop-and-frisk-judge-in-response.to.ruling.

Tesler, Michael. "The Spillover of Racialization into Health Care: How President Obama Polarized Public Opinion by Race and Racial Attitudes." *American Journal of Political Science* 56, no. 3 (2012): 690–704.

Tesler, Michael, and David O. Sears. *Obama's Race: The 2008 Election and the Dream of a Post-racial America.* Chicago: University of Chicago Press, 2010.

———. "President Obama and the Growing Polarization of Partisan Attachment by Racial Attitudes and Race." Paper presented at the annual meeting of the Midwest Political Science Association, Chicago, April 2010.

Tolchin, Susan, and Martin Tolchin. *Dismantling America: The Rush to Deregulate.* New York: Oxford University Press, 1983.

Twain, Mark. *The Adventures of Huckleberry Finn.* New York: Random House, 1885.

Tyson, Karolyn, William A. Darity Jr., and Domini R. Castellino. "Its Not a 'Black Thing': Understanding the Burden of Acting White and Other Dilemmas of High Achievement." *American Sociological Review* 70, no. 4 (2005): 582–605.

US Civil Rights Commission. "Voting Irregularities in Florida During the 2000 Presidential Election." Washington, DC: Government Printing Office, 2001. http://permanent.access.gpo.gov/lps13588/lps13588/main.htm.

US Department of Commerce, US Census Bureau. *The Diversifying Electorate—Voting Rates by Race and Hispanic Origin in 2012 (and Other Recent Elections)*. Washington, DC: US Department of Commerce, US Census Bureau, May 2013.

Valentino, Nicholas, and David Sears. "Old Times There Are Not Forgotten: Race and Partisan Realignment in the Contemporary South." *American Journal of Political Science* 49, no. 3 (2005): 672–688.

Vogal, David. *Fluctuating Fortunes: The Political Power of Business in America.* New York: Basic Books, 1989.

Walter, Jess. *Ruby Ridge: The Truth and Tragedy of the Randy Weaver Family.* US Department of Justice Report of the Ruby Ridge Task Force to the Office of Professional Responsibility of the Investigation of Allegations of Improper Government Conduct in the Investigation, Apprehension, and Prosecution of Randy C. Weaver and Kevin Harris. Washington, DC: Government Printing Office, June 10, 1994.

Weatherley, Charles (ed.). *Mandate for Leadership.* Washington, DC: Heritage Foundation, 1981.

Weiser, Wendy, and Margaret Chen. "Recent Voter Suppression Incidents." New York: Brennan Center for Justice at New York School of Law, November 3, 2008.

West, Cornel. *Democracy Matters: Winning the Fight Against Imperialism.* New York: Penguin Books, 2004.

Wilkerson, Isabel. "Detroit Drug Empire Showed All the Traits of Big Business." *New York Times,* December 12, 1988.

Williams, Patricia. *The Alchemy of Race and Rights.* Cambridge, MA: Harvard University Press, 1992.

Wilson, Carter A. "Policy Regimes and Policy Change," *Journal of Public Policy* 20, no. 3 (2000): 247–274.

———. *Public Policy: Continuity and Change* (Long Grove, IL: Waveland Press, 2013).

———. *Racism from Slavery to Advanced Capitalism.* Thousand Oaks, CA: Sage, 1996.

———. "Restructuring and the Growth of Concentrated Poverty in Detroit," *Urban Affairs Quarterly* 28, no. 2 (1992): 187–205.

Wilson, James Q. *Thinking About Crime.* New York: Vintage Books, 1985.

Wilson, William J. *The Declining Significance of Race: From Racial Oppression to Economic Class Subordination.* Lanham, MD: Rowman and Littlefield, 2006.

———. *The Truly Disadvantaged: The Inner City, the Underclass, and Public Policy.* Chicago: University of Chicago Press, 1987.

Wilson, William J., and Robert Sampson. "Toward a Theory of Race, Crime and Urban Inequality." In John Hogan and Ruth Peterson (eds.), *Crime and Inequality*. Stanford: Stanford University Press, 1995.

Wisely, Willie. "Who Goes to Prison." In Daniel Burton-Rose and Paul Wright (eds.), *The Celling of America: An Inside Look at the U.S. Prison Industry.* Washington, DC: Common Cause Press, 1998.

Wolfang, Marvin, Robert Figlio, and Thorsten Selling. *Delinquency in Birth Cohort.* Chicago: Midway, 1987 [1970].

Woodward, C. Vann. *Origins of the New South 1877–1913.* Baton Rouge: Louisiana State University Press, 1966 [1951].

Young, Iris. "Five Faces of Oppression." In Thomas Mappes and Jane Zembaty (eds.), *Social Ethics: Morality and Social Policy.* New York: Routledge, 2000.

Zeskind, Leonard. *Blood and Politics: The History of the White Nationalist Movement from the Margins to the Mainstream.* New York: Farrar, Straus and Giroux, 2009.

Court Cases

Adarand v. Pena, 515 U.S. 200 (1995).

Brown v. Board of Education, 347 U.S. 483 (1954).

Citizens United v. Federal Election Commission, 558 U.S. 310 (2010).

City of Pleasant Grove v. United States, 479 U.S. 462 (1987).

Civil Rights Cases, 109 U.S. 3 (1883).

Crawford v. Marion County Election Board, 553 U.S. 181 (2008).

Department of Housing and Urban Development v. Rucker, 535 U.S. 125 (2002).

Dorsey v. United States, 567 U.S. (2012).

Dred Scott v. Sanford, 60 U.S. 393 (1857).

Ewing v. California, 538 U.S. 11 (2003).

Floyd, et al. v. City of New York, et al., 813 F. Supp. 2d 457 (2013).

Furman v. Georgia, 408 U.S. 238 (1972).

Graham v. Florida, 560 U.S. 48 (2010).

Griggs v. Duke Power Company, 490 U.S. (1971).

Hill v. Snyder, case no. 10-14568 U.S. District Court of Michigan Southern District (2013).

Jacobs v. Scott, 31 F. 3d 1319 (1994).

King v. Smith, 392 U.S. 309 (1968).

League of Latino American Voters v. Perry, 548 U.S. 399 (2006).

McCleskey v. Kemp, 481 U.S. 279 (1987).

Miller v. Alabama, 567 U.S. (2012).

NFIB v. Sebelius, 567 U.S. (2012) 132 S. Ct. 2566.

Plessy v. Ferguson, 168 U.S. 537 (1896).

Ricci v. DeStefano, 557 U.S. 557 (2009).

Roe v. Wade, 410 U.S. 113 (1973).

Romer v. Evans, 517 U.S. 20 (1996).

Roper v. Simmons, 543 U.S. 551 (2005).

Rummel v. Estelle, 445 U.S. 263 (1980).

Shaw v. Reno, 509 U.S. 630 (1993).

Shelby County, Alabama v. Holder, 570 U.S. 193 (2013).

United States v. Blewett, 12-5226/5582 (May 17, 2013).

United States v. Morrison, 529 U.S. 598 (2000).

University of California Board of Regents v. Bakke, 401 U.S. 424 (1978).

Ward Cove v. Atonio, 490 U.S. 642 (1989).

Index

About the Book

The black/white gaps in income, education, and wealth are expanding. Prisons are crowded with black men. There is an increasing concentration of urban poverty. While individuals and communities reject biological determinism and find bigotry offensive, structural inequalities remain. Why? Addressing this fundamental question, Carter Wilson focuses on the elusive dynamics of contemporary racism.

Wilson documents the emergence of metaracism, a deeply embedded bias fueled by economic insecurity, entrenched (yet no longer publicly accepted) stereotypes, and shifts in public policy. He illustrates his argument with discussions of a broad range of policy issues. His provocative analysis offers new insights on both the roots of racism and its persistence today.

Carter A. Wilson is professor of political science at Northern Michigan University.